Martin K. Schermerhorn

Renascent Christianity - a Forecast of the Twentieth Century

in the light of higher criticism of the Bible, study of compartive religion and of the

universal prayer for religious unity

Martin K. Schermerhorn

Renascent Christianity - a Forecast of the Twentieth Century
in the light of higher criticism of the Bible, study of compartive religion and of the universal prayer for religious unity

ISBN/EAN: 9783337100155

Printed in Europe, USA, Canada, Australia, Japan

Cover: Foto ©Lupo / pixelio.de

More available books at **www.hansebooks.com**

ANNOUNCEMENT.

TWO IMPORTANT VOLUMES.
BY "A CLERGYMAN."
(Now ready.)

1.—"RENASCENT CHRISTIANITY, A FORECAST OF THE 20TH CENTURY."

[Widely known clergymen and other scholars who are among the leading representatives of Broad Church Christianity in England and America, to whom proof-sheet copies were sent for advance reviews, returned hearty commendations which will be found in full on the opening pages.]

"An earnest attempt to show that the Christianity of Jesus and of his Apostles was *eclectic*, and so Catholic or universal; that from the close of the second century has prevailed a 'tendency to revert and degenerate,' which accounts for all the superstitions and errors of the historic Church; and that all sectarian divisions, including that between *reasonable* Trinitarians and *conservative* Unitarians, may be healed by going back to 'the truth as it is in Jesus.'"

"*This is a brave, true, manly piece of work.*"
"*A breadth which emulates the Christianity of the late Bishop Brooks.*"
"*God speed to the potent new volume.*"

2.—NEW EDITION OF "ANCIENT SACRED SCRIPTURES OF THE WORLD."

[From a large number of scholarly reviews, made by some of our most reliable Newspapers and Periodicals, brief selections have been made and will be found, highly commending the volume, on the opening pages.]

"*An eloquent argument for that Catholicity which rises above creeds.*"
"*A valuable addition to every library.*"
"*It cannot fail to arouse interest.*"

The two are designed as companion volumes. The first is designated as "The Old Faith in Modern Form," and the second as "The Old Religion in Modern Words."

Uniform in size and style, large octavo of nearly 450 pages; extra paper and type. Price per volume, $2.50 and $2.00 according to binding.

₄ For sale by all booksellers. Sent by mail, postpaid, on receipt of price, by the Publishers.

G. P. PUTNAM'S SONS, PUBLISHERS
27 AND 29 WEST 23D STREET, NEW YORK;
24 BEDFORD STREET, STRAND, LONDON.

SINCERITY

STIMULATED BY SELF-FORGETFULNESS AND DIRECTED BY INTELLIGENCE IS THE SOURCE OF ALL VIRTUES.

The Creed and Pledge which are given on the following page may be found, with explanations, on pages 37 and 38 of "Renascent Christianity." They are repeated here with the hope that they may attract especial attention and also as a suitable connection of the two volumes, "Ancient Sacred Scriptures of the World" and "Renascent Christianity," both of which have been prepared as their amplification and enforcement.

In the ancient cathedral of Lubeck, in Germany, there is an old slab with the following inscription:

> "Thus speaketh Christ our Lord to us:
> Ye call me Master, and obey me not;
> Ye call me Light, and see me not;
> Ye call me Way, and walk me not;
> Ye call me Life, and desire me not;
> Ye call me Wise, and follow me not;
> Ye call me Fair, and love me not;
> Ye call me Rich, and ask me not;
> Ye call me Eternal, and seek me not;
> Ye call me Gracious, and trust me not;
> Ye call me Noble, and serve me not;
> Ye call me Mighty, and honor me not;
> Ye call me Just, and fear me not;
> If I condemn you, blame me not."

INSINCERITY

STIMULATED BY SELF-LOVE AND DIRECTED BY IGNORANCE IS THE SOURCE OF ALL SINS.

CATHOLIC CHURCH CREED

AND

PLEDGE OF FELLOWSHIP

FOR THE TWENTIETH CENTURY

CREED

I BELIEVE IN THE FATHERHOOD OF GOD.

I BELIEVE IN THE TEACHINGS OF JESUS THE CHRIST.

I BELIEVE IN THE GUIDANCE OF THE HOLY SPIRIT.

I BELIEVE IN THE CLEAN HEART.

I BELIEVE IN THE SERVICE OF LOVE.

I BELIEVE IN THE UNWORLDLY LIFE.

PLEDGE

I PROMISE TO TRUST GOD AND LOVE HIM SUPREMELY.

I PROMISE TO TAKE MY CROSS AND FOLLOW THE CHRIST.

I PROMISE TO ACCEPT THE HOLY SPIRIT AS MY GUIDE.

I PROMISE TO FORGIVE AND LOVE MY ENEMIES.

I PROMISE TO LOVE MY FELLOW MEN AS MYSELF.

I PROMISE TO HUNGER AND THIRST AFTER RIGHTEOUSNESS.

ADVANCE REVIEWS.

"RENASCENT CHRISTIANITY.—A FORECAST OF THE 20TH CENTURY."

Of twelve widely known clergymen and other scholars who are among the leading representatives of Broad Church Christianity in England and in America, to whom "proof-sheet copies" were sent for advance reviews, eleven responded as follows:

[*The MSS. of the reviews with the names of the reviewers are held by the publishers.*]

1.—" The cycle of the Seasons is typical of the cycle of the Centuries. In each is a Seed-time, a Summer, a Harvesting, and a Winter, during which a silent redistribution of values takes place, undiscovered till the Spring proclaims a re-incarnation.

'Renascent Christianity, A Forecast of the Twentieth Century,' is essentially a prophecy and a warning that the Spring-time of the Centuries is at hand.

It is, as well, a plea, that in things spiritual, we shall not be caught napping, secure in the pride of place and privilege, when the Sun of Universal Truth shall cast its light into the most hidden places and illume and lay bare their secrets.

With a breadth which emulates the Christianity of the late Bishop Brooks; with a scorn for that miserable self-love which, like a miasma, infects all it touches, the author makes Sincerity the touch-stone of religious unity and welcomes into a common fraternity all those who are intelligently sincere.

Science, long since, proclaimed the necessary unity of Truth. It is but now, however, that the 'Higher Criticism of the Bible and the study of Comparative Religion' has revealed to earnest students of Religion and Theology the same unity within their own sphere.

The author also emphasizes the dominant disaster of our day, as it has been that of other days of superlative progress and proficiency in things material. He sees, as other seers have seen, the monster Money, lying twined about the root of the modern tree-of-troubles.

Everywhere the corrupting influence of huge wealth has extended its pernicious tentacles, until neither the Church nor the State remains pure and undefiled.

It is indeed time that a halt were called, and this appeal by 'a clergyman' may, at least by its sincerity and outspoken candor, attract attention in those quarters which would be deaf to all ordinary petitions.

It is with this hope that all will bid God-speed to this potent new volume."

2.—" This volume called 'Renascent Christianity,' is written with prophetic earnestness. It is a plea for a return to the 'truth as it is in Jesus.' Its plea is based upon the novel ground that his teachings were eclectic and resumed in their simplicity all that was best in the world's sacred scriptures. This idea suggests that Christianity is a *pleroma* containing all that is best in all the other great religions of the world. The author's spirit is essentially catholic and irenic, and invites the coöperation of all liberal-minded people of whatever creed. He is very stern in his indictment of those 'reversions,' as he calls them, that have changed the character of Christianity from its original purity. Would not 'corruptions' be a better word than 'reversions'? More bent on driving home his message than on making a literary impression, he has drawn liberally on many writers for the confirmation of his principle.

The patience and the diligence that have gone into the structure of the book cannot be praised too much, and I sincerely trust that they will meet with their reward in a wide and cordial recognition of the spirit and the purpose of his work."

3.—" The subject of the book is one which must command the interest of all men who are in earnest about religion. The care, and reverence, and scholarly training with which the author has treated it will deserve respect and, it seems to me, interest among all faithful and conservative scholars."

4.—" This is a brave, true, manly piece of work. Brave—because it is so out-spoken as almost certainly to displease those who care chiefly for conformity and quiet. True—so true in its intents and purposes as to silence all questions of entire intellectual agreement. Manly—in that its breadth of sympathy is as wide as the world and excludes no child of the Heavenly Father.

Whether it is really the original Christianity or not this author so earnestly portrays, it is something so fine and sweet that all loving hearts will wish its purpose may be realized.

I welcome its clear challenge to intellectual as well as moral seriousness. Give us all this earnestness, this conservatism, this divine and all-inclusive sympathy and we may courageously and cheerfully lift up the cry—' *The Kingdom of Heaven is at hand.*'"

5.—" I respond with gratitude and 'God-speed.' So far as I gather from your line of thought and of argument, it seems to me the defense of a thesis to which the corrupters of the Religion of Jesus will find it difficult to make an answer."

6.—"*Renascent Christianity* is the title of a book which is a sign of the times. It is one more expression of the movement within Christianity towards a new birth—a reformation, a reconstruction of thought and of life. That there is such a movement at work in our midst, goes without saying. Every worthy expression of this movement is an added impetus to it. Such a work is that which aptly takes its title from this great tendency of our times.

The author, himself a Catholic Christian in the true sense of the word—having in his experience personally known widely diverse forms of Christianity, and found the common Christianity which is at the heart of them—wisely interprets the movement which he feels within his own spirit and recognizes all about him. He seeks to go back of Christianity to the Christ; back of institutionalism and dogmatic theology, to the life which gave birth alike to institutions and to systems of thought. He finds in the later developments of theology and ecclesiasticism much that is in the nature of a degeneration. Renewed life is, in his judgment, to be found in retracing the steps of thought and life back to the primal fount. To open this is to effect a regeneration of Christianity.

There is no question that in this he rightly expresses a wide-spread tendency of the times. Back through doctors and priests, through school-men and fathers and apostles to Jesus himself—this is the cry on every hand. In interpreting this original Christianity, the author shows himself in sympathy with the best tendencies of the movement which he expresses.

Intellectually he is a liberal of the liberals. While conservative in holding to the historic form of thought, the form of sound words, he is a liberal in reading those forms in the light of the truest and highest thought—that is the simplest and most essential thought of Christianity. How liberal the book is let two passages suffice to show. 'What then are the original sources of Christianity? *All the Holy Teachings of all the Religions of the World.*' Jesus the Christ was 'conceived of the Holy Spirit and born of the Virgin Mary,' in the sense that all who on earth shall attain to perfect holiness, *must be 'conceived in Holiness, and born of a pure mother in particular and of a pure ancestry in general.'*

While thus intellectually broad, he is ethical and spiritual, as must needs be the case with one who would go back to the Master. The book is instinct throughout with spiritual vitality,—the vitality of the teachings of Jesus. It is constructive and not merely destructive. It makes for a living faith.

The form in which the book is cast—that of short sections, intelligently headed—makes it easy for the average reader to follow understandingly its logical development.

The book is one which ought to help on the renascence of Christianity."

7.—"*Renascent Christianity* is the suggestive title of a volume whose advance pages I have examined. The author is evidently a man of wide observation and of many subjective experiences. He writes with fine flashes of insight, from the promptings of serious convictions, and with a passionate desire to recall Christianity to the simplicity of the Christ—the Christ of the ages and of the Saint; the Christ of Nature and of Grace.

Neither churchmen, dissenters, nor so-called liberals will agree with all the writer says. He waves away the churches with a scourge of small cords, and lays about him somewhat indiscriminately. But even those who read with resentment will be obliged to whet their eye-beams, to look sharply around and within, and to ask if these things are so."

8.—" I have been deeply interested in reading the scholarly work entitled *Renascent Christianity*. There is evidence on every page of a deep desire to ascertain the truth, and a fervid purpose to set that truth forth accurately for the benefit of Christianity. Students of historical religion are well aware that the original gospel has been greatly perverted. Simplicity has been sacrificed to mystery, and intricate intellectual process substituted for spiritual insight ; formalism has usurped the place of sincerity, and the broad message of Jesus has been narrowed to doctrinal and sectarian purposes.

He who ably presents the facts in this great matter, with stirring arguments and illustrations, is placing the modern thoughtful world under great obligations. The author of this admirable work has approached his task with combined earnestness and catholicity. He seeks to obtain the truth from errors, and with a sympathetic touch passes in review the degeneration which has occurred in Christianity. With no uncertain accent, he sounds the notes of warning at the same time.

There is evidence throughout of wide reading, and a throng of witnesses is summoned to attest the correctness of the positions herein maintained.

Such a volume ought to aid very much in clearing up misunderstanding with regard to genuine Christianity. It will thereby assist in directing more wisely the vast energies of the true gospel, and point out the quicker fulfilment of its glorious possibilities."

9.—" I hardly feel warranted in giving an opinion upon the treatment of subjects of so much importance where (on account of sickness) I have only had time to glance over the pages. But of this I feel quite sure, that, from your own experiences in the theological world, you cannot fail to give a broad, unsectarian, impartial, and truly religious view of what the Twentieth Century will ask in these matters."

10.—" You certainly treat your subject from the right point of view, and your position is an impregnable one. I wish I had time to read the plate-proof Copy more thoroughly, so as to be able to express myself more fully.

I thank you for your kindness in submitting it to me."

11.—[The following letter, written by his own hand, will explain why one of the twelve chosen was unable to review this volume. It will also be, in itself, of wide and permanent interest because of the venerable age as well as the exceptional intelligence and influence of the writer.]

"THE POLCHAR, ROTHIEMURCHUS, ABIEMORE, SCOTLAND,
"October 21, 1897.

". . . I have not forgotten our former correspondence with reference to the Memorial Church in Newport, R. I., and the best mode of turning to account for future generations the characteristics of Dr. Channing's thought and life. I rejoice to know that you are still engaged in the same work at an ulterior stage, and are bringing out this goodly volume in prosecution of it. I shall address myself eagerly to the study of it, if not too soon overtaken by 'the night in which no man can work.'

But in my 93d year, moving through my tasks at the slackened pace of a spent life, how can I expect or promise to qualify myself for an adequate review of a Treatise so comprehensive as is this one entitled *Renascent Christianity*. Here, on my study table before me, there are already in advance of yours seven or eight elaborate productions, of as many thousand pages; English, French, German, Dutch, sent me by their authors and waiting for review and judgment, which I cannot hope to give.

It is imperatively necessary for me to contract my remaining attempts within very narrow limits,—hardly going beyond the revision of my own reprints. I must not therefore undertake the office with which you entrust me. In declining it my comfort is, that with such allies as —— —— you cannot possibly gain anything from a worn-out co-worker that has dropped into the past. Nor can I think of any one whose good word would secure more attention for the volume than its own contents, with their lucid presentations, will of themselves secure.

. . . .

Though spared most of the infirmities of old age, I find the still-increasing claims upon me,—apparently a man made up of leisure,—more than I can meet. I have to depend on the forbearance of my friends for the many involuntary neglects with which I have to reproach myself.

I remain, with best wishes and thanks,

Yours very truly,
JAMES MARTINEAU."

NOTE.

The omission of names of Advance Reviewers, as of nearly all the recent Authors quoted from in this volume, has been especially assented to by all the parties concerned. This, as elsewhere explained, is not because of anyone's unwillingness to openly avow his sentiments; but rather to favor the strong desire of the Author that no names should be used in the entire volume except as some unusual demands of revered age, or high office, or *copyright* regulations should render it advisable or imperative.

THE AUTHOR.

Epiphany, 1898.

ACKNOWLEDGMENTS.

Among other volumes named elsewhere in the following pages from which citations, with the above understanding, have been made are those which follow: "Studies of the Inner Kingdom," "Things New and Old," "Talks About Jesus," "Faith and Self-Surrender," "God and Christ," "Our Heredity from God," "The Life in Common," "The Man Jesus," "What is the Bible?"

For these and all other helps, cordially extended for the preparation and issue of this volume, sincere thanks are here publicly offered.

Acknowledgments are hereby made, with thanks, to the following publishers: E. P. Dutton & Co., D. Appleton & Co., Geo. Ellis & Co., American Unitarian Association, Merrill & Baker, The Macmillan Co., Longmans, Green, & Co. Especial acknowledgments and thanks are due, and hereby are made, to Houghton, Mifflin, & Co. for their generous permission for the use of several of the shorter poems of John G. Whittier, but in particular of those used on pages 147–150 to form the "Model Sketch of Our Recent Prophet-Bard."

THE AUTHOR.

Epiphany, 1898.

Renascent Christianity

A Forecast of the Twentieth Century

IN THE LIGHT OF

Higher Criticism of the Bible
Study of Comparative Religion
AND OF THE
Universal Prayer for Religious Unity

BY

A Clergyman

During the past twelve years Rector in Succession of St. John's Protestant Episcopal
Church, Arlington, Mass., and of St. Mark's (Irving Memorial) Church
Tarrytown-on-Hudson, N. Y.; Formerly Pastor in Succession
of Channing Memorial Church, Newport, R. I., and
of Church of the Unity, Boston, Mass.

AUTHOR OF
"Ancient Sacred Scriptures of the World," etc.

ANNO CHRISTI 1898-2000

G. P. PUTNAM'S SONS

NEW YORK
27 WEST TWENTY-THIRD STREET

LONDON
24 BEDFORD STREET STRAND

The Knickerbocker Press

1898

COPYRIGHT, 1897
BY
G. P. PUTNAM'S SONS

The Knickerbocker Press, New York

TO HER WHO FOR NEARLY THIRTY YEARS HAS BEEN

THE SYMPATHETIC COMPANION OF MY LIFE

AND

TO OUR ONLY ONE WHO HAS GROWN

TO BE MY CHIEF LITERARY HELPER

I DO

HEREBY AFFECTIONATELY INSCRIBE THIS VOLUME

" Ye shall know Truth and Truth shall make you free." " Stand fast therefore in the Liberty wherewith the Christ hath made us free, and be not entangled again with the yoke of bondage."

" He is the freeman whom the Truth makes free.
And all are slaves beside."

" The voice mysterious, which whoso hears
Must think on what has been and what will be."

" Often as thy inward ear
Catches such rebounds, beware—
Listen, ponder, hold them dear ;
For of God—of God they are."

PREFATORY NOTES.

1. Thus far in the Evolution of Mankind the *credulous* has prevailed, to the repression and almost universal exclusion of the *critical;* especially so with reference to all subjects relating to Religion. By the "critical" is not meant *ignorant* rejection or unbelief, much less the *scoffing* spirit of Infidelity or the *scorning* spirit of Agnosticism: but a tendency *to look into* things, a spirit and habit of *inspection*. This was the original meaning of those shining words of the Bible —Prophet, Apostle, Bishop; they were names for those who were supposed to be inspectors or *lookers-into-things*.

> This of course refers to the generic meaning of the words. Their original significance was true to their derivation so long as Bible Religion was " pure and undefiled." Every recognized Prophet of the Old Testament, Apostle of the New, and Bishop of the first century was a "Skeptic" in such a pronounced sense of that word (in its generic meaning) as to be a "heretic," an "infidel" even, to the popular or "orthodox" party of his generation. When Christianity began to degenerate there were no more Prophets (except "false Prophets"), no more Apostles, and the word Bishop grew to mean a mere *overseer* or an official director of dogmatic and ecclesiastical affairs.

This critical spirit can only exist in highly *evolved* individuals, and can only prevail widely in highly *evolved* periods. Such individuals have been all those *true* Prophets, Apostles, and Bishops who (in all the Past and in every form of Religion) have "turned the world upside down" in its superstitions, stupidities, and sins; and have striven to inaugurate the Kingdom of Heaven on Earth through the agency of their Protestantisms, Revolutions, and Reforms. Thus far in History there has been no *period* so highly *evolved* as to enable this critical spirit to prevail widely. Most nearly approximating it were the first and second centuries and the sixteenth and seventeenth centuries of the Christian Era. (The periods of the Buddhistic, Socratic, Islamistic, and of the more ancient Confucian and Zoroastrian Reforms were approximations also; but limited in aspirations and local in attempts.)

But now, all the signs of the times indicate that the Evolution of Mankind has reached such an elevated stage as to render it possible to inaugurate a Protestantism of the *devoutly and reverently* Critical that shall so widely prevail over the *ignorantly and degradingly* Credulous as to virtually establish that Kingdom of Heaven upon Earth which John the Baptist, Jesus, and the Apostles introduced: and which the Protestant Reforms of the sixteenth and seventeenth centuries re-introduced. This conviction has so taken possession of the author as to be the compelling motive of every sermon preached, article written, and word of instruction spoken during the entire thirty years of his unceasing service as Minister of the Gospel of Jesus the Christ. He has ever tried to be a *true* Skeptic, that is, *a devout and reverent* looker-into-things. Moreover, he has increasingly believed that, in a new and wider sense than ever before, the Kingdom of Heaven is at hand. This belief finally suggested (as a possible forward-helping) this volume and dictated its contents—" Renascent Christianity, A Forecast of the Twentieth Century."

Renascent means reviving, renewing, or *newly springing up*. Renascent Christianity, therefore, means Original Christianity (*i. e.*, Christianity as taught by Jesus and his Apostles), reviving, renewing or *springing up anew*.

Explanatory of the general title is the additional one, A Forecast of the Twentieth Century. Forecast implies foresight: and foresight means power to foretell or to prophesy. In this sense this volume is a prophecy of the *kind* of Christianity that will prevail (or begin to prevail) in the Twentieth Century.

After the entire body of this volume was in permanent type, and these Prefatory Notes were in the printer's hands, the following met the author's eye for the first time: (" Our Heredity from God.")

" There is in human evolution also a great deal of what may be termed periodicity. Ideas and lines of thought run their courses in given periods. Religions have from the outset had a period of about five hundred years. Brahminism, itself a reformation of an antecedent faith, burst out simultaneously over Asia about 2000 B.C. The law-giving by Manu in Southern Asia, by Tschow in Eastern Asia, and by Moses in Western Asia, was spontaneous and simultaneous about 1500 and 1500 B.C. The song and psalm era of David and Homer was about 1000 B.C. Buddha in India, Confucius in China, Socrates in Greece, flashed forth about 500 B.C. Five hundred years later, Jesus, concentering all lines of evolution, symbolized the cosmopolitan unity of all future development. 500 to 600 A.D. the papacy was established, and Mohammed began his crusade of monotheism. 1000 A.D. the completed hierarchy was established by Hildebrand; 1500 A.D. the Reformation by Luther was kindled. As we near 2000, it seems certain that we are approaching the culmination and establishment of the age of Reason as the basis of Faith. . . . Through all these revolutions has there been evolution; and all religions have moved on The King's Highway to higher hopes and purer purposes."

2. The Author would classify himself as to Ecclesiasticism, Ritual, and Dogmatic Theology among the broadest of "Broad Churchmen." Episcopal Order of Government, so long as it does not degenerate into a tyranny of dictation or of control; Liturgical Worship, so long as it is intellectually sincere and spiritually elevating; Historic Theology, so long as it neither adds to nor takes from the simple teachings of Jesus the Christ, are all heartily accepted. Though much disliking (on account of their bigoted and persecuting associations) the words Churchmanship, Orthodoxy, and Trinitarianism, their truths (so far as they are clearly those enunciated by Jesus the Christ) are eagerly retained, while their errors are as eagerly rejected. The well-known Rector of Grace Church, New York City, has recently defined the position tersely and well—" Such unclassifiable thinkers are by no means so numerous within our ecclesiastical borders as might be wished. They come under the same sort of suspicion as that which overshadows the 'independent voter' in politics. Nevertheless their abiding in the ship inures to the benefit of the voyage. We are stronger and richer with them than we could be without them."

Among the last written words of the late Professor Henry Drummond were the following:

"The characteristics of Christianity are that it deals with the roots of things, with the heart and life; that it holds sacred the aspiration and the wants of man and man himself; that it recognizes above all social distinctions the universal brotherhood of the race, and over all legislation the one Golden Rule of Christ. While claiming no monopoly of this high spirit for Christian Liberalism, is it unfair to point out that the interests of Conservatism hitherto have been more centred on institutions than on men? Is it untrue to say that it has sought its sanctions in tradition rather than in the sense of justice and the educated intelligence of the people?"

Among the latest public utterances of Dr. John Watson are the following:

"When a preacher offers the beautiful verities of Christ and His salvation *as the hereditary treasure of our race*, then is the soul captivated and made eager for their acceptance. What it has long been seeking for, as in a mist, has now been revealed; what it has bitterly cried out for, as in a dry and thirsty land, is now within reach. When a preacher gathers together various elements of the Christian faith and demands that one should accept them all and at once with an alternative of punishment, then the kindly evangel is held as a pistol to the head and human nature is apt to rebel.

"The Gospel is never negative—an embodied threat—'refuse if you dare'; the Gospel is ever positive—a living promise, 'Come and be blessed.'

"Beyond all question and by the consent of all men the Bible has a voice of peculiar and irresistible majesty. Like the deep, mellow sound of a bell floating out from a cathedral tower on the violet sky of Italy and arresting for a brief moment at least the confused babel of the carnival below, so does the bell note of this book fall on the restless questions and fretful anxieties of the soul. Hearers are of a sudden hushed into reverence and are graciously inclined to submission, not by the ipse dixit of a fallible preacher, but because the mouth of the Lord has spoken it."

In a sermon recently preached by a scholarly "Trinitarian" clergyman in Columbus, Ohio, occurs the following:

"The truth is that whatever extravagance may be charged against the Higher Criticism, it has made it impossible for any intelligent Biblical scholar to hold the view of the Bible that was taught to me when I was studying for the ministry and that is held by a great majority of our church members to-day. *That view is simply not true.* The Bible is not the kind of a book that we once believed it to be. It is a better book, a diviner book as I believe; and the people of our churches have a right to know just what kind of a book it is."

A distinguished clergyman of the "Trinitarian" Faith, in a recent sermon preached in the city of New York, said:

"We are approaching an hour in the history of religious faith that may be called the hour before a revolution. All writers, speakers and thinkers are dealing with the subject.

"The day is at hand when the world must have a better interpretation of the Bible. The popular education of the people has been such that a revolution of faith is inevitable.

"New theology means the sum total of the aggressive thinking of centuries. This revolution in religion will make men better Christians in the broader sense of the word, and do away with ignorance and bigotry."

From various recent "orthodox" magazines and other periodicals have been gathered the following:

"Until we can put away from the minds of men the common error that the current Christianity of the Church is true Christianity, we can make but little progress in converting the world."

"It is generally acknowledged that there needs to be a waking up and a reformation in the Church at large. Christians need to be called back to the simple teachings of Jesus and to a Pentecostal sense of their mission for souls and for the world."

"The greatest necessity of our times is the *Christianization* of Christianity. Back to Christ, back to genuine Christianity!—this is the John the Baptist cry of the coming age and ages."

"It is my firm belief that the Church of Christ is on the eve of a mighty spiritual and moral upheaval, the incoming of a power that will make it truly Christian and sweep the world forward toward the Millennial dawn. For this the whole Church should pray, and in expectation of it move forward to the speedy conquest of the world for Christ."

A renowned Professor in one of our leading American Universities has recently said: "Not a mere shifting of lines, but a change of base; not a mere readjustment of details, but a reconstruction of Christian Theology is now necessary. There can be little doubt in the mind of the thoughtful observer, that we are now on the eve of the greatest change in traditional beliefs that has taken place since the birth of Christianity. But let us not be at all disturbed thereby. For as then, so now, change comes *not to destroy but to fulfil.*"

One more citation may be made illustrative of still broader interpretations: those of what we may term World-Theology, or the new, but already well established and widely studied science, known as Comparative Religion. That profound and honored scholar, Professor Max Müller, a few years ago concluded a personal letter to the author (which may be found on one of the introductory pages of the volume called *Ancient Sacred Scriptures of the World*) with these words: "There never was a false God, nor was there ever really a false Religion—*unless one may call a child a false man.* The true religion of the future will be the fulfilment of all the religions of the past—the true religion of humanity, that which in the struggle of history remains as the indestructible portion of all the so-called false religions of mankind."

The citations now made indicate the position, the method, and the spirit of all that will be found in the following pages.

3. "The originals are not original." Except in phrase, dress, fresh statement or re-arrangement "there is no new thing under the sun"—no *new* Thought, no *new* Truth. Whoever professes to be "original" displays mingled superficiality and conceit. Every wisest speaker or writer takes pains to say with Confucius, "I only hand on"; or with Jesus, "I came to fulfil." All truth "was in the beginning" as God's *eternal* Logos, "is now and ever shall be." There is no more, no less; except as the expanded vision enlarges its Revelation or the contracted vision shuts it out. It is

all a matter of the *enlargement* of vision; and this is all a matter of *clean* hearts and *clear* minds. "Thou shalt love the Lord thy God with *all* thy *heart* and *mind*." All true Seers *see* the same everlasting Truth; the *cleaner* their hearts and the *clearer* their minds the more expansive their vision. No true Seer can contradict another, for he *sees* the same things. Neither can he "add unto nor take away from": for Truth is a constant quantity—"the Alpha and Omega, the beginning and the end, the first and the last." Neither can he turn or change it into something new, for Truth *is* the "Father of lights, with whom is no variableness, neither shadow of turning,"—"the same yesterday, to-day, and forever." This scriptural and rational teaching will explain the following marked features of this volume:

(*a*) Its rejection of the common belief that there is an *exclusive* Revelation, a *chosen* line of Prophets, a *deposit* of Truth, a Faith *once for all* delivered to the Saints, a *favorite* People of God, or a *one and only* True Church.

(*b*) Its rejection of the common belief that the Seers of the Jewish and Christian religions saw *different* Truth from that which the Seers of other religions had seen—though doubtless they saw *wider*, and *deeper*, and *higher*, on account of that enlargement of vision which resulted from *cleaner* hearts and *clearer* minds.

(*c*) Its rejection of the common belief that *absolutely* new Truth is found in the Bible; and its constant affirmation that, *so far as they go*, all Religions reveal the same Eternal Truth.

(*d*) Its strong affirmation that "sacred" Scriptures are *modern* as well as ancient; that the "canon" of Divine Revelations has but just reached its Alpha Volume; that there are Seers to-day (or ought to be) as many and as great as ever were "raised up" in all the Past—nay, more and greater they *ought to be*: that Inspiration includes everything that is "pure, and beautiful, and good"; that all "holy" men (and *women*) are "inspired of God," and that the Old Testament Prophecy has, as yet, *only just begun to be ful-*

filled—" It shall come to pass in the last days, saith God, I will pour out of my Spirit *upon all* flesh; and your sons and your daughters shall prophesy, and your young men shall see visions, and your old men shall dream dreams; and on *all* my servants and on *all* my handmaidens I will pour out in those days of my Spirit; *and they shall prophesy.*" Such is the promised and *ever-ready-to-be-conferred*-Enlargement of Vision to all Mankind; so that *all* may be Seers whenever they fulfil the essential conditions—*clean* hearts, and *clear* minds. " Thou shalt love the Lord thy God with *all* thy *heart* and *mind*,"—then shalt thou too become one of God's Prophets, as well as one of His Saints and Sons.

> *" But when we in our viciousness grow hard,*
> *O misery on't! the wise gods seal our eyes*
> *. . . . . Make us*
> *Adore our errors, laugh at us while we strut*
> *To our confusion."*

" *The Lord* . . . *hath closed your eyes* . . . *and the vision of all is become unto you as the words of a book that is sealed.*"

"*Their eyes have they closed* . . . *but blessed are your eyes, for they see.*"

Blessed are those that are *both* pure in heart and clear in mind for they *do* see God.

What is true of *seers* or prophets in religion is equally true in every other department of human advancement. " The same idea, or invention, or discovery, has come about in many parts of the world at the same time. Strange views break out all over the globe by apparent spontaneity. Hardly ever is an important discovery made by one man alone. The correlation of force was simultaneously announced in three countries. The discovery of Neptune was announced by a Frenchman coincident with its determination by an Englishman. Chloroform was discovered on the same day by two men independently. Darwin and Wallace and Haeckel, without intercommunication, propounded simultaneously the hypothesis of evolution. It is as when mountain tops of equal height catch the morning sunbeam at the same moment. When races or individuals reach an equal height they touch the same ideas. Egyptians, Chinese, Mexicans, and Peruvians, all independently discovered the making of bronze. The Chinese, the Mayas, and the Germans invented the printing-press. Confucius, Zoroaster, and Jesus independently promulgated the golden rule." ("Our Heredity from God.")

4. In this volume (except in the introductory pages, and pages 19-22) no *names* of authors cited or quoted from are given. All citations and extracts are indicated by the usual quotation marks. The special reason for this is that no citations have been made or extracts included but such as are axiomatic or self-evident—to all who *combine* the three attainments of moral purity, intellectual honesty, and *unselfish* love of truth. For none others than those who have attained (or are hungering and thirsting to attain) these, is this volume designed. General reasons for this omission of names may be found in Section XXXV., page 53, "All Sacred Scriptures are Anonymous," and in Section XXXVI., page 54, "Hiding Self behind Truth."

5. An unusual number of italicized words, of words beginning with a capital letter, as also an unusual number of general marks of punctuation have been designedly used throughout the volume. The author has thus tried to make clear his meaning in passages that otherwise would (almost certainly) be wrongly understood, and unfairly represented by any sectarian or otherwise prejudiced person who might take the trouble to read or to glance through the pages. The mechanism of a book is of far less account than its meaning; and to be understood (especially in controverted or debatable statements) is of far greater importance than to follow approved methods of punctuating sentences or of printing words.

6. Sharp phrases and ofttimes seemingly severe (especially in the sections entitled Degeneration of Christianity, Tendency to Revert in Protestantism, Mercenary Conformity, Double-tongued Esotericism, and Hireling-Priests) will be found, and by some will be objected to. The author has been *conscience-compelled* in the use and retention of these. Many times did he propose to strike them out or to modify them. But, convinced that they were truths, and truths that *needed* to be spoken; convinced that it was only cowardice or fear of being criticised that suggested their omission or their smoothing down, at last the resolve was fixed to retain them, and to retain them unchanged. Every sharp

word and every severe rebuke, as well as every dissenting or (seemingly) heretical opinion expressed in this volume has been many times re-considered; and written and re-written "with all humility of mind and with many tears."

"Then answered one of the lawyers (Doctors of Divinity) and said unto him, Master, thus saying thou reproachest us also. And he said, Woe unto you also ye lawyers! for ye lade men with burdens grievous to be borne. . . . Woe unto you! for you build the sepulchres of the prophets, and your fathers killed them. . . . Woe unto you! for ye have had taken away the key of knowledge: ye entered not in yourselves, and them that were entering in ye hindred."

"You wish *pleasanter* words . . . and very likely consider my preference for such *plain* words a perverse sort of a partiality on my part . . . you wish I had not thrust them so butt-foremost at you,—you wish to use milder terms. Well, I admit there may be just a dash of perversity in their choice. The spectacle of the mere word-grabbing game played by the *soft-determinists* has perhaps driven me too violently the other way; . . . The question is of *things*, not of *eulogistic* names for them; and the best word is the one that enables men to know the quickest whether they disagree or not about the things. . . . Any other words permit of *quibbling* and let us, after the fashion of the soft-determinists, make a pretence of restoring the caged bird to liberty with one hand, while with the other we anxiously tie a string to its leg to make sure it does not get beyond our sight."—[Prof. JAMES in "The Will to Believe."]

. . . "'T is an unweeded garden
That grows to seed; things rank and gross in nature
Possess it chiefly."

"The time is out of joint; O cursed spite
That ever I was born to set it right."
(O blessed privilege that I may help to set it right.)

"Though all can never be wrong—the existence of even one faithful soul to recognize wrong, or to protest against it, means that something, at least, is right—yet there is always something wrong somewhere, which each of us was probably born to help set right. . . . When we examine it, moreover, we shall probably find that it is not something wholly new which we are required to do, but something in the line of what has been already done; developing and extending to a new case a principle already recognized."

"Divine Fatherhood and Human Brotherhood constitute the Religion of Jesus. This simple character Christianity retained for two centuries. Then the union of the Church with the State, its corruption by heathenism and its assumption of temporal power remanded the simple teachings of Jesus to the background and gave supernaturalism the control of Christianity for centuries. There have always been individuals and sects to keep alive in the Church the sacred flame of pure religion ; but the recovery of the primitive traditions, and the extensive reorganization of Christian doctrine in line with the simple teachings of Jesus must be the achievement of the twentieth and succeeding centuries. It is now high time to cut loose from sickly supernaturalism and lay all stress on the two great wholesome doctrines of Jesus—the Fatherhood of God and the Brotherhood of Man."

---

7. A word of apology may be added for the inclusion of so many citations, especially in the latter pages of the volume.

This has been done for a double reason :—the desire to present every essential aspect of the new interpretations of Christianity, and also to bring forward as many " witnesses " to these new interpretations as the reasonable limits of the volume would admit of. "Ye are my witnesses, saith the Lord." If "in the mouth of two or three witnesses every word shall be established," how much more profound the conviction when " we are compassed about with so great a cloud of witnesses"—comprising so large a proportion of the most scholarly, devout, and pure-hearted men and women of all the ages ; but of this introductory age of the twentieth century in particular.

8. As Virgil sang, and John the Baptist cried, and Jesus the Messiah prayed, and Paul the Apostle preached, and John the Revelator prophesied in the first century, so at the approach of the twentieth century should all Poets sing, and all Reformers cry, and all Messiahs pray, and all Apostles preach, and all Revelators prophesy:

" *The new era of Cumæan Song is now arrived,*
  The great Series of Ages begins anew."

" *The Kingdom of Heaven is at hand, Prepare ye the way of the Lord, make His path straight.*"

" *That they also may be One in us ; I in them and Thou in me, that they may be made perfect in One.*"

" *The times of this ignorance God winked at ; but now commandeth all men, everywhere, to repent.*"

" *The former things are passed away : and he that sat upon the throne said, Behold I make all things new.*"

9. With these prefatory notes carefully read and well understood, the elaborations of them in the following pages will be readily comprehended—however much they may be criticised or condemned.

If the sharp words which may be found in this volume, like the sharp teeth of the mouse in the fable, shall be able to gnaw even one of the strings of that vast net-work of Superstition which, for sixteen centuries, has been binding down the lion-strength of primitive Christianity, the author will be amply rewarded for his toil.

EXPLANATORY NOTES.

THE PASTORAL LETTER OF 1894.

Among various recent *tendencies to revert* from the "glorious liberty of the children of God" to the "yokes of bondage" imposed by systems and sects, is that signified by the widely known and much debated "Pastoral Letter of 1894."

Till then it was unheard of and undreamed of that the "Broad" school, or the "High" school, or any other school in the Protestant Episcopal Church of America should be subject to the direction of the Bishops as to honest interpretations of the New Testament, much less of the creeds and traditions of Historic Christianity. The Author entered this communion and ministry as a pronounced Broad Churchman. As such he was welcomed, confirmed, received, ordained, and nominated to his first Rectorship by the cordial and always gracious Bishop of New York. He came sincerely believing that the Episcopal Church, more than any other of the various "orthodox" Churches, was open to *new light;* and as such, offered the best *common ground* for that reconstruction of old Dogmas and reuniting of all who called themselves Christians into one truly Catholic Communion which was, as it still is, his chief prayer and hope. With this prayer and in this hope he has quietly labored in the Episcopal Ministry, with rarely a week or a Sunday of rest, during all these years till now. His first keen disappointment came with the issue of the Pastoral Letter of 1894. This seemed to be an open condemnation of all Broad Churchmen. Though pronounced by one of the Bishops, the Bishop of New York, as having "undoubtedly no conciliar authority" and "little more value than is expressed in the more or less close consensus of opinion of some half-dozen individuals" (Letter to the New York *Tribune*, February 15, 1895), it was reaffirmed by the House of Bishops at their last General Convention; and, in spite of the non-concurrence of the House of Deputies, has increasingly been accepted as the law of Dogmatic Interpretation to which all clergy of the Protestant Episcopal Church are bound to conform. Constant and unmistakable evidences of this reaction toward Dogmatism very painfully came to the Author's notice; and he was driven to the conviction that the hitherto progressive Protestant Episcopal Church had turned its face steadfastly backward.

For one he could not consent to go backward with it; neither could he, by keeping silence, even *seem* to stand with it in what appeared to be spiritual as well as intellectual reversion and degeneration.

Therefore, as an open protest against this and all similar "tendencies to revert and degenerate," and also as a hoped-for contribution (however slight) to the renascence or revival of New Testament and Apostolic Christianity, this volume was conceived and has been completed.

(1) *An Example for All Official Bodies of the Church Catholic.*

On page 254 was noticed a recent example, nobly illustrative of what the Bishop of New York, as quoted on one of the opening pages, earnestly commends and calls for—*the courage of one's convictions.*

At the date of this writing appears in all the public journals, with general approval, the responsive official action of the Corporation (referred to on page 254), practically withdrawing its censures, and granting entire liberty of thought and speech. The following extracts from the Resolutions may well be presented as a "text" for all official bodies of the Church Catholic:

> "It was not in our minds to prescribe the path in which you should tread, or to restrain your freedom of opinion or reasonable liberty of utterance. In this liberal and catholic institution all members shall enjoy full, free, absolute, and uninterrupted liberty of conscience, which includes freedom of thought and expression."

(2) *The Lambeth Conference of 1897.*

That which follows is from the Encyclical Letter just issued by the Lambeth Conference of 1897, composed of the bishops of the whole Anglican Communion:

> "That faith is already in serious danger which refuses to face questions that may be raised on the authority or the genuineness of any part of the Scriptures" (or of the Traditions, Formularies, or Creeds) "that have come down to us. . . . A faith which is always, or often, attended by a secret fear that *we dare not inquire, lest inquiry should lead us to results inconsistent with what we believe*, is already infected with a disease which may soon destroy it."

CONTENTS.

SECTION	TOPIC	PAGE
I.—	New Testament Sanctions	xxix
	Mission of the Higher Criticism	xxix
	Method of Comparative Religion	xxix
	Plea and Prayer for Religious Unity	xxx
II.—	Poetic Suggestions	xxx
III.—	Modern Sanctions and Suggestions	xxxi
IV.—	The Renascence	1
	"Behold, I Make All Things New"	1
V.—	Struggle for Existence—Survival of the Fittest	2
VI.—	Tendency to Revert is the Supreme Danger	3
VII.—	Degeneracy Universal in Religion	4
VIII.—	Degeneracy—Christianity no Exception, Six General Illustrations from History	6
		7
	The Twelve Disciples	7
	The Experience of St. Paul	8
	Statements of the Book of Revelation,	8
	The First Centuries	8
	All the Centuries	8
	To-day	9
IX.—	The Simple Truth as it was in Jesus	12
X.—	Back to First Principles	15
XI.—	The Original Sources of Christianity	15
XII.—	What of the New Testament?	17
XIII.—	The Renascent Bible	18
XIV.—	The Bible as Literature	19

SECTION	TOPIC	PAGE
XV.	How Myths Grow	21
XVI.	The Wheat Garnered—The Chaff Burned,	24
XVII.	Eclecticism, Inclusiveness, Catholicism, Christianity	27
	Three Analogous Conversations	27
	The Moral, as Drawn from the New Testament	28
	The Moral, as Drawn from other Ancient Sacred Books of the World	29
	Conclusion	30
XVIII.	Christianity is Religious Eclecticism	30
XIX.	Jesus no Sectarian—His Religion no Sect	32
XX.	Study of Comparative Religion Leads to Christianity	32
XXI.	Christianity a Vast Graded School of Religion	34
XXII.	Prove All, Hold Fast the Good	34
XXIII.	The Reliable Creed and its Essential Tests	36
XXIV.	The Living Creed and Pledge	37
	The Life Creed	38
	The Life Pledge	38
XXV.	Christianity the Supreme Religion	38
XXVI.	The World's Parliament of Religions	39
XXVII.	The Age of Comparison and its Test	42
XXVIII.	Religions Judged by their Fruits	43
XXIX.	Unprejudiced Testimonies	46
XXX.	The Verdict is for Christianity	47
XXXI.	Notwithstanding	49
XXXII.	What, then, is Christianity?	50
XXXIII.	Sacred Scriptures of the World, Modern as well as Ancient	50
XXXIV.	Modern Sacred Scriptures	52
XXXV.	All Sacred Scriptures are Anonymous	53
XXXVI.	Hiding Self behind Truth	54
XXXVII.	The Resurrected Jesus	56
XXXVIII.	New Meaning of Old Dogmas and Creeds,	57
XXXIX.	Questions of Criticism and their Answers	58

SECTION	TOPIC	PAGE
	THE CHARGE OF "HERESY"?	58
	REVIVING ANCIENT HERESIES?	59
	NEW WINE IN OLD BOTTLES, NEW CLOTH ON OLD GARMENTS?	59
	INCONSISTENT—A SORT OF HYPOCRITE?	60
	WHY NOT WAIT FOR COUNCILS, CONVENTIONS, OR AUTHORIZED COMMITTEES?	60
	THE "TRINITY," "NICENE CREED," ETC., WHY CONTINUE TO USE THEM?	63
XL.	ATTEMPT AT REASONABLE EXPLANATION	64
	1. THE TRINITY	64
	2. CHRIST	65
	3. JESUS CHRIST	65
	4. JESUS THE CHRIST	65
	5. CHRISTIANS	65
	6. SALVATION BY CHRIST	66
	7. JESUS CHRIST AS THE SAVIOUR	66
	8. SON OF GOD	66
	9. JESUS CHRIST THE SON OF GOD	66
	10. JESUS CHRIST THE ONLY SON OF GOD	67
	11. CONCEIVED OF THE HOLY SPIRIT, BORN OF THE VIRGIN MARY	67
	12. THE PRE-EXISTENCE OF JESUS	68
	13. BEFORE ALL WORLDS,—BY WHOM ALL THINGS WERE MADE	69
	14. GOD OF GOD, LIGHT OF LIGHT, VERY GOD OF VERY GOD: BEGOTTEN, NOT MADE,	69
	15. ONE CATHOLIC AND APOSTOLIC CHURCH,	69
	16. THE BIBLE IS THE WORD OF GOD	69
	17. THE HOLY SACRAMENTS OF BAPTISM AND THE LORD'S SUPPER	70
	18. THE HOLY GHOST	70
	19. RECEIVING THE HOLY GHOST	70
	20. ROSE FROM THE DEAD AND ASCENDED TO HEAVEN	71
	21. HEAVEN AND HELL	71
	22. SHALL COME AGAIN TO JUDGE THE WORLD, WHOSE KINGDOM SHALL HAVE NO END	71

SECTION	TOPIC	PAGE
XLI.	Still open to New Light	71
XLII.	Degeneration of Protestantism—Persistent Tendencies to Revert	72
XLIII.	The Protestant Reformation only the Beginning of Needed and Essential Reforms	75
XLIV.	"Though all Men should Forsake Thee, yet will not I"	77
XLV.	Renascent Christianity a Revival of Combined Piety and Morality	79
(a)	Piety and morality combined was Christianity as taught by Jesus	79
(b)	The two extremes	80
(c)	Religious ceremonialism and ethical proprieties	81
(d)	Partial truths accepted as the whole truth	82
(e)	Rome or reason	83
(f)	The golden mean	84
(g)	Jesus the great uniter as well as reformer	85
(h)	The old story of tendency to revert	86
(i)	Building on the side of Rome, or of reason, or on the "rock" between	87
XLVI.	Renascent Christianity a Re-adjustment of the Relations between Employers and those Employed, or between Capital and Labor	87
(a)	The re-adjustment stated	88
(b)	How the Christian employee should behave toward his employer	89
(c)	Peaceable and patient content with one's lot	90
(d)	"Vengeance is mine; I will repay, saith the Lord"	91
(e)	Burning sub-questions—indolence, pauper-spirited pride, ignorance, vice, violence	93
(f)	Special reforms favorable to the	

SECTION	TOPIC	PAGE

WORKING CLASSES WHICH RENASCENT CHRISTIANITY WILL INSIST UPON—LOWEST PRICES FOR ALL NEEDFUL COMMODITIES, EXTREMES OF WEALTH AND POVERTY RESTRAINED, SYNDICATES AND OTHER MONOPOLIES PUT DOWN, BUREAUS OF INDUSTRY, GOVERNMENT SAVINGS BANKS, SAME PAY FOR THE WORKING WOMAN AS FOR THE WORKING MAN 95

XLVII.—"FIRST PURE, THEN PEACEABLE" . . . 100
    (a) PURITY BEFORE PEACE 101
    (b) A TRUTH POSTULATED, A PROBLEM STATED, A THEOREM ENUNCIATED . . . 103
    (c) THE CAUSES OF FAILURES AND SUFFERINGS . 106
    (d) THE SWORD 108
    (e) MUCH TO BE DONE—ADVANCEMENT WILL BE SLOW 109

XLVIII.—HINDRANCES 111
    1. MERCENARY CONFORMITY . . . 112
    2. INSINCERITY 116
    3. DOUBLE-TONGUED ESOTERICISM . . 117
    4. HIRELING PRIESTS 118, 119
    5. CONSERVATISM OF INBORN STUPIDITY . 124

XLIX.—PREFATORY EXPLANATIONS AND TOPICAL CONTENTS OF THE NEW EDITION OF ANCIENT SACRED SCRIPTURES OF THE WORLD . 129

L.—A MODERN PROPHET-PRIEST—SKETCHED AS A MODEL 130

LI.—OUR RECENT PROPHET-BISHOP—SENTENCES SELECTED FROM HIS SERMONS . . . 144

LII.—A MODERN PROPHET-BARD—APPROPRIATE SELECTIONS 147

LIII.—REVERSIONS AND DEGENERATIONS WITH REFERENCE TO JESUS-WORSHIP AND MARIOLATRY 153
    CORRECTING QUOTATIONS 154

LIV.—REVERSIONS AND DEGENERATIONS WITH REFERENCE TO CONCEPTIONS OF THE HOLY GHOST 157

SECTION	TOPIC	PAGE
	CORRECTING QUOTATIONS	158
LV.	REVERSIONS AND DEGENERATIONS WITH REFERENCE TO CONCEPTIONS OF THE ATONING SACRIFICE	161
	CORRECTING QUOTATIONS	162
LVI.	REVERSIONS AND DEGENERATIONS WITH REFERENCE TO ARCHITECTURE AND ADORNMENTS AS CONSTITUTING A CHURCH	163
LVII.	REVERSIONS AND DEGENERATIONS WITH REFERENCE TO RITUALISTIC OR OTHER SENSATIONAL OR "POPULARIZED" FORMS OF WORSHIP	164
	CORRECTING QUOTATIONS	165
LVIII.	MODERN CONFIRMATIONS—A FEW OUT OF MANY	166
LIX.	ILLUSTRATIVE SELECTIONS FROM RECENT BOOKS BEARING ON THE HIGHER CRITICISM OF THE BIBLE	172
	1. THE INFALLIBLE BOOK	173
	2. IDEAS AND FORMS COMMON TO ALL RELIGIONS	174
	3. FALSE AND FANCIFUL INTERPRETATIONS	175
	4. INFALLIBLE BIBLES MUST BE INFALLIBLY PRESERVED	176
	5. THE TRANSLATORS MUST BE INFALLIBLE	177
	6. MIRACULOUS INSPIRATION NO LONGER CREDIBLE	177
	7. HIGHER CRITICISM RESCUES AND EXALTS THE BIBLE	178
	8. IMMORAL INFLUENCE OF THE OLD IDEAS OF THE BIBLE, ESPECIALLY UPON THE YOUNG	179
	9. THE ESSENTIAL TRUTHS OF THE BIBLE ARE, OF THEMSELVES, SELF-EVIDENT	180
	10. WHO ARE THE ENEMIES OF THE BIBLE?	181
	11. HOW TO VIEW AND USE THE BIBLE	181
	12. HOW THE BIBLE WAS FORMED	182

SECTION	TOPIC	PAGE
	13. THE BIBLE CANON ALWAYS AN OPEN QUESTION	182
	14. THE LONG PERIOD OF THE BIBLE'S GROWTH	183
	15. DATE OF THE BIRTH OF JESUS	184
	16. THE STORY OF THE MIRACULOUS BIRTH,	185
	17. THE MESSIANIC HOPE	185
	18. JESUS THE MESSIAH	186
	19. THE GOSPEL ACCORDING TO THE HEBREWS	187
	20. THE NEW TESTAMENT MIRACLES	188
	21. OUR SYNOPTIC GOSPELS	189
	22. THE FOURTH GOSPEL	190
	23. ST. PAUL'S CONCEPTION OF JESUS	191
	24. THE CORPOREAL RESURRECTION AND ASCENSION	192
	25. A PARABLE OF THE LIFE OF JESUS	194
LX.	MISCELLANEOUS CONFIRMATIONS — EXTRACTS FROM RECENT BOOKS	195
LXI.	EMPIRICISM AND EVOLUTIONISM VERSUS INSTITUTIONALISM AND CREATIONALISM	203
LXII.	TENDENCIES TO REVERT AND TO DEGENERATE HISTORICALLY CONFIRMED	208
LXIII.	THE PRESENT DEGENERATION OF OUR CHURCHES	211
LXIV.	TRUE TO ONE'S OWN SELF	215
LXV.	A RIGHTEOUS DISREGARD OF PUBLIC OPINION	217
LXVI.	THE GOLDEN MEAN OF CONTROVERSY	219
LXVII.	FRAGMENTS:	
	1. RISINGS AND FALLINGS OF MAN	221
	2. JESUS THE FRUITAGE OF THE AGES	224
	3. EXTERNAL PROSPERITY AND INTERNAL DECAY	225
	4. WHAT MANKIND MOST NEEDS	227
	5. ANSWERING OUR OWN PRAYERS	228
LXVIII.	THE SPIRIT AND NOT THE LETTER OF THE CREEDS	229
LXIX.	MODERN USE OF ANCIENT IDEAS AND TERMS	231

SECTION	TOPIC	PAGE
LXX.	Ideas and Terms Furnished by Evolutionary Science to Renascent Christianity	234
LXXI.	The Christian Church and its Worship in the First Century	238
	(a) prayer in the church down to the middle of the third century	240
LXXII.	Christology in the Church down to the Close of the Third Century	241
LXXIII.	Degeneration in the Church—how it Proceeded and Proceeds	246
LXXIV.	Degeneration of the Apostolic Ministry into Commercialism—as found at the Close of the 19th Century	250
LXXV.	Sermons made to Order	254
LXXVI.	Traditionalism as a Main Cause of Degeneration	257
LXXVII.	Credulity and Rome, or Faith and Reason—Which?	260
LXXVIII.	Evolution of the Triad as an Explanation of God	263
	(a) divine personality	265
LXXIX.	A Main Reason why so many Disbelieve in God and in Immortality	266
LXXX.	The Eclecticism of Christianity—Illustrations	269
LXXXI.	Renascent Christianity and Sacred Scriptures	
	(a) explanatory note	275
	(b) motives	275
	(c) the "retrograde movement"	276
	(d) special explanations as to translations of the bible	278
	(e) the "received text"	285
	(f) the polychrome edition	288
	(g) confirming citations	290
	(h) how the eclecticism of christianity renders it a world-religion	292
	(i) a parable of christianity as the religion of eclecticism	294

SECTION	TOPIC	PAGE
LXXXII.	MYSTERY OF THE DIVINE IN THE HUMAN—OR, JESUS THE CHRIST AS "GOD MANIFEST IN THE FLESH"	297
LXXXIII.	"FILLED WITH ALL THE FULLNESS OF GOD," AS THE PRIVILEGE OF EVERY MAN	301
LXXXIV.	ILLUSTRATIVE SELECTIONS FROM MANY RECENT AUTHORS	304
	(*a*) OPTIMISTIC FOREGLEAMS	305
	(*b*) COURAGE AND HOPE	307
LXXXV.	ILLUSTRATIVE NOTES	
	1. SUCCESS AND FAILURE	321
	2. FICTION AND FACT	321
	3. A MOST ANCIENT STATEMENT OF THE DOCTRINE ON THE TRINITY	321
	4. HOW IGNORANCE EVER MISCONCEIVES THE CHARACTER OF GOD	321
	5. AS IN RELIGION SO IN EDUCATION, COMMERCIALISM PREVAILS	323
	6. SENSATIONALISM IN THE CHURCHES	324
	7. IT PAYS	325
	8. COMMERCIAL BRIGANDS	326
	9. PUNISHMENT MEANS PURIFICATION AND REFORM	327
	10. GOLDEN ERAS IN RELIGION NO EVIDENCE OF SUPERNATURALISM OR OF PERMANENTLY SUPERIOR WORTH	329
	11. CHURCHES AS SPIRITUAL HOSPITALS AND MORAL REFORMATORIES	330
	12. INSINCERITY THE ONLY UNPARDONABLE SIN	332
	13. BONDAGE TO TRADITIONS	333
	14. TRUE RELIGION IS CATHOLIC, AND AS SUCH INCLUSIVE	335
	15. TENDENCIES TO POMP, LUXURY, AND WEALTH AMONG THOSE WHO ARE CALLED MINISTERS OF CHRIST	336
	16. THE RESULTS OF PARTISANSHIP IN RELIGION AS SEEN IN OUR MISSIONS AND CHURCHES THE WORLD OVER	338

SECTION	TOPIC	PAGE
LXXXV—Illustrative Notes—(*Continued.*)		
	17. What then is the remedy, and where?	339
	18. Sectarianism and Catholicity	341
	19. Decay in all Religions and their constant need of Reform	342
	20. The Critical Faculty and its Benevolent Use	344
	21. Mercenary Motives	344
	22. Melioration and Meliorators	345
	23. Another Voice in the Wilderness	347
	24. "On, Honor, Honest"	352
	25. Gradual Extension of "The Real Presence" as a Doctrine of the Church	352
	26. "The Truth, the Whole Truth, and Nothing but the Truth"	353
	27. Free Churches and the Gospel "without Price"	355
	28. The "Established Order" and the "Protestants"	358
	29. Scylla and Charybdis	359
	30. The Ruling Motive	366
	31. Beliefs, Theoretical and Practical	369
	32. "Repent Ye"	371
	33. Closing Confirmations	373

ADDENDA.

1. Explanations to Readers 383
2. To the 20th Century—an Open Appeal . . . 386
3. To all who Seek the Christ 391
4. The Rapid and Baneful Growth of Tradition . 392

"Lord God of Hosts be with us yet,
Lest we forget—lest we forget."

INTRODUCTORY QUOTATIONS.

I.—NEW TESTAMENT SANCTIONS.

(a.) *Mission of the Higher Criticism.*

"REPENT ye; for the Kingdom of Heaven is at hand.
. . . .
The voice of one crying in the wilderness,
Make ye ready the way of the Lord,
Make his paths straight."

"From this time began Jesus to preach, and to say, Repent ye; for the Kingdom of Heaven is at hand."

"Thy Kingdom come, Thy will be done on the Earth as in Heaven."

(b.) *Method of Comparative Religion.*

"Jesus cried and said, He that believeth on me, believeth not on me, but on Him that sent me." "For I have not spoken of myself; but the Father which sent me, He gave me commandment what I should say, and what I should speak." "If any man hear my words and believe not, I judge him not: for I am not come to judge the world, but to save the world."

"Why even of yourselves judge ye not what is right."

"Whosoever doeth the will of my Father, who is in Heaven, the same is my brother, and my sister, and my mother."

(c.) *Plea and Prayer for Religious Unity.*

"And other sheep I have which are not of this fold; them also I must bring, and they shall hear my voice; and there shall be one fold and one shepherd."

"Holy Father, keep them whom Thou hast given me in Thy name, that they may be one even as we are. Sanctify them in the truth; Thy word is truth. Neither for these only do I pray, but for them also that shall believe on me through their word, that they all may be one, even as Thou, Father, art in me, and I in Thee, that they also may be one in us—I in them and Thou in me, that they may be perfected into one."

II.—POETIC SUGGESTIONS.

"If some new phase of truth thy toil discover—
   Thine inmost eye with some bright vision blest—
Conceal it not, proclaim it as a lover
   His love proclaims. Awhile, thine honored guest—
Thy new-found thought—secret perchance may hover
   Near Thee alone! But there it must not rest."
—Sir William Hamilton.

"What if cherished Creeds must fade?
   Faith will never leave us;
God preserves what God has made,
   Nor can Truth deceive us.
Let in light—the Holy Light!
   Brothers, fear it never;
Darkness smiles and wrong grows right;
   Let in light forever!"
—Whittier.

"All before us lies the way,
   Give the past unto the wind.
All before us is the day,
   Night and darkness are behind.

> Eden, with its angels bold—
> Love, and Peace, and Purity—
> Is not an ancient story told,
> But a glowing prophecy."
>
> —WHITTIER.

III.—MODERN SANCTIONS AND SUGGESTIONS.

"It is almost certain that the Church will soon begin the reconstruction of Dogma, and that men are living who will have share in the enterprise. The material is rapidly accumulating for the work, and the Church will soon demand that the results of the New Criticism and the New Exegesis be gathered and stated to the world. . . . This is a time for which many are praying. . . . It is to be hoped that every branch of the Christian Church will soon exact no other pledge of her teachers than a declaration of faith in Jesus as the Son of God and the Saviour of the world, and a promise to keep His commandments; and otherwise to grant to them the fullest freedom of thought and expression."—*The Rev. John Watson, D.D.* [Ian Maclaren] *in the Lyman Beecher Divinity Lectures at Yale University,* 1896.

"The Fatherhood of God and the Brotherhood of Man—that is the simple creed that has given inspiration to every religion that has ever struck its roots deep down in the human heart; and no other belief to-day is so dominant among the forces that are making civilizations over again. It marks the point of divergence from the old religions and social systems whose fundamental thought was, 'God made man, therefore He has a right to damn him.' 'Not so,' say those who speak for a new interpretation of the old dogmas. 'Rather let us say, God made man, therefore He will bless him.' The old creed has always driven men apart: the new creed will draw them together."—*From a recent editorial of the New York Tribune.*

[The following, from a recent Sermon by Bishop Henry C. Potter, D.D., is as true of our religious as it is of our social and political conditions—as applicable to the Church as it is to the State:]

"This is a universe of order, not of chance nor of freak. Just because behind it there is the sovereign Source of all laws, therefore no mere human caprice can suspend those laws. Into this universe of fixed laws the Author of it has introduced a being with the mysterious and inestimable gift of moral freedom. To him has been vouchsafed not only will, but freedom of the will. He may work, or he may dream. He may sow wheat or tares. But 'whatsoever a man soweth, that'—not something else—' shall he also reap' . . . *the harvest whose seed he has sown;* not the harvest which he has merely wished for, or coveted, or imagined. . . . As in imperial Rome, glutted with the wealth of her conquests, and drunk and dizzy with the infamy of her vices, there has risen, with much material prosperity, the loathsome spectacle of manhood without virtue, of womanhood without shame, of a people glorying in its degradation, and rotten to the very core. Harvests, plenty, wealth: what are they but the possible instruments of an unutterable degradation, save as they are held as a stewardship for highest ends, and used as agencies for man's service and God's honor? . . . This may seem a harsh statement, but its substantial accuracy is very easily tested. . . . For what, in one word, is our condition? I maintain—and I challenge contradiction of that statement—that it is one in which *independent action has largely perished.* Largely, but not wholly, thank God! The other day on the floor of Congress a member who had convictions gave expression to them, and announced his intention of voting, whatever his party might do, in accordance with them. Said a fellow-member, as he sat down: 'You are right, and I agree with you. *If I too had the courage of my convictions, I should do as you will do. But I have not; and so, I shall not.*'

"A poor creature, we say! A coward, without principle; or, at least, *with principles too weak to make him do his duty!* Yes; but who is responsible for him? Again I say, *my brother, you and I.* . . . There are wrongs to be righted which, because they have sometimes been exaggerated by rash and reckless men, cannot, nevertheless, wisely be ignored. . . . Above all, there is a noisy and aggressive self-confidence which may well make us tremble. . . . Ours is a heritage of great ideals. It is these that we must sow in the hearts of the people. . . . Let us not be slow to do it."

"A sturdy stock that suffered exile rather than forego the right of free thought and free speech. These are the people who are the salt of the earth. And yet as I read history I see that they are the people who have been hunted with dogs and followed by armed men carrying fagots. . . . Take from America the Puritans, Huguenots, Quakers and other like-minded reformers of Church and State, and it is no longer the land of the free or the home of the brave."

[*The following are recent words by the Rector of St. Peter's Episcopal Church of Albany, N. Y.*]:

"In every department of thought a new theory or fact is a disturbance and an affront. It intrudes upon men's leisures. It breaks crystallized thought and dislocates mental habits. With the mass of people, a new fact, and especially a new theory, is an intellectual tramp who is unceremoniously turned out of doors with an exhortation to work for his living. This is especially true in regard to facts or theories which compel men to revise those interpretations and opinions which, while not authorized by, are more or less associated with the traditional religion. *The new theory or fact has, therefore, got to fight and turn out of doors the orthodox belief before it can take and occupy its place.*"

"Obviously, then, one needful part of the process of reformation in theology which is now happily in progress, is to emancipate men's minds from *the tyranny of creedal language*, and bring them back to the simplicity of Biblical language. This will greatly help to make religion more true than it has been to the actual facts of human life, relations, and experience. Heartily do we wish success to the new reformation."

RENASCENT CHRISTIANITY.

IV.—THE RENASCENCE.

"Behold, I make all things new."

IN these days of new science, new thought, new methods, new aspirations—in short, of a new universe to all who have widely observed and profoundly meditated—the above prophecy is being fulfilled as never, in historic times, has it been fulfilled before. With the "new Heavens," which astronomy is creating for us, and the "new earth," which evolutionary science is creating; with the new history of mankind which geology and archæology are unfolding, and the new nature of man which both physiology and psychology are revealing, must come, surely and quickly, new religion, new ethics, and a new Church. In these latter departments there is at present (and quite naturally) chaos. The uncertainties and the pangs of a new birth are upon us. The void and darkness of a new creation are before us and around. In all highly civilized communities of the earth there is to-day such a commotion of enquiry, doubt, and unbelief as no other epoch in the history of theologies, of systemized morals, or of ecclesiastical cults ever experienced —the first four Christian centuries not excepted. In this dissolving, formless, and re-creative condition of things any honest and reasonably intelligent attempt to purify original sources, to reform institutions, to reconstruct creeds, and to restore the ever-living Christ with his vitalizing religion to the world ought to be cordially welcomed. Human agencies indeed cannot re-create, but they can and must "prepare the way." Without this preparation the kingdom of God never has come to the world and never will. Chaos will continue, void and darkness will prevail "upon the face of the deep." But in proportion as human agencies vigorously co-operate, the Divine Agency will fulfil its prophetic promise, "Behold I make all things new."

"The spirit of God moved upon the face of the waters. And God said, Let there be light, and there was light. And God saw the light, that it was good, . . . and the evening and the morning were the *first period.*"

V.—STRUGGLE FOR EXISTENCE—SURVIVAL OF THE FITTEST.

"What I say unto one, I say unto all, Watch." This was the Divine Master's oft-repeated injunction. In Religion as elsewhere, Eternal Vigilance is the price of Liberty. In Religion as elsewhere prevail the universal, inviolable laws of Struggle for Existence and Survival of the Fittest. The Hebrew Scriptures everywhere symbolized these laws by "the shedding of blood, without which there could be no remission"; and the Christian Scriptures everywhere symbolize the same by the Cross, without which there can be no Crown. "Strait is the gate and narrow the way which leadeth unto Life, and few there be that find it." Therefore "struggle." Connected with these there is another equally certain and equally universal law, in Religion as elsewhere:— Tendency to Revert, with consequent Deterioration and Decay. These three great laws, Struggle for Existence, Survival of the Fittest, and Tendency to Revert (or to Degenerate) are fundamental in Soul, as in Mind and Body; in systems, theories, and practices of Religion as in everything else. No intelligent person any longer questions these laws as existent in the realms of Body and of Mind. And no intelligent student of the Bible, of the Sacred Writings of all nations, of Christianity (through its few bright and many dark ages till now), of the various religions of the world which have risen and decayed, can fail to be convinced—whether he be prepared to acknowledge it or not—that the same great laws prevail in the Soul of Man, and in all those institutions and products of religion through which the Soul of Man seeks to evolve and express itself.

VI.—TENDENCY TO REVERT IS THE SUPREME DANGER.

As an unquestionable fact, in Christianity as in every other form of religion, there has been from the first a persistent and unceasing Tendency to Revert. The tendency of the masses, headed and guided by priest-craft, always has been, still is, and doubtless always (till the Millennial Ages) will be, to degrade religion into superstition, to transform both worship and morals into pantomimic routines and into dramatic exhibitions. To select one example out of a multitude. The original religion of Eleusis, in ancient Greece, was rational, lofty, and solemn; but soon it became interwoven with fables, corrupted by tradition, and controlled by priest-craft. To please and (as it was supposed) edify the masses, it was permitted to go gradually downward till we see it transformed at last into such spectacles as that of countless multitudes of devotees with eagerness and transport gathered to witness "Venus rising from the waves,"—the courtesan Phryne personating Venus by entering and emerging from the sea at Eleusis, while priests recited litanies and the breathless multitude gazed, wondered, and adored. "To this came at last the once sublime and elevating religion of Delphi and of Olympia." So tends every religion downward—and Christianity is no exception—unless ceaselessly guarded by reformers and diligently purged from ever accumulating fables and corrupting superstitions.

In ancient Greece, such men as Æschylus and Sophocles, Socrates and Plato sought to reform the popular religion by rejecting its irrational fables, dogmas, and rituals, retaining only the essential truths which were beneath them. Had they succeeded in this attempted reform then the noble religion of Greece—later that of Rome, and later still that of Christendom as well—might have been saved from degenerating into senseless stories of nymphs, dryads, and dæmons; of fairies, gnomes, and hobgoblins; of spooks, witches, and devils; of charms, amulets, and saving sacraments; of magic shrines, magic relics, and supernatural visions; of miraculous healings, inerrant holy books, and infallible popes; of apostolical successions of priests, infallible edicts of official theologians; and "many other such like things" which, in ever-varying forms and versions, are found in all the religions of the world.

The popular religion, which is always the religion of the majorities, to-day as ever, here as elsewhere, strongly and persistently tends to revert. Only by the unsparing rejection of its senseless fables, childish rituals, and irrational dogmas (retaining always the essential truths which are hidden beneath them)—only thus can this tendency be restrained from utter deterioration and hopeless decay.

VII.—DEGENERACY UNIVERSAL IN RELIGION.

"Tendency to Revert" is a law of universal application so far as the present earth and its various products are concerned. There are certain observations of science and also of history which have now settled into such unquestionable facts as to be self-evident. We may call them axioms. Among these a few may be cited as follows:

1. All moving bodies, unless vigorously and unceasingly propelled, tend to become again inert and motionless.
2. All living organisms, unless vitally sustained and renewed, tend to decay and death.
3. All domesticated plants and tamed animals, unless assiduously cultivated and restrained, tend to return to their original wildness and ferocity.
4. All civilized communities of men, unless constantly incited and urged forward to a more perfect civilization, tend to fall back to their primitive savagery of tastes and habits.

5. All enlightened minds of men, unless ever moving upward in intellectual culture, tend to their primal stagnation and stupidity.

6. All elevated characters of men, unless persistently aspiring to higher and ever higher ideals of virtue, tend to become grovelling and vicious again.

These all are recognized as axioms of science and of history, and are confirmed by every thoughtful person's observations and experience.

To these six axioms we add a seventh:

7. All teachings and institutions of religion, unless ceaselessly guarded, purified, and reformed, tend to revert to the corruptions and follies of grossest heathenism.

Attempting now to apply these axioms to *individual* persons, societies, teachings, and institutions, we are almost invariably repelled with the reply—"Yes, it is all unquestionably true *in general*. But *I* am an exception: *my* Country, *my* Society, *my* Doctrines, *my* Religion, are exceptions. *I* could never revert to a savage condition! *my* country could never become barbarous, *my* institutions debased, *my* Religion heathenish again!" So exclaims the average American, European, Asiatic, African, Sea Islander—of every State and Tribe—with equal self-assurance and emphasis. As to Religion in particular the average Christian, Jew, Mohammedan, Confucian, Buddhist, Brahman, Zoroastrian—of every sect and school—with equal self-esteem and bigotry would exclaim, "*I* am, *we* are, an exception!" Christians, like all the others, perhaps (on account of their prevalent conceit that they are "God's chosen people" and theirs "the true and only true Religion") even more than the others, are disposed to make an exception of Christianity, and especially of their own Christian sect and selves. The average Christian is highly indignant at any comparison of Christianity with any of the other Religions of the world, all of which he contemptuously spurns as Paganism or Heathenism, between which and Christianity "there is fixed an impassable gulf." It is as much as any man's reputation is worth (in some "Catholic" countries or communities as much as his life is worth) to venture a suggestion that Christians are *not* " God's chosen people " in any exclusive sense. They forget or reject St. Peter's affirmation, " God is no respecter of persons, but in every nation he that revereth Him and worketh righteousness is accepted by Him." Who ever yet heard a sermon preached in any reputable " orthodox " Christian Church from this text—except it were to undervalue it and explain it away? What reputable " orthodox " Christian Preacher, Priest, Bishop, or Theological Professor can to-day be found who even dares to openly advocate the *impartial* study of Comparative Religion—all the Religions of the world gathered in one Parliament—with all their Sacred Books open side by side, and all their representative men accorded the equal courtesy of free and honest speech?

VIII.—DEGENERACY—CHRISTIANITY NO EXCEPTION.

So much as to the fact that the average Christian (like the average Jew, Mohammedan, or other bigoted Religionist of the world) strenuously asserts that *his* Religion is " an exception," both as to its Teachings, which are infallible, and as to its institutions, which are not subject to the law of Tendency to Revert. But let us pass from Christianity as one of the great religions of the world to Christianity as divided into numerous sects and schools. The average adherent of each one of these sects and schools makes this claim, as against all the others, that his sect or school is certainly " an exception." The average Roman Catholic affirms this. Protestantism may indeed revert—in fact, has already half reverted—to Heathenism. But Roman Catholicism revert—the one and only true and infallible Church revert to Heathenism? *Never!*

The average Greek Catholic affirms the same of the " Most Holy, Blessed, and only Orthodox Church " to which he belongs, as against both Roman Catholicism and Protestantism. The average Protestant affirms the same as against both Roman Catholicism and Greek Catholicism.

Those who call themselves Anglican Catholics, or Church of England Protestants, or Protestant Episcopal affirm that, without the "Apostolical Succession" and certain other essential characteristics which they claim to possess, there is no "true Church"; hence the average "Churchman" will have no "dealings" with any of the other Protestant "sects" —counting them all as degenerate and likely to degenerate more and more. The same they affirm (but with much less severity) of the Greek and the Roman Churches; while of their own "Catholic and Apostolic Church" they affirm such a degree of infallibility as renders it impossible for *it* ever to revert to its original Heathenism. On the other hand the average adherent of any one of the hundred or more Protestant sects affirms substantially the same of his own sect as against all the others. And finally, as we have already suggested, all average Christians, of all the Protestant sects as well as of the Greek Catholic and Roman Catholic, are united in this one respect (and in this one only) that they persistently believe all other religions of the world already so degenerate as to warrant their being called False Religions; and so rapidly degenerating that they are, all alike, certain of speedy collapse and utter decay; "but Christianity—*never!*"

Is then Christianity an exception to the otherwise universal law of degeneration or tendency to revert? Does this law find no application here? Is there no danger, need there be no anxiety *here*—though everywhere else there is alarming danger and cause for ceaseless anxiety? Let us glance at a few of a thousand facts of history which plainly show how futile and foolish is this claim that "Christianity is an exception."

To begin with:—1. Christianity's first and greatest apostles, the Twelve Disciples, reverted so quickly and degenerated so rapidly that one of them sold his Master for money; all the others deserted him and fled in his time of sorest extremity; while the chief one of them all, St. Peter, thrice lied and with profane curses and oaths, in the presence of Pilate, denied that he was even acquainted with the man whom, a few days before, he had saluted as "Messiah the Son of the Living God." And many years later, this same St. Peter so reverted and degenerated again that "for fear of the Jews he dissembled" and played both the coward and the hypocrite in refusing to stand by his previously professed convictions of Christian toleration and charity.

2. The saintly St. Paul was so painfully conscious of this tendency to revert and degenerate that he testifies to "beating till it is black and blue" (a free translation) his body, in order to hold it in subjugation; and even in his old age he exclaims: "I exceedingly fear and tremble lest, after I have preached to others, I myself shall become a castaway."

3. In the Book of Revelation, which closes the New Testament canon, we find it recorded that large portions of the Christian Church—indeed every one of its seven great geographical divisions to which the Apocalypse was addressed—had already reverted so far as to deserve severe reprimand for various heathenish corruptions and errors to which they had returned, while others had so rapidly degenerated as to become "Anti-Christ." And future Anti-Christs were foretold and pictured in most repellent and horrible forms.

4. The reversions and degenerations of the second, third, fourth, and every succeeding Christian century—increasing and deepening as the centuries came and went—are too numerous, too sad, and too well known for us here to recount. Coming down to the eve of the twentieth century, let us glance at the condition and tendencies of Christianity as we find it to-day.

5. After nearly nineteen hundred years of zealous efforts at self-propagation, "making disciples," not always with the method of Jesus, by "preaching the Gospel to every creature," but, as well, by proselyting, bribing, driving, compelling—resorting to sword and rack and dungeon, to anathema and scorn and contempt, to proffers of wealth and position and honor, to promises of heaven and threats of hell hereafter—after all these many centuries of such zealous efforts at self-propagation, by methods of mingled good and ill, what has Christianity accomplished *so amazingly different*

from what other great religions have accomplished, as to entitle it to reprobate them all as "false religions," while it alone is so infallibly true as to be "an exception" to otherwise universally prevailing laws? Putting aside the past, what are the *actual* conditions and tendencies of Christianity at the close of this nineteenth century?

Roughly stated, according to statistics, three fourths of mankind are still zealous adherents of the pagan or "false" religions. One fourth of mankind are *nominally* Christians. Of this one fourth of mankind who are *nominally* Christians, three fourths are zealous adherents of Roman and of Greek Catholicism. So, one fourth of mankind are *nominally* Christians; and one fourth of the *nominal* Christians are *nominal* Protestants. Of these *nominal* Protestants three fourths are not *professed* Christians. So, of *nominal* Protestants only one fourth are *professed* Christians. Of these *professed* Protestant Christians—such an insignificant fraction of mankind—it is not for us to judge how many there are to whom the Divine Master—in his now invisible but ever-present personality—is saying, as he said to the pious formalists and ritualists of old, "Ye hypocrites, how can ye escape the condemnation of Hades?" and again: "I never knew you: depart from me ye that work iniquity." Professed Christians are by no means the same thing as *genuine* Christians, whether Protestant, Roman Catholic, or Greek Catholic. Most Protestants think that there are very few, if any at all, of *genuine* Christians outside of the Protestant Churches. The Roman and Greek Catholics not only so judge with reference to each other, but join heartily to return the compliment—with redoubled emphasis—to all the Protestant sects. Though there is doubtless a great deal of truth in the counter-charges, it would be better for all sides to observe the injunction of the Divine Master—"Judge not."

6. With these rough estimates and these counter-charges as to genuineness before us, disheartening as it is, we are still more disheartened by learning from recent statements of the "great Evangelist" of *orthodox* Protestantism, publicly made at revival meetings in the city of New York, that

40,000,000 of souls in Christendom (more likely to be 100,000,000) are to-day unreached by any form of Christianity, to say nothing of the three fourths of mankind who are still pagans! Moreover, he assures us that "last year in two Protestant denominations alone, 3000 churches report no accessions." From other sources we learn that, in the United States of America, all the churches and chapels and mission halls taken together do not provide sittings for one third of our population. Of these sittings for about one third of our population, on an average, fully one half remain unoccupied on every Sunday, except on some such special occasions as Christmas and Easter Day, *when the decorations and music are to be especially fine.* These sittings for about one third of our population, not more than half of which, on an average, are occupied, are—as any observer in any part of our country must have often noticed—occupied by at least six girls and women to one man, with rarely a young man or a child to be seen. The men, as a rule (and large numbers of women also), especially those of the more scholarly, refined, and moral classes, are practically not influenced, and seemingly will never be, by what is known as Orthodox Christianity. What is true of the United States of America, in the above regards, is substantially true of all Protestant communities everywhere; and, largely true, also in all the more civilized and intelligent communities of Roman and Greek Catholicism. To these general statements is added another from unprejudiced and authoritative sources with reference to the arrested growth of what are known as Foreign Missions. What these Missions have accomplished to date, so far as statistics of converts are concerned, may be inferred from a glance at Asia alone. Three fifths of the entire population of the earth—more than 700,000,000 of souls—inhabit Asia; and all these, to-day as firmly as ever, adhere to the Buddhistic, Confucian, and Mohammedan Religions—except about a half million of Protestant, and ten millions of Roman and Greek Catholic Christians. After so many years and so much money spent in zealous propagandism, only about a half-million out of more than seven hundred millions of souls are drawn to Protestant Christianity; and these are, as a rule, from the lowest intellectual and social classes. Moreover, we are assured by almost the united voices of all the higher intellectual and social classes of this immense population of Asia (three fifths of the entire population of the earth) that no form of what is known as Orthodox Christianity will ever be accepted or can hope to make any noticeable progress among them. Their own religions, so far from decaying, are reviving. Their magnificent Temples of Worship are being restored and new ones erected. Their priests are becoming more learned, noble, and pure. Their worshippers are growing more intelligent, moral, and devout. They are even beginning to return the compliment of their Christian friends by sending missionaries to Christian lands to proclaim, not that Christianity is a "false" religion and all Christians "heathen" (which no well-bred or intelligent Asiatic would ever think, much less teach), but to show to Christians what is best in their much maligned religions, and to convince them of the verity of their own Scripture—"Of a truth I perceive that God is no respecter of persons; but in every nation he that feareth Him and worketh righteousness is accepted with Him": adding, perchance, some needed instructions upon one of their own beautiful Scripture texts, "He who is beloved of God honors every form of Religious Faith." Thus are we not only humiliated as to what our beloved Christianity has actually accomplished in the world, but are brought to a certain conviction also, that it is "no exception" to all other things in the universe, so far as concerns its essential conformity to the three great laws known as Struggle for Existence, Survival of the Fittest, and Tendency to Revert. This last law is the one that has been most disastrously forgotten. "Degeneration" has wrought its deadly havoc with the pure, simple, and lofty teachings of Jesus all adown the ages. Heathen fables, traditions, and methods, have always been permitted to intertwine and interweave themselves. From the first century and increasingly down to the present century, the Christian Church has been very largely

Pagan. Christians have, for the most part, worshipped Heathen Deities under Christian names. The prophets have prophesied falsely and the people have loved to have it so! The mild but radical Jesus has been so grievously misconceived, and so untruthfully presented that he would hardly recognize himself in any of the popular creeds, sermons, or even Bibles wherein he has been portrayed for so many centuries; and, more than any other teacher the world has ever known, would have reason to exclaim, "Save me from my friends!" Such already has been Christianity's tendency to revert, and so will it continue—even to a final and entire return to Heathenism—unless it renounces its heathenish errors and retains nothing except the simple truth as it was taught by Jesus. It is high time that this should be done. Certain Bishops of the Church of England not long ago were keenly satirized by a famous essayest of their own church for tragically declaring "It is high time that something should be done for the honor of our Lord's Godhead!" Not this is what is needed—too much, by far, of this already! But what *is* needed and what, in the twentieth and succeeding centuries, *must* come—is beginning to come already—is Renascent Christianity.

IX.—THE SIMPLE TRUTH AS IT WAS IN JESUS.

"The simple truth as it was in Jesus" is Christianity pure and true. To get hold of this Truth as best we can, and bring it forth, and make it live and flourish again is Renascent Christianity. This, and this alone, is the sacred object, the holy aim of what is now widely known as Higher Criticism of the Bible. Jesus had no system, wrote or dictated no creed, suggested no cult, imposed no dogma, insisted upon no essential doctrine. His "doctrines" were simple teachings which every child might understand—beatitudes, parables, commendations of sincerity and charity, condemnations of hypocrisy and of self-love, ethical maxims, theological axioms, beautiful affirmations of eternal life to the truly righteous, and sad warnings of eternal death to those who persist in unrighteous deeds or in unholy desires and thoughts. These, together with his foundation teachings, his corner-stone truths, of the Fatherhood of God and the Brotherhood of Man, constituted His Gospel—His entire Gospel. "Go ye into all the world and preach *this* Gospel to every creature; whosoever receiveth it and *openly* maintains it [is baptized] shall be saved; whosoever rejecteth it shall be condemned." This was all. And had it remained all, the kingdom of God would have come and His will would have been done on earth, as in heaven, a thousand—yes, fifteen hundred years ago!

But hardly had the Divine Voice of Jesus ceased to be audibly heard before "degeneration" set in. The same voice continued to speak in the unceasing whispers of the Spirit of Truth—the Holy Spirit—which had been promised. The holiest of the Apostles and first disciples listened to it and, for the most part, followed its dictates. They too constructed no system, composed no creed, organized no cult—beyond such simple offices, methods, and symbols as Jesus himself had suggested—compounded no dogma, imposed no essential doctrines, wrote no sacred book, but simply "preached the Gospel to every creature," as Jesus had preached it to them. "Repent, accept this Gospel of Jesus, openly practise and promulgate it, and thus work out your own salvation and the salvation of mankind." This was all we hear of in the Apostolic Church of the first quarter-century after the visible departure of Jesus. Had it remained all, we repeat, the kingdom of God would have come and His will would have been done on earth as in heaven, a thousand—yes, fifteen hundred years ago! But poor human nature, alas! Its tendency to revert is even stronger and more persistent in religion than in any other thing. As the half-domesticated flower or plant tends strongly to become the wild flower or plant of the prairie or field again; as the half-tamed bird or colt tends strongly to become free and ferocious again; as the half-civilized African or Indian tends strongly to become a drivelling and roving savage again; as the half-illumined mind and the half-elevated character tends strongly to revert to intellectual stupidity and to moral stagnation again—so the half-domesticated, half-tamed, half-civilized, half-illumined, half-elevated soul tends strongly to revert to the sensuous and senseless superstitions of its original Heathenism. Like Milton's lion half-embedded in slime and pawing to be free—whenever it ceases *to paw for its* freedom, it sinks downward and is lost again. So it has come to pass in every one of the many religions of the world. Every one of them started as pure, simple, and reasonable reforms. The leader of every one of them was, in some sense or degree, a Christ of God—an "anointed," a divinely accepted and sanctioned redeemer and saviour of mankind. While the Divine Leader or Master remained visible among his little band of followers all went well. When he was seen no more, and the Spirit of Truth which had spoken audibly through him began to speak only in inward whispers "to teach and to guide" those who would listen "into all truth," only a few souls of men were found pure enough and lofty enough to listen, and to be taught and guided by its holy dictates. When these "few" passed away degeneration always began, and from century to century increased ; so that every religion of the world has again and again reverted to Heathenism, needing unceasing reformers and unending reforms in order to rescue it from hopeless decay. To all this, again we say, Christianity has been, *is* no exception. The "degenerates," in Christianity as in every one of the other great religions of the world, plead super-naturalism. "*Ours* is a super-natural religion, the true, *the one and only true* religion. God incarnated Himself as a man in order to reveal and establish *it*, and so *it*, cannot decay. He appointed infallible guardians, authoritative keepers, an inerrant book, holy sacraments, heavenly ceremonials, saving mysteries, divine agencies, and directions of every sort, so that *all is exactly as He desires it to be* in *our* religion." So affirms the "degenerate" of every form of religion the world has ever known. In one phrase or another he defies the reformer with the assertion—*my* religion is founded on a rock and the gates of hell shall not prevail against *it !* He listens not to the primal cautions and warnings which the Divine Founders of all the religions have joined to give to their followers. "Take heed that ye do not as the heathen do. . . . Watch; what I say unto one I say unto all, watch." Neither will he hearken unto what "the spirit saith unto the churches"—alike to the churches of every religion the world has ever known. Such is the *insistent* hardness of heart and blindness of mind—" Their eyes have they closed and their ears have they stopped, lest they should see and hear and be converted and I should heal them "—of the leaders and supporters of degenerate religion the world over. *And Christianity is no exception.*

X.—BACK TO FIRST PRINCIPLES.

"*Back to first principles; back to the original sources; back to the simple truth as it was in the Divine Founder!*" This must be the loud and the unceasing cry of every true religious reformer. And the Reformer of Christianity can not be an exception.

XI.—THE ORIGINAL SOURCES OF CHRISTIANITY.

Christianity is a Religion, *the* Religion of Eclecticism. Its founder was the great Religious Eclectic of the World. He taught nothing new, but culled from every field. His epoch was at the meeting and parting of all the ways. The land in which he lived was overrun with representatives of every religious faith. The writings or verbal teachings of all the Divine Masters of all the Divine Religions of the earth were before his eyes or sounding in his ears. Not an accent of the Holy Ghost was he heedless of. All fell as so much good seed into the fruitful soil of his lofty mind and heart, and forthwith sprang up unto a Hundred-fold Harvest. He utterly disclaimed the teaching of any *new* Truth. "To this end was I born, and for this came I into the world, that I should *bear witness* to the Truth. . . . The words that I speak unto you I speak not of myself. . . . It is written.

... And again it is written. ... He that is not against me is on my side. ... He that doeth the will of my Father who is in Heaven, the same is my brother, and my sister, and my mother." So spake and proclaimed again and again this great Religious Eclectic of nineteen centuries ago. As the invisible Spirit of Truth, during all these centuries He has been speaking and proclaiming the same thing—" My doctrine is not mine. ... The words which ye hear are not mine " but His " who sent me," and who " has not left Himself without *the same* witness in any nation or among any people."

What, then, are the Original Sources of Christianity ? *All the Holy Teachings of all the Religions of the World.* Everything in all Holy Books or Holy Traditions of Mankind which was *genuinely* good, and beautiful, and true, the Divine Jesus seized upon by a sort of omniscient faculty of mind and soul; appropriated it—in the name of the Common Heavenly Father—and wrought it into those Teachings which constitute the sum and substance of his Everlasting Gospel. There is nothing new under the sun. All Truth that is *necessary to man's spiritual elevation* had been revealed by the Holy Spirit, and spoken by the holy prophets and sages of all nations before Jesus came. Not a Truth, nor a fragment of a Truth, *entirely* new did he utter or profess to utter. All that he said had been said, in other ways, before. " Search the Scriptures " of every Ancient Religion that has survived till now, and you will find it all. " These are they that testify of me." Christianity itself was Universal Religion *renascent*. Jesus was " its resurrection and its life." His mind was the crucible and his soul the alembic, in which was fused and from which was distilled *in new form*, the Eternal Truth of God; which Truth had been a common " Deposit " of all the Great Religions,—a " Faith," not " once," but *ever and forever*, " delivered to the Saints."

So we arrive at the fact, which needs to be constantly repeated, that Christianity is *a* Religion, *the* Religion of Eclecticism ; and Jesus its founder, *the* great Religious Eclectic of the World.

XII.—WHAT OF THE NEW TESTAMENT SCRIPTURES?

Christianity, "which was Universal Religion *renascent*," existed long before there were any New Testament Scriptures. How *long* before no one can exactly tell, for "God buried *the body of this* Moses, and no man knoweth of his grave to this day!" Sufficient is the fact that Christianity *could* exist, *does* exist, and *can* exist without any *especial* Holy Book *peculiar* to itself. All books are its Holy Books, and all Truth is its Revelation.

But, within a generation or two after the *visible* and *audible* retirement of its Divine Founder, Christianity—which had already spread over the known earth—seemed to need the support of some Written Records. So "many took it in hand to write." Who they were nobody exactly knows, and it matters not. The things that were written were so numerous and, for the most part, so spurious and worthless, that after perhaps two hundred years, a few of the more helpful and reliable of the manuscripts were sifted out, and gathered into what is now known as the Canon of the New Testament. As to their *special* inspiration or inerrancy, not a claim was made by any of their writers nor by any of those who compiled them into a single volume or "Canon." They were issued and everywhere known as simple Biographies of Jesus and Letters to Churches. As such they were, and are, Literature—*sacred* Literature indeed, but still Literature. So they were held to be for two or three centuries, at which time Christianity began to revert to Heathenism so rapidly that these Writings were soon transformed into a Charm or Fetich: and, more and more as Degeneration progressed and the centuries went on, they were idolized instead of "searched." Finally they were united in one volume or "Canon," with those Selections from Ancient Hebrew Literature which had come to be known as the Old Testament Scriptures; and the two Collections of Writings combined were called the Bible. A next step was to pronounce them the Word of God: and a next, to hold them inerrant and infallible—*God's miraculous and only Revelation to Mankind!* From this point of downward tendency, all the rest was natural and easy. "*Facilis est descensus Averni.*" Anathemas upon all who should question or doubt; Salvation for all who meekly received; and Damnation for all " Jews, Turks, Infidels, and Heretics" who should dare to reject! Apostolic, Nicene, and Athanasian Creeds which, "whosoever believeth shall doubtless be saved, and whosoever believeth not shall doubtless be damned!" Sacraments, without which there can be no Salvation! Rituals of Worship, without which no man can please God! An infallible Church, outside of which all are without God and without hope! Vicarious Blood, without which all mankind must eternally perish! Intercession of saints, without which none can receive the mercies of God! Infallible Popes for Roman Catholics! Infallible Councils for Greek Catholics! An infallible Apostolic Church for English Catholics! And, for all orthodox Protestant sects alike, an infallible Book! Such has been the tendency to revert, and such its appalling results. And all because it was supposed that Christianity—which arose, flourished, and gloriously prevailed for two hundred years without any Holy Book, and for half a century without any recognized New Testament writings at all—could not possibly get along without some "infallible" book, church, council, or Pope, to compel and sustain it. A heathenish principle adopted to begin with; and, Heathenism rampant ever since, as a consequence.

But now 't is time, high time, to return to "The Truth as it was in Jesus." And all broadest minds and greatest souls of humanity are demanding the return. The twentieth century will be the opening age, not of any Protestant Reformation merely, but of a Religious Reform *world-wide and eighteen centuries deep;* and this reform will be—in spirit, not in name—*Renascent Christianity.*

XIII.—THE RENASCENT BIBLE.

With the written records called the Bible this reform has vigorously begun, and shall more vigorously continue. The Bible, not as an infallible or as a supernatural book, but as a volume of Sacred Literature: one of many, but *probably* best of all and containing the Truth of all,—as the vastly superior results of its teachings have thus far seemed to indicate— this is the first position taken, and now to be maintained, by the Higher Criticism. As an indication of what is already astir in the Christian world regarding this great impending Reform, a quotation just taken from a leading book review is here added, with the remark that the list of names given contains for the most part those of *ultra-conservative* workers in the cause of Biblical Revision and the New Criticism.

XIV.—THE BIBLE AS LITERATURE.

"*The Bible as Literature* is a compilation of articles upon the subject by Professor Richard G. Moulton, Ph.D., Rev. John P. Peters, Ph.D., Rev. A. B. Bruce, D.D., Rev. Henry Van Dyke, D.D., Professor W. J. Beecher, D.D., Rev. William E. Griffis, D.D., Rev. William H. Cobb, D.D., Professor Max Kellner, D.D., Professor Lewis B. Paton, M.A., Professor Marvin R. Vincent, D.D., Professor George Frederick Wright, D.D., Professor George B. Stevens, Ph.D., D.D., Rev. Samuel T. Lowrie, D.D., Professor M. S. Terry, D.D., and Professor Albert S. Cook, Ph.D. It may well be imagined that some pointed things are said by these writers, who represent progressive theology in this country. Professor Moulton declares that the Bible, the very name of which may be translated as 'literature,' is a 'literature smothered by reverence,' and he goes on to say: 'To the devout reader the Bible has become a storehouse of isolated texts, of good words. He scarcely realizes that it exhibits the varieties of literary form familiar to him elsewhere— essays, epigrams, sonnets, stories, sermons, songs, philosophical observations and treatises, histories and legal documents. Even dramas are to be found in the Bible, and also love songs; nay, so far does dumb show enter into the ministry of Ezekiel that some of his compositions might fairly be described as tableaux-vivants. The distinction between things sacred and things secular, which exercises so questionable an influence upon our times, seems unknown to the world of the Old Testament. Its literature embraces national anthems of Israel in various stages of its history, war ballads with rough refrains, hymns of defeat and victory, or for triumphant entrance into a conquered capital; pilgrim songs, and the chants with which the family parties beguiled the journeys to the great feasts; fanciful acrostics to clothe sacred meditations or composed in compliment to a perfect wife; even the games of riddles which belong to such social meetings as Samson's wedding. With the single exception of humorous literature, for which the Hebrew temperament has little fitness, the Bible presents as varied an intellectual food as can be found in any national literature.'"

As another indication of "what is astir" in the way of trying to fulfil the prophetic words and method of the Divine Founder of Christianity, we add here another quotation from the same recent book review as that inserted in the section immediately preceding.

"Warfare of Science with Theology."

"The aim of the author of this work, Hon. Andrew D. White, late President of Cornell University, has been, in his own words, 'to try to aid in letting the light of historical truth into the decaying mass of outworn thought which attaches the modern world to mediæval conceptions of Christianity, and which still lingers among us—a most serious barrier to religion and morals, and a menace to the whole normal evolution of society.' Behind this barrier he sees the flood of increased knowledge and new thought rapidly rising with the danger of a sudden breaking away, distressing and calamitous, sweeping before it not only outworn creeds and noxious dogmas, but cherished principles and ideals, and even wrenching out most precious religious and moral foundations of the whole social and political fabric. 'My belief is,' he says, 'that in the field left to them—their proper field—the clergy will more and more, as they cease to struggle against scientific methods and conclusions, do work even nobler and more beautiful than anything they have heretofore done. And this is saying much. My conviction is that science, though it has evidently conquered dogmatic theology based on Biblical texts and ancient modes of thought, will go hand in hand with religion; and that although theological control will continue to diminish, religion, as seen in the recognition of 'a power in the universe, not ourselves, which makes for righteousness,' and in the love of God and of our neighbor, will steadily grow stronger and stronger, not only in the American institutions of learning, but in the world at large."

The Christian Bible, like the other sacred Scriptures of the world, is henceforth to be reckoned and treated as literature. As such every intelligent and honest student of it will, not only profoundly revere it (as containing most sacred Truth), but also must sharply inspect, critically investigate, and unsparingly sift it, in order to help gather the wheat into the garner, but to burn the chaff in quenchless fire. There is much to be done; exactly what, can here only be indicated.

XV.—HOW MYTHS GROW.

A typical illustration may be presented which will suffice to show how myths grow; and how tradition should always be suspected, credulity restrained, and the records of traditional literature examined critically and sifted unsparingly.

Even while he was yet alive our own Emerson had occasion frequently to correct misstatements of his sayings that were rapidly and widely circulated,* as also to deny fables that

---

* The author has preserved a letter which painfully reminds him of his own agency in this matter. Ministering one Sunday at the old Unitarian Church of Concord, in either the morning or evening services, he made reference to a sentence which he had caught, as he supposed, from Mr. Emerson's lips during a lecture he had recently delivered in Music Hall, Boston, on the subject of Immortality. The next morning he received a politely worded letter from Miss Ellen Emerson, who had been present at both the services, saying she had

had already begun to grow concerning his personality and his doings. After his decease these misstatements and fables continued not only to prevail, but also to increase; so that his various biographers—even within ten years of his decease—have been obliged to sift the evidences and sharply distinguish between truth and fiction. This is by no means uncommon; indeed, it is constant and universal, even in these latter days. How much more so in the former days; and *increasingly* so, century by century, as we go backward to the ages of *unwritten* history, and of records preserved only in uncertain memories, and handed down by wonder-loving, and—almost always—party or partisan-regarding lips!

Everybody knows how, even while they lived, and much more after they were dead, the personalities, deeds, and words of Peter the Great, Napoleon, and Wellington; of Walter Scott, Wordsworth, and Carlyle; of Washington, Webster, and Lincoln—as, indeed, of every other of the greatest men and women of modern centuries down to this day—have quickly and persistently been distorted, perverted, or, obscured by mysteries, fables, and myths. And no intelligent person will now read a history or a biography or any volume of general literature—recognized fiction alone excepted—which has not been sharply examined and thoroughly sifted in order to separate facts from fancies, exaggerations from realities, the genuine from the spurious. So is being fulfilled John the Baptist's prophecy concerning the Living Christ—who has been and is the refining, purifying Spirit of all the ages—" Whose fan is in his hand, and he will thoroughly purge his floor, and gather his wheat into the garner; but he will burn up the chaff with unquenchable fire."

<small>reported the quotation of the sermon to her father; that he wished to thank the preacher for the honor, but also to assure him that neither the words nor the exact thought were his. Immediately the preacher, *being entirely certain* that he had heard accurately and quoted correctly, called upon Mr. Emerson—whom he already had the honor of knowing—to convince him of the truthfulness of his report. The result was that, *by reference to the manuscript*, the sentence was found to be as Mr. Emerson had affirmed.</small>

As an additional hint of the fact that Myth-weaving and Fable-making are still widely and rapidly going on—even among "enlightened Protestants"—with reference to both Christianity and the Christian Bible, we may notice two general facts. The Theology of such books as Milton's *Paradise Lost*, and the Christology of various Religious Novels, like *Prince of the House of David* and nearly every one of the many *popular* Lives of Christ, have insensibly so shaped, and colored, and changed original Christianity, the original Christ, and the original meanings of the Bible, that with every age of Protestantism—as truly though not as completely as with the ages of Roman and Greek Catholicism which preceded it—*reversions* to Heathenism and consequent *degeneration* have been and *are now* going on. The popular Book Reviews of to-day are announcing whole *crops and floods* of *popular* Novels by *popular* Novelists who "have been engaged at enormous prices" to produce—for the Demetrius-Publishers, to be used for the *diversion* of the Great-is-Diana-of-the-Ephesians reading Public—various 'Silver Shrines for Diana" in the way of Popularized Lives of Christ! If such reversions and degenerations are permitted to continue, the Holy Bible will soon become a mere *Gemara*, like that which ruled the Jewish Church in the days of Jesus; and The Christ will be transformed into a mythic Achilles, Heracles, or Jove, as were the real heroes and shining Saints of Ancient Greece who, *to divert the masses*, were permitted gradually to degenerate into the "gods" of degenerate Greece, whose degenerate Holy Book came at length to be the Homeric Hymns to the Gods and the Theogony of Hesiod—the former the Old Testament and the latter the New Testament of their *Bible for the Masses!*

This is *the* Age of Fiction. Such another has never before been known in History; not excepting even that of St. Paul's time, when "all the Athenians and the strangers sojourning there spent their time in nothing else, but either to tell or to hear *something new*." As a confirmation, note such an announcement as this, just made in a thousand periodicals and newspapers all over Christendom: "The popular novelist —— has engaged to write a new story to be called ——; and, though he has not yet set pen to paper to produce it, he has already been paid $27,000 in advance for the work." Story-writers, Novelists, and Authors of Fiction—all commendable in their proper spheres and helpful under reasonable limitations—are the heroes, sages, and divinities of to-day. They furnish ninety-nine one hundredths of the popular *pabulum*. They amass fortunes in a year and live in splendid luxury, as did the *sophists* and literary *clients* of ancient Greece and Rome. Meanwhile the *genuine* philosopher, the *truthful* historian, the writer on exact or *actual* Science, the author of *realistic* Literature, the teacher or preacher of *genuine* Religion " pure and undefiled before God the Father " now as ever—relatively speaking *more* than ever—must wear the " tattered cloak " and live in humble poverty and retirement. Verily, the danger of to-day, *above* that of any previous age that History tells us about, is, that *Religion and all will end in Fiction*—as transpired in the Ancient Empires of Greece and of Rome, and in every other decayed or decaying Empire and civilization of the Past. Who will " come up to the help of the Lord, to the help of the Lord against the mighty?"

XVI.—THE WHEAT GARNERED, THE CHAFF BURNED.

This prophecy must also and specially be fulfilled with reference to: *first*, the Bible itself, and then to the whole mass and body of Religious Literature, Theology, Dogmas, Traditions, Sacraments, Rituals, and Ecclesiasticism, wherever existing among civilized people upon the whole earth.

" Now also the ax is laid unto the root of the trees ; therefore every tree which bringeth not forth good fruit, is hewn down and cast into the fire." This is the perpetual *renascence* of the living Christ ; and this the " prepare ye the way," which all intelligent, reverent Christians ought henceforth to hear and to heed. The need of this sharp examination and of this thorough and unsparing sifting, overturning, pruning, and purifying, is greater by far as we approach the various records, traditions, and institutions of ancient times. We see myths growing, superstitions arising, and prevailing all about us even in these days of exact records, and of immediate and impartial investigation. In spite of our amanuenses and reporters; in spite of our wondrous modern arts, inventions, and appliances, of Photography, Phonetics, Phonographics, Telegraphy, Telephonics; in spite of our Omnipresent Press and Omniscient Eye of public inquisitiveness, introspection, sharp discernment, and unsparing judgment, ("quick and powerful, and sharper than any two-edged sword, piercing even to the dividing asunder of soul and spirit, and of the joints and marrow, and is a discerner of the thoughts and intents of the heart," so that there is "no creature that is not manifest, but all things are naked and open")—in spite of all these astounding characteristics of our century, (which, more than all the preceding eighteen centuries combined, indicates the presence of the Living Christ, and proclaims the Kingdom of Heaven at hand,) even here and now—(right before our face and eyes)—we see myths growing, superstitions arising and prevailing. How must it have been then in the Bible-forming, dogma-fashioning, ritual-building, creed-making, cult-organizing ages! Among untutored, semi-civilized, and highly imaginative Orientals! When legend and fable, extravagance, exaggeration, and supernaturalism were the very nutriment of the popular mind, and the very atmosphere in which everybody lived and moved! When nothing was *written down*, but everything *called to remembrance*, then circulated from mouth to mouth, from group to group, from country to country, and from generation to generation; till some well-meaning writer—himself also a product of his credulous age and a victim of his myth-loving environment—should "take it in hand to set forth, in order, a declaration of those things which are most truly believed among us!"

What need to add any further reasons for the Higher Criticism? What need of other enforcements of the sacred demands that are upon all intelligent students of the Bible, as of the other Sacred Scriptures of the world—to be, not only profoundly reverent, but also, (in the name and spirit of the Living Christ), sharply critical, and unsparingly honest and true, both in their own private investigation, and in whatever instruction they may find opportunity to give to others.

Now as in all preceding ages, in Christianity as in Judaism and all other forms of Religion, in Protestantism as in Catholicism, in the United States of America as in other States and Countries of the Earth, degeneration continues and persists. *The popular forms of Religion are always Reversions.* Simply because they *are* Reversions they become and remain popular. "The people love to have it so" —*therefore* the hireling-priests, now as ever, and ever as now, "prophesy falsely." Such is the rise, progress, and *numerical* success of "popular" Religion the World over, and History through. The purest things are always unpopular. Truth is always in the minority. Wide is the gate and broad is the way that leads to *Degeneration*; strait is the gate and narrow the way that leads to Holiness and Truth.

To-day the same as ever, here the same as in ancient Judea, the radical teachings and methods of Jesus are everywhere and urgently needed :—" Howbeit in vain do they worship me, teaching for doctrines the commandments of men." . . . For laying aside the commandments of God, ye hold the traditions of men, as the washing of pots and cups; and many other such like things ye do." . . . "And He said unto them, Full well ye reject the commandments of God, that ye may keep your own traditions." . . . "Making the Word of God of none effect through your tradition, which ye have delivered; and many such like things do ye." . . . "Every tree that bringeth not forth good fruit is hewn down and cast into the fire." . . . "And it came to pass, when Jesus had ended these sayings, the people were astonished at his teachings; for he taught them as one having authority and not as their scribes."

"Ye are the salt of the earth; but if the salt have lost its savor, wherewith shall it be salted? it is thenceforth good for nothing, but to be cast out, and to be trodden under foot of men. . . . Think not that I am come to destroy the Law as delivered by prophets; I am not come to destroy, but to fulfil. For verily I say unto you, Till heaven and earth pass, one jot or one tittle of the Law shall in no wise pass, till all be fulfilled."

So spake, *and speaks*, the Living Christ.

XVII.—ECLECTICISM, INCLUSIVENESS, CATHOLICISM, CHRISTIANITY.

THREE ANALOGOUS CONVERSATIONS.

(a) *Sectionalism and Cosmopolitanism.*

First American.—"You say that all countries of the earth are interesting and beautiful. Why then do you not go and reside in them?"

Second American.—"For three reasons. *First.* This is the country of my adoption and home. *Second.* My friends and interests are chiefly here. *Third.* To me this is the *most* interesting and beautiful country of the earth. Therefore, I prefer to continue my residence here."

(b) *Sectarianism and Catholicism.*

First Churchman.—"You say that all denominations of Christians are parts of the true Church. Why then do you not become a member of them?"

Second Churchman.—"For three reasons. *First.* Ours is the church of my adoption and communion. *Second.* My associations and anticipations are largely confined to it. *Third.* To me it is *more nearly* Christian in its beliefs and methods than is any other of the denominations. Therefore, my duty is to remain where I am."

(c) *Exclusivism and Christianity.*

First Christian.—"You say that there is divine truth and goodness in all Pagan religions. Why then do you not become a Mohammedan, Jew, Confucian, Buddhist, Brahmin, or Zoroastrian?"

Second Christian.—"For three reasons. *First.* Christianity is my native and life-long faith. *Second.* My spiritual life is quickened and purified by its teachings. *Third.* To me its truth is *more completely* divine than that found in the other religions. Therefore, it is my duty, my preference, and my choice to remain a Christian."

THE MORAL—AS DRAWN FROM THE NEW TESTAMENT.

JESUS AS A JEW.—"*He that is not with me is against me. . . . The woman was a Greek, a Syrophenician by nation; and she besought him that he would cast forth the evil spirit out of her daughter. But Jesus said unto her, Let the children first be filled: for it is not meet to take the children's bread, and to cast it unto the dogs. . . . I am not sent but to the lost sheep of the house of Israel.*"

JESUS AS THE CHRIST.—"*And John answered and said, Master, we saw one casting out evil spirits in thy name; and we forbade him, because he followeth not with us. And Jesus said unto him, Forbid him not: for he that is not against us is for us. Whosoever shall do the will of God, the same is my brother, and sister, and mother. And other sheep I have, which are not of this fold: them also I must bring; . . . and there shall be one fold, and one shepherd.*"

THE DISCIPLE AS A SECTARIAN.—"*And they went, and entered into a village of the Samaritans, to make ready for him. And they did not receive him. . . . And when his disciples James and John saw this, they said, Master, wilt thou that we command fire to come down from heaven, and consume them.*"

THE DISCIPLE AS A FOLLOWER OF THE CHRIST.—"*Then Peter opened his mouth, and said, Of a truth I perceive that God is no respecter of persons: But in every nation he that feareth him, and worketh rghteousness, is accepted with him.*"

Paul as a Denominationalist.—"*I gave my voice against them. And I punished them oft in every synagogue, and compelled them to blaspheme; and being exceedingly mad against them, I persecuted them even unto strange cities.*"

Paul as a Christian.—"*There is neither Greek nor Jew, circumcision nor uncircumcision, Barbarian, Scythian, bond nor free. . . . There is no difference between the Jew and the Greek: for the same Lord over all is rich unto all that call upon him. . . . As he saith also in Osee, I will call them my people, which were not my people; and her beloved, which was not beloved. And it shall come to pass, that in the place where it was said unto them, Ye are not my people; there shall they be called the children of the living God.*"

The Moral—as drawn from other Ancient Sacred Books of the World.

"*Have the religions of mankind no common ground? Is there not everywhere the same enrapturing beauty beaming forth from many thousand hidden places? Broad, indeed, is the carpet God has spread, and beautiful the colors He has given it. . . . There is but one lamp in this house, in the rays of which, wherever I look, a bright assembly meets me. . . . O God! whatever road I take joins the highway that leads to Thee.*"—Persian Scriptures.

"*What doth the Lord require of thee, but to do justly, and to love mercy, and to walk humbly with thy God.*"—Hebrew Scripture.

"*The catholic-minded man regards all religions as embodying the same truths; the narrow-minded man observes only their differences.*"—Chinese Apothegm.

"*Altar flowers are of many species, but all Worship is one; systems of Faith are different, but God is one.*"—Hindu Apothegm.

"*He who is beloved of God honors every form of Religious Faith.*"—Buddhist Scripture.

"*God is by nature the Father of all men; and all best men He calls his sons.*"—GRECIAN SCRIPTURE.

"*Amid all the conflict of opinions there sounds through all the world one consenting law and idea,—that there is One God, the Ruler and Father of All. . . . I do not blame the variety of representations, only let men understand there is but One Divine Nature; let them love One, and keep One ever in their thoughts.*"—ROMAN SCRIPTURES.

"*If thou art a Mussulman, go stay with the Franks; if thou art a Christian, mix with the Jews; if thou art a Shuah, mix with the Schismatics. Whatever is thy religion, associate with men of opposite persuasions. If thou canst mix with them freely, and art not the least angered whilst listening to their discourse, thou hast attained peace, and art a master of creation.*"—ARABIAN SCRIPTURES.

"*To him who on these pinions has risen and soared away to the throne of the Highest, all religions are like—Christians, Moslems, Guebers, Jews;—all adore Him in their several way and form.*"—PERSIAN APOTHEGM.

CONCLUSION.

Eclecticism is Inclusiveness. Inclusiveness is *true* Catholicism. True Catholicism is *genuine* Christianity.

XVIII.—CHRISTIANITY IS RELIGIOUS ECLECTICISM.

True Christianity "was in the beginning, is now, and ever must be" Religious Eclecticism. All intelligent and unprejudiced study of Comparative Religion must lead to Christianity —that is, to Religious Eclecticism *as a method*. One of the gravest errors that all the ages have thus far made, is that of supposing Jesus to have been a Sectarian and his Religion a Sect. Every man is likely to portray his Master or Leader in Religion, as he does his God, after his own pattern. The masses of men have always created God " in *their* own image and after *their* own likeness." An elephant, a tiger, a monkey, a snake would quite naturally (and quite excusably) do the same. Exactly so the great Masters and Leaders of Religion have always been conceived of by the masses, by the ninety-nine out of a hundred, we may say, as nearly if not altogether like unto themselves. Ninety-nine out of a hundred are bigoted; being so, they build fences about their own Religious Conceptions and shut themselves *in*, and all who have different Conceptions *out*. They, and all the rest who are *inside*, are adherents of the one only and true Religion—the true Church. "The Chosen of God" are they; while all *outside* are Schismatics, Heretics, Infidels, Pagans, Heathen. Naturally these ninety-nine out of a hundred—whether Buddhists, Mohammedans, or Christians—always have done, and, so long as they continue bigoted, always will do, the same with their chosen Master's personality and teachings. Around Gautama, Mohammed, and Jesus alike they have built—from the beginning till now—fences of Fables, Traditions, Ecclesiasticisms, Dogmas, and Creeds. All who should choose to come within those fences would be The Faithful, holding the True and Saving Faith; all others would be "Anathema." In order to justify themselves they have claimed that *secret orders* were somehow communicated by their great Leaders to some Chief Apostle, or to his successors, commanding these "fences" to be built and diligently kept up. No records, no tradition even, of such a command or of such "secret orders" are anywhere to be found. But bigotry in general, and priest-craft in particular, always falls back upon infallible Councils, on infallible Churches, or infallible Popes whenever the infallible Book proves insufficient. So has it been in all the Religions. Gautama, Mohammed, Jesus, and all the great Masters have been alike treated in this as in almost every other respect. Human nature is human nature everywhere. The masses are always the masses. Priest-craft is everywhere priest-craft. Bigots, like thorns, brambles, and weeds, cover the earth.

XIX.—JESUS NO SECTARIAN, HIS RELIGION NO SECT.

In spite of all this, Jesus was no Sectarian, and his religion was no Sect. As wide as humanity were his sympathies, as old as human history was his Church. No "fences," except those of humility and of penitence—of a desire to be pure in heart and of an aspiration to hunger and thirst after righteousness—did he build or tolerate. He was the friend of publicans and sinners, of Samaritan heretics, and of theological outcasts. His only detestations were for pompous, self-conceited "Saints," who glorified themselves and despised others. His only rejections were those of "Scribes and Pharisees, Hypocrites" and "Priests and Levites passing by on the other side"—using terms of to-day, hypocritical clergymen, self-parading Doctors of Divinity, bigoted and cold-hearted Church officials, and the front-seat-always-on-hand Church members who "devour widows' houses and for a pretence make long prayers." These, and these only, he detested and rejected, saying: "Woe! woe!—Therefore shall ye receive the greater condemnation. . . . Thieves and harlots shall go into the Kingdom of God before you." Jesus then was a sectarian only in the sense that he excluded all hypocrites, bigots, and religious formalists. His religion was a "Sect" so broad that it included—the earth over and humanity through—all who were humble, loving, and sincere. This is the eclecticism of *genuine* Christianity to-day, "as it was in the beginning and ever shall be, world without end. Amen."

XX.—STUDY OF COMPARATIVE RELIGION LEADS TO CHRISTIANITY.

As we have already said, to this *genuine* Christianity, whose *method* is religious eclecticism, all intelligent and unprejudiced study of Comparative Religion must lead. "To which of these religions do you belong? To all, for all combined constitute the genuine religion." These are well known words of Goethe. They may be taken as the Universal Creed of all *greatest* scholars, poets, prophets, sages, and saints, including Jesus. Jesus himself formulated the

Creed so far as its substance was concerned. Goethe only condensed the whole life, and Gospel, of the Divine Nazarene into a single sentence when he composed those words. Indeed they are almost an exact rescript of the only Creed of Jesus that the New Testament traditions have handed down to us: "Who is my mother? and who are my brethren? Whosoever shall do the will of my Father who is in Heaven, the same is my brother, and sister, and mother." Upon the mind of the writer of these pages these words of Jesus made a deep impression in his early youth, and gradually shaped his Theology and directed his Religious life. While a schoolboy, a devout member and communicant of the Presbyterian Church, he heard a sermon preached by what was called a "loose though scholarly" Presbyterian minister upon the above words, and in the above spirit (though cautiously worded "for fear of the Jews"). That sermon helped him more than all the other sermons listened to during his student days. One figure used by the preacher he never could forget: Truth has been broken into a thousand fragments; every Religious sect and school has a fragment or two, at which they are tugging away, supposing it to be the whole Truth. What all great minds and Christlike souls are seeking to do is, to put an end to the janglings and strife by bringing the fragments together into One United Truth. This was a good figure. Similar ones have since met the writer's eye:—"Religious Truth is a Shield (not of two only but of a thousand sides); view *every* side, then will you have the Whole Truth."—"All Religions are the same wine in different colored glasses." This from Emerson would be a more exact figure if thus stated:—All *forms* of Religion are the same wine *in different dilutions* and in different colored glasses. Oriental figures are:—"The many rays emanating from one central lamp"—"The various colors of the beautiful carpet God has spread"—"Altar flowers are of many species, but all Worship is one."—"To him who on these pinions has risen and soared away to the throne of the Highest, all religions are like; Christians, Moslems, Guebers, Jews, all who are humble and sincere, adore Him in their several ways and forms." To which may be added the saying of that Chief Apostle of Jesus, St. Peter, "Of a truth I perceive that God is no respecter of persons; but in every nation he that revereth Him and worketh righteousness is accepted with Him."

XXI.—CHRISTIANITY A VAST GRADED SCHOOL OF RELIGION.

While accepting all these and similar figures as helpful, the writer finds more of comprehensiveness and of exact correspondence to World-wide, History-through facts in this similitude.—A great, complex, various, and ever varying System of Education adapted to every degree of intelligence and of culture; ranging from the Nursery and Kindergarten departments up through the Primary and other various grades to the College, the University, and the Post-University; with instructors and instructions adapted to each—like teachers like pupils, "like priests like people."—Such, in the wise Providence of the Eternal, is the Universal Religion of Mankind with its numerous and diversified Schools or Sects. If this Providential Scheme could only be recognized; if each department would attend to its own work and not attempt to dictate to, monopolize, or absorb (much less to anathematize) the others; if Priests, Ministers, or Teachers in the several grades would gracefully accept their especial stations and seek only *to advance* their congregations, and to *graduate* them upward as rapidly as possible—then all sectarianism, bitterness, rivalry, and hatred would cease and the Kingdom of God would *at once* be here. This was the Gospel of Jesus; it is time for us to go (as the first disciples did) into all the world and preach it to every creature. This is the Eclecticism of Christianity as Jesus taught and founded it. And this is Renascent Christianity.

XXII.—PROVE ALL; HOLD FAST THE GOOD.

While yet a student in Williams College, but more especially in the Union Theological Seminary of New York and in the Yale College Divinity School, the writer was frequently reproached by his fellow-students for his habit of closely questioning and often refusing to accept, the Calvinistic Dogmas of his Presbyterian Sect, Text-books, and Professors. "These profound books, these learned instructors, our dignified and respectable Presbyterian Faith—who are you, a mere schoolboy, to question them!" The response always was,—Yes, but every one of the fifty or more Protestant Sects claims that *it* has profound books, learned instructors, a dignified and respectable Faith. The Roman Catholics claim the same; so do the Greek Catholics; so do the Jews; so does every one of the various schools and sects of the Mohammedan, Buddhistic, Confucian, Brahmanistic, Zoroastrian, and other Religions of the World. All alike claim and proclaim their wisdom, scholarship, and wide influence. As a fact there *are* learned men, influential men, and saintly men in them all. What then shall I do? To whom listen? Which especial System or Sect shall I unquestioningly accept? The one in which I was born? Then—"By the simple accident of birth I might have been High-Priest to Mumbo Jumbo."

No! I will listen to *all;* will question every one; and from them all will accept whatever I intelligently and honestly can. "*Prove all things; hold fast that which is good.*"

The great question is—not Which Religion, Church, Sect, School, System *suits me best;* to which can I *most conveniently and agreeably belong?* This may do as a starter; may be excusable until one can find time and opportunity to become broader and wiser, so as to make choice from his own *intelligent conviction.* But the "great question" is, What, *in each and in all,* can I accept as true, and conscientiously make into a Creed by which to guide and inspire my life? Of course such a Creed cannot be arrived at in a day or in a year. So every creed should be a *gradual* and a *growing* one—always open to new light, eager for improvement, like the busy bee "gathering honey from every flower," and ready to be changed or even retracted should growing *intelligence and holiness combined* demand it.

"What! Changed your mind so soon? Not *I.*
But *it;* that, changing to my thoughts, has changed my mind."

"Yesterday you wore a cloak: Why not to-day?" "Yesterday was cold—to-day is warm." Consistency is more frequently the fool's excuse, the sluggard's plea, or the coward's boast than the watch-word of those who are wise, devoted, and brave.

"*Constancy in Error is Constant Folly.*"

In Religion—which is, more than anything else, a matter of *unfolding* intuitions, of *widening* wisdom, and of *evolving* Spiritual Life—all this is especially pertinent and true.

XXIII.—THE RELIABLE CREED AND ITS ESSENTIAL TESTS.

But how perplexing it all is; and, after all, who can hope ever to arrive at any permanent certainty! To these very natural exclamations answers may be made as follows: *First*—No creed is of any account that has not a practical side to it; in fact, that is not *far more* practical than theoretical. So nothing should be accepted, or sought for, except that which will surely *elevate and inspire*, as well as broaden and brighten one's every-day life. If you are *not* inspired and elevated, are *not* growing sweeter and better, suspect your Creed and hasten to correct it. *Second*—No Creed is of any account which has not an *intellectual* side to it, and does not grow out of one's *first-handed* investigations and convictions. "Thou shalt love the Lord thy God, with all thy *mind*, as well as soul and strength, is the first and great Command." Therefore never repeat a Creed like a parrot, nor accept one without serious questioning, nor *continue to accept it* without unceasing inspection, and readiness to enlarge or improve. *Third*—In studying Comparative Religion adopt the Platonic test of an otherwise credible Belief;—What the *wisest and best* men have always and everywhere affirmed, on questions of Theology and of Ethics, is likely to be true. Whatever is common to the *fundamental* teachings of all the Great Religions may be gathered into a Creed of Mankind and accepted as Truth. This was the method of Jesus and this is Christianity. *Fourth*—That great and Divine Eclectic who was the founder of Christianity has left two Condensations of Divine

Truth, of which all the rest of the Gospels and the Epistles of the New Testament are only elaborations—*namely*, The Beatitudes, and the Two Commandments. These, like all the rest of his Divine Teachings, are Eclectic and (in other phrase) are common to all the Great Religions of the World. So, on the Platonic basis, as well as because they are *self-evident* to what we may term the Universal Human Mind, they may be accepted as Truth. As such they may constitute a Creed with which all who seek to be pure in heart, and who hunger and thirst for righteousness, may at least *start* the inspiration and direction of their every-day lives. These Beatitudes and Commandments, however, need a constant study of the whole Christian Bible (of which they are only a summary) for their illumination and enforcement.— The Christian Bible *expurgated and corrected* we mean; for it—(like all other ancient books) is cumbered with much of traditional accumulation and *débris*, which Higher Criticism is now Providentially commissioned to remove.

The expurgated and corrected Sacred Books of the other Great Religions of the World should also be studied; not only because they so wondrously confirm all the essential teachings of the Christian Bible, but also, because they furnish those varied statements and beautiful illustrations of the Common Truth, which nothing can supply so well as Oriental Piety and Oriental Imagery combined.

XXIV.—THE LIVING CREED AND PLEDGE.

The Beatitudes and Two Commandments of Jesus, being accepted as the summary of the Christian Bible, and of all the other Bibles of the world, might (as they are found in the New Testament) be taken as the Common Creed of Mankind. However, greater brevity and simplicity may be an advantage for ordinary concerted, and individual, use.

In a recent volume of notable Sermons entitled *The Mind of Christ*, a well-known clergyman of Scotland has suggested such a simplified Creed joined to a Pledge of equal spirit and simplicity. Venturing to add two or three clauses to each, to change a few words, and to give a more Creed-like and Pledge-like form to both, they are here added.

The Life Creed.

I believe in the Fatherhood of God.
I believe in the Teachings of Jesus.
I believe in the Guidance of the Holy Spirit.
I believe in the Clean Heart.
I believe in the Service of Love.
I believe in the Unworldly Life.

The Life Pledge.

I promise to trust God and love Him supremely.
I promise to take my Cross and follow Christ.
I promise to accept the Holy Spirit as my Guide.
I promise to forgive and love my Enemies.
I promise to love my Fellow Men as myself.
I promise to hunger and thirst after Righteousness.

XXV.—CHRISTIANITY THE SUPREME RELIGION.

Thus far Christianity is Supreme. Spite of its many, great, and persistent degenerations; spite of the Commercial Spirit—inherited from Judaism,—of Priest-craft—common to all Religions,—of stupid Conservatism—the "block-head" mystery prevailing everywhere;—spite of all these reversions, and perversions, Christianity has proved itself superior to all the other Religions of the World. This superiority is evident from even the brief study of Comparative Religions that intelligent and unprejudiced scholars and observers have, up to date, been able to make. The comparative study of Sacred Books, of Literature drawn from or growing out of those Books, and of grades of advancing or receding Civilization that may fairly be said to be *essentially* or *inseparably* connected with them—this is our field of observation and of judgment. Of the superiority which we claim there have been various notable opportunities for public manifestation during the Christian

Centuries; some of them, we confess, very unfavorably resulting, for Christianity—as, for instance, during all the Mediæval Centuries, when the Scholarship, Morality, and higher Civilization of the world belonged, unquestionably, to Islamism in particular, and to Confucianism, Brahminism, and Parseeism in general. But, spite of these many centuries of decadence the partial renascence of Christianity, known as the Protestant Reformation, and the much more radical and complete one now in progress, together with the thriving scholarship, morality, and civilizing influences of the first three Christian centuries, have so combined to rescue the Divine Religion of Jesus from reversion and decay that, to-day, it stands before the world unquestionably supreme.

XXVI.—THE WORLD'S PARLIAMENT OF RELIGIONS.

Without doubt the most notable manifestation of this superiority that has ever transpired was that known as The World's Parliament of Religions, held in connection with the recent Columbian Exposition in Chicago. Not "three wise men from the Orient" only, but a large assembly of wise men—the wisest, the most saintly, the most noble, the *best* as we may truthfully call them—out of every civilized nation under heaven, representing every highest or more intelligent form and phase of religion, from every continent and corner of the earth, were there gathered together to witness—they knew not what at first! But in the end, as in the providence of God it proved, to witness the transcendent power of Christ's personality, and the supreme glory of his religion, as compared with all the other personalities and religions of the world. Not as on that greatest of historic Epiphanies, the day of Pentecost, when those gathered were representatives only of various tribes, sects, and proselytes of the Jews scattered abroad among all the nations who had "come up to Jerusalem for to worship"—this assembly was composed of representatives from all the great nationalities, and all the ancient as well as most recent religious faiths of the civilized world.

This most remarkable manifestation is not only "most remarkable," but is also bound to have most wide reaching, world illuminating, and history transforming results.

After nineteen centuries of historic illumination, transformation, and evolution, what has the world to say about Christianity? Let us examine and answer this question in the light of the nineteenth century, as focused in the recent "World's Parliament of Religions."

At the very beginning we are met by an objection thought by some to be unanswerable; an old objection and yet very new; an objection many times answered, and yet forever pressed upon us not only by Jews, Pagans, and Skeptics, but also by many honest enquirers among those who—in some sense—call themselves Christians. The objection is this: The claim of superiority is a claim that long has been and still is made with equal sincerity and emphasis by the devotees of all the other great religions of the world, Jewish, Persian, Buddhistic, Confucian, and Mohammedan—all say the same thing,—claim the same superiority.

No doubt that all the representatives of the great religions of the world, from the most ancient Hindoo and Parsee faiths to the most recent of the Protestant Christian sects, crossed seas and continents coming up to this World's Parliament of Religions, each with this thought in his heart and this word on his tongue,—*My* Religion is supreme! In view of this fact there were many of "the most straitest sects" of all these Religions (our own Christian Sects included) who doubted of the benefits, to say nothing of the reverence, of such a World's Parliament of Religions. Others of the most liberal, or what one may better term "free-thinking," Sects concluded that the time had come (and the Parliament of Religions would settle it) when the indefinite article "a" should be substituted for the definite article "the"; so that all the claims would be right and none wrong—My Religion is *a* Superior, not *the* Superior Religion. This they thought should be done as a timely compromise, in the interests of universal peace and good will. It is time, they said, that we acknowledge the good in all Religions—and not any longer set up one as true and try to pull down all the others as false. What is now demanded is an acknowledgment, on all hands, that there are "Lords many" and that all forms of Religions are equally authentic and divine; or better still perhaps that all put together make the True Religion—the Universal Religion.

A famous essayist of this free-thinking sort (Thomas Wentworth Higginson), in a well known essay entitled "The Sympathy of Religions," has written this: "The main difference between the various Religions of the World is, that each fills some blank space in its creed with the name of a different teacher. The Parsee, for instance, wears a pure white garment bound around with a certain knot; and whenever this knot is undone, at morning or night, he repeats the four main parts of his creed, which are: 'To believe in one God and hope for mercy from Him only; to believe in a future state of existence; to do as you would be done by.' Thus he keeps on the universal ground of Religion. Then he drops into the language of sectarianism and adds 'to believe in Zoroaster as a supreme teacher.' The creed [he continues] thus furnishes a formula for all Faiths. It might be printed in blank like a circular, leaving only the closing name to be filled in. For Zoroaster write Christ and you have Christianity; write Buddha and you have Buddhism; write Mohammed and you have Mohammedanism. Each of these is true Religion *plus* an individual name. It is by insisting on this *plus* that each Religion stops short of being universal the World over." So say all "free thinkers." To claim that there is one Superior Religion—that any one of the Religions is *essentially* superior to the others, is narrowness, sectarianism, bigotry. It is time, they say, for a Universal Religion, and a Universal Religion must be the residuum of all the great Religions of the World fused into one. This is what some thought the Parliament of Religions meant, or would come to mean. But it proved otherwise. Every representative was cordially received, and equal civilities and rights of speech were granted to all. They were simply invited to come and compare their Religions—not so much as to their original teachings as in their actual historic results. It thus became a study—a most interesting, important, and timely study—in Comparative Religion. It was indeed a World's Exhibition of Religion—not of religious theories but religious results. What has your religion accomplished? Show us its superior fruits and we will then believe in its superior worth.

XXVII.—THE AGE OF COMPARISON, AND ITS TEST.

Happily we are now living in an age of the World in which the test, which Jesus himself gave, can be applied, and is being applied, in its most impartial and universal sense,—the test I mean, "By their fruits shall ye know them."

Our age is an age of Comparisons. All our World's International and National Exhibitions are exhibitions of comparative values. All our literature and ever advancing civilization means a sifting of values and an exhibition of superior worth by means of the comparative method. Which of several pieces of machinery shall have the medal? Place them side by side and see how they work. Which of various theories of Political Economy, of National Government, of Science, of Sociology, of Ethics, is worthy of ultimate or of exclusive adoption? Place them side by side, compare their practical workings, and, after a reasonably prolonged and impartial witnessing of results, judge as to superiority. So the whole civilized World is doing to-day. We have entered upon the age and the ages of Comparisons. " By their fruits shall ye know them."

This test is being applied, whether we know it or not, first of all, among the various denominations of our own Christianity. Men are beginning to look about them and inquire for the Christian body or name that can show, not the most, but the best fruit; not Antiquity, Creeds, Cathedrals, Sum Totals, but real fruit—souls saved, characters regenerated, society uplifted, the world advanced. Mankind, here and now, are beginning to listen to the teachings which are enunciated, not by the most oracular or pretentious theologians or ecclesiastics, but by those who are most like the Divine Master—simple, loving, and wise. The Christian World is beginning to believe not in the institutions which *talk* most, but in those which *do* most, and do it most effectively. Christian "orthodoxy" is no longer tested by creeds, but the creeds themselves are being tested by their results. Those interpretations of the Bible which are found to have the greatest power over—not the tongues or professions, but—the consciences and lives of men, are beginning to be received as the true interpretations, and that form of Christianity which, after the test of centuries, has shown its superior power to refine and elevate and purify, is being accepted—*must henceforth be accepted*—as superior. This is what is going on among the various Christian communities. The same is the test, and the only real test of Christianity as against the other great Religions of the World. " By their fruits shall ye know them."

XXVIII.—RELIGIONS JUDGED BY THEIR FRUITS.

Christianity must stand or fall, must be ranked as superior or inferior—now after this lapse of nineteen centuries, simply on the ground of comparative merit, or of relative worth. It is no longer—as it once was and doubtless had to be—a question of Antiquity, Prophecy, or Supernatural Sanctions, chiefly or exclusively. It is no longer a question, as it used to be, of Numerical Strength, or of Institutional Grandeur, or of Political Domain. All these are broken earthworks, decayed fortifications of the Past, which modern culture, and wisdom, and purity, and humanity are forcing us to abandon. The question of to-day and of the future is, not what are the Sanctions or Accessories of this or that religion, but *what is it?* What has it done? What is it doing and what does it promise to do? We as Christians will no longer permit other Religions to reckon up the Antiquity of their Faiths, figure up their Prophecies, add their Miracles, count their Adherents,—as they have always been doing,—and thrust their sum-totals in our face, or in the faces of one another, as final evidences that they are superior or divine. We will no longer permit this. Neither must we permit ourselves to do the same to them. If we do, we shall continue to find that almost every other great Religion can thrust back a sum-total of these very boasts or claims at least equal to our own; while infidels will meanwhile stand by and scoff to see us worsted with the weapons of our continued choice. Neither may we claim, as some have claimed, that Divine Truth has been revealed *to us alone*, in the sense that God has deigned to send Prophets to us only. For, studious research has already drawn forth many a golden treasure from those "rubbish heaps of superstition,"—the Sacred Books of the Ethnic Religions. Impartial criticism is more and more proving the truth of our own blessed Bible, that "God is no respecter of persons," and that He has "never left Himself without witness among any people, but has from time to time raised up prophets among them all such as they were able to hear."

None of these methods of the past are to be continued as the methods of to-day or of the future. Rather, now and hereafter, must be adopted the New Testament method—"By their fruits shall ye know them." Recognizing gladly all that is good, or beautiful, or true, in other Religions; conceding to their great teachers all the authority which they can, rightfully, claim; we are to place them side by side with the Religion of Jesus; and, by witnessing their practical workings—their relative civilizing, regenerating, ennobling, and purifying influences and results—are thus to determine, in these "latter ages of the world," which is the best Religion, which is truest, and—as a reasonable inference—which is most divine. This henceforth is the only tenable as well as the only truly Biblical ground upon which we may base our claim for the great superiority of the Christian Religion. Prophecy, Miracles, Inspiration, Martyrdoms—all of these, as many and as great are claimed by the other Religions.

Of course we may believe that ours are true and theirs mistaken or false. But however much we may *believe* this, we have no adequate method of demonstrating it except by pointing to the unique, the transcendent power of Christianity, as seen in its incomparable triumphs, as a co-operating agency at least, in regenerating and civilizing the World.

And now, for the first time in History, we are able to demonstrate this with a great and ever increasing power of demonstration. Till quite recently the Sacred Books of the various Religions of the World were sealed to our view. Within the past twenty-five years they have been unsealed and are now open to us all. Till now, too, the true history and the real progress of civilization among the so-called Pagan nations of the World has been hidden from us. Inaccessible, shut in and shut out each from the other, and from all the rest of the World, how could they be known or how could any right comparison be instituted? But Christian Missions first, Christian Commerce second, Christian Education, Invention, and Enterprise third, have battered down all partition walls, have demanded and secured "open sesame" to every corner of the world, have piled upon our book shelves and placed before our eyes the materials for an adequate and just comparison. China, India, Persia, and the Islands of the Sea, with their inhabitants, customs, institutions, laws, and grades of civilization—their past progress and future promises are now definitely placed before us. Railroad, and inter-oceanic and telegraphic and telephonic communication have made us next door neighbors to every tribe and people of the earth. Hence to all who read, study, and observe, *with intelligence and candor*, the Argument from Comparisons has become cumulative. So overwhelmingly is it on the side of Christianity that it seems well-nigh absurd even to re-state the claim. This is what our World's Exhibitions, held, every one of them, in Christian lands, originated and sustained by Christian intelligence, industry, and enterprise, have meant. Providentially they all have been Epiphanies of Christianity. Japan, China, India, Persia, Africa, and the Islands of the Sea have sent representatives to them who have returned—as did those sent in ancient times to spy out the Promised Land—bearing tokens substantial and convincing of the superiority of Christian institutions. From the last World's Exposition—grandest and best of all,—especially from that department of it known as the "World's Parliament of Religion," returned many an intelligent, devout, and truth-loving delegate who exclaimed, as did the Queen of Sheba, returning from the court of Solomon, "Behold the half was not told me."

XXIX.—UNPREJUDICED TESTIMONIES.

And all this is not, as some of the scoffers might say, "American spread Eagleism" or "nineteenth century brag" or the "partisan boastings of Christian bigotry." As one of our prominent Christian ministers, heard and known all over the earth, has recently said, "It is the religion of Jesus that has abolished slavery, emancipated childhood, uplifted womanhood, and fought all battles for human freedom and the rights of man. All that distinguishes the workingman of America and Europe from the Chinese coolie, the Hindoo pariah, the Egyptian fellah, and the proletare of ancient Rome is due to Christianity. Christianity has promoted intelligence, has been the mother of science, the nurse of art, the promoter of invention. Industry in its greatest sense—the industry of steam and electricity—which defies time and space, does not exist except in Christian lands."

Lest this should be called the "special pleading" of interested parties—of clergymen and others who are paid to say it—let us quote also the recent language of one who is not an ecclesiastic, nor a theologian, nor even an "orthodox" Christian,—one of our most distinguished American scientists, doctor of laws, professor of chemistry and mineralogy in Harvard University :—

"As modern science dates from Newton, so all that is noblest and best in man, all that is most pure and lovely in life, all most unselfish morality, all most heroic chivalry, all most holy charity is dated Anno Domini. Looking at

Christian Institutions simply as outward facts—without regard to sanctions of doctrines, dogmas or creeds of any sort —what do we see? No less than this: that everything in the world that is loftiest and profoundest in thought, which is most ennobling and heroic in character, which is bravest and most unselfish in action, which is purest and loveliest in art, which is most consoling and hopeful in philosophy; and above all this, every form of most beneficent charity, every great movement for the amelioration of mankind, every influence most sanctifying to family ties, dates from one conspicuous and definite epoch of the world's history from which civilized men began to count again the revolving years. Who can speak the matchless worth of Christianity."

These are fair and honest statements of the results, to date, of this science which is now widely known as the Science of Comparative Religion. But, lest this too should be considered partisan, or be classed among the Exclusive Statements of Sectarian Religionists, let us add one of many statements from those who have been born and bred in other Religions. One of the distinguished delegates to the World's Parliament of Religions in Chicago, a reformed Brahmin of India, afterwards made scores of addresses in various parts of this country, every one of which was a fervent eulogy of Christianity. His favorite quotation was that of his great fellow reformer of India: "How we wish that Jesus had been born in India! We should have devoted an epic to his glory, sung his name through every city and village, comforted the weak in their sorrows and the dying on their death beds with his holy words, remembered him in every act of daily life, and died finding consolation and strength in his blessed example. We wish indeed that Jesus had been born in India."

XXX.—THE VERDICT.

So it is that even the chief representatives of so-called Pagan Religions are joining in the testimony; are coming to acknowledge not only that Christian civilization is supreme, but also that it is verily the personality of Jesus and the promulgation of his gospel upon which, as a chief corner-stone, Christian Civilization is built. The great masses of truth lovers and truth seekers, impressed with the supreme majesty and dignity of Jesus, convinced of his superior wisdom, authority, purity and grace, have taken his Gospel—the Gospel of the Fatherhood of God, the Brotherhood of Man, the Forgiveness of Sins and the Immortal Hope—and, upon this for nineteen Centuries have been building, and building "better than they knew," a great kingdom of light, and love, and humanity. They have proclaimed the teachings of Jesus, perpetuated his memory, immortalized his deeds, and exalted his example; so that now, more than ever, he stands out in glory, with all the world wondering before him. They have taken the name of Jesus, "name of wondrous love, name all other names above," and crying out "All hail to its power," have been singing all through the centuries—and to-day with a louder, fuller, sweeter voice than ever: a voice heard in millions of temples all over the earth, yes, in every corner of every continent and in every habitable island of the sea—are singing the old hymn, the *one united, unbroken* Hymn of Christendom, we may call it:

> " Jesus shall reign where'er the sun
> Does his successive journeys run ;
> His kingdom stretch from shore to shore,
> Till moons shall wax and wane no more.

> " To him shall endless prayer be made,
> And praises throng to crown his head ;
> His name like sweet perfume shall rise
> With every morning sacrifice.

> " People and realms of every tongue
> Dwell on his love with sweetest song ;
> And infant voices shall proclaim
> This early blessing on his name.

> " Blessings abound where'er he reigns ;
> The prisoner leaps to burst his chains,
> The weary find eternal rest,
> And all the sons of want are blest.

> "Let every creature rise, and bring
> Peculiar honours to our King:
> Angels descend with songs again,
> And earth repeat the loud Amen."

XXXI.—NOTWITHSTANDING.

All this *in spite of* the many, great, and persistent Degenerations with which *genuine* Christianity has been cumbered; and by which, from the Second Century *increasingly* until now, its progress has been impeded! What then must have been the inherent, latent, as yet largely undeveloped and widely misapprehended power of *original* Christianity! What it *was* may be inferred from what it *accomplished* as a world-conquering, world-regenerating Religion, "pure and undefiled before God and man" during the First Century. What it *is*, may be, and *shall* be, may be gathered from the title of this volume, *Renascent* Christianity—Christianity *springing up anew*. Had original Christianity escaped the universally prevailing law of Tendency to Revert, had it remained pure and uncorrupted, as it issued from the lips and life of its Divine Founder! verily, verily, his Holy Dream, and that of all his Apostles and first zealous followers, would have actually been accomplished—the Kingdom of God *would have come* and His Will *would have been done*, on Earth as in Heaven, long before the Nicene and Athanasian Creeds were imposed as yokes and goads upon the *degenerate* Christians of the *degenerate* Christian Church! And now, should Christianity become *truly renascent*—springing up again as it did in the First Century, and *so continuing*—verily, verily, the long dreamed of Millennium would actually be here before the close of the Twentieth Century!

"Even so, Jesus Master, come quickly!" "Repent, Prepare the Way"—so shall the "Kingdom of Heaven" *verily be* "at hand."

XXXII.—WHAT THEN IS CHRISTIANITY?

What then *is* Christianity? Why is it, as we have shown, *essentially* superior? In all truthfulness we are reminded that it "*was* inferior during several Mediæval Centuries." We are also told that it only *happens* to be at the top now: and why may it not again revert to Heathenism so completely as to become inferior again to one or more of the Pagan Religions? We answer—This sad Reversion may indeed take place again, and repeatedly. There will doubtless come yet many fallings away as Jesus and his chief Apostles repeatedly predicted. But "Truth crushed to earth shall rise again." Simply because Christianity is "Truth" in a *broader*, as well as purer, and higher form than is found in any of the other forms of Religion, *therefore* has it been—as in the Protestant Reformation—still more now is, in the present Reformation, and promises more and more to be as Scholarship, Culture, and Civilization increase—a *ceaselessly renascent* Religion.

But why *is* it a "*broader*, purer, and higher form of Truth"? Simply because it was in the beginning, is now, and ever must be an *Eclectic Religion*—and the only one of the Great Religions that was, is, or can be eclectic. This claim has been made and substantiated in a previous section, and so need not be further considered here. As an Eclectic Religion it *still* as at first, and *forever* as now, claims, takes possession of, and appropriates as its own, *all Truth wherever found*.

Thus it is that the Spiritual Fruitage of all the Ages, the genuine Inspirations and Products of the Holy Ghost everywhere and always, "world without end," belong to *genuine* Christianity. If those who call themselves Christians will only recognize this and permit *renascent* Christianity to claim and appropriate its own, then will it soon become and to the end continue, in fact as in name, The One Holy Catholic and Apostolical Religion of Mankind.

XXXIII.—SACRED SCRIPTURES OF THE WORLD—MODERN AS WELL AS ANCIENT.

Christianity as an Eclectic Religion, as the only Eclectic Religion, still as at first, and *forever* as now, claims, takes possession of, and appropriates as its own, *all* Truth wherever *found*. As such, its " Bible " is comprehensive and enlarges itself, ever and ever, to take in " all Truth wherever found." Hence it has, and must have, its Sacred Scriptures " new and old "—*modern as well as ancient*.

The word Scriptures means, of course, Writings, or Things Written. The word Sacred means venerated, highly valued, or held in highest esteem. " Sacred Scriptures of the World " then, as a title, means those writings of the world which are or are worthy to be venerated, highly valued, or held in highest esteem. In a lower sense all writings which contain any Truth or Beauty are Sacred Scriptures. But, by common consent of all people and ages, the word Sacred is reserved for writings which bear on *highest* Truth and Beauty—which universally are recognized as those only which relate to Religion and Ethics; or to Piety and Morals. So, in any Collection of Sacred Scriptures of the World, nothing can be wisely included but such writings as relate to the Supreme Being and to Mankind in their nature and relations.

Such writings however are modern as well as ancient. It is a serious practical error as well as an outgrown superstition to suppose " a deposit " of Sacred Truth and Beauty made in ancient times once for all, and never to be added to, repeated, newly adapted, or changed. " The faith once delivered to the Saints " has been delivered not once only, but countless times—indeed, unceasingly, and *increasingly*, as the ages have gone by. Possibly there have not been so many " Saints "—that is, persons of such high attainments in Holiness—in some of the modern as in some of the ancient ages, through whom the Holy Communications could fittingly be delivered, but in all the ages there have been some. " God hath *never* left Himself without witness." In these latter ages there have unquestionably been those of equal attainments in Holiness, and of vastly wider and more profound intelligence. Through these has been " delivered " to the World that deeper Truth and higher Beauty of which he prophesied who said to his disciples, " I have many things to say to you, but ye cannot bear them now. Howbeit when

He, the Spirit of Truth, is come He will guide you into all Truth."

It is high time then that we should have not only a volume, but volume upon volume, of recognized and so designated *modern* Sacred Scriptures of the World. The growing intelligence, the lessening superstitions and narrowness of the world, as well as its more widely-prevailing and perfectly-balanced saintliness, demand, more and more, such a recognition and such a designation. As a response to this evident demand a volume has recently been collected and edited, and will be duly issued under the title, *Modern Sacred Scriptures of the World.* The same editor has previously collected and published a companion volume under the title, *Ancient Sacred Scriptures of the World.*

XXXIV.—MODERN SACRED SCRIPTURES.

No especial merit is claimed by the compiler and editor of this volume soon to be issued for his share in the work. Out of several volumes of his own manuscript notes entitled "Quotations and Thoughts"—accumulated during forty years of reading and meditation—he has simply selected such brief, pointed, and luminous portions as seemed to him best fitted to be called "Sacred" Scripture and best adapted to make up a single volume. This volume he has called by a new name indeed; many of its arrangements and some of its contents are also new; but otherwise it claims no merit above that of other Selections and Anthologies which have —in less methodical ways—sought to condense the Religious and Ethical Literature of Modern Times into a single volume for devotional and practical purposes.

Had all been included which the editor has accumulated under the title of "Quotations and Thoughts" during his many years as student, theologian, and clergyman—all of which he highly values as quickening to his own private aspirations and resolves—not one volume only, but three or more, would have been offered to the publishers as a result. This accumulation, however, is but a fraction of what might be gathered—of equal, and in some cases doubtless of still higher value—from the vast bulk of Sacred Writings both in Poetry and Prose, which holy men and women have "in these last days" produced. Thus may be indicated what inexhaustible treasures remain for succeeding editors to draw from;—to say nothing of those "deposits" which shall unceasingly be made, as the future centuries and generations shall come and go. The volume referred to is but the gathering of a few pebbles from the sea-shore. The *novelty* of its title and method may be a beginning of those days when wise men shall not only realize for themselves—as an *esoteric* treasure—but also boldly teach to the world, that Divine Revelations have never ceased; that wherever a holy soul is found there is an Oracle of God; and that "Sacred Scriptures of the World" include everything, in all writings, that are genuinely "true and beautiful and good."

XXXV.—ALL SACRED SCRIPTURES ARE ANONYMOUS.

Besides the *novelty* of the title and of the general method of the volume to be known as Modern Sacred Scriptures, the editor has ventured upon another—which in the *Ethnic* Scriptures of the previous volume he also adopted—that of withholding all names of those who are, or are reported to be, authors of the various Quotations and Thoughts. This is a *novelty* indeed so far as Modern Literature is concerned. Among the ancients, to be, and to remain *anonymous* was highest genius and most beautiful humility combined. He who forbade his disciples to make him known, charging them, again and again, "See that thou tell no man"; who consented to leave no record of his deeds or words, except in the characters and memories of those with whom he lived and to whom he spoke; who provided for no such record, except as it might spring forth as inspiration from the lips and pens of others after he should disappear; even instructing his disciples—as he doubtless did—to forbear adding their own names as biographers or as authors, so that nearly all the New Testament writings remain to this day as practically *anonymous:* thus is he, the Supreme Man, here as elsewhere, our supreme authority and example. How surprising that those who call themselves his followers have—in these modern times—so rarely been willing, in this regard as in many others, to obey his authority or to follow his example! The author of that "Second Bible," commonly known as the Dramas of Shakespeare, is one of a very few who, in recent centuries, has sought, like his Divine Master and his Disciples, to hide himself behind his words so that the world might not consider *him*, but only the Truth and Beauty his words are designed to reveal. But the time is approaching, or rather, is reapproaching, when all Highest Thoughts and Deeds shall be, and remain, *anonymous*. The lower—that is "profane" or secular—thoughts and deeds doubtless need the backing of their author's name, in order to make them comprehensible or authoritative. Their authors, too, need the glamour and glitter of notoriety, in order to feel *adequately compensated* for their effort or toil. But highest Truth and Beauty, which alone are worthy to be called "Sacred," are—like axioms and intuitions—self-evident. As such *they* need no backing of an author's name; and *their* authors, like themselves, are too lofty to need or to accept, as compensation, the glamour and glitter of notoriety.

> "Things done are won;
> Love's joy lies in the doing."

XXXVI.—HIDING SELF BEHIND TRUTH.

To apprehend Truth in somewhat of its highest Grace and Beauty, and to be privileged to disclose somewhat of that apprehension to the World—this, *and nothing else*, is what all loftiest souls desire. Attaining this, they seek for, ask for, no other reward. "I say unto you, rejoice, not that the spirits are subject unto you; but, rejoice rather, that your names are written in Heaven." Divine approval, not human; God's praises, not the praises of men; eternal attainments and accomplishments, not temporal commendations and rewards, is what all holiest and highest souls desire, and seek. Over this *they* rejoice, and over this only. In the Old Scriptures it is written God buried Moses so that no man knoweth of his sepulchre to this day. In like manner has God buried all who have been His accepted prophets. God's highest mediums of communication with mankind have always been *incognitus:* who exactly they were no man knows "to this day." The authorship of nearly every book of the Bible, as well as of the other most Sacred Scriptures of the World has been contested; and even when the *name* of the author has been conceded, the author himself, in all the details of his personality, remains to this day practically unknown. So should it be! 'T is the Divine Method—the Method of Grace as well as of Genius! Why obscure self-evident Truth and Beauty with the shadow of an author's name? an author who, at his best, is only a mouth-piece or a medium. It is a hindrance, and an impertinence besides. There is but *one* Author—the Supreme Wisdom and Love. Him alone should men consider and adore. Better far will it be when the names of Moses, David, Ezekiel, Isaiah, Matthew, Mark, Luke, John, Paul, Apollos, Homer, Zoroaster, Confucius, Gautama, and the whole line of Sacred Writers, down to "Shakespeare and Bacon," and the geniuses and saints of to-day, are entirely forgotten *as authors*, so that God, the Outshining Central Sun "may be all in all." Then will men no longer enquire for Authors in order to do them homage, but only for Truth and Beauty in order to adore them, and be themselves transformed into their "image and likeness."

"Wherefore henceforth know we no man after the flesh; yea, though we have known Christ after the flesh, yet now henceforth know we him no more." "And when all things shall be subdued unto Him, then shall the Son also himself be subject unto Him that put all things under him, that God may be all in all."

Of a stately Temple or an artistic Palace it may gratify idle curiosity to know who was the architect, or who is the owner. But only those who appreciate least, stop to ask or require to know this. The stateliness of the Temple, the beauty of the Palace speak for themselves to all most intelligent observers; and so lost are *they* in study and admiration of *these*, that mere curiosity as to architect's or owner's name finds no place in them. The watch, not the watchmaker; the machine, not the mechanic; the statue, the painting, the invention, the self-evident theory, the demonstrated problem, the luminous saying, the convincing proposition, the irresistible book—not the artist's, inventor's, student's, or writer's name, is what the Higher Intelligence of this and of all coming ages will, *increasingly*, call for.

" Proverbs are sayings without an author."

" The originals are not original."

" For neither now nor yesterday began
  These thoughts, which have been ever, nor yet can
  A man be found who their first entrance knew."

XXXVII.—THE RESURRECTED JESUS.

" Behold, there was a great earthquake; for the angel of the Lord descended from heaven, and came and rolled back the stone from the door and sat upon it. His countenance was like lightning, and his raiment was white as snow: and for fear of him the keepers did shake and become as dead men. And the angel answered and said unto the women, Fear not ye; for I know that ye seek Jesus, which was crucified. *He is not here, for he is risen*, as he said. Go quickly and tell his disciples that *he is risen from the dead*. And they departed quickly from the sepulchre with fear and great joy; and did run to *bring* his disciples word.

"And Jesus came and spoke unto them, saying, All authority is committed unto me in heaven and on earth. Go ye therefore and teach all nations, baptizing them into the name of the Father, and of the Son, and of the Holy Spirit; teaching them to observe all things whatsoever I have commanded you. *And lo, I am with you always, even unto the end of the world. Amen.*"

XXXVIII.—NEW MEANING OF OLD DOGMAS AND CREEDS.

Among "orthodox" Christians there are in common use now—as there have been since the fourth century—certain doctrinal words and phrases, which demand adjustment to Renascent Christianity and to the new interpretations of the Bible known as Higher Criticism. The volumes prepared by the writer, entitled *Ancient Sacred Scriptures of the World*, and *Modern Sacred Scriptures of the World*, are both prepared in the interests of Renascent Christianity and of Higher Criticism of the Bible. Any readers of those volumes, and all students of the Bible and of other Sacred Books of the World, will be much assisted by any reasonably intelligent and reverent attempt to *revitalize*—if not to reconstruct—the Dogmas and Creeds which are yet in common use. The following attempt is certainly made in a "reverent" spirit. He who makes it believes himself to be "reasonably intelligent" with reference to the subject in hand. He hopes that it may, *by its very inadequacy if for no other cause*, be the means of stimulating other attempts and many; until finally "new bottles" shall be *fittingly* prepared for the "new wine," and "new cloth for the new garment."

"In vain I turned, in weary quest,
Old pages, where—God give them rest!—
The poor Creed-mongers dreamed and guessed,
And still I prayed, 'Lord, let me see
How Three are One, and One is Three!
Read the dark riddle unto me!'

"Then something whispered, 'Do'st thou pray
For what thou hast? This very day
The Holy Three have crossed thy way.
Do not the gifts of sun and air
To good and ill alike, declare
The all-compassionate Father's care?
In the white soul that stoops to raise
A lost soul from its evil ways,

Thou seest the Son, whom angels praise !
The still small voice that spoke to thee—
The bodiless Divinity—
Is the Holy Spirit's mystery !

" In Love, and Sacrifice, and Grace,
The *Trinity* stands before thy face !
'T is thus in this and every place,—
The Father, seen in rain and sun :
The Christ, in good for evil done :
The Voice Within,—the Three are One !'

" I shut my Book of Doctrines fast—
The monkish gloss of ages past :—
The Schoolman's Creeds aside I cast :
And my *heart* answered—Lord I see
How Three are One and One is Three !
The riddle hath been read to me."

XXXIX.—QUESTIONS OF CRITICISM AND THEIR ANSWERS.

The author, in penning this section in particular, is certain that he will meet with violent outcries from the traditionally "orthodox." From those *hopeless* ones, especially, belonging to that class of "scribes and pharisees" who exclaimed to Jesus, " Art thou greater than our father Abraham ? Whom makest thou thyself ?"—these violent outcries are certain to come. The old reply of Jesus and of all the prophets must be returned *to them :*—

" This people's heart is waxed gross, and their ears are dull of hearing, and their eyes they have closed ; lest at any time they should see with their eyes, and hear with their ears, and should understand with their heart, and should be converted, and I should heal them."

But to open-eyed, opened-eared, open-hearted objectors and enquirers the following questions with their answers are submitted :

First Question.—Are you not opening yourself to the charge of " Heresy " ? *Answer.*—There are no terrors in this charge, as it has been a familiar one to the author from

College and Theological Seminary days. "After the way which they call heresy, so worship I the God of my fathers" for these thirty years past.

Second Question.—But are you not reviving "ancient heresies" which were long ago and repeatedly condemned? *Answer.*—Yes; but it is always in order "to move a reconsideration."

Third Question.—But are you not disregarding the injunction of Jesus, "Put not new wine into old bottles. Sew not new cloth upon an old garment"? *Answer.*—*Temporary expedients* are always allowable, and sometimes are advisable. Till the new bottles are made, it is wise to tie up the old "wine-skins" as best one can; till the new garments are patterned and prepared, it is necessary to patch up the old. This, however, not as a finality, but only as a *makeshift*.

Jesus himself and his apostles used nearly all of the outworn forms, formularies, and symbols of the Jews with *an entirely new meaning*. For three centuries the "orthodox" party, with their *Judaizings* as to circumcision, bloody-sacrifices, priestly-successions, temple-worship, and other such "essentials" and "essential meanings," was overwhelmingly uppermost in the Christian Church. St. Paul fought an almost single-handed battle with them throughout his entire life; insisting upon using the old forms, formularies, and symbols in a new and rational way. After his death, St. Paul's successors of like spirit and method rapidly increased and finally prevailed. Then, but not till then, the new wine was put into new bottles; the new garments were made out of new cloth. The same was the case at the time of the Protestant Reformation,—that *beginning* of the Renascence of Christianity. Two centuries before Luther, individual priests and saintly scholars began to use, and to insist upon using, old forms, formularies, and symbols, with meanings entirely new. Till Protestantism was a fact, organized and established, this rational use of irrational rituals, creeds, and sacraments was persisted in *by individuals;* till, at length, the various corporate bodies of Protestantism were compelled to accept the rational meanings and adopt new forms of ritual, creeds, and sacraments appropriate to them. So has it been ever, and everywhere, and in all classes of reforms. Never an *abrupt* transit from the old to the new; but gradual changes—first in the spirit, then in the letter. Not *revolution* but reform is the meaning of Renascent Christianity; Christianity springing up into renewed life, and the renewed life, in due time, assuming its appropriate forms—*re-forming itself*. In this view of the matter our next question may be very briefly answered.

Fourth Question.—Are you not inconsistent—indeed, a sort of hypocrite—to remain officially, or even nominally, connected with a religious body which almost unanimously adheres to the old spirit as well as letter of its beliefs? *Answer.*—Reform comes *never* except through the agency of self-consecrated, self-forgetting reformers, who are *inside* the needing-to-be-reformed religious body ; and who insist upon the right to remain inside, *as long as free interpretation and free speech are granted them.* "Give me a platform upon which to stand, and I will shake the world," said Archimedes. But there is no platform given—in the present life—except *inside* the world. When we are driven out, then—of course we must go!

Fifth Question.—But why not wait for councils, conventions, or authorized committees, of the great religious bodies to do the "tying-up" and the "patching," if they so much need to be done? "By what authority *doest thou* these things?" *Answer.*—One of the best known, most scholarly, most saintly, and venerable of the clergymen of America has recently given a reply to this always and everywhere proffered question—proffered especially by the "scribes and pharisees, hypocrites," who always "urge it vehemently."

"Always there is the same danger when you trust to priests and Levites instead of bidding every man testify for the truth. The priest goes on his side of the way on his decorous journey. The Levite goes on his. It is the outside Samaritan who listens to the voice of God. The Mormon Church of yesterday, or the Roman Catholic Church of the dark ages or any of its little Protestant imitators, are all in the same condemnation. From the nature of the case they look backward and despise the word of prophecy. Most dangerous, as I believe, to liberty of conscience is a compact organization where wealth, and dignity, and prestige, combine to insist that Middle Age dogmas shall be clamped over the mouth of the preachers of to-day,—men who have been taught by Hamilton and Le Conte, Darwin and Agassiz, Maurice and Robertson, Martineau and Stanley, Channing, Emerson, and Brooks."

To which we add :—In Religion as elsewhere, the Individual has rights as well as Corporations ; among which is the right of Free Conscience and Free Speech. For sixteen centuries the *autocratic* Church and Churches have tried to suppress this right ; but in these enlightened days, and in this enlightened land especially, " Ecclesiastical Authorities " can no longer be slave-holders or slave-drivers. " The word of God is not bound " any longer. Emancipation of thought and tongue has been proclaimed in Church as in State. Slave-holders and slave-drivers, in remote and degraded communities and " communions," still resist ; and there are many of the newly manumitted who cravenly hug their broken chains and, slave-like, dare not speak as the Spirit *seeketh* to give them utterance. Notwithstanding, to all who are willing to be freemen, the Declaration of Spiritual Independence is an accomplished fact forever. Original Christianity was this Declaration ; through eighteen centuries of warfare it has been contested ; Protestantism was its first signal victory ; *Renascent* Christianity is, and will be, its complete achievement and permanent establishment. " Brethren, ye have been called unto Liberty . . . Stand fast therefore in the Liberty wherewith Christ has made you free, and be not entangled again with the yoke of bondage. . . . For where the Spirit of the Lord is there is Liberty. . . . The glorious Liberty of the children of God."

All Reform is a return to, or *toward*, First Principles. This has never been secured, in the History of any Religion, except by individual *insistency*—supplemented, often, by the *persistency* of combined Protesters, or of organized Dissenters, who have been conscience-compelled or persecution-compelled to combine or to organize.

In one of a series of Advent Sermons, just now being preached in St. Paul's Church, New York City, the scholarly and bold preacher has drawn bitter criticism, and the pouring out of vials of wrath upon himself, by venturing to say many things that a Prophet-Priest ought to say in rebuke of common opinion and practice. Among the more notable of them is the following:—" Never yet have the Officials or the Authorized Leaders among the people recognized the signs of the times." This is a great fact of Universal History—in Religion *more* than in other things, in Church *more* than in State. Who have been the Reformers and true Builders-up of Religion in all ages? Not the High-Priests, who belonged to the Aaronic Succession; nor the Scribes and Rabbis who sat in Moses' Seat; not Popes, Cardinals, Arch-Bishops, Bishops, nor well-paid Professors in Theology, nor popular Doctors of Divinity. But *mocked* Elijahs, *men-of-sorrow-and-acquainted-with-grief* Isaiahs, *despised-and-rejected-of-men* Jeremiahs, *unauthorized* John the Baptists, the *unordained* Jesus, *non-commissioned* Sauls of Tarsus, *anathematized* Monks of Erfurt, and Prophet-Priests of like Spirit; ordained and approved of God, though not of man—these everywhere and ever, have been the Reformers and true Builders-up of Religion.

From Moses and all the Old Testament prophets down to Jesus and Paul, and from these down to Luther and to-day; in Judaism, in Christianity, and in every other form of Religion, it has been the Individual—never the Council, Convention, or Authorized Committee—that has "turned the World upside down" in its Errors and Wrongs, and ushered in all the new Light and Life that have ever come to Mankind. It is not Egotism, nor presumption—as commonly affirmed—to be true to one's convictions. Every *commissioned* teacher, especially, should speak the Truth as God has revealed it to him by His Holy Spirit—and " speak it boldly as he ought to speak." One's light, even if it be but the light of a *farthing candle*, is not his own; and he is bound to put it "not under a bushel, but on a candlestick." Never yet has the Holy Ghost spoken through Council, Convention, Committee, or Church until it first had spoken in the "still small voice" to Individuals who, like Elijah and Paul, were "not disobedient to the heavenly vision." No one is so small or humble—be he truly sincere, pure-hearted, and devout—but that the Spirit of Truth will speak to him; and not an accent should be lost. "What ye hear in the ear, that preach ye upon the housetops."

Such are some of the main reasons why no Prophet-Priest, however humble his name or station, should dare await the cumbrous, tedious, and uncertain action of Ecclesiastical Officials—however much esteemed and revered—before giving, to whomsoever will receive it, whatever new Light has *clearly* shined into his soul through the agency of that Spirit of God, which "lighteth every man that cometh into the world."

Sixth Question.—But why continue the use, at least, of such Un-Scriptural terms as The Trinity; and of such Un-Apostolic formularies as The Nicene Creed; and of much of the language common to both the written and extemporaneous Devotions of "Orthodox" Christians—the mediæval and modern meaning of which is so *widely* different from that which you, and multitudes of others, now believe; and which—as you claim—neither Jesus nor any of the more spiritual and intelligent Christians of the first two centuries believed? *Answer.*—By analogy, an answer is furnished us in recent words of a celebrated American Physician, who, in a profound book on Pathology, has defended himself for the use of ancient medical terms—which have long since ceased to have their original meaning—as follows: "Nearly all our Medical Terminology expresses our ignorance, more than our knowledge. Despite all our progress in Medical Science we are yet obliged to retain old terms, which are very inadequate, for even our best known diseases. But, *provided we understand what they mean now and to us*, there is no serious objection to their use. Indeed, their retention is a matter of necessity, until such a time as the fuller nature of the various diseases shall be unveiled ; then, these old and largely meaningless terms can be, and will be, *gradually abandoned*."

Exactly so we say of Theological Terminology. Such terms as The Trinity, such Creeds as The Nicene, and such dogmatic or symbolic words as those so much and widely used in "Orthodox" Instruction as well as Devotion, express "ignorance more than knowledge." Despite all our progress we are "yet obliged to retain them" although "very inadequate" to convey our higher meanings. As we seek—not Revolution but—*Re*-form, we must retain them until our own knowledge, *and also the knowledge of those whom we are called upon to guide and instruct*, is more complete. There is no serious objection to this "provided we understand," and also *try to make those whom we guide and teach* understand, "what they mean now, and to us." In this sense their retention is allowable, and perhaps essential, "until such a time as the fuller nature" and meaning of Theological Truth "shall be unveiled." Then, "these old and largely meaningless terms can be, and will be, *gradually* abandoned."

XI.—AN ATTEMPT AT REASONABLE EXPLANATION.

1.—*Trinity*.

The Trinity is a common and helpful phrase wherewith to designate those Historic Manifestations of the Divine Being which are known as Fatherhood, Sonship, and Inspiration. Fatherhood is God seen in Creation ; Sonship is God recognized in Man ; Inspiration is God enthroned in the Soul. Looking upward to the Universe we behold God the Father ; looking about to Mankind we behold God the Son ; looking within to Spiritual Holiness we behold God the Holy Ghost. *And these Three are One.**

* NOTE.

The word Trinity, in its original, means, any three-fold manifestation—as the length, breadth, and height of a cube ; all are equal and all are aspects of

2.—*Christ.*

The word Christ is a Greek form of the Hebrew word Messias, which means *anointed;* that is, set apart or consecrated. Priests, Judges, Kings, Rulers, Officials of any sort, who were *anointed,* set apart, or consecrated, were called Messias in the Old Testament Scriptures—which is, being interpreted, Christ.

3.—*Jesus Christ.*

Jesus Christ is he who—living in Judea nineteen hundred years ago—set himself apart or consecrated himself *unreservedly* to God for the Service of Mankind. To signify this he called himself, and allowed himself to be called, Messias, or Christ.

4.—*Jesus the Christ.*

Because Jesus *was* the first, and *is* the only one, of men who has *unreservedly* consecrated himself to God for the Service of Mankind, he is called, and deserves to be called, The Christ.

5.—*Christians.*

Christians are those who, like Jesus, *consecrate themselves to God for the Service of Mankind.* Strictly speaking, no one has a right to the name who has not so consecrated himself. Whoever is so consecrated, wheresoever found, is a Christian. And those who are the most *unreservedly* consecrated are most truly Christians.

one thing. As a figure, or as a *means of apprehension,* its use is helpful and allowable. But as the Dogma of a Triad, or of an Actual Tri-Personality of Divine Being, it is a degradation both of thought and theology. This Dogma is found as a teaching in the Sacred Books of all the Ancient Pagan Religions (except in the Koran of Islamism), but is not so much as hinted in the Bible—except by impossible and far-fetched inferences. The one passage which has long been quoted as a proof-text, that of the Three Witnesses, has always been considered spurious; and is now rejected as such by the Revised New Testament. The dogma of Tri-Personality came from the Pagan Religions and (most unfortunately) was adopted by Christianity during its "Philosophical Period" of the 3d, 4th, and 5th Centuries.

6.—*Salvation by Christ.*

As Christ means Messias, or Anointed, or set apart, or consecrated, " Salvation by Christ " means the same as does the term Christian—*Consecrated to God for the Service of Mankind.* All who are so consecrated are being saved. All who are not so consecrated are being lost. In proportion as one is *unreservedly* consecrated he *is* saved. In proportion as one is *not at all* consecrated he *is* lost. Such is Salvation always and everywhere. And there is no other way. There is none other name given on Earth, or in Heaven, whereby we must be saved but "Christ," that is, Consecration.

7.—*Jesus Christ as the Saviour.*

Jesus was the first of the Holy Teachers of the World who clearly taught, and personally illustrated, this way of salvation; therefore he, above all, is Saviour. As he was and is the *only* Saviour who *unreservedly* consecrated himself to God for the Service of Mankind, therefore is he worthy to be called " *The* Saviour."

8.—*Son of God.*

A son of God is one who, having *consecrated himself to God for the Service of Mankind*, is accepted into that high approval and relationship which belongs to a son. The consecration to God is called being " born " of God, and the acceptance is called " adoption." Strictly speaking, none but those who have *consecrated themselves to God for the Service of Mankind* are entitled to consider themselves His Sons. And all who are so consecrated, always and everywhere, are " Sons of God."

9.—*Jesus Christ the Son of God.*

Jesus Christ is " The Son of God," because, having *unreservedly* consecrated himself to God for the Service of Mankind, he was *fully* and *forever* accepted of God, by the Adoption of Sonship, as " the first-born of many brethren " through whose leadership and example all men *may*, in like manner, become Sons of God;—as the Scriptures teach, "Beloved now are we the Sons of God," and "As many as are led by the Spirit of God, they are Sons of God." *

10.—*Jesus Christ the Only Son of God.*

Jesus Christ is the "only" or "only-begotten" Son of God in the sense that, inasmuch as he is the *only one* of men who has *unreservedly* consecrated himself to God for the Service of Mankind, therefore is he the *only one* whom God has *fully* and *forever* accepted by "the adoption of Sonship" as—in the highest sense—His Son. Therefore is he worthy to be called God's only or "only-begotten Son"; according to the Scriptures, "He learned obedience by the things that he suffered," and "Thou art my Son, this day have I begotten thee," and "*Wherefore* God also hath highly exalted him, and given him a name which is above every name: That at the name of Jesus every knee should bow, of *things* in heaven, and *things* in earth, and *things* under the earth; and that every tongue should confess Jesus Christ is Master to the glory of God the Father."

11.—*Conceived of the Holy Spirit, born of the Virgin Mary.*

Jesus Christ was "Conceived of the Holy Spirit and born of the Virgin Mary" in the sense that all, who on Earth shall attain to *perfect* Holiness, must be conceived in Holi-

---

*NOTE.

Alexander the Great in the Temple of Ammon was saluted by the High-Priest as Son of God. Alexander respectfully accepted the salutation, but added: "God is by nature the Father of all; it is no wonder then that all best men may, without irreverence, be called His Sons." So (but in an unspeakably higher and holier sense) Jesus Christ as the *supreme*, the *ideal* man called himself and is rightly called THE Son of God. Among the Romans, Greeks, and Hebrews, for centuries before the Christian era, the phrases "Sons of God" as applied to all good men, and "The Son of God" (or "a god," or "a god in human form," or "*logos* incarnate," or "word made flesh") as applied to the best, greatest, or *ideal* man, were in common use. So Christianity added nothing new when, by its Divine Method of Eclecticism, it adopted and made use of these phrases.

ness, and born *of a pure mother in particular and of a pure ancestry in general.* The "Holy Spirit," or Spirit of Holiness, is the *quickening* power of God in man—pre-natal as well as post-natal.*

12.—*The Pre-existence of Jesus.*

Jesus was "The Word—or Logos—of God Incarnate" in the philosophical or metaphysical sense of Neo-Platonism, as found in the Proem of the Fourth Gospel. This doctrine is not taught in any other part of the Bible. Neither as a dogma nor as a widely received teaching was it known in the Christian Church of the first two Centuries. Therefore, in the view of Higher Criticism, *it may or may not be received.* But "The Pre-existence of Jesus" is everywhere

---

* NOTE.

In other respects Jesus may have been born by natural agencies, as have been all other men. His birth *was* supernatural in the above sense. But in that sense only, so far as Historic Confirmations are concerned—*that is*, his own claims, the claims of his parents, the testimony of his Disciples, the writings of his Chief Apostle St. Paul, or of others who ought to have known ; and who, *had* they known or *believed* it, would most certainly have proclaimed it widely as the first and chief Supernatural Sanction of Christianity. Of all this nothing *reliable* or sufficiently confirmed is found in the Bible. The claim of Prophetic Announcement (as that of Isaiah) is fanciful and unfounded. The beautiful accounts of The Annunciation and The Birth, are the Poetry of Admiring Reverence, which must be interpreted and believed *simply as* Poetry. For a hundred years after The Annunciation and The Birth not a word is heard of them, not a hint is found, except in the Apocryphal Marvels, which ignorant men wrote and ignorant people believed. One of these "Apocryphal Marvels" happened to be retained in (or, more probably, added to) the opening Chapter of Matthew's Gospel as an Addendum of the *largely* Apocryphal Genealogy of Jesus. Except here, and in a single interrogation found in the first Chapter of St. Luke's Gospel thirty-fourth verse, not a reference to or hint of any such a Supernatural Conception or Birth as is popularly claimed is found in the entire New Testament. Without its recognition the Christian Church was founded, organized, and (for two of its most important and holy Centuries) flourished. If it could be dispensed with then, certainly it can be now. It is not *incredible*, and whoever *must*, may believe it. But it is certainly not *historically verified ;* and all who have given up the dogma of the *Verbal* Inspiration of the Bible, must also reject the dogma of the Supernatural Conception and Birth of Jesus (in the sense of popular "Orthodoxy") as *binding* upon the Faith and Consciences of *intelligent* Christians.

taught in the New Testament, and was everywhere held in the Early Christian Church. So also is the Pre-existence of all Human Souls everywhere taught, or implied, or taken for granted, in the whole Bible; as it was also an almost Universal Belief of the Early Christian Centuries.

13.—*Before all Worlds;—By Whom all Things were made.*

The above explained teachings of the Bible render it comprehensible and reasonable to believe that Jesus the Christ was "begotten of his Father before all worlds"; and that he was the *logos*, or *word*, "by whom all things were made."

14.—*God of God, Light of Light, Very God of Very God: begotten, not made.*

In a *general* sense *every* man whom "God created in His own image and after His own likeness"; in a *special* sense every "new born" or spiritually *re-created* man; but, in an *unspeakably higher* sense, Jesus the Christ is "God of God, Light of Light, Very God of Very God: begotten, not made." In this Bible sense, as well as philosophically and rationally, Jesus the Christ *is* God; and it is proper to obey and adore him as such.

15.—*One Catholic and Apostolic Church.*

There is "one Catholic and Apostolic Church" in the sense of the Scriptures, which teach that "God is no respecter of persons, but in every nation he that feareth Him and worketh righteousness is accepted with Him," and "Whosoever doeth the will of my Father who is in Heaven the same is my brother, and my sister, and my mother"—which teaching is beautifully expressed in the Communion Office of the Book of Common Prayer of the English—or Episcopal—Church in the words "The blessed company of all faithful people."

16.—*The Bible is the Word of God.*

The Christian Bible is "The Word of God" in the sense that it has thus far proved itself to be chief and supreme among those manifold Divine Revelations concerning which itself teaches "The invisible things of Him from the Creation of the World are clearly seen, being understood from the things that are made, even His eternal power and Godhead"; and "God, who at sundry times and in divers manners spoke in times past unto the fathers through Prophets hath, in these last days, spoken unto us through a Son."

17.—*The Holy Sacraments of Baptism and the Lord's Supper.*

Baptism by the use of water is a "Sacrament" in the sense of an "outward sign of inward Grace" proffered, accepted, and diligently retained "till life's end." The Lord's Supper is also a "Sacrament" in the sense of a "remembrance that Christ died for us, feeding on him in our hearts by faith with thanksgiving." According to all the teachings of the New Testament Scriptures, and of the Church of the Early Centuries, these two, and these only, are "The Holy Sacraments" of The Christian Religion.

18.—*The Holy Ghost.*

"The Holy Ghost" is The Spirit of God, or The Spirit of Truth, or The Spirit of Holiness, which—forever and everywhere—seeks to enlighten, inspire, guide, comfort, and save the souls of men; with the one and only condition that they will devoutly proffer acceptance, welcome, and eager co-operation.

19.—*Receiving the Holy Ghost.*

Such *hearty* and *entire* acceptance and welcome of The Spirit of God, or The Spirit of Truth, or The Spirit of Holiness, and such ceaseless co-operation as to result in God's *enthronement* in the soul, is "receiving the Holy Ghost." Whosoever has not thus *enthroned God in his Soul*, has not been "born of the Spirit. And "whosoever is not born of the Spirit, cannot enter into the Kingdom of God."

20.—*Rose from the Dead and Ascended to Heaven.*

Jesus Christ "rose from the dead and ascended into Heaven" in the sense of the Scriptures, which teach that "there is a Spiritual Body" over which Death hath no power; that "Flesh and Blood cannot inherit the Kingdom of God"; and, that all who live and die in Holiness shall, in like manner, "rise from the dead and ascend into Heaven."

21.—*Heaven and Hell.*

The alternatives of human choice and destiny are "Heaven" and "Hell," in the sense that they are "within" us, as holy or unholy characters which will "comfort" us or "torment" us forever, without regard to locality, or to external conditions—which was emphatically the teaching of Jesus and of his chief Apostle, St. Paul.

22.—*Shall come again to judge the World, whose Kingdom shall have no End.*

Jesus The Christ and The Only Son of God—as already explained—is *the* "highly exalted" of God and *the* "Teacher," *the* "Example" and *the* "Saviour" of Mankind. As such he must also be "Our Judge." Himself said "I will not leave you; I will come unto you; Lo! I *am* with you always even unto the end of the World." In this sense—though physically invisible—he is the *ever-living, ever-present* Christ; and Christendom is his rightful "Kingdom," and shall be, "World without end, *Amen*." In this, his Rightful Kingdom, he, for eighteen centuries, has been, is now, and ever shall be enthroned as "Judge of the World." *Amen* and *Amen*.

XLI.—STILL OPEN TO NEW LIGHT.

The mere Hireling in Religion as in other things, may say —as a Hireling Politician is represented as saying,—"These, my constituents, are my *sentiments;* if they do not suit you they—*can be altered!*" But the Truth-lover and Truth-loyalist always says, These are my *convictions;* they can be altered, *but only by the suggestions of The Spirit of Truth* speaking anew, and more audibly, through my own increased Intelligence and Holiness.

"He that believeth on me, as the Scripture hath said, out of his belly shall flow rivers of *living* water. This spake he of The Spirit, which *all* who believed on him should receive."

"Howbeit when He, The Spirit of Truth, is come, He shall guide you into *all* Truth."

"And they were *all* filled with the Holy Spirit; and began to speak . . . as The Spirit *gave them utterance*."

"In *like manner* The Spirit also helpeth *our* infirmities."

"For *as many* as are led by The Spirit of God, they are Sons of God."

"The Spirit Himself beareth witness with *our* Spirit."

"And it shall be in the *last days*, saith God,
I will pour forth of my Spirit upon *all flesh*:
And your sons and your daughters shall prophesy,
And your young men shall see visions,
And your old men shall dream dreams:
Yea and on my servants and on my handmaidens in those days
Will I pour forth of my Spirit; and they shall prophesy."

These promises and assurances only *began* to be realized at Pentecost. Since the Second Century they have been either widely perverted or largely forgotten. Renascent Christianity is to be their *revival* and *gradual-leading-on*, through the ages, to a final and full Realization.

XLII.—DEGENERATION OF PROTESTANTISM—PERSISTENT TENDENCIES TO REVERT.

When the scholarly, broad-minded, warm-hearted Chaplain of the departing *Speedwell* and *Mayflower* said to his weeping flock—about to leave him forever—"There is more light yet to shine from the Word of God," he scattered the first seed of that Advanced Protestantism which has ever since been springing up and *trying* to flourish—in spite of the unceasing efforts of "Orthodoxy" to trample it down and root it out.

Till then, it was generally conceded that Protestantism as Luther, Henry VIII., Cromwell, and Laud left it, was the final stage of Christianity's Evolution. In its Rituals of Worship *probably*, in its Ecclesiastical Methods *possibly*, but in its Doctrines or Dogmatic Statements *certainly* it should never be changed. The Ultima Thule had been reached. No navigator would ever venture beyond; should he be so fool-hardy, certain disaster and ruin would await him. The end had been attained; the height, depth, length, and breadth of Divine Truth fully and forever compassed. The three Creeds, and especially the Athanasian, contained it all; whosoever should doubt it, "let him be Anathema"—without question he should "perish everlastingly."

Such were the common, seemingly almost unanimous, conceptions of all "Orthodox" Christians. "The Reformation" had settled it all: no more questions were to be asked. The Earth on the back of the Elephant, the Elephant on the back of the Tortoise; Sixteenth Century Protestantism on the back of Fourth Century Theology, Fourth Century Theology on the back of Judaism—that explained it all. To enquire any further, certainly to expect any further changes, was "to fly in the face of Providence." On such or similar suppositions, Lutheranism organized itself in Germany and in Scandinavia; Anglicanism and Presbyterianism in Great Britain; Puritanism in New England; Episcopacy and all the other Denominations in the United States of America. All were one in this, and in this only, that all alike fixed about them a Faith-line (in military phrase a Death-line). This Faith-line fixed about them was in triangular form: *unalterable* Ritual on this side, *unchangeable* Ecclesiasticism on that side, and *infallible* Doctrines on the other side. True, every one of the hundred or more "orthodox" Sects, as they sprang up, differed as to the nature and limits of the first and second sides; but as to the third they were, and are, united. Each, of its own triangular boundaries, said, sternly, *Thus far and no farther*.

In this way Protestantism became, virtually, another Papacy or Patriarchate;—with endless popes and patriarchs instead of one. So too, in its degeneration, it soon came to repeat the intolerance and even the persecutions of the Autocratic Romanism whence it sprang. It hung Quakers, burnt Witches, banished Baptists and Romanists alike, in one portion of its domain; and, in all portions and among all its "orthodox" Sects alike, inhibited a free Religious Press, prohibited free Theological Speech, bound Reason, gagged Conscience, stifled Conviction, suppressed Enquiry, just as always had been done by degenerate Christianity back to the Fourth Century. True, on the part of most of the Protestant Sects, the triangular boundaries have been *slightly* extended now and then; but this only as compelled by indignant and influential Protesters *from inside*. True also that the prohibitions and penalties have grown less numerous and less severe; this, also, only as compelled, and in like manner. But the boundaries are still *fixed*, with their accompanying prohibitions and penalties; and none but the boldest and bravest ever venture to disregard them. As to the "penalties," they have changed in form, but hardly in substance, from those of Maternal Romanism. Ostracism (social as well as religious) has taken the place of Anathemas. Expulsions or depositions have superseded gibbet, and pyre; heresy-trials the inquisition, and *whispers-of-heresy* the thumb-screw and rack. The persecutions of mediæval Romanism, nay, even the stones and the cross of First Century Judaism, were, after all, easier for a genuine hero to bear than is the pusillanimous ostracism, the pestering heresy-trials, and the *un-get-at-able* suspicions which now are the punishments of all accused of "heterodoxy" or charged with Theological Unsoundness.

All this and much more—so painful to recall, and yet demanding to be recalled, in order to warn against continued degeneration—indicates the past and present Degeneration of Protestantism; it shows also how strong, *even in it*, is the old, universal, always persistent Tendency to Revert—*in Religion as in everything else*.

"Mine hand shall be upon the prophets that see vanity, and that divine lies:

"Because, even because they have seduced my people, saying, Peace; and there was no peace;—

"To wit, the prophets of Israel which prophesy concerning Jerusalem, and which see visions of peace for her, and there is no peace, saith the Lord God."

"Think not that I am come to send peace upon the Earth; I came not to send peace, but a sword."

"The Wisdom that is from above is first, pure—then peaceable."

XLIII.—THE PROTESTANT REFORMATION ONLY THE BEGINNING OF NEEDED AND ESSENTIAL REFORMS.

When Christianity began to revert, it began, and till now has continued, to revert in three general directions. Its Symbolism (or Ritual) grew toward that of Heathenism; its Ecclesiasticism grew toward Despotism; and its Dogma grew toward the Superstitions of Paganism. The Protestant Reformation began, and has continued, as only a partial Reform of the first, a very slight Reform of the second, and no Reform at all of the third. (*a*) The Ritual of all the Protestant Sects is a marked advance upon that of the Mediæval Churches—Roman and Greek Catholicism. (*b*) The Ecclesiastism of all the Protestant Sects is a *slight* advance; the same tyranny (in councils, conventions, and other officialisms) exists in *modified* forms; instead of one Pope or Patriarch, there have come to be hundreds or thousands called by various names. (*c*) The Dogmatism of the Fourth Century, increasing in popular favor down through the Dark Ages till now, remains *essentially* un-reformed, except among those Protestant sects known and condemned as Heretics—the Unitarians, United Brethren, Christians, etc. What is now needed, called for, and *demanded* by rapidly increasing Protestants of the Higher Order (the most scholarly, virtuous, and reverent Christians of Christendom) is a *Completed* or, at least, a rapidly *Completing* Reform. Away with the Symbolisms or Rituals of *essential* Heathenism! Down with Tyrants and Tyrannies in Church *even more* than in State! Banish to the shades of the past all Dogma or Forms of Dogma that bind Christianity to the superstitious beliefs of the *degenerate* Religions of Paganism! This is, and more and more is to be, the Three-fold Cry of those "Protesters" who represent, and will continue more and more to represent, the Highest Intelligence, Morality, and Faith of the Christian World.

"And while he lingered, the man laid hold upon his hand . . . and they brought him forth, and set him without the city.

"And it came to pass, when they had brought them forth abroad, that he said, Escape for thy life; look not behind thee, neither stay thou in all the plain."

"I will overturn, overturn, overturn . . . until He comes whose right it is."

"And Jesus said unto him, No man, having put his hand to the plough, and looking back, is fit for the Kingdom of God."

"I know thy works, and thy labour, and thy patience, and how thou canst not bear them which are evil: and thou hast tried them which say they are apostles, and are not, and hast found them liars:

"And hast borne, and hast patience, and for my name's sake hast laboured, and hast not fainted.

"Nevertheless I have somewhat against thee, because thou hast left thy first love.

"Remember therefore from whence thou art fallen, and repent, and do the first works; or else I will come unto thee quickly, and will remove thy candlestick out of his place, except thou repent.

"He that hath an ear, let him hear what the Spirit saith unto the churches: To him that overcometh will I give to eat of the hidden manna, and will give him a white stone, and in the stone a new name written, which no man knoweth saving he that receiveth it.

"As many as I love, I rebuke and chasten; be zealous therefore, and repent."

XLIV.— "THOUGH ALL MEN SHOULD FORSAKE THEE, YET WILL NOT I."

It is hard for a Leader to be deserted and left to stand alone. Almost as hard is it for a follower to stand alone, or almost alone, with his deserted Leader. The most tragic incident in the life of the Divine Founder of Christianity was that of Calvary; when, deserted by all the world and his few bosom friends besides, he felt himself, for a moment, deserted by his Heavenly Father too! The next most tragic incident was that of Gethsemane, concerning which he spoke prophetically: " Behold, the hour cometh, yea, is now come, that ye shall be scattered, every man to his own, and shall leave me alone: and yet I am not alone, because the Father is with me "; and during which he said, so piteously, to his sleeping *chosen three*, " What, could ye not watch with me one hour?"

But even more *trying* to faith and courage, though not so impressive to the world, was that incident recorded in the sixth chapter of the Fourth Gospel: " Many therefore of his disciples, when they had heard *this*, said, This is an hard saying; who can hear it? . . . From that time many went back, and walked no more with him. Then said Jesus unto the twelve, Will ye also go away?"

Deserted by all the rest because of his " hard sayings," he turns—imploringly and yet defiantly—to the twelve and asks, What are you going to do? Will you stand by me? If so, most glad shall I be; if not, *so must it be!* I will not retreat, I will not prevaricate, I *will stand alone!* Almost as brave were the twelve, who at once responded: " Master, to whom shall we go? Thou only speakest the words of Eternal Life." He who was mouthpiece for the twelve on this occasion, on another equally trying one still more bravely exclaimed, " Though all men should be offended at [forsake] thee, *yet will I not*."

This spirit of disregard for the *number* of one's adherents or co-adherents; this unconcern as to majorities and popularities; this willingness to stand with the few; this resolve to stand even *all alone* with Truth—as God reveals it to the soul through that "Spirit of Truth" which He ever "gives freely" to all who seek it *in pureness of life and sincerity of heart*—this spirit is the one and only test of a *genuine* Christian. Who has little of this has little of Christ. Who has much of this has much of Christ. Who rule and direct the whole life according to it—let men "take knowledge of them that they have been with Jesus."

The great leader of the Protestant Reformation proclaimed himself a follower of Jesus in no other words more truly than when he exclaimed—"Here I stand, I cannot otherwise, so help me God!" and again—in the very face of an impending martyr-death—"If every tile on every roof were a devil, I would go forward!" All that has ever been wrought for God, and Truth, and Humanity—from the day of faithful Abraham to the day of The Christ, and from the day of The Christ till now—has been wrought in this spirit of *genuine* Christianity. 'T is hard to stand in the small and scattered ranks of the always unfashionable, always despised minority. Many there are, even in this "wicked and adulterous generation," who know well, from bitter experience, what are the self-sacrifices and sorrows that belong to Truth-seeking; and what the obloquy and shame that belong to Truth-speaking. But there are, as they also well know, the unspeakably higher compensations of a good conscience; so that one can gladly as well as boldly say, "If there are but ten people in the world who deal with Religion intelligently and honestly, I am resolved to be one of the ten." They also find comfort in remembering that all who have been noblest in themselves, and most helpful to the world, have stood among the despised minority and endured, as martyrs, the cross and the shame. He who was derided by Pharisees and Sadducees; whose followers "went back and walked with him no more"; whose disciples "all forsook him and fled"; and who, in his extremity, cried out "My God, My God, why hast Thou forsaken me?"—even he is our Divine Example of steadfast loyalty to honest convictions of Duty and Truth.

He who wrote that sublime Epistle to the Hebrews, teaches and exhorts us out of his own brave, blessed experience: "Wherefore Jesus also, that he might sanctify the people with his own blood, *suffered without the gate*. Let us go forth therefore unto him *without the camp*, sharing his reproach. . . . For God hath said, I will never leave thee, nor forsake thee. So that we may boldly say, The Lord is my helper, and I will not fear what man shall do unto me."

XLV.—RENASCENT CHRISTIANITY A REVIVAL OF COMBINED PIETY AND MORALITY.

(a) *Piety and Morality combined was Christianity as taught by Jesus.*

Among the first words of Jesus was the injunction, Seek ye the Kingdom of God, and His righteousness—that is, God Himself as an object of love and worship, and God in his characteristics or virtues as a model of human character; in short, piety or internal religion, and morality or external religion. Both of these, as mutually related and mutually dependent, are to be sought, sought with great diligence and persistency as that word would imply, and sought as first both in order of time and order of importance. "Seek ye *first* the Kingdom of God and His righteousness."

True Christianity is piety and morality combined; or more exactly, is morality based upon piety and growing out of it. Observe: not morality the basis and piety the outgrowth, but the opposite. Piety, *i. e.*, recognition, reverence, worship, and love of God, is the ground, the soil, the womb from whence all true morality must spring. *True morality:* not meaning by that the morality of respectability, of policy, of æsthetics, which is the morality of man; but the morality of principle, of righteousness, of holiness, which is the morality of God. If a man is moral merely because it is respectable or politic to be so, or because he thinks it beautiful, as a pretty face is beautiful, his morality is only skin deep, pocket deep, public-sentiment deep; and like the seed in thin soil it will be scorched and withered as soon as the sun is up. But the man who is moral from principle, moral because his recognition of the omniscient holiness of God inspires him to rectitude, and purity, and truth; rectitude of heart, as well as of life; purity within, as well as without; truth in secret thought and silent motive, as well as in profession and in deed;—the man whose morality is thus based upon his soul's conscious and constant recognition of God, is the truly moral man; his is the morality of piety, as deep-rooted as God Himself, because planted in him; and, like the seed in good soil, it shall bring forth fruit unto everlasting life.

This is what we mean by saying that true religion of any form, but true Christianity in particular, is a combination of piety and morality; or more exactly, is morality based upon piety and growing out of it.

(b) *The two Extremes.*

Now, as a matter of fact, the two extremes towards which the masses of mankind have always been tending, the Scylla and the Charybdis against which they have alternately been dashing, the two opposite directions of that "broad road" which at either end terminates in destruction, have been these two elements or components of true religion—piety and morality—divorced and made to stand at a distance; while the "golden mean," the "mid-stream," the "narrow way," that leadeth to everlasting life, and which "few" have been able to find, has been a combination of the two. Piety *without* morality—theoretical belief in God, formal worship, verbal adoration, professional love,—without any particular emphasis upon personal righteousness as the fruit and substance of all—this has been one extreme towards which the greater multitude has always been tending.

Morality *without* piety—without practical recognition of God, without conscious communion with Him, without worship, or adoration, or love; in other words, moral character emphasized: goodness, blamelessness in the sight of man, external rectitude, the commandment "Thou shalt love thy neighbor," observed without any particular regard to the first commandment, "Thou shalt love the Lord thy God,"—this has been the other extreme towards which the lesser multitude has always been tending. While piety *and* morality, God *and* His righteousness, worship *and* fidelity, adoration *and* goodness, love *both* in sentiment and in life, *both* to God and to man, the first and second commandments *combined*—this is the Golden Mean which, as the old Chinese sage used to say, "few have been able to attain." Nor do we wonder that few have attained it when we remember how much easier it is for everybody to run to extremes than to hold themselves in equilibrium; how much less effort is required to drift with the breeze and the impetuous current than to pull at the oars of self-regulation and restraint; how much more *natural* it is to seize a half of the truth or a little portion of it and make a "hobby" of that, than it is to wisely seek and patiently practise the truth in its completeness.

(c) *Religious Ceremonialism and Ethical Proprieties.*

To transform religion into a sentiment and a ceremony on the one hand, and to transform it into a routine of external proprieties on the other, is much easier, requires much less effort, is much more in accordance with the inclinations of human nature than is the practice of that true religion which comprehends both God and man; both devotion of soul and devotion of life; both piety of the heart and morality of character. This, as Plato says, "is a most difficult thing," and just because it is *difficult* the masses of men have always been shrinking from it and satisfying themselves with being either very pious to the neglect of morality or very moral to the neglect of piety. And so the world has been forever drifting, now to one extreme, now to another; now toward superstition, and now toward infidelity; now toward gross ceremonialisms and idolatry, and now toward theoretical irreligion and open atheism.

Jerusalem, as Jesus found it, "a whitewashed sepulchre, filled with dead men's bones," a house of God transformed into a den of thieves; Athens, as Paul found it, "wholly given up" to senseless superstitions and gross idolatries; Germany, as Luther found it; England, as Wickliffe and Wesley found it, full of religious institutions and churches transformed into organizations of debauchery and intrigue—these have been the final results of piety divorced from morality. Imperial Rome as it was in the time which succeeded Epicurus and the Stoics, full of heroisms, but at the same time full of inhumanities, suicides, and despairs; France, revolutionized by infidelity, as it was in the time of Mirabeau and Robespierre, when God, religion, and immortality were not only practically but theoretically discarded—these have been the final results of morality divorced from piety; or of an attempt to direct individual character and human events without a positive recognition of God and a devout reliance upon Him for wisdom and help.

(d) *Partial Truths accepted as the Whole Truth.*

A partial truth adopted as a fundamental principle, or emphasized with an emphasis which belongs only to the whole, is always dangerous, both to individuals and communities; its immediate results may not be so perceptible; but, if persisted in, its final results must be disastrous. And the main reason why the moral and religious history of the world is a history of disasters and failures is because men have always been emphasizing partial truths, building up theories, characters, institutions upon them, when they ought rather to have sought "the truth, the whole truth, and nothing but the truth." Now the partial truths of religion are piety and morality divorced, with an emphasis placed upon one or the other which belongs only to both combined.

"Fear God and keep His commandments," was the whole truth as propounded by the ancient teacher of Wisdom. But one class of religionists have taken only the first clause as their motto, and with "Fear God" upon their banners, they have always been leading their ecclesiastical hosts into all sorts of gross and sensuous as well as senseless superstitions. The other class, in their reaction, have caught only the last clause, "keep the commandments," and giving the main, sometimes the whole emphasis to this, have led their smaller but equally mistaken hosts, first, into a religion of pure humanitarianism ; second, into religious skepticism; third, into infidelity, and fourth and finally, into theoretical and practical atheism. Jesus re-stated this old truth in its wholeness at the very beginning of his ministry, when he said : Seek the kingdom of God, and Seek the righteousness of God. But one class of men seized the first half of his truth and construed it into ceremonial piety, while another class seized the last half and construed it into external morality. So history has always been repeating itself down to the present day, and is now repeating itself as faithfully as ever before, in that superficial method and tendency of the multitude to get hold of a fraction of the truth and run with it into dangerous and disastrous extremes.

(e) *Rome or Reason.*

There has never been a time in which there was a wider separation between ceremonial piety and external morality, as distinct characteristics of two opposite tendencies in religion, than there is at present throughout most of the Christian world. Ritualists, on the one hand, are emphasizing ritualism, as though it were the all-important thing. Rationalists, on the other, are emphasizing reason and its codes of ethics, as though these were all-important. And toward the one or the other of these extremes the multitude of individuals and of organizations seem to be tending. "Rome or Reason" is the question which almost all religious thinkers are putting to themselves, with the supposition that they must necessarily take one road or the other; while almost no one seems to dream that the whole truth is, not Rome *or* Reason, but Rome *and* Reason. Almost no one seems to comprehend the fact that Rome has run mad with half the truth, and Reason has run mad with the other half. The right way is to cast the devil out of both, and bring them together into one complete truth of religion and reason, piety and morality, the fear of God and works of righteousness conjoined. We speak of "Rome and Reason" in this connection because, historically and practically, piety has been the distinguishing feature of Romanism and morality the distinguishing characteristic of Rationalism. And these two bodies are the two extremes toward which, naturally and logically, all must tend, in proportion as piety is emphasized more than morality or morality more than piety. Both are partial developments produced by the unnatural repression of certain parts of religious truth, and by the unnatural stimulating of other parts; and, like all partial developments they are both, relatively speaking, monstrosities and deformities.*

(f) *The Golden Mean.*

Now, between these two, as between all extremes, there must be a Golden Mean, a "mid-stream current," a posi-

---

* As an illustration we may take the following from the New York *Times* of the date of this writing:

"SAW THE 'DEVIL' BURNED.

"A PERFORMANCE AT THE SALVATION ARMY HEADQUARTERS.

"Visitors to the Salvation Army Headquarters last night saw the 'devil' dismembered and dissected by Major ——, and also saw him burned to a crisp, from his cloven hoof to his horn-topped head. Incidentally they also heard the Major's physiological lecture on the several parts of the 'devil's' anatomy.

"His heart was called deceit, his wings were labeled as the ungodly amusement of prize fighting, his tail was composed of a pack of cards fastened end to end, his internal organs were composed of a string of whisky bottles and tobacco pipes. Each part or portion represented some supposed evil against which the army is waging war.

"As a finality the lights were turned out and red fires ignited, and in the midst of the flame appeared the 'devil,' who was quickly consumed and then vanished.

"The performance was preceded by a parade of the army through the streets in the vicinity of the hall with the usual music."

Almost every day, and in almost every News Publication, similar reports of the doings and sayings of the popular Religious Bodies are made. Verily, Protestantism has already reverted to the Ages of Miracle Plays when, for instance, they enacted "*God the Father being waked up to come and see the rascally Jews murdering His Son!*"

tion of equilibrium, in which piety and morality can be made to counterbalance, or to equiponderate, the one against the other.

As we study the history of Christianity and of all religions, we find this position of equilibrium has been attained by individuals in all ages, and approximately, now and then, by religious organizations. David, Pythagoras, Socrates, Paul, Luther, Wesley, Channing, are only a few representative names taken at random from that large number of individuals, known and unknown, of all religions and ages, who have both feared God and wrought righteousness; who have, in theory and practice, emphasized both piety and morality with an equal emphasis; and hence have become at the same time fervently devout toward God, and beautifully blameless and pure in the sight of men.

Now and then, too, Institutional Religion has approximated to, and in some cases has been made for a time to occupy, this position; indeed all great religious reformations have been an attempt to arrest Institutional Religion in its wild rompings, its frantic dashings hither and thither, and bring it back to a just equipoise between Piety and Morality. This was what Moses attempted to do, when he established among the Israelites both an elaborate religious ritual *and* an elaborate code of morals; and though, on account of the inwrought stupidity of the people, his attempt was a perpetual failure, it nevertheless came nearer being a success than any other attempt of ancient times. Buddha too, Pythagoras, and Mahomet sought to draw the masses of their countrymen from superstitions on the one hand, and infidelity on the other; and to bring them, through sincerity of worship *and* purity of character, into organized harmony *both* with God and with one another.

(g) *Jesus the great Uniter as well as Reformer.*

Jesus especially, of all religious reformers, made it the object of his reformation to institute a religion with God *and* Humanity as its corner-stones—with recognition of *both*, love for *both*, service of *both*, blamelessness in the sight of *both* as its supreme characteristics and its fundamental truths. "The kingdom of God is at hand, therefore repent." "Be born again of spirit and of water." "Be pure in heart," and "Hunger and thirst after righteousness." "Love God with all your heart and mind and strength," and "Love your neighbor as yourself." "Pray to God always," and "Do good to all men." This was the well-balanced Gospel—the truth in its wholeness and completeness which Jesus spent his life in teaching, which he commissioned his disciples to teach, and which he made the "Rock" upon which he desired his followers to build his church.

(h) *The old story of Tendency to Revert.*

But hardly had the building commenced, hardly had the foundation been laid, when all but a few solitary workmen deserted it, and, with partial truths as new foundations, according to their own extravagant fancies, began to build on the one side Dogmatisms, Ceremonialisms, and Superstitions; and on the other, Rationalisms, Humanitarianisms, and Infidelities: and so it has been through all the centuries down to the present time. There has been, indeed, an Apostolic Succession of well-balanced reformers, who, planting themselves firmly upon the rock of Faith *and* Works, of Piety *and* Morality which Jesus himself established, have there been building, slowly but surely, the True Church against which "the gates of hell shall not prevail." But the multitude of Christians, both individually and institutionally, have always been tending to extreme positions. They have always been building either on the side of Rome or on the side of Reason; either with ceremonial piety, or with external morality, as their corner-stone. And the farther from that true foundation which combines them both in a living, well-wrought, well-balanced truth they have been able to get—whether to the one side or the other—the greater has seemed to be their satisfaction and their content. And so it is in a great degree to-day.

(i) *Building on the Side of Rome, or of Reason, or on the "Rock" between.*

Should we attempt to give an illustration of the geographical distribution and relation of the various religious organizations of Christendom at the present time with reference to this "true foundation" we should say: Romanism is on the extreme right, and over against her are built all those who emphasize Dogma and Ritual more than they do Reason and Morality; Rationalism is on the extreme left, and over against her are built all those who emphasize Reason and Morality more than they do Doctrine and Worship; while all those who, with Jesus, emphasize both Faith and Works, Piety and Morality, with an equal emphasis are standing upon the true foundation itself, where the true Church of Christ is being built; and where, when built, it shall stand and shine forever. In short, now, as always, in proportion as individuals or organizations emphasize one side of religious truth more than another, in that proportion they are building upon another foundation than that which Jesus laid. His foundation was God and Humanity; God first and Humanity second, but both conjoined in service and in love. Only those who stand with their feet firmly planted upon these two stones, believing in God and believing in Man, loving God and loving Man, serving God with fervent piety and serving Man with blameless devotion—only these—and all these, without regard to sectarian distinction or name—building upon the true foundation "which is Jesus the Christ."

This *was* Christianity as Jesus founded it; and *Renascent Christianity is its revival.*

XLVI.—RENASCENT CHRISTIANITY A RE-ADJUSTMENT OF THE RELATIONS BETWEEN EMPLOYERS AND THOSE EMPLOYED OR BETWEEN CAPITAL AND LABOR.

(a) *The re-adjustment stated.*

Of the twentieth Century *the* burning question will be, that which has smouldered beneath the smotherings and quenchings of Hierarchism, in Church and State, for sixteen centuries, but is now bursting forth with threatenings of fury and devastations everywhere in the civilized communities of the world. The relations between Employers and those Employed or between Capital and Labor is, and more and more is to be, that "burning question." Among the first of all the *practical* issues which renascent Christianity will meet and mend is this. It *must* be true to its Divine Founder; and his *first words* of practical Holiness were words that concerned this primal relation of man to man. Himself a laboring man, a carpenter by trade, and toiling in that trade for his daily bread unceasingly, until within about two years of his martyr death, quite naturally his sympathies were with the working classes to which he belonged. From the first utterances that Tradition has preserved for us, down to the last, he was the tender, helping friend of the poor, the unfortunate, the oppressed, the outcast, the "publicans and sinners": whom the rich and oppressive Pharisees and Sadducees, as Employers and Capitalists, held ever in iron grasp and beneath their compelling heels. "The Spirit of the Lord is upon me, because he hath *anointed* me to preach the Gospel to the poor; he hath sent me to heal the broken-hearted, to preach deliverance to the captives, and recovering of sight to the blind, to set at liberty them that are bruised." Such was the opening sentence and the substance of his initial sermon as a Reformer. Such also was the spirit and sum of all his sayings and doings for the entire two and a half years of his holy life as a public teacher. What exactly his position was on the question before us is well shown in the two central sentences of the Beatitudes taken from his matchless Sermon on the Mount. To the employers or capitalists he said, "Blessed are the merciful; for they shall obtain mercy." And to those employed or the laborers he said, "Blessed are the peacemakers; for they shall be called the children of God." In these two Beatitudes lies the whole question of the readjustment of relations between "the classes and the masses" so much agitated just now—and more and more to be agitated as the centuries shall come and go.

(b) *How the Christian Employee should behave toward his Employer.*

The parable of Jesus about The Laborers in the Vineyard was intended to illustrate, if we may so speak, the sacredness of a bargain between man and man. The master of a vineyard had made a bargain with certain laborers. When the work was done they thought they ought to have more than their stipulated wages. Their reason was that they saw others were getting more, or more in proportion; so they seem to have extemporized a sort of secret labor organization, or there may have been one already organized —who knows?—and possibly it may have been called "The Knights of Labor"—for things that have been are, and things that are have been, and there is nothing new under the sun. At any rate, they talked it over together, and appointed or commissioned a spokesman to act as their leader and present their complaint, practically demanding higher wages. To this complaint their employer answered: "Friend, did I not agree with thee for so much?"—as much as to say, A bargain is a bargain, business is business. I agreed with you and with the others for a certain amount per day. I cannot, or I choose not, to pay more. If you prefer not to come another day, very well; I will employ others. There are your wages for to-day. I do thee no wrong. Didst thou not agree with me for so much?

Now, what are these dissatisfied employees going to do about it? If they are Christians and gentlemen—a gentleman is a Christian always and a Christian is always a gentleman—if they are Christians and gentlemen, they will follow the advice of John Baptist to the laborers, tax-collectors, and soldiers of his day: advice which Jesus enforced in all his teachings; as also did St. Paul, even to sending back the run-away slave, Onesimus, whom he called his beloved "friend and brother," and even his "son," sending him back to his master; because in running away he had broken a compact which he had made, or which the existing laws of the state had made for him—which laws, however unjust while they existed, ought to be reverenced; and which compact, however offensive, ought not by violence or rebellion to be broken.

The advice of John Baptist was: "Do violence to no man. . . . Be content with your wages." The two sentences thus coupled together would seem to imply this: Be content with your wages as long as possible, as long as you can manage to live on them and cannot do better elsewhere. But at any rate, do violence to no man; your present employers, or your late employers, or anyone else. Go quietly and seek other ways of living; by all means, other remedies than violence for your wrongs. This advice the protesting employees of the parable of The Laborers in the Vineyard, would certainly follow if they were Christians and gentlemen. If they were atheists and loafers, nihilists and anarchists—as most of the bomb-throwing, dynamite-using leaders of modern strikes and mobs, and of social revolutions generally, are said to be—they would be likely to do most anything that is violent and revengeful. Believing in no God, they will assume to be gods themselves, and take matters in their own hands. Let us see, by illustrations, what the Bible and Christian way is. We must remember that those employees to whom Jesus and John the Baptist and St. Paul addressed themselves, were oppressed with double oppression, either of which was far more burthensome than is any form of modern oppression. The Jewish yoke of national exactions and the Roman of civil exactions joined to make poverty poorer, toil severer, and compensation far less adequate than any yoke of modern times—even than those of Russia on the necks of its peasantry, or of Britain on the necks of its subjects in Ireland and India are said to be to-day.

And yet Jesus, John the Baptist, and St. Paul joined with all others whose words we find recorded in the New Testament to recommend peaceable and patient content with one's lot.

(c) "*Peaceable and patient content with one's lot.*"

What does that mean? Why, it means belief in two things: *first*, in this statement of the Psalmist, "I have been young and now am old, yet have I never seen the righteous forsaken nor his seed begging for bread." And *second*, it means belief in the statement found everywhere throughout the Bible, but especially emphasized by Moses, and the Psalmist and St. Paul, "Vengeance is mine; I will repay, saith the Lord." As to the first of these statements, to this day who ever saw a righteous man or woman—a man or woman who had loved and practised righteousness from youth up—who ever saw such an one utterly deserted, or his or her seed, *nurtured and trained in righteousness*, begging for food? No one. Utter poverty and want are always the punishment of sin; we may be sure of it; sins of omission if not of commission, secret if not open, forgotten if not remembered. So the truly righteous have nothing to fear, as to utter poverty and want, however small their wages may be. With St. Paul they may exclaim, "Having food and raiment, let us therewith be content": "Though we have nothing, yet do we possess all things": Or with the Psalmist, "I have been young and now am old, yet have I never seen the righteous forsaken, nor his seed begging bread."

(d) "*Vengeance is mine; I will repay, saith the Lord.*"

That is a thunderbolt of Divine threatening hurled at the head of all human oppressors, and the Christian, believing it to be such, is content to leave Almighty God to do His own work in His own good time. As the Psalmist again says: "I saw the prosperity of the wicked . . . pride compassed them about, violence covered them, their eyes stood out with fatness, they had more than heart could wish; they spake wickedly concerning oppression, they prospered in the world, they increased in riches"—and yet what was their end? "Surely thou didst set them in slippery places. Thou castest them down to destruction. Now are they brought into desolation as in a moment they are utterly consumed with terror. God shall suddenly shoot at them with a swift arrow and they shall be wounded. And all men that see it shall say, This hath God done, for they shall perceive that this is His work. But the righteous shall rejoice in the Lord, and put their trust in Him; and all they that are true of heart shall be glad." The Bible is full of such expressions. "O! earth, earth, earth, hear the word of the Lord. Thus saith the Lord, write this man childless, a man that shall not prosper in his days; for no man of his seed shall prosper." "Thou fool, this night thy soul shall be required of thee; then whose shall these things be?" "In hell he lifted up his eyes, being in torment." "Go to now, ye rich men, weep and howl, for your miseries that shall come upon you. Your riches are corrupted and your garments are moth-eaten. Your gold and silver is kankered, and the rest of them shall be a witness against you, and shall eat your flesh as it were with fire. . . . Behold the hire of the laborers who have reaped down your fields, which is of you kept back by fraud, crieth; and the cries of them which have reaped are entered into the ears of the Lord of Sabbaoth. . . . Be patient therefore, brethren, unto the coming of the Lord . . . behold the judge standeth before the door." And not only is the Bible full of this, but also history is full of illustrations and confirmations of it.

There is a tradition that the Israelites in Egypt, when compelled by their oppressors to make brick without straw, used to comfort and encourage one another by quietly whispering as they met or passed:

> "There is One who sees,
> There is One who sees;
> He will punish them,
> He will punish them."

There was One who saw; there was One who punished. And there was One also who, in due time, delivered, and prospered, and blessed the patient Hebrew toilers, who tried to be content with their lot. On the banks of the Nile, travellers, we are told, may now hear these same words rhythmically repeated by hard toiling, poorly paid men, women, and children. As they toil they cheer each other by singing the ancient words of trust in Divine care and over rulings:

> "There is One who sees,
> There is One who sees;
> He will punish them,
> He will punish them."

Not only in ancient times, but now; not only on the banks of the Nile in the days of Pharaoh, but on the banks of the Nile in these days—now and always, here and everywhere—there is One who sees, One who will punish: One who in due time will deliver, and prosper, and bless, all who are truly righteous, and who put their trust in Him. "Vengeance is mine; I will repay, saith the Lord." This, then, is the Bible and Christian way—the Bible and Christian attitude of the employé toward the employer.

(e) *Burning Sub-Questions.*

But there are some burning sub-questions of to-day which we of to-day must look squarely in the face, and consider the right way to meet and answer them—questions affecting the welfare of that vast body of employees, of all civilized States, who are citizens; and, as such, holding in hand the ballot—hold, if they only would realize it, the righting of their own wrongs; and, under Providence, the shaping and securing of their own present as well as eternal welfare. Some of these sub-questions let us glance at. But, lest our words of sympathy for and encouragement of the working classes should be misunderstood, let us first say that there are three or four things that a genuine Christian can have no sympathy with, and no toleration for, in either the working classes or the wealthy classes—the poor or the rich.

1. *Indolence.* The rich man's indolent son or daughter who, without toil, lives upon another's toil; and the striker or the tramp who eats another's bread rather than work even for the smallest wages—even for ten cents a day, or for the poor crust he eats—these both, and both alike, all should condemn

and detest. If a man will not work—it matters not who the man is—it is a shame for him to eat. And of an indolent *woman*, whether rich or poor, the same is equally true,—God's truth, not man's.

2. That *pauper pride* or pride of pauperism,—whether in rich or in poor,—which permits one to live in dependence upon others, merely because the work which he or she finds to do is supposed to be too humble, or servile, or socially degrading. There is nothing so degrading as voluntary or avoidable dependence upon others: and, whoever has a spark left of manhood or of womanhood will dig in the ditch or scrub in the kitchen rather than be an idle, worthless parasite—sustained by the toil and sweat of parents, relatives, neighbors, or friends, to say nothing of public charity.

3. Avoidable *ignorance and vice*. The two generally go together, whether among the rich or among the poor. The empty-headed, dissipated children of wealth, whose leisure hours are devoted to fashionable amusement and folly; and the working classes, who spend their leisure hours on street corners, in groggeries, in sensational theatres, and in other idle and empty ways—and get up strikes chiefly because they want more money for strong drink and for other means of dissipation—for both of these classes and for both alike nothing but condemnation and contempt should be felt and expressed.

4. Those who attempt to secure their rights by *violence of any sort;* whether it be by rebellion against established laws—so long as they are established laws—or by threatening mobs—with their daggers, pistols, dynamite, bombshells, and infernal machines—or by labor organizations—which devise secret machinations, refusing to show their hands, and seeming to prefer darkness rather than light—or by one man or body of men commanding or even requesting another man or body of men to "strike," or to cease work merely because they themselves have chosen to do so. All of these things are impudent interferences with law, and order, and personal rights; and, especially on the part of Christian citizens, ought not for a moment to be

resorted to or tolerated. Especially not on the part of *American* citizens. Why? Because American citizens, above all others, hold in their hands the ballot, and by this can—if they will wisely work and patiently wait—rectify their wrongs and secure their rights.

A Roman senator being asked how to secure public reform, answered: "Agitate, agitate, agitate!" In this American democracy, where the laboring classes are and always must be the overwhelming majority, and where impartial suffrage is and always must be universal; here especially the way, and the only Christian way, to secure public reform is to *agitate, agitate, agitate ;* and, in addition, to *legislate, legislate, legislate ; vote, vote, vote !*

(f) *Special Reforms Favorable to the Working Classes which Renascent Christianity will insist upon.*

Having thus suggested the way by which reforms favorable to the working classes are to be sought and secured, let us now enumerate, with briefest comments, some reforms which appear to be not only timely, but also pressing necessities. As such every *genuine* Christian will join in efforts to secure them.

1. That rent, food, clothing, and all needful commodities may be reduced to the very lowest prices for the advantage of the working classes. Public Revenues must be secured and Taxes paid chiefly if not entirely by the wealth of our country. To this end the working classes must demand at the ballot-box this four-fold method of relief:

Tariff or import duties only on the luxuries of life. Protection or export restrictions only on the necessities of life. Graduated Taxation, so that as wealth increases the per cent. of tax shall increase in regular proportion; *with severe penalties for any misstatements as to one's taxable property.* This is necessary: for as the famous revivalist says, "More lies are told about money in general and about tax-lists in particular than about anything else in the world."—And, finally, large Succession Duties imposed upon all devised and inherited estates. With reference to this last it is sufficient to quote the following from one of the leading daily papers:

"The chancellor of the exchequer has received $1,100,000 as succession duty on the property of the late Duke of Buccleuch." The above is from a cablegram from London to New York, and is worthy of note. A more just and equitable tax cannot possibly be levied than that of "Succession." Why should our rich men's heirs enjoy money they never earned without paying a tax upon it? In this fourfold way let the working classes demand, and at the ballot-box secure, reduced prices for all the needful commodities of life, to begin with.

2. Then let them demand—*and at the ballot-box secure it*—that the present wide gulf between luxurious wealth of employers and depressing poverty of employees—the extremes of capital and labor—be narrowed by some system of co-operative wages, whereby all employees shall share both the prosperity and the adversity of their employers. "If one member suffer, all should suffer with it; if one member rejoice, all should rejoice with it." This must be the law in Christian business as well as in the Christian church. As it now is, what have we in our Christian (?) communities all over the earth! The same extremes of luxurious wealth and of depressing poverty, which characterized, degraded, and at length destroyed, the mighty civilization of pagan Rome, and of all other pagan states to this day.

Let us take some everywhere familiar examples. On a certain railroad, employees are getting $1.50 a day for from twelve to fifteen hours of hardest, most disagreeable, and dangerous work; and sometimes are months left without their pay at that; while the president is regularly drawing $30,000 a year for a few hours per day of sitting in a business office. The president in his easy-chair a few hours each day must regularly draw his $100 per day; while the breakman, trackman, coal-heaver must toil at $1.50 for fifteen hours of hard and dangerous work! Take another case. The receiver of a railroad—no wonder they are called *receivers*—received one-quarter million of dollars for a few months' overseeing of the road, while hard-worked employees, from conductor and engineer down, were hardly able to keep their families from starving; and, worse still, thousands of widows and orphans all over the country were deprived, nay robbed, of their little stores put aside for a scanty livelihood by the "insolvency" of the Corporation which solicited their subscriptions, and then managed to "legally" transfer them to their own already swollen purses! Widows and orphans may be cheated, and hard-working employees' families half starved: but the employers, and especially the *receivers*, must *receive* all they can manage to lay their hands on! And the worst of it is, that the laws of our Christian (?) land are made and executed *in favor* of these high-handed robberies and oppressions. Another illustration, this time a wholesale one. Presidents and directors of banks and of insurance companies; of gas, water, telegraph, telephone companies; presidents and directors of mining and milling, of manufacturing, of commercial and of extensive farming companies, pile up millions, live with every luxury, have more than heart can wish—while those who *do the work* and really *earn the money*, cramped and stinted, are driven to toil from dawn to dark; and when humbly asking an hour or two taken off their long day, or a shilling or two added to their scanty wages, are gruffly told that the "company cannot afford it!" The company cannot afford it! It can afford to its well-dressed, easy and luxurious officials *everything they ask*—to its hard-working, self-denying employees—*nothing!* And, if ever the times are hard and the companies' income reduced, how do they manage it? By asking the wives and daughters of the rich officials to try and get along with fewer elegancies, and the officials themselves to smoke less expensive cigars and drink less expensive champagnes? No, no! this cannot be done! but by telling their workmen that their wages must be reduced a shilling a day, and they must be content to wear their ragged coats, and their wives and daughters their shabby dresses "during these hard times." Nay, they go further. If they must live in a cellar henceforth instead of in a garret as now; and, Lazarus-fashion, beg crumbs upon the doorsteps and from the rich tables of Dives—Dives being a president or vice-president, or director or other official of the company—let them do it " during these hard times " !

> " Dives in robes, Lazarus in tatters ;
> Half-starved Lazarus, Dives full fed.
> Dives' children plump and ruddy,
> Lazarus' gaunt and pinched for bread.
>
> " Dives in a gorgeous palace—
> Guilded ceilings, marble floors ;
> Lazarus lying on his door-steps,
> With the dogs to lick his sores.
>
> " Let *his* starving children shiver,
> Pinched and blue with Winter's cold !
> Mine in furs shall still be mantled,
> And *their* pockets filled with gold."

Yes, now as in our Saviour's day ; now, as in the days of " Rome's proud climax tottering to its awful fall," Capital—and Christian (?) Capital, as often as that which is called Pagan or Infidel—is " a monster gorged 'mid starving populations."

In proud Rome, as in many another proud state and city, small fortunes were spent on a single meal ; and ladies, like the famous Leullia Paulina, wore robes covered with pearls and emeralds costing a million of dollars; while tens of thousands of human beings in Italy and in other lands were without daily bread, or even a warm tunic to protect them from the winter's cold. So is it now. See the cartoons, read the recitals of poverty, for instance, in recent New York, London, Paris, Berlin, daily papers—then walk up and down the fashionable avenues in cities and towns all over our land ! We must acknowledge that shiftlessness, indolence, and vice have much to do with it ; but not all, not even chiefly :—It is for the most part depressing, disheartening wages, and the great gulf fixed between capital and labor—the extremes of luxury and poverty represented by employers and employees—that must bear the guilt and blame.

The remedy must be some system of co-operative wages by which the prosperity of capital shall ensure a proportionate prosperity of labor—the employer and employee *rising together as well as falling together.*

Some remaining demands which must be made, favorable to the laboring classes, need only be stated.

3. Christian governments should protect and encourage labor by suppressing all syndicates, or other monopolies, which exist for the purpose of centralizing capital and controlling markets. Such are syndicates for the ownership of lands; syndicates for the control of manufacturing industries; syndicates for speculation in grain, coal, oil, and other commodities. As a rule, "syndicates" are only a reputable name for gangs of robbers and dens of thieves. What can a small farmer, manufacturer, mechanic, merchant, or other laborers with little capital do in the face of these giant monopolies? They are gradually transforming the working classes into slaves and serfs: they can no longer produce anything themselves; they must be overshadowed, crushed out, and forced to go at the beck and call of concentrated capital. Let the word *syndicate* and the thing which it stands for, become a by-word and a hissing in the land, with millions of workingmen's ballots aimed at its vile heart until it is destroyed. This we say, and pray, in the name of the Ever-living Christ—*Amen.*

4. In every city, town, and village of Christian lands governments must establish and control bureaus of industry,—employment offices, not almshouses,—for aiding employees in finding suitable employment; and, in particular, for guaranteeing that work, at reasonable prices, shall always and everywhere be furnished to those who cannot secure it themselves. Not charity, but work; not alms, but respectable labor, at reasonable prices, is what Christian government must henceforth provide for all able-bodied men and women who are in need of it and cannot find it for themselves.

5. In addition governments must organize and sustain such institutions as savings banks, guaranteeing *absolute security* for the small savings of the working classes; which must be free, of course, from taxation.

6. And finally, the working *women* must demand for the *same work* the *same pay* as the working man: in schools, factories, stores, everywhere. How shall the working woman demand this, as she has no vote and almost no voice in public affairs? She may demand it *now* by her private appeals and influence; and ere long, let us hope, Christian governments will become so *truly* Christian, that they will give and guarantee the ballot to woman, the same as to man.

But now to sum up. While atheists and anarchists will doubtless continue to try and right their wrongs by mobs, violence, and revenge—all to their own harm—no one who is a Christian or a gentleman—nay, no one who is a humanitarian or a patriot in any true sense—will have anything to do with such methods of relief. *They* will stand by their bargains, and be content with present compensations, as long as they can. And when they *must* do otherwise, they will seek their ends quietly, leaving vengeance and compulsion to Almighty God. Trusting ever in a kind and wise over-ruling Providence, they will adopt and prescribe peaceful agencies for righting their wrongs—such as agitation, legislation, the ballot-box.

Through these agencies it is now high time to seek vigorously the reforms mentioned; bearing ever in mind the workingman's Beatitude, falling sweetly from the lips of him who was The Ideal Working Man—" Blessed are the peacemakers; for they shall be called the children of God." The same lips pronounced also the Beatitude which must mould the methods, temper the spirit, and direct the life of every *truly* Christian Capitalist or Employer—" Blessed are the merciful; for they shall obtain mercy."

XLVII.—" FIRST PURE, THEN PEACEABLE."

This may be—nay, *must* be—taken as the Motto, the Watch-word, and also as the War-Cry of Renascent Christianity, as it was of original Christianity. Among the first utterances, and the most emphatic, of the Divine Founder of Christianity was the famous text, "Think not I am come to send peace on earth; I came not to send peace, but a sword." The Angel-Cry of Christianity in its first announcement was, as it now is and ever must be, "Glory to God in the highest; and, on earth, peace to *good-willing* men." To all others "there is no peace"—never was, never can be. "No peace, saith God, unto the wicked!"—"*First* pure, *then* peaceable."

"After long intervals of peace, wars ever enter the stage," as truly in Religion as elsewhere. In Church as in State applies the sentence of the Puritan preacher,—"Till the Lord hath created his universal and everlasting peace in the world, men ought to be in readiness, not only to pray but also to fight for the peace of Jerusalem."

(a) *Purity before Peace; the World must be made Pure before it can become Peaceable.*

When Napoleon the First stepped from the top of the Alps to the throne of France, grasped the throat of the Revolution in one hand and drafted his code of French law with the other, he supposed that the problem of anarchy was solved forever; the ruffian mob held *down* by force; the higher and better inclined citizens held *in* by law; the neighboring powers held *off* by alliances, treaties, and threatened retaliations: this was the First Consul's solution of the problem of peace. But, hardly were his figures concluded and his result announced before the "scarlet robe of France began to drip again with human gore"; all his bonds of force, law, and policy were broken; another revolution projected him from his throne, and raised again "a bloody-fingered Bourbon" to his place. Insurrections, upheavals, and reactions, in the midst of external prosperity and refinement,—like frequent eruptions from a volcano whose sides are covered with foliage and skirted with flowers,—was for the succeeding half-century the history of the French monarchy and the French republic. Then came a second great upheaval, shaking Europe to its centre, filling the civilized world with sympathy and alarm; spilling the best blood, expending the richest treasures, destroying the noblest monuments of the once imperial France; and terminating in a "Reign of Terror," which almost repeated the horrors which succeeded the overthrow of the Girondists under the ferocious leadership of Robespierre and his revolutionary accomplices. Hardly had we as American citizens begun to moralize upon the causes of *our* recent Rebellion, and to consider how to prevent the recurrence of commotion and bloodshed in our own country, when that international and civil conflict of Germany and France burst like a thunder-cloud over Europe. The whole world, Pagan as well as Christian, was startled by it. Prussia, though victorious, was scathed and scarred and demoralized. And France, the champion of nations, foremost in art, superior in science, exalted in civilization, unrivalled in gayety, polish, and grace; built, as her citizens supposed, upon a foundation of adamant; adorned, as they believed, with imperishable beauty; surrounded, as they imagined, with defensive bulwarks which might defy the armies of the world,—France, as "in the twinkling of an eye," was thrown from her pedestal of grandeur; and so marred was her countenance and exhausted her strength, that it must even yet be generations before she can hope to re-attain her former position of beauty and prosperity.

These and similar events which have been, and are, transpiring in this last half of the Nineteenth Century are not causeless. Neither are their causes, as most men suppose, freaks of Nature or mysteries of Providence. They are not insoluble, except to those who refuse to study them. Their causes are not hidden, except to those who are unwilling to search them out. The inferences which they suggest and the lessons which they teach are designed to increase wisdom in this and all succeeding generations. They are the time-spirited events which, though Sphinx-faced, stand postulating truths for humanity to consider, stating problems for humanity to solve, enunciating theories for humanity to demonstrate. If humanity *will not* consider, if the problems are unsolved, and the theories unproved,—then will the voice which in all the past has been thundering them out, wax louder and louder. But whosoever will have courage and wisdom to attend, shall deduce magnificent results, and receive splendid rewards; working out, meanwhile, with the sureness of the stars, a superb destiny for themselves and for human-kind.

(b) *A Truth postulated, a Problem stated, a Theorem enunciated.*

Of these "postulated truths" let us select one which is most important :—*Purity before Peace.* Of these "stated problems" let us present one which is both most difficult and most comprehensive :—*First pure, then peaceable.* Of these "enunciated theorems" let us press into the foreground one which is most practical and fundamental :—*The Church first, and the World second, must be made pure before God will permit them to have Peace.* Let us state the matter concisely and consecutively.

The most important truth for Church and State alike to learn, is, *that every human event has a human, as well as a divine, cause.*

The most important problem of every age, is, to find out *what are the causes of its failures and sufferings.*

The most important proposition which the logic of history and the facts of to-day are waiting to prove, is,—

That the great evil is, not failure or suffering, but the causes of these; and that until these causes are removed, failure and suffering will continue to be in the future what they have been ever in the past,—both the warning and the lesson, the scourge and the balm, the curse and the blessing of mankind.

One of the most curious facts of history is, that the Natural has been so swallowed up in the Supernatural; Human agency, as a correlation of the Divine, has been so completely lost sight of; Mankind has been so entirely discarded as one of the powers, factors, efficient and morally responsible forces of the universe, as practically to transform the human race into a complicated machine, all of whose clatter and clang, confusion, tangles, breaks, and disasters are attributable alone to that Invisible Hand which in the beginning invented it, set it in motion, and still drives it on. Theories have been considered rather than facts. Self-conscious freedom, cause and effect, individual volition, the fruits of neglect or wrong, the good results of doing good, and the ill results of doing ill; the praise or blame connected therewith, and the lessons of prudence and wisdom to be drawn therefrom,—all these facts had been overlooked in the intense supernaturalism which has prevailed. Men have delighted to "shirk" responsibility, and to "shoulder" the blame of all calamity and suffering upon the Almighty. When the plague devastated the army of the Greeks before the walls of Syracuse, they said, "The gods are fighting against us," but thought nothing of their camps swarming with vice and all manner of sanitary neglect. When Sparta, Athens, Carthage, Rome, fell, the people said, "The deities are avenging some impiety or some neglected sacrificial offering," but thought not of the licentiousness and luxury which were gnawing at the vitals of their national life, as the worm gnaws at the stem of a plant, until both flower and branches lie withering upon the earth. When Jesus was weeping over Jerusalem, which he saw quaking upon its corrupt foundation, as a city upon the crater of a volcano, the Jews, instead of heeding his warning and "repenting" of their evils, were praying at the street corners, and offering sacrifices in the temple. When the contagion was sweeping through Spain in the last century, the citizens of Madrid persecuted the "innovators" who proposed to cleanse the loathsome streets of their dirt and filth, and spent their time, meanwhile, in consulting physicians, saying mass, and repeating prayers.

The language of old Achilles to the assembled Greeks, inspired, as Homer represents, by the "white-armed goddess Juno," may be taken as the universal language of the past, in all times of calamity and suffering,—

> "Ye sons of Atreus, here at once
> By war and pestilence our forces waste.
> But seek we now some prophet or some priest,
> Or some wise vision-seer, who may the cause explain,
> Why with such deadly wrath Apollo fires;
> If for neglected hecatombs or prayers
> He blames us; or if the fat of lambs and goats
> May soothe his anger and the plague assuage."

No need to come down to the plagues, diseases, disasters; to the riots, insurrections, and revolutions of which even the nineteenth century is full, and which many—calling them the "inscrutable providences of God"—have been inclined to doctor with fast-days, humiliations, and prayer. No need to cite instances with which all are familiar, in our own age, of both beseeching and blaming Heaven for calamities brought on by the most reckless violation of all sanitary, social, moral, and humane laws. No need to come so near home, or so near the present time for historical illustrations of this almost universal tendency on the part of men to "shirk" responsibility, and to "shoulder" both the burthen and the blame upon God. Happy are we to believe that, though this tendency is still strong and prevalent, the increasing intelligence and better common-sense of the civilized nations of to-day are beginning to react against this old, old superstition, and by their reaction are drawing men into a moral consciousness, both of self-reliance and of self-responsibility. Men are beginning in these days to understand what is the meaning of that old maxim, "God helps him who helps himself"; they are beginning to understand that whether there be "God o'erhead" or not, there is a god of this earth, and that god is *man himself*,—so absolutely its god, that if he neglects its control, it will fly into chaos; if he neglects to use it wisely for *his* good, *it* will use him; and, using him, will play the tyrant, making him both its victim and its slave. In short, men are beginning to learn that there is a humanity as well as a "divinity" in all human events, and that the "rough-hewing" must be done by humanity, while the "shaping" may be left to the divinity.

To worm, fish, and fly a thunder-storm, an earthquake, a cyclone is, doubtless, and must remain a miracle. But this is no reason why these things should be and remain miracles to intelligent men. The more intelligent human beings become the more natural is everything, *inside* as well as outside *the Bible;*—the less of freak, fable, mystery, and myth; the more of law, order, reasonableness, and naturalness there is to the entire Universe, as studied or observed.

(c) *The Causes of Failures and Sufferings.*

When this truth is sufficiently comprehended, men will begin to inquire understandingly into the causes of their failures and sufferings.

St. James in the Scriptures long ago answered the question. "Come they not hence, even of your lusts?" *All human failures and sufferings are a culmination of some particular evil; or else result from a complication of various evils.* This statement will be made more clear by an illustration. Here is a man who is a "fast liver," in the fast sense of that term. All his bodily instincts, both natural and artificial, are gratified to the utmost; with full speed he drives along the highway of sensual enjoyment. Suddenly he falls sick; a council of physicians, after a careful examination, announce that it is no disease in particular that ails him, but all diseases in general,—a complication of diseases, resulting from the general and prolonged violation of the laws of health; and little can be done except to allow the attack to take its course, until it shall terminate either in convalescence or in death. So, every failure and every suffering—individual or general—is brought on by repeated violations of the laws of personal, or social, or physical, or intellectual, or spiritual, well-being. When the paroxysm has once begun, as all history shows, you can do but little, except to let it take its course, until it terminates either in convalescence or overthrow. Not *during* the failure or suffering, but *before* it, or *at once* after it, is the time to consider its causes and seek their removal.

We who call ourselves Christians, and Christian nations, have "failures and sufferings" back of us in history—a long, dark, disheartening record. And now is the time—if we have any wisdom or prudence or humanity left—for us to figure profoundly upon that hard old problem, What were the causes of those failures and sufferings, and how shall we remove them? Thank God, we *are* beginning to figure and to "figure profoundly" upon this problem. A few men among us have, at least, approximated its solution. Phillips and Garrison, in their theories of political reform; Sumner, in his statesmanship; Peabody and Cooper, in their social benevolence; Horace Mann and Henry Barnard, in their plans to educate and elevate the masses; and last, but not least, an increasing number of liberal theologians, in their broad gospels of Renascent Christianity. Such men as these have *theoretically* approximated the solution of the much-vexed problem, What are the *causes* of Christianity's many, long-continued, oft-repeated failures? After nineteen centuries, why has the Kingdom of God *so signally* failed to come?

And now if the people who call themselves Christians can only be brought to hear and to heed such teachings, we shall have—even during the twentieth century, perchance—the "New Jerusalem descending out of Heaven from God," bringing to the world *permanent prosperity and enduring peace.*

We may not dwell upon this point except to remark that, while the causes of failure are manifold, they may be grouped into the three following divisions:

(1.) The ignorance and vice of the masses. (2.) The luxury, selfishness, and oppression, ecclesiastically and socially, of what are called the "upper classes." (3.) And, principally, the time-serving bigotry and intrigue of covetous and ambitious rulers, both in Church and in State. These are the main styes from which the miasm of all calamity is wafted through the Church and the Nations. These are the chief fountains whence all the bitter waters flow; and so long as these are permitted to remain, the language of Jesus will be the language of every true reformer: "Think ye that I am come to bring peace upon the earth? I tell you nay, but a sword."

(d) *The Sword.*

"*Out of His mouth went a two-edged sword.*" "*Repent therefore; or else I will come to thee quickly, and will fight thee with the sword of my mouth.*"

The *sword*, whether of the hand or of the mouth—of the intellect, or of the spirit—is God's instrument of rebuke and medium of reform. It is, at the same time, the bitter drug and the sharp blade by which, when all other remedies fail, the diseases and wounds of humanity must be healed. Like the remedies of those physicians mentioned by Sophocles,—

"Who bitter choler cleanse and scour,
With drugs as bitter and as sour,"—

the *sword*, when the necessity for it arises, only denotes that there is a bitter "choler" back of it, which demands an equally bitter remedy in order to its removal.

One of our distinguished fellow-citizens is reported to have said, "If all the drugs of the apothecaries in this city were thrown into the sea, it would be better for the health of our inhabitants." If he had included in this rash remark all the physicians, surgeons, and nurses, his proposition would have been about as wise as is that of those "peace-loving fools," who, while all the causes of failures and sufferings remain undisturbed, pass a wholesale condemnation of wilful mischief-making upon agitators and agitations, upon reformers and reforms—crying out "peace, peace, where there is no peace." When all men become wise enough and good enough to strictly obey sanitary laws, and when all *causes* of disease are permanently removed, then, but not till then, drugs—with those who now make and administer them—may be "cast into the sea." Men talk of beating swords into ploughshares, and transforming the metal of cannon into church-bells. This may do as a prophecy of bright things to come; but as a proposition of to-day, it would be as wise to beat the surgon's knife into knitting-needles, or transform the physician's cruse into a jar for sweetmeats. While humanity remains imperfect; at least, while ignorance, vice, crime, selfishness, ambition, and irreligion hold sway in the world, the *sword* must come.

Not the *sword* are we to condemn, *but its causes.* Here let men bestow their curses, offer their opposition, make their prayers, pour their tears, and expend their energies! Here let the strong arm be lifted and the melting heart poured out! Here,—in efforts to elevate the masses, to repress social evils, to disarm caste and selfish pride; especially in efforts to reform the ballot-box, to straighten crooked judges, to exorcise corrupt officials, to regenerate the social life and broaden the religious spirit of the people—here is both the Thermopylæ and the Marathon of Renascent Christianity. Here let philanthropists and benefactors lay down their lives,—pouring out, if need be, their blood! Here, upon the battle-field of truthful words and honest deeds, let the "red flowers of martyrdom" henceforth grow! So shall the Church militant become the Church triumphant: and long-expected, long-enduring peace, like the golden sun of morning, with stately and majestic stride shall come walking o'er the earth.

(c) *Much to be done—Advancement will be slow.*

But this, all, is prophecy! Long time yet will it be before these bright days shall come, because there is so much for us to do meanwhile. Nature, in her progressions, never "makes a leap." So is it in the progress of social and of religious life; here, as everywhere else, all grand achievements, at least all permanent achievements, must be attained by hard work in connection with slow and gradual approximations. To elevate the masses both in intelligence and virtue, to break down selfishness and social oppression, to cleanse official injustice and intrigue—in Church or in State —as all past experience demonstrates, is by no means an easy task; but it is, nevertheless, a task which God has given humanity to do. It cannot be done in a year or a century, perhaps not in many centuries; *but it must be done ;* and humanity, divinely commissioned, must do it, before any Church or nation of the earth can permanently enjoy the reign of peace. God never does by a miracle for us what he has once committed to the industry and prudence of his creatures. One might as wisely stand upon the banks of the Mississippi or the Amazon, " waiting for the river to flow by," as to stand waiting for God to establish His Kingdom of Heaven upon earth before men have eagerly and fully *prepared the way.* One might as well think to hold back the tide of the ocean by throwing in sticks and stones, as to think to prevent sin and sorrow in the world merely by offering protests, holding conventions, preaching sermons, and repeating prayers.

You cannot stop contagion in a city whose streets are heaped with filth, and whose inhabitants are living in constant violation of sanitary laws; you cannot prevent pain and exhaustion in a body filled with disease ; you cannot give a virtuous and beautiful exterior to a character which is internally corrupt; you cannot quench the lightning while the atmosphere is surcharged with electricity; you cannot smother Vesuvius with the palm of your hand, or hold back Niagara with your finger. No more, while degradation is among the masses, while selfishness reigns in society, while wrong triumphs in the nation, while bigotry, insincerity and oppression hold sway in the Church, can you prevent those upheavals and revolutions, those failures and sufferings, those sins and sorrows which, now as ever and ever as now, depress and curse the world.

> " Not with the burial of the sword,
> Dire war shall cease."

Not by beating swords into ploughshares or transforming cannon into church-bells, but *by removing the causes* of these evils, shall be brought to pass that happy time when " Nations shall no more lift up a sword against nations, neither shall they learn war any more." Till then, it matters not how loud the cry for " peace," *there can be no peace.* Till then, war "must needs come." Till then, in the language of Joel, let men "beat their pruning-hooks into spears." Or, in the language of Jesus, "let him that hath no sword sell his garment and buy one,"—*not the sword of the flesh, but of the mind and soul; of the heart and lips, and life.*

Such was the Spirit, and such were the demands and methods, of original Christianity. Renascent Christianity must possess, adopt, and continue the same—until "every valley shall be filled, and every mountain and hill shall be brought low; and the crooked shall be made straight, and the rough ways shall be made smooth; and all flesh shall see the salvation of God."

XLVIII.—HINDRANCES.

Of *genuine* Christianity, as of *genuine* Religion of every form, there are various prevailing and popular hindrances—holding it ever down from its Heaven-born manifestation to the world, keeping it ever back from lofty accomplishments in the interests of Mankind. Of these hindrances the main ones may be designated as follows—Mercenary Conformity, Insincerity, Double-tongued *Esotericism* (or Private Interpretation), Hireling-Priests (or Priestcraft), and Conservatism of Inborn Stupidity. To somewhat assist in "preparing the way," perchance, for Renascent Christianity, these five main hindrances are here noticed; and it will be excusable if the writer "notices" them with sharp, cutting, John-the-Baptist rebukes. "Ye generation of vipers! Who hath warned you to flee from the wrath to come? . . . Behold now the axe is laid at the root of the tree; every tree that beareth not good fruit shall be hewn down and cast into the fire."

1.—*Mercenary Conformity.*

"*Jesus answered and said, Verily, verily, I say unto you, Ye seek me, not because ye care for the works which I do, but because ye did eat of the loaves, and were filled.*"

"*A certain man named Demetrius . . . who made sil-*

ver shrines for Diana and brought no small gain to the craftsmen . . . said, Sirs, ye know that by this craft we have our wealth. . . . And when they heard this . . . all, with one voice, about the space of two hours, cried out, Great is Diana of the Ephesians."

Such is the spirit of Mercenary Conformity the world over and History through. Jesus, like all other Messiahs of God, recognized it: and, among his first words to the world, as among his last, he declared that every worldly motive, and every selfish advantage, must be completely and forever renounced by everyone who would become a Christian. To his first disciples he said plainly, If you follow me you must leave all; I have nothing to give (but a good Conscience), nothing to promise (but the approval of God). "Birds have nests and foxes dens but the Son of Man hath not where to lay His head. . . . The disciple must not seek to be above his Master." Poverty and Persecution are mine: you too *must be willing to accept them* for the Kingdom of Heaven's sake—otherwise ye cannot be my disciples! We are told this was said to the disciples *only:* to the *few* who were to be the *first* Apostles and Confessors of Jesus! Not to the world in general, not to us especially, was it said! "And there *went great multitudes* with him; and he turned and said to them *all*, If *any man* come to me, and is *not willing* to forsake his father, and mother, and wife, and children, and brethren, and sisters, yea, to lay down his own life also, he cannot be my disciple. And *whosoever* doth not bear his cross and come after me, he cannot be my disciple." Thus to *all*—to all the world and to all times did Jesus speak, rebuking the Mercenary Spirit in religion, and affirming that no man *could*, or *ever can*, be a Christian who (however secretly or little) is influenced by desire of worldly advantage or hope of worldly gain.

So, in like manner, have taught and declared all the Holy Prophets of all the Religions of the world. From righteous Abraham, who left all and went out "he knew not whither": and devout Moses, who "forsook Egypt, choosing rather to suffer affliction with the people of God than to enjoy the pleasure of sin for a season": and Sākya Muni, who forsook his kingdom and spent a long life in poverty, friendlessness, and suffering for the attainment of Holiness and the uplifting of his fellowmen: and Socrates, who, rejecting bribes of large wealth and great public honors, cheerfully accepted a Martyr's death rather than *by a word* betray Heavenly Wisdom and Virtue. "And what more shall we say? Time would fail us to tell" of the prophets, saints, confessors of all Religions and ages—women, children, and men, "a great multitude whom no man can number"—who, leaving all to follow Sacred Convictions of Truth and Duty, "were tortured, not accepting deliverance; that they might obtain a better resurrection: and others had trial of *cruel* mockings and scourgings, yea, moreover, of bonds and imprisonment: they were stoned, they were sawn asunder, were tempted, were slain with the sword: they wandered about in sheepskins and goatskins; being destitute, afflicted, tormented (of whom the world was not worthy): they wandered in deserts, and in mountains, and in dens and caves of the earth."

All these, in all the ages to this day,—the martyr-spirited, self-renouncing, self-forgetting souls of every Religion and time—join with the Holy Jesus to rebuke the Mercenary Spirit; and to affirm and re-affirm the everywhere-always-and-to-everybody-applicable Truth, that *No man can be a Christian (that is an accepted Son of God) who is (however secretly or little) influenced by desire of worldly advantage or hope of worldly gain.*

Spite of all this, in these as in all times, Commercialism prevails, in Religion as elsewhere. How much will you give me? What pay? What advantage? What reward? These are first, middle, and last questions: from the minister who stipulates for his salary, and the missionary for his stipend, down to "the grocer, the baker, and the candlestick maker," who profess Religion because it is *more respectable* to do so; and adhere to the sect or church that promises the largest dividends of personal advantage, "both for the life that now is and for that which is to come." Not *all* ministers, missionaries, and professors of religion are of this commercial spirit. Everybody knows of some, in every religion and sect of the world, who, *utterly regardless of results to themselves*, are completely consecrated to Truth and Holiness. Everywhere upon the earth can be found some, of every religious faith, who (having no "eye to the main chance," no thought of "what people will say," no care for social station, popular applause, or pecuniary reward) are willing to live unhonored and die unsung, in humble devotion to that which they believe to be God's command and Humanity's good. Who cannot recall some with whom they have chanced to meet in the various paths of life, who verily answered to this description—a "Christian who loves his cause well enough to throw into it all that he has; and, not deeming that enough, throws himself?" Nevertheless, the mercenary spirit *prevails*, in Religion, as in everything else. Alas! poor Human Nature, in its upward Evolution, is so little removed, as yet, from the ox who moves only for the lash, and the dog who serves only for the bone. But a man should not *remain* a brute; he may, perhaps must, *start* down there; but to wish, or even to be willing, to *remain* there, is shameful, and will degrade him more and more. So Jesus, with all the Lofty and Holy of the world to join in his words, says: "If *any man* come to me, and is *not willing* to forsake his father, and mother, and wife and children, and brethren, and sisters, yea to lay down his own life also, he cannot be my disciple." Notwithstanding these Divine words, which have come thundering as well as ringing down the ages, the mercenary spirit *has* prevailed, and *prevails*. "What will ye give me, and I will deliver him to you?" said one of Jesus' own chosen disciples to the rich, fashionable, pious, orthodox Religious Body of that day—which called itself the True Church, and despised all others. Centuries later, to a similar Religious Body (which for a thousand years had lived and flourished chiefly by means of threats and bribes), Henry IV. responded, "A crown is worth a mass." These are two *marked* illustrations out of a multitude that cover the pages of Christian history

—nothing being said of the greater multitude unrecorded, which await the day when the secrets of men's hearts shall be revealed. Henry IV. bid *higher* than did Judas Iscariot, but both alike betrayed their Master, and were Traitors to Truth. Mercenary conformity, whether for "a crown," or for "thirty pieces of silver," or for only "a piece of bread," is always and everywhere Treason to Truth. Truth, whether incarnate in a Holy Man (as it was in Jesus), or embodied in a Holy Cause, or enunciated in a Holy Proposition, or speaking in a Holy Conviction, is as divine as God Himself; nay, *is* God Himself—"The Word made Flesh and dwelt among us full of grace and truth." In these, or in any other of the various forms of Truth, whoever knowingly betrays it for worldly advantage or for self-seeking aims, is a Traitor to Truth. Whoever in any thing, but in his religion above all, thinks one thing and (deliberately) says another, believes one thing and (deliberately) professes another, betrays his Christ as basely as Judas did, and deserves that Historic Traitor's infamy and shame. Bribes are everywhere proffered. Satan tempts every man as he did Jesus. Bread, applause, riches, glory, position, smiles of friends, popularity, patronage, prosperity,—these are proffered as inducements to conform. As threats against non-conformity, their opposites—poverty, reproach, starvation perhaps, domestic oppositions, social criticism; especially Church opprobriums and Ecclesiastical anathemas, such as the cry of Heretic, Infidel, Atheist, Agitator, Communist, Outlaw, Peculiar, Eccentric, Crank! So coax with rewards, or alarm with threats, the Devil and his Agencies, now and ever. And whoever yields is lost. Whoever would be saved from the awful, the "unforgivable Sin" of Mercenary Conformity— the Sin against the Holy Ghost, the Ananias-and-Sapphira Sin of lying, not unto men, but unto God—must *resist to the death*. As Jesus did, so must he repel all these tempters with such words as, "Get thee hence, Devil, for it is written, Man shall not live by bread alone, but by every word that proceedeth out of the mouth of God. And again it is written, Thou shalt worship the Lord thy God, and Him alone shalt thou serve."

2.—*Insincerity.*

The deadliest foe of Truth (whether it be of Science, of Philosophy, of Ethics, or of Religion) always has been, is, and must be, Insincerity. To say one thing and think another, to profess one thing and believe another, is, not only to *betray* Truth, but also to build a cross and openly crucify Truth upon it. When it comes to that most sacred of all forms of Truth, Religious Convictions (the dictates of the Holy Ghost, God's voice in the Soul), what an unspeakable crime it is to publicly pervert or openly misinterpret that! "Verily I say unto you, all sin shall be forgiven unto the sons of men, and blasphemies wherewithsoever they shall blaspheme; but he that shall blaspheme against the Holy Ghost hath never forgiveness, but is in danger of eternal condemnation."

As to Religious Belief, one *need not* speak, *may* keep silent; but, if he *does* speak, by all that is sacred, let him speak what, in the most sacred depths of his heart, he honestly believes. As to Ecclesiastical Conformity, one *need not* conform; but if he *does* conform, by all that is sacred, let him conform to nothing that violates his settled convictions of what is true and right. As to Theological Creeds, one *need not* profess; but if he *does* profess, by all that is sacred, let him profess nothing (with hand, or posture, or lips) that does not correspond with the innermost sincerities of his soul.

Insincerity is the hypocrisy of "Scribes and Pharisees, hypocrites," upon which the Divine Jesus poured out all his vials of wrath. To him there was, in reality, but *one sin*—the fertile, fiendish Mother of all sin; and that sin was religious insincerity. He called it the sin against the Holy Ghost. His chief apostle, St. Peter, said of it, "Thou hast not lied unto men, but unto God!" Even those who are called Pagans have everywhere most bitterly denounced it. Everybody may recall those two *lines of fire* from Homer:

> "Who dares think one thing and another tell,
> My soul detests him as the gates of Hell."

Nothing more heroic and grand, but, also, nothing more reproachful to the hypocrite, can be found, in any literature, than is the following, translated from the ancient Persian:

> "Ottāyá from his earliest youth
> Was consecrated to the Truth,
> And if the universe must die
> Unless Ottāyá told a lie,
> He would defy the Fates' last crash,
> And let all sink to one pale ash,
> Or ever from his truthful tongue
> One word of falsehood should be wrung."

3.—*Esotericism.*

Nothing is more cowardly or more wicked than all this talk, imported from Heathenism, and now so much in vogue among "Orthodox Christians"—ministers and the better educated laymen—about *esoteric* and *exoteric* beliefs—beliefs which one may keep secret, or speak only to an inner circle of kindred minds who are practically sworn to secrecy; and beliefs which one may profess and teach in public. "Esotericism" has been the method and the excuse of priestcraft, Papacy, and tyranny, as well as of hypocrisy, in every religion and in all the ages. Its importation into Protestant Christianity (merely to quiet the consciences and save the reputations of those who profess to be "orthodox" when they know, and to their secret circles confess, they are not)—is a certain sign of degeneration, a growing evidence of reversion to Heathenism.

The cowardice and shame of such a double-tongued orthodoxy was what the "pagan" Homer, in the lines already quoted, so strongly rebuked. But it is more than cowardice and shame. It is sin against the Holy Ghost. It is "Lying to God." It is stifling holy thoughts, smothering holy convictions, the "Infanticide of Sacred Beliefs."

The truth and nothing but the truth should be sought for in the Bible as in all other writings; in religion as in other things. And when truth is found it should be openly proclaimed to the world; in defiance of personal advantage, of popular demands, and even of the threatened wreck of systems venerable and strong. The time to give truth to the world is whenever the Spirit of Truth gives it to us. Not ours to enquire for *consequences*. Leave consequences to Him who rules and overrules! Man's duty is to do right *and also to speak the Truth* "though the Heavens fall." "What ye hear, that preach ye upon the house-tops," is the commission of Jesus to all who claim to be his disciples.

> "Paid hypocrites, who turn
>   Judgment aside, and rob the Holy Book
> Of those high words of Truth, which search and burn
>   In warning and rebuke!
> Woe to such Christians! Woe
>   To those whose hire is the price of blood,—
> Withholding, darkening, changing, as they go,
>   The searching Truth of God!"

> "A glorious 'remnant' linger yet,
>   Whose lips are wet at Heavenly Fountains,
> The coming of whose faithful feet
>   Is beautiful upon the mountains!
> Men, who the Living Gospel bring
>   Of Holiness and Love forever,
> Whose joy is an abiding Spring,
>   Whose peace is as a flowing river."

The Reverend Make-Believe is, in religion, what the Honorable Make-Believe is in politics—never a *reformer*, always a *caterer*. He makes it his business, for *his own* peace and policy, to suit Truth to the tastes of his constituents—not to demand (as he ought to) that his constituents *shall cultivate and adapt* their tastes to Truth.

"Lift up your voice like a trumpet and cry aloud, spare not," and proclaim the Word of God to men, "*whether they will hear or whether they will forbear.*" This is the old, the new, the everlasting command of God.

4.—*Priest-Craft or Hireling-Priests.*

"*And it shall come to pass, that every one that is left in thy house shall come and crouch for a piece of silver and a morsel of bread; and shall say, Put me, I pray thee, into one of the priests' offices, that I may eat a piece of bread.*"

Since penning this quotation from the Book of Samuel, the daily newspaper has been read and from it extracted the following:

"*Many After This Pulpit.*"

"It is said that the official board of the —— Church, in —— Street, near Madison Avenue, has received more than two hundred applications from pastors of Churches located in cities and towns in the vicinity of New York city since the resignation of the last Pastor."

Were this a *rare* report it might be passed without particular notice. But similar ones are so common as to excite the sorrow and shame of all who revere that Apostolic Christianity, the only cry of whose Ministers was, "Woe is me if I preach not the gospel"; whose only glory was the "Cross of Christ"; and whose only boast, "I have coveted no man's silver, or gold, or apparel. Yea, ye yourselves know that these hands have ministered unto my necessities, and to them that were with me."

We learn from every source and from all over the Christian World that the *scramble* for place, and pay, and fame, is as great among the Clergy as it is among the Politicians. The same methods are resorted to—Advertisements, Personal Presentations, *Wire-pulling*, Diplomacy.

In addition to this eager place-hunting, consider the luxurious living, and mountain, seaside, across-the-continent, across-seas, over-Europe, and around-the-world Tourings-for-Pleasure of most of those who have the large salaries, the *high* places, and "who seem to be pillars!" Contrast all this with the camel's-hair raiment, the seamless coat, the threadbare cloak, the coarse sandals, the empty wallet, the roofless homes, the scant food, the long pedestrian journeyings, and the ceaseless preaching of the Gospel in every place and every day, "without money and without price,"—with only the Heavenly Compensation of unceasing persecutions of men and the unfailing approval of God—which characterized Christianity as Jesus and his Prophet-Priest predecessors and successors established it! *Prophet-Priests and Hireling-Priests—what a contrast!* To be sure "the people love to have it so": for the *rich* supporters of *rich* Churches, as a rule, demand soft words and "smooth things" now as ever. Ease, luxury, and comfortableness they *will have*, in their Churches as in their homes; no Clergyman is acceptable who will not provide them with this, and they are willing to pay him his price. Alas, that the supply should be *greater* than the demand—two hundred-fold greater, sometimes, as the Newspapers and Church Officials report! Where the Churches are not already rich and "fashionable," their main desire, as a rule, seems to be to become so. Answering to this demand the Hireling-Priest makes it his first object to secure money for a *finer* edifice in a more *centrally* located neighborhood. His next object is—as a sort of auctioneer—to sell, to let, or to otherwise *fill* the Pews. This secured, he becomes—like all other smooth-tongued, oily-mannered Priests whom the "Scribes and Pharisees, hypocrites," patronize and approve! Our picture does not single out *any one* Congregation or Priest. Our garment is not *made to order.* But wherever the reader of these pages sees the resemblance, let him smite it! Wherever the garment will fit, let it be put on!

The "great evangelist" of orthodox Protestantism says many true things—when he lets Theology and the Bible alone—and says them wondrously well. Among recent true and well said things the newspapers report the following:

"The trouble is we have too many man-sent men, and some of them are devil-sent."

"I am tired of silver-tongued people. I have been going around Christendom for years, and I never found one of these silver-tongued preachers who amounted to anything."

"The way in which the *fashionable* and *popular* Clergymen chase the Devil out of their Churches, reminds me of the way I once saw dogs chasing swine out of a field—the dogs were ahead, and kept so far ahead that the swine were none of them in sight."

The Prophet-Priest—like the true Physician of the body, the true Reformer, Patriot, Scholar, each in his department—has but one desire and aim; which is, to cure permanently, to render vital and sound. The Hireling-Priest—like all other Charlatans and Quacks—seeks only to give present relief; and so ministers with soothing words, hypnotic gestures, narcotic rituals, somnolent dogmas, and anodynous creeds—anything, everything—within the bounds of reason—that his *parishioners* or patrons may ask, and *be willing to pay well for!*

> *Rich-Parishioner*—" Do you see yonder cloud that's almost in shape like a camel?"
> *Hireling-Priest*—" By the mass, and 't is like a camel indeed."
> *Rich-Parishioner*—" Methinks it is like a weasel!"
> *Hireling-Priest*—" It is backed like a weasel."
> *Rich-Parishioner*—" Or like a whale!"
> *Hireling-Priest*—" Very like a whale."

The Hireling-Priest is not by any means always found in the *high* stations; but he *is* always aiming to get there. If conscious of inferior talents—of diplomacy,—and of unfavorable environments—lack of influential patrons,—he will, *for the nonce*, be satisfied with a "piece of bread." For a mere livelihood—if he can get no more—well seasoned with flattery and applause, he will, for a while, be content to mildly say that white is black and that black is white. Or, if not quite so submissive, he will compromise the matter by saying that white is only a pleasant aspect of black and black only an unpleasant aspect of white. But, not long, is he content with an humble position and small pay. His ideal is, to secure—by hook or crook—a rich and "fashionable" parish; with a "magnificent" church edifice, an imposing and "enriched" service, a "snug" salary with large "perquisites," a "comfortable" parsonage or rectory; and—what is sure to come with these—with male parishioners to take him on excursions and invite him frequently to dine, and with devoted ladies to embroider his slippers and—if he be a Ritualist—to make and adorn his many-colored Vestments. Nor does his ideal end here. It includes, besides, the hope of soon being called "Rabbi, Rabbi," by receiving the title of Doctor of Divinity for his name; and the aspiration, some day, to secure even the chief office of his sect or church—Chairman, President, Ruling-Elder, Bishop, Archbishop, Cardinal, or Pope. Again we say: Our picture does not single out *any one* individual of *any one* Religion. Our garment is not *made to order*. But wherever the reader of these pages sees the resemblance—whether in the Buddhistic, Moslem, Jewish, or Christian Priest—let him rebuke it! Whoever the garment will fit, let him put it on. And we may be sure of the *fitting* and the *resemblance* whenever we hear a Priest angrily or bitterly condemning them.

Not to one age, religion, or sect alone, but to every age, religion, and sect applies the pathetic and reproachful exclamation of the brave Prophet-Priest, Jeremiah—"A wonderful and horrible thing is committed in the land. The prophets prophesy falsely, and the priests bear rule by their means; and my people love to have it so: and what will ye do in the end thereof?"

THE VOICES.*

Hireling-Priest—
"Why urge the long, unequal fight?
  Truth's lamp lies trampled in the street!
Why lift anew the flickering light,
  Quenched by the heedless millions' feet?"

Prophet-Priest—
"I'll do my work; it shall succeed
  In mine or in another's day;
And, if denied the victor's meed,
  I shall not lack the toiler's pay."

Hireling-Priest—
"Give o'er the thankless task: forsake
  The fools that know not ill from good;
Eat, drink, enjoy thy own, and take
  Thine ease among the multitude."

* See special acknowledgement on page 9 of opening pages.

Prophet-Priest—
"My meal unshared is food unblest;
　I hoard in vain what love should spend;
Self-ease is pain; my only rest
　Is labor for a worthy end."

Hireling-Priest—
"Live for thyself; with others share
　Thy proper life no more; assume
The unconcern of summer air
　For life or death, for blight or bloom."

Prophet-Priest—
"Free-lipped the liberal streamlets run,
　Free shines for all the healthful ray;
The still pool stagnates in the sun,
　The lurid earth-fire haunts decay."

Hireling-Priest—
"Thy task indeed seems over hard,
　Thou scatterest in a thankless soil;
Thy life, as seed, has no reward
　Save that which duty gives to toil."

Prophet-Priest—
"Faith shares the future promise; Love's
　Self-offering is a triumph won;
And each good thought or action moves
　The dark world nearer to the sun."

Hireling-Priest—
"The world is God's, not thine; let Him
　Work out a change—if change must be;
The hand that planted, best can trim
　And nurse, the old, unfruitful tree."

Prophet-Priest—
"Break off Love's sacred chains! Turn
　On myself my thought and care!
Myself mine own mean idol! Burn
　Faith and Hope and Charity there!

"O God! let us Thy servants dare Thy Truth in all its power
    to tell;
Unmask the priestly thieves, and tear the Bible from the grasp of
    Hell!
From hollow rite, and narrow span of Law and Sect, by Thee re-
    leased,
O teach us that the Christ-like man is, everywhere, Thy holy
    priest.
Chase back the shadows, gray and old, of the dead ages, from
    our way;
And let our hopeful eyes behold the dawn of Thy Millennial
    Day,—
That day, when fettered soul and mind shall know the Truth
    which maketh free,
When he who Christ-like serves his kind shall, Child-like, claim
    the love of Thee."

5.—*The Conservatism of Inborn Stupidity.*

"Which say to the seers, See not; and to the prophets, Prophesy not unto us right things, speak unto us smooth things, prophesy deceits."

This is the fifth of our "main hindrances" to Renascent Religion of every sort, but to Renascent Christianity in particular.

"Inborn" traits or defects are not to be *blamed* so much as *regretted*. We must exercise great forbearance toward them, and yet point them out and patiently seek to reform them. Every aspiring, progressive, mind and soul knows what an almost hopeless obstacles in the path of advancement the Conservatism of Inborn Stupidity is, and how difficult to deal with. Everything has a use, we are assured; but the use of this is one of the deep mysteries. The famous Rev. Dr. Chapin used to explain it, in his lecture on Columbus, thus: "The Conservatism of Stupidity was probably permitted as a block upon the wheels of Reform; but still the mystery remains—why such a multitude of conservative blockheads are needed!" They are found everywhere, always, and in every department of human life. They are officials as well as constituents, representatives as well as patrons, priests as well as people.

Their further characterization and reproof let us leave to the following quotations—one from a recent edition of the Protestant Episcopal *Church Standard*, and the other from the closing book of the New Testament:

"THE POWER OF DULNESS."

"There is a certain power and weight in dignified dulness which the prudent man will consider.

"There is nothing more unsafe than brightness. The man who sees clearly and speaks clearly, the bright, bold, alert man, whose mind works rapidly, is a very unsafe man. The world is always suspicious of him. He has new ways of looking at things, new ways of saying things. He startles and annoys people. His reasoning may be very clear; his conclusions very conclusive; his method bright and to the point; but his clearness and precision, and brilliancy of comprehension and statement, are against him.

"The general average of humanity does not see clearly, nor think clearly, nor express itself clearly. It is a very muddled affair generally. If it is to be taught and influenced, it must be on its own ground. It has the conviction that muddle and confusion are the normal state of things. It is very suspicious of the man who undertakes to disentangle the confusion, and bring precision out of the muddle. It resents his pretence that anything can be clear which is not clear to itself. It pronounces him 'an able man, perhaps a brilliant man, but an *unsafe* man.'

"It turns with a sense of relief from him and his ways to the safe timidity, the decorous dulness, the dignified and solemn heaviness of respectable commonplace, which disturbs nobody, and against which not a word can be said.

"In the pulpit perhaps there is nothing that at times has greater influence. When decorous and solemn commonplace occupies that position, and gravely confines itself to large round platitudes, it is a positive relief to a man of nervous temperament. He can close his eyes and go to sleep quietly, satisfied that when he wakes everything will be as he left it. There is a sense of serene rest and calm, as if a man were removed from all the turmoil of the wicked world, when he can incline his head at a comfortable angle, and let the round and balanced sentences lull him to his rest.

"We entered once, awhile since, a church which shall be nameless. The pew backs were very high. They were well-cushioned. The preacher stood in a thing shaped like a giant's wine-glass. There were seventy-five heads before him, exclusive of our own, all gray or bald. These seventy-five heads just appeared above the backs of the pews, clothed in their venerable gray crowns of glory, or shining in their bareness, where sermons by the hundred had hit and glanced off to the next pew. The venerable heads were calmly reposing in that sweetest of all sleeps since infancy—a Sunday sleep in a well-stuffed pew—all except perhaps a half dozen whose consciences or ledgers kept them awake. It was only at rare intervals that a noise, as of one in an uneasy dream, disturbed the solemn cadences of the preacher.

"He was preaching on the duty of reading a chapter in the Bible every day. It was a thoroughly safe subject, and he handled it in a thoroughly safe way. The sentences were all round and well finished after the approved pattern, and they rolled out with a full and musical intonation, as if the speaker enjoyed the sound of his admirable voice. Evidently he was 'the right man in the right place,' a man of weight and influence, a thoroughly safe man, to whom those dignified gentlemen could intrust the preaching of the Gospel in *their* church, satisfied that all was well, while 'drowsy tinklings lulled the fold.' It was a touching sight to see the quiet confidence those world-weary men reposed in their chosen shepherd; with what infantile simplicity they dropped to rest, as if each one said, 'The doctor is preaching. It is all right. He will go through that manuscript in a way to command any man's confidence and respect. We can go to sleep like lambs while *he* guards the sheep-fold.'

"To be sure it is only fair to say that sometimes there come crises in social and political life which set all rules at defiance, and your dull man looks on with a dazed and imbecile look in his glassy eyes which is really tragical and pitiful. There is need of something more than dulness then, or things go very badly. But as soon as the crisis is over, dulness assumes its ancient worship, and clothes itself in all its primeval dignity.

" In literature the influence of dulness is not given, we are sorry to say, its due consideration. Readers are getting into a bad habit of impatience with it. They have been known to condemn it, and speak bitterly and sarcastically about it—to resent it almost as a personal injury. This is the case in general literature, however. Religious literature has not thus cast off all regard for the past, and abandoned itself to new-fangled ways.

" The religious book, or the religions publication, being in some sort akin to the sermon, retains still due respect for dignified and solemn dulness. It is read as a duty, sometimes as a penance perhaps, and the reader resents any attempt to render his toil lighter or his penance less penetential. He wants to go in the old respectable and decorous path and the ponderous periods of a grave discussion, ponderously involved and elaborated, have a great weight with him. They sound very magnificent and learned, and, at all events, are thoroughly safe ; and his religious book or religious newspaper must first of all be *safe*. ' Whatever is is right,' must be their motto. The same venerable straw must be threshed over again and again with the same regular and grave beat of the wooden flail. The writer must not disturb his reader with any subject on which there is a difference of opinion, or with any view or any question later than his venerable great-grandfather.

" We know religious papers, for instance, which owe their weight and consideration, and both are considerable, to the fact that they never had an opinion and never will have ; that they never expressed themselves on any matter on which there is greater doubt than on the propositions that ' honesty is the best policy ' and ' virtue is its own reward ' ; whose secret of influence is the owl-like gravity and highly-respectable dulness with which they repeat Mother Grundy's oracular utterances to an over-awed world. So, as we have taken the liberty to say, he is a very thoughtless man who underrates the high position which dulness holds in the minds of men, or the dangers and the failures of brightness.

"We cannot ourselves see why the pulpit should be dull, why religious books should be unreadable, why religious newspapers should be stupid. We do not see the connection between piety and owliness, nor understand why necessarily brightness should be condemned as hostile to religion.

"But though we cannot see the subtile bond of connection, we recognize the fact."

"And unto the angel of the church of the Laodiceans write; These things saith the Amen, the faithful and true witness, the beginning of the creation of God; I know thy works, that thou art neither cold nor hot: I would thou wert cold or hot. So then because thou art lukewarm, and neither cold nor hot, I will spue thee out of my mouth. . . . As many as I love, I rebuke and chasten: be *zealous* therefore, and repent."

"Now too oft, the priesthood wait at the threshold of the great,—
Waiting for their beck and nod; servants of men, not of God.
Fraud exults, while solemn words sanctify its stolen hoards;
Slavery laughs, while ghostly lips bless his manacles and whips.

"Not on them the poor rely, not on them looks liberty,
Who with fawning falsehood cower, to the wrong, when clothed with power.
O, to see them meanly cling, round the master, round the king,
Sported with, and sold and bought,—pitifuller sight is not!

"Tell me not that this must be: God's true priest is always free;
Free, the needed truth to speak, right the wronged and raise the weak.
Not to fawn on wealth and state, leaving Lazarus at the gate,—
Not to peddle creeds like wares,—not to mutter hireling prayers,—

"Nor to paint the new life's bliss on the sable ground of this,—
Golden streets for idle knave, Sabbath rest for weary slave !
Not for words and works like these, priest of God, thy mission is ;
But to make earth's desert glad, in its Eden greenness clad."

XLIX.—PREFATORY EXPLANATIONS AND TOPICAL CONTENTS OF THE NEW EDITION OF ANCIENT SACRED SCRIPTURES OF THE WORLD.

The Prefatory Explanations and Topical Contents of the new edition of Ancient Sacred Scriptures of the World (which may be found in that volume) were prepared and inserted for two reasons: One, that they might furnish suggestions as to *methods* of Translation, of Expurgation, of Correcting, and of Compiling, to students in general, of Higher Criticism of the Bible and of Comparative Religion. The other, that by their *very faults and defects*—as initial and novel efforts—they might stimulate wiser and more effectual attempts on the part of others in the interests of Renascent Christianity. The author of these Prefaces and Contents claims no superior scholarship, and assumes the possession of no extraordinary intellectual or spiritual insight. He simply has felt that certain things in the interests of Higher Criticism and Comparative Religion Studies needed to be said and done; he has waited long for others to say and do them in both a *reverent and a radical* spirit— which, in these enlightened times, is the only spirit in which they can be *effectively* said and done. After many years of waiting—with *scoffing* Radicals on one hand turning the Bible and all Religions into ridicule, and *orthodox* Conservatives on the other making them still more ridiculous to all who are *intelligently* reverent or *reverently* intelligent— he could no longer resist the *sense of duty* that impelled him to open efforts for the *renascence* of Christianity and of its Holy Book, however bitter the criticism or severe the condemnation he might thereby draw upon himself.

"*Let me perish, but let Truth survive.*" Whatever reproach or loss may result to *himself*, the Truth-lover irresistibly must be a Truth-speaker. "*I cannot otherwise. God help me.*"

From the first this has been the *Compelling* Spirit of *genuine* Christianity. Its Divine Founder made it the closing and climax of his Beatitudes: "*Blessed are ye, when men shall revile you, and persecute you, and say all manner of evil against you falsely, for my sake. Rejoice, and be exceeding glad; for so persecuted they the prophets which were before you.*"

He himself was Truth-compelled even to the Cross and the Sepulchre. "*I have not spoken of myself; but the Father which sent me, He gave me a commandment what I should say, and what I should speak. I have given you an example that ye should do as I have done.*" And all his disciples, except Judas Iscariot who betrayed him, *did as he had done.*

"But that it spread no further among the people, let us straitly threaten them, that they speak henceforth to no man in this name.

"But Peter and John answered and said unto them, Whether it be right in the sight of God to hearken unto you more than unto God, judge ye.

"For we cannot but speak the things which we have seen and heard.

"And now, Lord, behold their threatenings: and grant unto thy servants, that with all boldness they may speak thy word."

L.— A MODERN PROPHET-PRIEST—SKETCHED AS A MODEL.

"He was despised and rejected of men."

He was friend and benefactor, though in less signal ways perhaps, to many other churches besides his own; indeed, he was a sort of Bishop in its best sense, a Shepherd in its genuine New Testament sense, of all Churches in America. Not one ever appealed to him for counsel or help in vain; his sympathy, his words, his efforts were with all; freely offered, nay gladly, eagerly offered. So heart and soul and head and life consecrated to his cause was he, that no Macedonian cry, "Come over and help us," ever fell unheeded upon his ear. For nearly half a century he came and

---

* Chiefly from "What is the Bible?" and "The Man Jesus," and "The Religion of Evolution."—By special permission.

went, with his richest thoughts, his devoutest efforts, his deepest and purest love—sacrificing his home comforts, spending his money, risking his health; heedless indeed of everything but *that* which he might help or *those* whom he might bless.

His whole ministerial life might be called an uninterrupted Labor of Love. And, as was fitting, a "labor of love" ended his life. For, called to a distant city of the West, to speak in advocacy of his cause, and also to preach the dedication sermon of a new church, neither his age, nor his bodily infirmities, nor the severity of the weather, nor the length and weariness of the journey withheld him; but, as in his earliest days, he left his home and went, discharged, with even unwonted inspiration and grace, the duties there laid upon him; and then, stricken with disease, returned—to die.

Of him was true what long ago Homer sang of his never-yielding, never-resting hero:

> "Whose soul no respite knows
> Though years and honors bid him seek repose.
> But now the last despair surrounds our host,
> No hour must pass, no moment must be lost."

Not only his own bereaved church in New York, but also all Churches of America owe tributes of affection and gratitude to his most precious memory.

In his varied labors, his wide and numerous circles of intercourse, he had gained a host of personal friends. It is impossible that one should be both loved and admired more intensely and more sincerely than was he, by those who enjoyed the rare privilege of his acquaintance and friendship. He had the wondrous faculty without deceitfulness, flattery, or pretense of seeming to be the particular friend—the most particular friend—of each one of his friends; so that he was unaffectedly a father, a brother, nay even a lover, to every one who knew him well.

The author's acquaintance with him began when a student at the Presbyterian Theological Seminary in the city of New York. He chanced to drift into his church one morning and was at once drawn in admiration toward him;

chiefly, because his appearance and manner were so strikingly similar to those of the venerable President of Williams College—from which institution he had just graduated—who, up to that time, had been the most paternal and sympathetic, as well as most majestic, manly, and scholarly of all the preachers the author had enjoyed the privilege to know or to hear. Very soon a personal acquaintance was sought. The young student was received warmly, taken into his fatherly counsels, adopted, as it were, into his family, drawn to his heart and held there, more and more closely, until the hour of his death. What he was to one he was to many others of the younger clergymen. All who knew him clung to him as a wisest, dearest friend—even as the sons of the prophets in ancient times clung to Elijah. And when he was parted from them and carried up out of sight, they all stood gazing after him and exclaiming, " My father, my father, the chariot of Israel, and the horsemen thereof." Many there are who can join in thus testifying to the honor, excellence, integrity, genius, and worth of this bishop of so many churches, this shepherd of such a multitude of souls.

One of his own distinguished parishioners,—whose character no doubt was very largely shaped, and whose sentences and songs were, in some measure at least, inspired by the eloquent teachings, the sublime influences, the sweet, pure, and beautiful examples of his life-long pastor and friend, sang of all good and noble men in general, but prophetically of this good and noble man in particular—

> " Let the light
> Stream on his deeds of love, that shunned the sight
> Of all but Heaven ; and in the book of fame
> The glorious record of his virtues write
> And hold it up to men, and bid them claim
> A palm like his, and catch from him the hallowed flame."

When Jesus said of the approaching Nathaniel : " Behold an Israelite indeed," he doubtless meant to say, Behold a man !—a true, well-endowed, well-balanced, and well-developed specimen of manhood. Such a man in any age is rarely found, and when found he attracts the attention and wins the admiration of all who observe him.

Now and then there appears a man who seems to be a god descended to earth in human form—so large is his pattern, so majestic his endowments, so superior his developments of body, mind, and soul. It was to such as these that Napoleon the First referred when he exclaimed, "How rare are men! in all Italy I have found only two."

It was to such as these that Shakespeare referred when he said,
> "But thou, O thou
> So perfect and so peerless, art
> Created of every creature's best."

And again,
> "There's nothing ill can dwell in such a temple."

It was to such as these too that Pope referred when he said,
> "'T is not a lip, an eye, we beauty call,
> But the joint force and full result of all."

When a man answering to these descriptions appears among men, so rare an apparition is he that there is no wonder he becomes at once a sort of divinity, whom all delight to honor and revere. It is simply the homage which mankind pays, and rightfully pays, to typical or ideal manhood.

We have been told that Mr. Gladstone, who, for a half century nearly, has above all others been admired, almost adored, by his fellow-citizens of Great Britain, is a man of this peerless pattern and mould,—every inch a man, which is much higher praise than to say "every inch a king." And those who have known them both well, have said that this "Modern Prophet-Priest," though moving in quite a different sphere, was the Gladstone of America—if not of the American people, certainly of the American pulpit. Though a preacher instead of a statesman, he was nevertheless every inch a man, as all who saw him much or heard him sympathetically hastened at once to acknowledge. Nature had endowed him, to begin with, not only with a "sound body," but also with a noble, graceful, commanding form and figure; with a massive head, an intellectual brow, a winsome as well as intelligent and penetrating eye, a countenance soft and serene but capable of expressing the wrath of Mars or the indignation of Jove, a voice, as musical as a harp and as gentle as a purling stream, but adapted also to the swelling anthems of his thoughts and the sending forth of his occasional thunderbolts of argument or rebuke. Seen upon the streets, or in whatever promiscuous crowd, the observing eye would at once single him out as a superior man. To look in his face was both to love and to fear him; and to listen to the accents of his voice was to know that there was authority back of it—the authority both of a great heart and of a giant mind.

Such were the rare physical or mechanical endowments with which Nature had generously furnished him; and no one could know better than he how to use them to their best advantage—to their most efficient and excellent results.

In this sound and noble body dwelt a correspondingly sound and noble mind; indeed the body was only the mould in which the mind had cast itself—the coarser, less beautiful and less perfect outer image of his own inner self.

"The mind is the measure of the man": but you can take, or at least begin to take the measure of the mind from the shape, outlines, and expressions of its materialistic mould, its physical representation, the body. And no one who knew this Prophet-Priest even a little, much less they who knew him well, could fail to be convinced that his body was no mask or disguise, but as perfect an exhibition as flesh and blood could give of the personality within. *The " word" made flesh and dwelling among us full of grace and truth.*

Intellectually, he was not what is called a profound mind; which generally means narrow and deep. But he was well-balanced, many-sided, comprehensive, broad; and also deep enough for the seeds of wisdom and thought to take root, to be well nourished, and to grow mightily and beauteously to the bringing forth of abundant fruit. And this, as all history and observation show, is the manly type of mind—

the type of those who have been and are, in the highest sense, the thinkers, teachers, and leaders of the world.

He had a thorough classical education to begin with, graduating while yet almost a boy from Harvard University. Afterwards he studied theology with an open mind and a free range of inquiry and of thought—tied to no essential creed, anchored to no pre-determined set of doctrines, pledged to no system, school, or sect, responsible to no one but to God, and caring for nothing but to seek, and find, and know, and do, God's truth and will. Thus studying, with all books wide open before him, with all good and wise men as his teachers, and with his own conscience as his own and only monitor, he laid firmly and broad the foundation not only for his professional career, but also for that many-sided culture, that wide-reaching wisdom, that everything-appropriating, all-comprehending intellectuality which fitted him well to be what he finally was—a teacher of teachers in almost every department of thought, and a leader of leaders in almost every social, industrial, charitable, political, and educational, as well as ecclesiastical department of activity and life.

His was a splendid mind; and, by contact with the world in a hundred ways, by wide, various, and intimate relationships with men and women of all stations and nations, as well as by classical culture and the wisdom of books, he had been educated widely and well. His superior, with reference to *versatility* of education, in its best sense, could not be found. He was at home on all subjects, was posted on all topics, was fully prepared both to appreciate and to communicate wisdom with reference to almost everything. He was no specialist—deeming it necessary to know only one thing in order to know it well; but rather deeming it essential to know many things, nay, so nearly as possible, to know everything in order to know even one thing of importance, as it ought to be known. Thus, not "narrow and deep," but broad and comprehensive was his education—a true, effective, manly education. Manly endowments, character, and culture he was possessed of to almost a miraculous degree.

But all the virtues have never yet been granted to any one man; a portion has always been withheld from each, as a sort of "thorn in the flesh," lest, as Paul said, they should be exalted above measure. Though not a "saint" in the sense that we may apply that word to some who have lived, he was certainly a saintly man; though not possessed of miraculous spirituality he was always and in all things spiritually-minded. All his springs were in God. He was rooted and grounded in the faith of Jesus Christ. His conversation was in heaven, in all holiness and godliness; and in his everyday practice, as well as in his preaching, the kingdom of God and His righteousness were ever foremost and supreme.

The pathos of devotion that marked his prayers, his sermons, his ordinary conversation even, running like a current of inspiration through every sentence, through every word, indicated that in his innermost soul was a closet of prayer, with closed doors, wherein he uninterruptedly communed with the Father who seeth in secret and rewardeth openly.

Theologically speaking he was not an *angel with one wing*, as so many of the "angels of the church" always have been and are. He was not radical to the exclusion of conservatism, nor conservative to the exclusion of radicalism; he was not a skeptic to the exclusion of belief, nor a believer to the exclusion of skepticism; he was both—radical and conservative, a believer and a skeptic. The two organs of his brain, "destructiveness" and "constructiveness" seem to have been harmoniously and equally developed, so that there was nothing partial, one-sided, or incomplete about his religious convictions or theories. He possessed the rare faculty of discrimination; of being able not only to detect error and to reject it but also to discover the truth and to conserve it. This is why to extremists on both sides he often seemed inconsistent; now, from some utterance in which he pointedly criticised or discarded an error, the extreme radical would claim him for his side; again, from some utterance in which he zealously defended some ancient method or truth, the dogmatic conservative would claim him for his side; and when he refused, as he always did, to be counted in on either side, both would join to condemn him as illogical, inconsistent, unreliable. "To which of these religions do you belong? To all, because all combined constitute the true religion," said Goethe in his *Wilhelm Meister*. This is what our prophet-priest was always saying; and because the dogmatists—both radical and conservative—could not comprehend him, they charged him with poor logic, inconsistency, unreliableness. They looked only upon one side of the shield, he upon both sides; they considered only one phase of the star or the planet, he all phases. Then too, he understood well, and practised well, what Goethe in another place says—"If you have got any faith, for God's sake give me a share of it; but your doubts you may keep to yourself, I have plenty of my own." His skepticism he reserved like a hidden instrument for the secret workings of his own mind; his faith, positive and sincere, was all that he felt called upon to give public or promiscuous expression to. Results, not processes; ends, not means; the refined gold and not the alloy, or the methods of refining were the stock in trade of all his pulpit teachings, of all his public instructions and ministrations. No better illustration of this prime characteristic of all his theology and theological methods could be cited than that furnished us in one of the last sermons that he preached, and the very last that was printed—the sermon entitled "Christianity Unchanged," preached a few weeks before his decease at the dedication of a church in St. Louis. We may quote here two or three selections from it, though the entire sermon is needed in order to furnish a complete illustration :—

"Be sure, then, it is really upon its merits that Christianity rests. If it had not maintained that ground all other kinds of evidences would long ago have broken down. Let its enemies crowd together and pile up the proof of the inconsistencies, infirmities, persecutions, dogmatic extravagances and incredible opinions, or indefensible usages of the historic church, and make of them as ugly and awful a heap as they can. It only redounds more to the strength of the constitution of Christ's religion that it has borne these sicknesses and survived the weight of these burdens, and the sorrow of these tears, and comes down to us, in spite of the perversities of its ignorant or imperfect supporters, its rash interpreters, its unreasoning defenders, in the purity and power with which it survives." . . .

"There are too many glorious and beautiful traditions of the church universal; too many saints and martyrs; too many signs of divinity in its hymns and prayers and festivals, in the mystic faith hid often in its harsh creeds; in the meekness and patience and loving kindness of the Christian saints and apostles of the past, to make it anything less than a dangerous impoverishment of spiritual wealth to dissever the hereditary connection with and direct descent from the freest modern Christianity and its historic ancestry in the Church of Christ." . . .

"Christianity is even greater, diviner and richer—surer in its sway than its loudest champions suppose. They encumber it with assumptions, bolster it with defences, deform it with claims it neither owns nor needs. If anyone can conceive or anticipate the appearance of a spirit holier, lovelier, or more spiritually illumined than Jesus, or one whose example, temper, faith, heroism, could be fitter to elevate and guide the moral and spiritual fortunes of humanity, he may expect with reason a new revelation and a new religion. But the universe must be rich indeed if it holds another soul like his. Meanwhile, we cling confidently to the hem of his garment. He is the nearest to God the holiest history has handed down. The instincts of civilization have crystallized about him. The church is the setting of the jewel that sheds its lustre far beyond its frame. But let us protect and strengthen the setting, and not disown it if it bear some marks of the antiquity in which its earlier efforts were made; for it holds up before new generations the splendor and glory of the one name that has hitherto had power to hold the reverence and confidence of the race, and to whose pre-eminence, and rightful honor, and mastership, we can see no end. Therefore, we in the midst of modern light, and children of reason, sons of progress, do from our heart of hearts call him Master and profess our unfeigned faith in his teachings, and in the Church he planted."

Turning from the general to the more particular and personal there are a few special delineations of his grace and worth that we may make. Who that has ever been a guest in his home, or had him as a guest in their homes, can soon forget the charm and the cheer that emanated from and surrounded his personality! It was like the mellow radiance or the soft glow of a summer morning;—the birds began to sing, the flowers to open, the valleys to smile, the hills to dance, the trees to murmur their gladness, the floods to clap their hands, the heavens and earth, and all nature to rejoice as soon as his beaming face appeared, or his tender voice, with its always warmly welcoming, affectionately solicitous, love-inspiring and love-compelling greetings, fell upon the ear. Nor is this a mere rhetorical figure of personal and perhaps extravagant admiration; it is the exact experience of everyone who has ever spent a day in his home, or had him as a guest for one day in theirs. Now and then there is a person of that rare calibre and gift that literally carries sunshine everywhere; no darkness but that recedes, no sorrow but that vanishes, no burden but that falls, no tear that is not dried, no sigh that is not changed to singing, no pessimism that does not become optimistic, hopeful, and glad in the presence of such an one. " Did not our hearts burn within us as he talked with us by the way and sat with us at meat?" said the two disciples of Emmaus when, their eyes being opened, they found they had entertained an angel unawares. What heart-burnings of purity, wisdom, hope, and gladness have we not experienced, in common with all who ever walked by the way with this modern prophet-priest, or sat with him at meat! The grace of his manner, the tenderness of his words, the wisdom of his speech, the immaculateness of his ideas and ideals; together with the inspiration of his eye, the expressiveness of his countenance, and the wonderful eloquence of his eloquent tongue—the combined effect, who can forget it, or fail to be forever wiser, purer, and happier on account of it!

"He was only with us one night," said the father of a family not long ago, "but he left in our home an atmosphere of sweetness and purity which the children as well as ourselves did not cease to recognize and enjoy for weeks and months thereafter." How many heads of families not only all over America, but also in various parts of Great Britain, France, Switzerland, Germany, where at different times he travelled, and was invited or received as a guest, would gladly testify to the same beautiful, almost divine influences left behind in their homes like the lasting perfume of flowers, or the odor of sweet-smelling incense—cassia, spikenard, and myrrh, very costly and very precious! This personal, domestic, and social influence and inspiration, so widely spread and long continued, was by no means the least important outflow, benediction, or blessing of his life. It was moreover the basis of all his public, the fountain-head of all his professional ministrations; he carried the same well-rounded, many-sided, to-all-and-to-everybody adapted personality with him wherever he went. Chief among equals was he, as well as chief among inferiors. He was the chief organizer, counsellor, director, and inspirer of his own Christian denomination, throughout the entire forty years of his public ministry: and that by common consent, not by his own election or choice. And so it was that hardly nowhere, from Maine to California, could a church edifice be dedicated, a pastor installed, a convocation called, or an assembly held, without his presence being solicited and his leadership if possible secured.

He was always the recognized leader. He was captain of the craft, always at the wheel, always on the watch; and at the same time was the "*placidum caput*" above the tempestuous waves, ever to rebuke their violence and reduce them to a calm. A natural born leader was he, spontaneously chosen and unanimously recognized, not only in the church but also in every department of life to which his activities were given. The Sanitary Commission, the the most splendid charity of our age, he organized, and, as a historian has said, "was not only its parent, but also its never-flagging spirit and its daily slave." Time would fail to speak of the charities, the industries, the humanities, the reforms, in church, city, and nation, which he organized, or helped to organize, and became the heart and soul of. In everything that he attempted the advocacy or advancement of he was, or soon became, by the persistent wish and will of all, *the* man.

As a reformer, in church, society, or state, one sentence as applied to him may express it all, " Nobility is insensibility to opinion." He invariably sought not the praises of man, but the praise of God; and though no man could be more tender of the feelings of others than was he—as tender as the fondest mother of her dearest child—yet such was his loyalty to Truth and Right, that he spared the feelings of no one; nay, mortified, wounded, crucified his own feelings, if circumstances required, in order to stand by what his intellect assured him was true, or to defend what his conscience pointed out as right. From his pulpit, and from whatever position, public or private, he assumed, in other language he continually exclaimed—"Aloft on the throne of God, and not below in the footprints of the trampling multitude, are the sacred rules of right, which no majorities can misplace or overturn." And this is why he was never the preacher, teacher, or leader of the masses; was never in any way or sense, what we call *popular*. His head and his heart, his intellect and his conscience, his theories and his principles were too lofty for the masses to reach; and he was too God-like, for the sake of mere popularity, to abandon them and come down.

It is without doubt providential that among the teachers of the world, especially among religious teachers, both intellect and conscience are so graded as to constitute a sort of Jacob's ladder, whose bottom rests on the earth but whose top at the same time touches Heaven. Upon the uppermost rounds of this ladder stand a few of God's most highly favored and endowed, whose mission it is to take directly from Him revelations of truth and duty and hand them down to a succession of less highly favored and endowed, grade by grade, until at length they reach the earth. In their transmission they become, of necessity perhaps, perhaps providentially, less and less heavenly,—more and more of the earth, earthy; so adapting themselves to the less and less heavenly, more and more earthy-mindedness of the different grades of teachers and of men; until finally, *in some diluted form*, they reach and are received by the masses. The preachers, teachers, leaders of the masses *must of necessity* be more or less like the masses, of the earth, earthy. "From that time many of his disciples went back and walked no more with him. Then said Jesus unto the twelve, will ye also go away?"

This modern Prophet-Priest was one of the chosen few, one of the *Anointed* of God, whose station is appointed to them upon the topmost round of the ladder of Heavenly Revelation. To desert that station and come down would be not only to leave a gap in the line, but also to debase and degrade the sublime endowments wherewith God has providentially, and for providential purposes endowed them.

Why did he not resort to the tricks and devices of the ministerial trade, to fill his church, Sunday after Sunday, with an applauding multitude! Why did he consent patiently, nay even submissively, to speak his best words—which, to those who had ears to hear them, were the words of God's highest angels—much of the time to half-filled pews; or even, at times, as did Jesus at the well of Samaria, to a single listening auditor? Why did not he, endowed as he was with so large a measure of the wisdom of Plato, the eloquence of Demosthenes, the piety of David, the faith of Paul and the tender, glowing heart of love of the Master himself—why did not he, thus endowed, grow envious of some of the great congregations which thronged the churches about him, and enter the list as a rival of ministers whose name and fame were upon everybody's lips?

"Then the Evil One taketh him up into an exceeding high mountain, and sheweth him all the kingdoms of the world, and the glory of them; and saith unto him, all these things will I give thee, if thou wilt fall down and worship me: and Jesus said unto him, get thee hence, Satan; for it is written, thou shalt worship the Lord thy God, and Him only shalt thou serve."

He loved men and the approbation of men, but he loved God and the approbation of his own conscience far better; this is why he did not, why he could not descend to become either the idol or the mouth-piece of the masses. He knew that it was his mission to be a teacher of teachers;—to teach and charm those who were to teach and charm others, which others were in the end to teach and charm the multitude; and true to his mission he was; though all his life long it caused him to stand comparatively deserted, and at times— with God—alone! And yet, what a band of the very elect, small in numbers though it was, he gathered and held ever about him.

New York city directly, and indirectly New York state, and all the states in this union of states, owe more, in intellectual, moral, social, and political influence, *of the highest leadership and type*, to the past half-century's personalities, words, and works of the congregation of the church of which this Prophet-Priest was pastor—than to any other half-dozen churches combined in New York city or Brooklyn, we may venture to affirm.

Distinguished names might be mentioned as confirmations, and many facts might be adduced to strengthen the confirmation; such as the leadership which he himself and his prominent parishioners had, and have, ever bravely assumed and persistently held, over almost every organization, project, or movement which had in view the radical remedy and reformation of public affairs.

The Sibyl of ancient times wrote her prophecies on the loose leaves of trees, and made the winds her messengers, to bear them everywhere. Such, not in fable but in fact, is the influence which this modern Prophet-Priest exerted for more than forty years upon his city, his country, the world.

May similar priests—similar in spirit and method if not in endowments and power—in ever increasing numbers— arise to lead and feed the flock of Christ, and to hasten on that *Renascence* of Christianity which shall be a glorious fulfilment of his prophecy, who said, "There shall be one fold and one Shepherd."

LI.—OUR RECENT PROPHET-BISHOP—SENTENCES SELECTED FROM HIS SERMONS.

"*I shall grow* so that I shall be able to understand vastly more of what God is and of what He is doing. God also *will be ever doing new things*. . . . Therefore each year grows sacred with wondering expectation. . . . *Be ready for any overturnings,* even of the things which have seemed most eternal, if by these overturnings God can come to be *more the King of His own Earth.* . . . A universal Commerce is creating common bases and forms of thought. For the first time in the history of the world there is a manifest, *almost an immediate possibility of a universal religion.* . . . Our ordinary life so hangs fast in the dull middle regions of *conventional propriety and selfish expediency,* that it becomes, not the fountain, but the grave of individuality. . . . Let us put aside everything that hinders *the highest from coming to us.* . . . He who takes any new word of God *completely* gets both a *new* truth and a new duty—*is continually seeing new truth* and accepting the duties that arise out of it. . . . Oh, if you could only know two things about yourself: first, that you are a different creature from any that the world has ever seen; and second, that *you are a real utterance of the same Spirit of Life out of which sprang Isaiah and St. John.* . . . God has been here, and *God is here still.* . . . That miracles have ceased is a *sign of increasing spirituality.* . . . It is not for us to *catalogue and inventory* Deity. . . . Oh, in this world of shallow believers and weary, dreary workers, how we need the Holy Spirit! The power of the Holy Spirit—*an everlasting spiritual presence among men!* What but this is the thing we want? . . . *Insist on having your soul get at God and hear His voice.* . . . Be profoundly honest. Never dare to say, . . . through conformity to what you know you are expected to say, *one word which at the moment when you say it you do not believe.* . . . Seek great experiences of the soul, and *never turn your back on them when God sends them,* as He surely will.

... Revelation is not the unveiling of God, but *a changing of the veil* that covers Him. For man to accept the pattern of his living absolutely from any other being besides God in all the universe *would be for him to sacrifice himself and lose his originality.* ... Because no other being ever was or ever will be just the same as you, and because precisely the same conditions never before have been and never will be grouped about any other mortal life as are grouped around yours, *therefore for you to do and be what you, with your own nature in your own circumstances, ought, in the judgment of the perfect mind to do and be*, that is originality for you. ... There is an Atheism which still repeats the Creeds—*a belief in God which does not let Him come into close contact with the every-day life.* ... Many who call themselves Theists are like the savages who, in the desire to honor the wonderful Sun-dial which had been given them, built a roof over it! *Break down the roof; let God into your life.* ... This has always been true, *that the new idea has been born of the old*,—not by flinging their nets out into the heavens in hopes to catch a star, but by digging deeper into the substance of the earth on which they stood, *and finding there a root.* ... And that is what we have to look for in the future. You and I cling to the old historic statements of our faith. ... What is our feeling as we hold fast there? We stand *expecting change and progress, new truth, new light.* ... *We believe that the new truth must come out of this old truth, the perfect truth out of this partial truth*, some day. ... Only he who consents to enlarge his own conception of the possibilities of faith with God's can calmly watch the everlasting *growth of Revelation and see the old open into the new.*
... To discriminate between the eternal substance of Christianity *and its temporary* forms; to bid men see how often forms have perished *and the substance still survived;* to make men know the *danger of imperfect and false tests of faith*, and to encourage them to be not merely resigned *but glad as they behold the one faith ever casting its old forms away*, and by its undying vitality *creating for itself new*—

that is to open wide the great gates of the Divine Life, and make the way more clear for the children to their Father. Every *new* experience is a *new* opportunity of knowing God. Every *new* experience is like a jewel set into the texture of your life, *on which God shines and makes interpretation and revelation* of Himself. You hang a great rich dark cloth up into the sunlight, and the sun shines on it and shows the broad general color that is there. Then, one by one, you sew great precious stones upon the cloth, and each one, as you set it there, catches the sunlight and pours it forth in a flood of peculiar glory. A diamond here, an emerald there, an opal there; the sun seems to rejoice as he finds each moment a new interpreter of his splendor, until at last the whole jewelled cloth is burning and blazing with the gorgeous revelation. . . . A much-living life is like a robe that bursts forth of itself to jewels. *They are not sewn on from the outside. They are born out of the substance of that life* as the stars are born out of the heart of the night. *And God shines with new revelation upon every one.*"

"We cannot kindle when we will
  The fire which in the heart resides,
The Spirit bloweth, and is still—
  In mystery our soul abides :
*But tasks in hours of insight will'd,
Can be, through hours of gloom, fulfill'd.*

"With aching hands and bleeding feet
  We dig and heap, lay stone to stone ;
We bear the burden and the heat
  Of the long day and wish 't were done.
*Not till the hours of light return
All we have built do we discern.*"

LII.—A MODERN PROPHET-BARD.*
Appropriate Selections.

"To us have Prophet-Bards of old,
Their deep and constant sorrows told;
The same which earth's unwelcome seers
Have felt in all succeeding years.
Sport of the changeful multitude,
Nor calmly heard nor understood,
Their song has seemed a trick of art,
Their warnings but the actor's part.
With bonds, and scorn, and evil will,
The world requites its prophets still.

So was it when the Holy One
The garments of the flesh put on !
Men followed where the Highest led
For common gifts of daily bread,
And gross of ear, of vision dim,
Owned not the godlike power of Him.
Vain as a dreamer's words to them
His wail above Jerusalem,
And meaningless the watch He kept
Through which his weak disciples slept.

Yet shrink not thou, whoe'er thou art,
For God's great purpose set apart,
Before whose far-discerning eyes
The Future as the Present lies !
Beyond a narrow-bounded age
Stretches thy prophet-heritage,
Through Heaven's dim spaces angel-trod,
Through arches round the throne of God !
Thy audience, worlds !—all Time to be
The witness of the Truth in Thee !"

" Our common Master did not pen his followers up from other
    men :
His service liberty indeed, he built no Sect, imposed no Creed ;

* See special acknowledgement on page 9 of opening pages.

But, while the boasting Pharisee made broader his phylactery,
As from the synagogue was seen the dusty-sandalled Nazarene
Through ripening cornfields led the way upon the awful Sabbath day,
His sermons were the healthful talk that shorter made the mountain-walk,
His wayside texts were flowers and birds, while mingled with his gracious words
The rustle of the tamarisk-tree and ripple-wash of Galilee.

"With noiseless slide of stone to stone, the mystic Church of God has grown.
Invisible and silent stands the temple never made with hands,
Unheard the voices still and small of its unseen confessional.
He needs no special place of prayer whose hearing ear is everywhere;
He brings not back the childish days that ringed the earth with stones of praise,
Roofed Karnak's hall of gods, and laid the plinths of Philæ's colonnade.
Still less He owns the selfish good and sickly growth of solitude;
Dissevered from the suffering whole, love hath no power to save a soul.
Not out of Self, the origin—but, out of Others saved from sin,
The living waters spring and flow, the trees with leaves of healing grow."

"I ask no organ's soulless breath to drone the themes of life and death,
No altar candle-lit by day, no ornate wordsman's rhetoric-play,
No cool philosophy to teach its bland audacities of speech
To double-tasked idolaters, themselves their gods and worshippers,
No pulpit hammered by the fist of loud-asserting dogmatist,
Who borrows for the hand of love the smoking thunderbolts of Jove.
I know how well the fathers taught, what work the later schoolmen wrought;

I reverence old-time faith and men, but God is near us now as
  then ;
His force of love is still unspent, his hate of sin is imminent ;
And still the measure of our needs outgrows the cramping
  bounds of creeds ;
The manna gathered yesterday already savors of decay ;
Doubts to the world's child-heart unknown question us now
  from star and stone ;
Too little or too much we know, and sight is swift and faith is
  slow ;
The power is lost to self-deceive with shallow forms of make-
  believe.

" We walk at high noon, and the bells call to a thousand oracles.
I lay the critic's glass aside, I tread upon my lettered pride,
And, lowest-seated, testify to the oneness of humanity.
He findeth not who seeks his own, the soul is lost that's saved
  alone.
Not on one favored forehead fell of old the fire-tongued mira-
  cle,
But flamed o'er all the thronging host the baptism of the Holy
  Ghost ;
Heart answers heart ; in one desire the blending lines of prayer
  aspire ;
' Where, in my name, meet two or three,' The Christ hath said,
  ' I there will be ! '

" So sometimes comes to soul and sense the feeling, which is
  evidence,
That very near about us lies the realm of spiritual mysteries.
The sphere of the supernal powers impinges on this world of
  ours."

THE ANSWER.

" True Worship's deeper meaning lies in mercy and not sacrifice,
Not posturing of penitence, but love's unforced obedience.
The Book and Church and Day are given for man, not God,—
  for earth, not heaven.
The blessed means to holiest ends, not Masters are, but helping
  friends ;

And the dear Christ dwells not afar the King of some remoter star,—
Listening, at times, with flattered ear to homage wrung from selfish fear :—
But here, amidst the poor and blind, the bound and suffering of our kind,
In works we do, in prayers we pray, life of our life, he lives to-day."

"What care I that the crowd requite
 My love with hate, my truth with lies?
'T is but to Faith, and not to sight,
 The walls of God's true Temple rise!

"I 'll faint not, falter not, nor plead
 My weakness: Truth itself is strong:
The lion's strength, the eagle's speed,
 Are not alone vouchsafed to wrong.

"My nature, which, through fire and flood,
 To place or gain may fight its way,
Hath equal power to seek the Good,
 And Duty's holiest call obey.

"So, haply, when my task shall end,
 The Wrong shall lose itself in Right,
And all my week-day darkness blend
 With that long Sabbath of the Light."

"Grown wiser for the lesson given, I fear no longer, for I know
That, where the share is deepest driven, the best fruits grow.
The outworn rite, the old abuse, the pious fraud transparent grown,
The good held captive in the use of wrong alone,—

These wait their doom, from that great law which makes the past time serve to-day;
And fresher life the world shall draw from their decay.

"Take heart!—the Waster builds again,—a charmèd life old Goodness hath;
The tares may perish,—but the grain is not for death.

" God works in all things ; all obey His first propulsion from the
    night :
  Wake thou and watch !—the world is gray with morning
    light ! "

    " Blow, winds of God, awake and blow
      The mists of earth away ;
    Shine out, O Light Divine, and show
      How wide, and far we stray !

    " Our friend, our brother, and our Lord,
      What may thy service be ?—
    Not name, nor form, nor ritual word,
      But, simply following thee.

    " No fable old, nor mythic lore,
      Nor dreams of bards and seers,
    No dead fact, stranded on the shore
      Of the oblivious years ;

    " But warm, sweet, tender—even yet
      A present help is he,
    And faith has still its Olivet,
      And love its Galilee.

    " The letter fails, and systems pall,
      And every symbol wanes :
    The Spirit, over-brooding all—
      Eternal Love remains."

" If ye have precious truths that yet remain
  Unknown to me, Oh teach me them ! Each way
  Into my soul I open wide, that they
  May enter straightway, and belief constrain.
  But urge no fear of loss, nor hope of gain—
  Hell's terrors, nor Heaven's joys—to essay
  To force my soul's belief, or quench one ray
  Of inward Light ! such self-born faith would pain
  The Holy Ghost within—who asks assent
  Not even to simplest truths until the hour,
  Arrives of their belief-constraining power."

"I have not seen, I may not see,
My hopes for man take form in fact ;
But God will give the victory
In due time ; in that faith I act :
And he who sees the future sure,
The baffling present may endure ;
And bless, meanwhile, the Unseen Hand that leads
The heart's desire—beyond the halting step of deeds."

"O loving God of Nature ! Who through all
Hast never yet betrayed me to a fall,—
While following Creeds of men I went astray,
And in distressing mazes lost my way :
But turning back to Thee, I found Thee true,
Thy love unchanged and fresh as morning dew,—
Henceforth on Thee, and Thee alone, I rest,
No warring sects shall tear me from Thy breast.
I doubt no more, nor trust in man-made creeds :
Thy Light I trust, and follow where it leads."

"O friends, with whom my feet have trod
　　The quiet aisles of prayer,
　Glad witness to your zeal for God
　　And love of men I bear.

"I trace your lines of argument ;
　　Your logic, linked and strong,
　I weigh as one who dreads dissent,
　　And fears a doubt as wrong.

"But still my human hands are weak
　　To hold your iron creeds ;
　Against the words ye bid me speak,
　　My heart within me pleads.

"Who fathoms the Eternal Thought ?
　　Who talks of scheme and plan ?
　The Lord is God ! He needeth not
　　The poor device of man.

"I walk with bare, hushed feet the ground
  Ye tread with boldness shod;
I dare not fix with mete and bound
  The love and power of God.

"O brothers, if my faith is vain,
  If hopes like these betray,
Pray for me, that my feet may gain
  The sure and safer way!

"And thou, O Lord! by whom are seen
  Thy creatures as they be,
Forgive me if too close I lean
  My human heart on Thee!"

LIII.—REVERSIONS AND DEGENERATIONS WITH REFERENCE TO JESUS-WORSHIP AND MARIOLATRY.

The most emphatically quoted and enjoined of all Old Testament Scripture, by Jesus as also by all New Testament writers, was, "The first and great commandment" which forbids, as idolatry, all *worship* offered to any other than the one and only God. Who this one and only God is, Jesus constantly explained as Our Father or The Father. "Then saith Jesus unto him, Get thee hence, Satan; for it is written Thou shalt worship the Lord thy God, and Him only shalt thou serve. . . . God is spirit; and they that worship Him must worship Him in spirit and in truth. . . . The true worshippers shall worship the Father. . . . The Father seeketh such to worship Him. . . . When ye pray, say Our Father." All Old Testament worship was of The One God Jehovah alone; and all New Testament worship was of the One God the Father alone. And yet the masses of Protestants to-day worship Jesus *almost to the exclusion* of the Father, even as the masses of Romanists worship the Virgin and the Saints almost to the exclusion of both Jesus and the Father. Jesus-Worship is the popular worship in all the "Orthodox" Protestant Denominations as Mary-Worship is in the Roman Church. Both alike, and equally, are idolatry; both are reversions to Heathenism. Praying *in the name of*—" Calling upon the name of "—Jesus, or of Mary, or of any real saint; reverencing, admiring, adoring one, or all, of these is one thing. Worshipping them, praying *to* them, confusing or confounding them with the Father—The One and Only God—*whom alone men are commanded to worship and taught to pray to*, this is quite another thing. The former is Scriptural and reasonable; the latter is unscriptural, heathenish, idolatrous.

Corrective Quotations.

" Ill-informed persons are apt to suppose, that the disciples were accustomed to worship their Master as God, even while he lived familiarly among them in Galilee and Jerusalem—a conclusion utterly unfounded and untenable. Thus we read, 'Then came to him the mother of Zebedee's children, worshipping him.' The word used in this and other such cases does not denote religious worship, but only the respectful salutation or obeisance which one person might offer to another, probably by prostration in the oriental manner. This may be clearly seen from a parallel expression in the same Gospel, relating to the unforgiving servant and his lord: 'The servant, therefore, fell down and worshipped him saying, Lord, have patience with me, and I will pay thee all.'

"We have in these cases examples of the old and well-known meaning of the English word 'worship'—that is all. The Greek verb strictly and exclusively denoting religious worship is a different word, and this is *never* applied to Jesus. It will be found that in no instance was Jesus the object of religious worship during his lifetime. Even after his resurrection, when it is said that his disciples saw him 'and worshipped him,' the word used is the more general word, expressive of respectful and reverent salutation. An excellent illustrative example occurs in Genesis xxxvii. 6, where the sheaves are said to have 'made obeisance' to Joseph's sheaf. The word thus rendered is, in the Septuagint version of Genesis, expressed by the *same* Greek word which, in the English N. T., has been so often and so indiscriminately rendered 'worshipped,' as applied to Jesus and other highly respected persons in common.

"Of any other kind of worship than this being offered to Jesus there is no trace anywhere in the New Testament. We know that it was a charge brought by the Jews against the Christians in later times, when probably the worship of Jesus was growing up into an established practice. It is impossible that it should not have been brought forward by the bigoted enemies of the early Christianity, had fitting occasion been afforded to them. But there is no trace of it in the Book of Acts, or in any other book of the New Testament. The inevitable inference is, that during the first century such a charge was not thought of, and could not be made, in the face of the fact that the disciples did *not* speak of Jesus Christ as God, nor pay him religious adoration.

"When Jesus taught his disciples to pray, he said nothing about the adoration or worship of himself. He told them to say, 'Our Father which art in heaven.' He even said to them that, after he was gone from them, they were to ask him nothing, but to ask the Father in his name. He said to the woman of Samaria in clear and precise terms, which it might be thought that no one could misunderstand or explain away, that 'the true worshippers shall worship the Father in spirit and in truth.' In the Book of the Acts we find a prayer of the disciples recorded, and to whom is it addressed? 'They lifted up their voice to God with one accord and said, Lord, thou art God, which hast made heaven, and earth, and the sea, and all that in them is.' It is unnecessary to quote more, for it is evident to whom the prayer of the assembled disciples was here offered, and that it was in no sense to Jesus Christ. Similarly, on the evening before his crucifixion, Jesus himself, according to the fourth Evangelist, prayed and said, 'Father, the hour is come; glorify thy Son, that thy Son also may glorify thee. . . . And this is life eternal, that they might know THEE, the only true God, and Jesus Christ whom thou hast sent.'"

"Wherever, in short, there is any clear statement in the New Testament as to the prayers or the worship of the first Christians, it is always to the same effect. It is in no case Jesus that is addressed. The great Object of religious worship is everywhere God, the Heavenly Father, even 'the God and Father of Jesus Christ.'

"It was nearly two hundred years before that peculiar development of Christianity, since known as Jesus-Worship, reached predominance, at and through the Council of Nicæa. But such an advance as this, or anything like it, can nowhere be seen within the limits of the New Testament. Let any one compare the abundant and varied evidence of the worship of Jesus found in hymns and liturgical forms of the time of Tertullian in the third century—let any one compare and contrast that with the total absence of everything of the kind from the Christian books. It requires nothing more to show that the worship of Jesus, like that of the Virgin Mary, was the growth of a long period of time, and of a credulous and superstitious period. It requires nothing more to show how highly unjustifiable, on Scriptural grounds, is the modern practice of the Churches of uniting Jesus Christ in an equal offering of worship with Him 'who is above all,' whom Jesus himself habitually worshipped, and whom, even in the fourth Gospel, he is recorded to have addressed in prayer as 'the Only True God.'

"When the grand hereditary truth of Judaism, which is transmitted to Christianity, was lost sight of in the third and fourth centuries of our era, polytheism and idolatry in new forms sprang up forthwith, and multiplied with rapid increase through the whole mediæval period. First, the Son, then the Virgin Mother, and at length countless hosts of saints and martyrs, rose into the rank of Deity, and were invoked with fervent prayers—the last personage so exalted being usually the most popular object of worship; till, finally, at the altars which filled the churches before the Reformation, the name of the Father Himself was never heard.

LIV.—REVERSIONS AND DEGENERATIONS WITH REFERENCE TO CONCEPTIONS OF THE HOLY GHOST.

The common conception of the *coming* and *presence* of the Holy Ghost has reverted and degenerated from that lofty one found in the Bible to something like the following:— The God-Family from all Eternity consisted of three Persons. These three kept close and continual companionship until the necessity came for one to go and try to save the fallen and perishing Human Race. The second Person of the Trinity offered to go and remain on Earth thirty-three years; the third Person, meanwhile, to remain with the first Person to help Him, and to keep Him company. This "scheme" was accepted and fulfilled:—with the understanding, however, that, when the "expiatory work" was done and the "body of flesh and blood" brought back, by the second Person, into Heaven, "there forever to dwell," the third Person would be spared to go and complete the "Redemptive Scheme." Hence it came to pass that, about forty days after the Ascension of the second Person, came the Descension of the third Person,—*His first appearance upon Earth*. The second Person has, ever since, "remained at the right hand" of the first Person "on High"; while the third Person has been trying to carry forward the redemptive work of Mankind. On the "Day of Pentecost" the Holy Ghost descended *for the first time;* before that day no one had ever "received the Holy Ghost"; since that, all who believe on Jesus as an "Atoning Sacrifice" and are baptized with water in the Triune Name—and none others—also "receive the Holy Ghost." That this is not travesty—much less scoffing or ridicule—let any intelligent and honest person prove by listening to the preaching, teaching, and worship in the "orthodox" Churches of all denominations and names. In five out of six he will probably gain this as the popular conception.

Correcting Quotations.

"Our English words *Ghost* and *Spirit*, the one of Anglo-Saxon, the other of Latin origin, correspond to and represent only *one* word in the original Scriptures, Hebrew and Greek respectively. This should unquestionably everywhere be rendered by 'Spirit,' especially in the New Testament, the word *Ghost* being, in our days, by no means free from objectionable associations. It can only tend to convey false impressions to many English readers, to use sometimes the one, sometimes the other, in an English version of the New Testament, the original word being always, without exception, the single neuter substantive πνεῦμα.

"This 'Holy Spirit' has been upon the Earth and in the souls of men from the beginning till now. In the Old Testament all life, intelligence, mental energy, and mental skill, were of its operation. 'The Spirit of God moved upon the face of the waters' at the dawn of creation, and reduced the chaos into order. The same inspiration upholds us in being, gives us understanding and strength to do whatever man is capable of doing; and when that Divine power is withdrawn, we die and return to the dust.

"It is evident that, in all such representations, what is really meant by the term in question, is no other than God Himself. It is the Almighty Being, inscrutably putting forth His power in the creation, support, control, inspiration, of the universe of animate and inanimate things—acting upon us and in us by the operation of His living and will energy. There is nothing to shew that the ancient writers of the Old Testament, in thus speaking of the active power of God, ever attributed to it a separate personal existence. Nor has this, in fact, ever been maintained. The Holy Spirit, in the older Scriptures, is indeed the Divine Being in His action upon the material world, and in communion with the soul of man; but this fact will not justify us in saying that it is 'God the Holy Spirit,' as though it were a something distinct, something to be thought of and named as God, apart from Him who alone is Jehovah and The Father. The personal conception, if admitted into the Old Testament, would manifestly tend directly to weaken or destroy the proper monotheistic idea of the Mosaic religion. It will be found, that nothing approaching to so dangerous an infringement of the great characteristic principle of that religion is anywhere to be met with throughout the Hebrew Books.

"The truth of these statements may be shewn by a reference to various expressions which occur in the New Testament. When Jesus reasoned with the Jews respecting his own authority as a Divine teacher, and the power by which he wrought his miracles, he said to them, as reported by the first Evangelist, 'If I cast out devils by the Spirit of God, then the kingdom of God is come unto you.' In the parallel place in St. Luke, the same saying is reported thus : 'If I with the finger of God cast out devils, no doubt the kingdom of God is come upon you.' The two forms of expression were evidently understood by the Evangelists to mean the same thing. What that meaning is cannot be doubtful, and is well illustrated by the words of the fourth Gospel, where Jesus says on another occasion, 'The Father that dwelleth in me, he doeth the works.' But this, again, cannot reasonably be taken to mean that the Infinite Father was in Christ, in the Evangelist's conception, in any other way than by the Divine help and power which He gave him; or, also, by means of the indwelling Logos; and such forms of expression simply amount, in fact, as already observed, to the statement of the Apostle Peter at the Pentecost. The Almighty Father was manifested in Jesus, and, in the Apostle's conception, was seen to be so, 'by miracles and wonders and signs which God *did by Him*.'

"It is thus clear, that the 'finger of God' and the 'Spirit of God' are simply God Himself, the Heavenly Father, acting in and through the Christ; and it is no more necessary, or allowable, to make a separate person of the Spirit, than it is to suppose such a distinction to be hidden or implied in the phrase 'the finger of God.'

"There are still one or two facts to be mentioned which are wholly unaccountable on the supposition of the truth of the popular teaching on this subject. First, there is no doxology, or ascription of praise, to the Holy Spirit, in either the Old or the New Testament. Nor is there any instance, we believe, on record, in all the Scriptures, of any prayer having ever been addressed to the Holy Spirit *as a separate personality*. It is inconceivable that this should be the case, had this Divine power been regarded in the early Christian times as *separately* God, a definite personal being, even as much so as the Almighty Father.

"It is, indeed, in the second place, to be remembered, that no example can be adduced, from the first and second centuries, of the Holy Spirit being made an object of worship, or perhaps even of its being spoken of as a distinct existence —as distinguished, that is to say, from the idea of it as a power, gift, blessing, conferred by God. Even in the Apostles' Creed, which probably comes down from the end of the second century, the Holy Spirit does not appear in a *personal* character. It may be questioned whether it does so in the original Nicene Creed, although at the time when this was composed (A.D. 325), the doctrine of a Trinity *of equal persons* was beginning to be held by some of the more speculative of the Church Fathers. The absence of the fuller definition of the Spirit from the Nicene Creed proper is well known. It was the Council of Constantinople (A.D. 381) which introduced the longer form now found in the English Prayer Book.

"No reasonable mind can suppose that the Spirit of God is confined in its movements within the limits of Churches, one or all of them; that it can only visit the humble, waiting soul through the medium of a 'Sacrament' or through the person of a 'priest.'

"All true religion, whether in 'Church' or out of it, is founded upon, is identical with, the sense of the Living Presence of God with and in the human soul—that alone. Such is also the evident foundation of Christianity, as recognized in almost every act and word of the Christ and his Apostles. With them, the Heavenly Father is the all-pervading Spirit of the universe, a living God, who can hear our prayers, and see our efforts to do His will; and who, by His Spirit, can help, enlighten, and comfort the souls of all that faithfully look to Him, whether they shall bow down in the humblest meeting-house, or in the grandest cathedral of human Art. Not, indeed, in the presence of elaborately or superstitiously observed formalities, any more than amidst fanatical noise and excitement, can we think that the Spirit of God most effectually visits the waiting soul, or lets the 'still, small voice' of His presence be most clearly and touchingly heard within the heart. It is rather in the hour of quiet and lonely meditation that this will come to pass:— when we think with penitence about our past sins, when we reflect upon the duties we have to do, and how best we may do them, when we strive and pray to give ourselves up to all God's will concerning us; then will the communion of His Holy Spirit be ours; 'the grace of Jesus Christ' be with us, and the Divine Love be shed upon us. Then, too, shall we know that we are true disciples of His Son, acceptable servants and children of our Father which is in Heaven."

LV.—REVERSIONS AND DEGENERATIONS WITH REFERENCE TO CONCEPTIONS OF THE ATONING SACRIFICE.

Not less and less, but more and more, the entire public Worship of Roman (and Greek) Catholicism is becoming *one unceasing* "Mass"; a perpetually reoffered Sacrifice of the body and blood of Christ upon the Altars of Cathedrals and Churches: without participation in which no human soul can be saved. Not less and less, but more and more, the Anglican and Protestant Episcopal Churches are tending to this same reversion and degeneration. Rarely now can be found a Communion Table; all are "Altars." Rarely now do we hear of a preacher, or a prophet, or even of a minister; all are "Priests." All the paraphernalia, and ceremonies, and vestments, and Altar-adornments, and fastings, and genuflections of Romanism are slowly but surely creeping into the Anglican and Episcopal Churches all over Great Britain and America, and their outlying Mission Fields in common. They call it the "enrichment" of their services. Among the "Denominations" or "Sects" there is, happily, an almost universal tendency *upward*—instead of *downward* —in this regard. We must except, however, the Revivalistic Sects and the Salvation Army, and similar organizations whose singing, preaching, and praying are all about "the atoning blood"—*even more than ever.*

Correcting Quotations.

"On the subject of the death of Christ, it may be enough to remind the reader that this is nowhere in the New Testament, or in the Apostolic Church, represented as possessed of a propitiatory or expiatory efficacy, *in the old heathen sense of such expressions.* It was simply the Providential means by which the admission of the Gentile world was secured to the faith of the Gospel. The phraseology in which it is spoken of is, indeed, at times very largely figurative—arising naturally out of the Levitical ideas and institutions of the Jews. But, while this is true, one literal fact is usually expressed by it. That fact is what has just been stated—not the incredible doctrine that the All-merciful God, in His 'wrath,' required to be propitiated by the death of an innocent victim; nor the equally incredible doctrine that Christ's death has redeemed men from everlasting sufferings in hell, because he has borne their punishment, and thus given 'satisfaction' to Infinite Justice. No such barbarous ideas as these are anywhere either plainly stated in the New Testament, or veiled and conveyed, as in a parable, under its more figurative expressions.

"It follows by necessary consequence, that the Romanist and high Anglican doctrine of the Sacrament of the Lord's Supper, as also the common doctrine of the 'Atoning Blood,' are perversions of Christianity and reversions to Paganism. All these miserable animosities and controversies to which these doctrines have given origin have been only so much energy misapplied and wasted, or worse. There is no Scriptural evidence whatever, no evidence at all which rises above the character of early Christian superstition, by which the Lord's Supper can be shewn to be of the nature of a sacrifice for sin, requiring to be perpetually renewed by a 'sacrificing priest.' There is no evidence, in truth, worthy of the name, by which it can be shewn to be anything else, in its institution and nature, but a simple service of devout commemoration. 'Do this in remembrance of me,' are the words of Christ himself, when he founded the rite. Whatever, in modern doctrines concerning it or concerning the nature of Christ's death, passes beyond this, in form or in spirit, can only be set down as misunderstanding, or as the inherited remains of ancient error."

LVI.—REVERSIONS AND DEGENERATIONS WITH REFERENCE TO ARCHITECTURE AND ADORNMENTS AS CONSTITUTING A CHURCH.

When the Disciples directed their Master's attention to the magnificent Temple in Jerusalem, they doubtless still retained some of the prevalent conception that the value, or truth, of a religion is signified, if not measured, by its external glory and show. The Master quickly rebuked this erroneous conception by his pointed reply: "Not one stone shall be left upon another." Never were the externalities of the Jewish Church—Temple, Synagogues, throngs of devoted worshippers, immense offerings of the rich, zeal for Orthodoxy and for Ritual and for the True Church—so magnificent or flourishing or intense. And yet all was "a whitewashed Sepulchre full of dead men's bones." So may it be in all days, and to-day and here. Certain it is that, everywhere, chief emphasis is now being placed on finely constructed and adorned church edifices; and more and more so. If you have not these you are nobody; having these you have (practically) everything! Grinding demands upon the purses of poor and rich alike are made to secure these; and crushing burdens of debt are imposed, rendering the one unceasing object of the Church seemingly to be—*to raise money!* And with it all, so often, a *decrease* of Spiritual Life! As our Prophet-Bishop used so often to exclaim: "All this complicated Machinery and magnificent Equipment of the Christian Church, while *the fires beneath are smouldering or gone out!*" If this be true, or in proportion as it is true, of any Church it is surely reverting and becoming degenerate. And "not one stone shall be left upon another that shall not be thrown down."

Said Epictetus: "If you have a mind to adorn your city by consecrated monuments, first consecrate in yourselves that most beautiful of all monuments, a character formed to purity, justice, and benevolence. Not by raising magnificent temples will you confer the greatest benefits upon mankind, but by exalting magnificent souls. Do not variegate the structure of your walls with Eubæan and Spartan stones only, but adorn yourselves with culture and virtue, for God is honored by the characters of those who worship him, not by wood or stone."

The original *church* was the *people* without reference to the place; they might meet in an upper room, in a private house, beneath a tree, in an open field, in a cave or cavern of the earth, it was all the same a church:—not *it* but *they*, the people assembled. To such churches as these Paul wrote all his letters; and through the agency of such churches,— not aided by magnificent piles of architecture, nor by architecture of any sort, but aided simply by the enthusiasm of Humanity and of the Divine Spirit which had taken complete possession of them—through the agency of such, houseless, homeless, roofless churches, (*assemblies of devout people*, organized and co-operating for devout purposes), was brought about that wonderful reformation of the first and second centuries we call the introduction and propagation of Christianity.

LVII.—REVERSIONS AND DEGENERATIONS WITH REFERENCE TO RITUALISTIC OR OTHER SENSATIONAL OR "POPULARISED" FORMS OF WORSHIP.

When the tempter said to Jesus "If thou be the Son of God cast thyself down," he simply proposed to him the adoption of the popular methods of degenerate Religions the world over. By parade, trick, or show, attract the crowd and secure success! Wherever, whenever, or *howsoever* this is done it is a yielding to the Devil, and is a reversion to

Heathenism. Elaborate Ritual is only a more refined form of that *many-formed* Sensationalism by which the Church and Religion are made popular so *as to catch and please the masses.* This is the "wide gate and broad way that leads to" *Degeneration;* "and many there be that go in thereat."

Correcting Quotations.

"In the ruder stages of national and individual life, men are educated religiously by and through the aid of sensuous imagery, either in outward embodiment, or in those ceremonial observances which suggest and typify the inward and recondite truths aimed at,—which Paganism everywhere uses, which with a nicer application and a wiser forelook made up the Hebrew polity, and which the Church of Rome now so largely retains in her ritual,—or in those less gross and ideal forms which make the staple of our modern creeds and practices; and it remains yet a profound problem, whether, dispensing with them, society could have attained the spiritual culture and intellectual elevation which now characterize it. Yet, with all the admitted advantages which have flowed from such a machinery, it has been liable to the most serious abuse, when not closely watched and guarded by divine counteractants, in landing the devotee into the depths of a degraded and besotted idolatry. The reason is apparent: between the idea or truth aimed at, and the human mind on which it is to be impressed, stands the symbol, the rite, the agency, the instituted means; by ceremony, by picture, by cross, by altar, by temple, by whatever of sensuous appliance designed to aid the imagination and impress the sensibilities, which tradition or custom may have introduced and sanctioned. Here intervening as by authority, they gain for themselves a lodgment, which gradually obscures the truth they were originally designed to symbolize; and so the agency supplants the principle, and what was intended as the scaffolding comes in process of time to be regarded as the building. *And, by a degeneracy easily understood, the imagination dominates every other faculty, and leads to the worship of the altar, instead of God; the cross, instead* of Him who died on it ; or wastes the sensibilities in an absurd flutter of robes and tippets of sacred millinery, and the ritualistic posture—putting of head and hands and knees to ape the external form of a devotion which has wholly escaped the heart.

"The religious sense turned awry, all is disordered and out of harmony. Egypt—Greece—Rome! what a sad worship, and a sadder morality, when the keen eye of Paul rested on the Acropolis, or scanned the magnificence of the palaces of the Cæsars! And just as the religion of mankind is withdrawn from common life and practice, and becomes a thing of parade and priestcraft,—a liturgical and transactional economy carried on for its own sake, and apart from the people,—it becomes an institution builded—every wall, and tower, and turret—to subserve the personal or corporate power and aggrandizement of those who conduct its mysteries or minister at its altars! And lo! we have at once repeated a historic picture of Dagon and Juggernaut, the priestcraft of India, Egypt, and Rome. Yet all this spiritual darkness and despotism, which has rested so long upon the nations, originated in a simple perversion of the religious instincts of humanity, from supplanting the substance by the symbol, and enthroning the means in place of the end."

LVIII.—MODERN CONFIRMATIONS—A FEW OUT OF MANY.

"*Out of the heart of Nature rolled*
The burden of the Bible old."

"Our highest Orpheus walked in Judea eighteen hundred years ago. His sphere-melody, flowing in wild, native tones, took captive the ravished souls of men ; and, being of a truth sphere-melody, still flows and sounds, though now with thousand-fold accompaniments and rich symphonies, through all our hearts, and modulates and divinely leads them."

"Let knowledge grow from more to more,
 But more of reverence in us dwell;
 That mind and soul, according well,
May make one music as before,
But *vaster.*"

"The truth-seeker is the only God-seeker.

"The curse of both religion and science, in all ages, has been the thought that there was somewhere an ultimate,— a place to stop. Here we are, finite minds in the midst of infinity. And, for the finite that is moving toward infinity, there is nowhere a place to anchor, but only the privilege and the opportunity of endless exploration."

"Beneath all the various widespread and disconnected labors, discoveries, and experiments of the great body of scientific workers, there is the common belief that all scientific truth is one; that the universe is all of one piece; that distant truths are only different parts of one divine pattern that runs all through the whole visible garment of God. This scientific faith is grander than any that the religious world has yet attained. But we must come to this. Religious truth is one, as God is one. Go forth, then, ye religious explorers, and seek only for truth; knowing that all truth-seekers are brothers, and must come to hand-clasping and looks of recognition by and by!"

"I apprehend that there is but one way of putting an end to our present dissensions; and that is, not the triumph of any existing system over all others, but the acquisition of something better than the best we now have."

"We search the world for truth, we cull
 The good, the pure, the beautiful
 From graven stone and written scroll,
 From the old flower-fields of the soul;

> And, weary seekers of the best,
> We come back laden from our quest,
> To find that all the sages said,
> Is in the Book our mothers read."

"After all that Biblical critics and antiquarian research have raked from the dust of antiquity in proof of the genuineness and authenticity of the books of the new Testament, credibility still labors with the fact that the age in which these books were received and put in circulation was one in which the science of criticism as developed by the moderns—the science which scrutinizes statements, balances evidence for and against, and sifts the true from the false—did not exist; an age when a boundless credulity disposed men to believe in wonders as readily as in ordinary events, requiring no stronger proof in the case of the former than sufficed to establish the latter, namely, hearsay and vulgar report; an age when literary honesty was a virtue almost unknown, and when, consequently, literary forgeries were as common as genuine productions, and transcribers of sacred books did not scruple to alter the text in the interest of personal views and doctrinal prepossessions."

> "The word unto the prophets spoken
> Was writ on tables yet unbroken;
> The word by seers or sibyls told,
> In groves of oak or fanes of gold,
> Still floats upon the morning wind,
> Still whispers to the willing mind.
> One accent of the Holy Ghost
> The heedless world hath never lost."

"The two indispensable conditions of a nobler and truer theology for the time to come, are, first, a thoroughly honest use of learning—a determination never to ignore or evade whatever criticism history or science demonstrates to be *fact*, however it may upset our preconceived notions or unsettle our traditional belief; and, secondly, to cultivate with the utmost veneration and tenderness that spiritual element of our being which brings us into living communion with God, and which, though wonderfully nourished and strengthened by the teachings of Scripture, flows from the same divine source, and is only another working of one and the self-same Spirit which uttered Scripture itself."

"The fact, so much lamented over by the clergy and the religious press, that so many of the most intelligent minds of the country are already turning their backs upon Christianity, clearly finds an explanation to no small extent in the blind folly of Christianity in continuing to demand that men must subscribe to the belief in an infallible Bible or else stay outside the Christian fold. Why does this folly continue? Is Christianity bent upon intellectual suicide? Can it be possible that it does not see that it is putting itself in a position where men who read and think for themselves on religious subjects, have no alternative left them?—they must either subscribe to what they do not believe to be true, or else they must turn their backs on Christianity!"

"The collection of writings which forms the Bible is, in its greater part, the remains of the ancient Hebrew literature. It is not a Creed nor a Creed-book, which men are called upon to receive under penalty of damnation. It nowhere claims to be so. Nor is it a body of immutable laws for our time, or for any other. Many of its ideas on creation, on the Divine Being, and His intercourse with men, and on various other subjects, are simply such as were suited to the infancy of the human race. The Bible may nevertheless, if wisely used, be a help and an influence to guide and enlighten the conscience; as it is a channel through which the Unseen Spirit has often spoken to men, and may still speak to us, if we will listen."

"The experience of many ages of speculative revolution has shown that while knowledge grows and old beliefs fall away, and creed succeeds to creed, nevertheless that Faith which makes the innermost essence of Religion is indestructible."

"No one would venture now-a-days, to quote from a book, whether sacred or profane, without having asked these simple and yet momentous questions: When was it written? Where? and by whom? Was the author an eye-witness, or does he only relate what he has heard from others? And if the latter, were his authorities at least contemporaneous with the events which they relate, and were they under the sway of party feeling or any other disturbing influence? Was the whole book written at once, or does it contain portions of an earlier date; and if so, is it possible for us to separate these earlier documents from the body of the book?"

"Neither shall ye tear out one another's eyes, struggling over 'Plenary Inspiration' and such like; try rather to get a little even Partial Inspiration, each of you for himself."

"An Inspiration as true, as real, and as certain, as that which ever prophet or apostle reached, is yours if you will."

"Jesus came to reveal the Father. But is God, the Infinite and Universal Father, made known only by a single voice heard ages ago on the banks of the Jordan or by the Sea of Tiberias? Is it an unknown tongue that the heavens and earth forever utter? Is nature's page a blank? Does the human soul report nothing of its Creator? Does conscience announce no Authority higher than its own? Does reason discern no trace of an Intelligence, that it cannot comprehend, and yet of which it is itself a ray? Does the heart find in the circuits of creation no Friend worthy of trust and love?"

"Our own religion takes a place not distant from, but *among*, all religions, past or present. Its relation to them, is not that they are earth-born, while it alone is divine, but it is the relation of one member of a family to other members, who 'are all brothers, having one work, one hope, and one All-Father.'"

"Every race above the savage has its Bible. Each of the great religions of mankind has its Bible. These books contain the highest and deepest thoughts respecting man's relations with the Infinite above him, with his fellows around, and with the mystery of his own inward being. In them are found the purest expressions of faith and hope, the finest aspirations after truth, the sweetest sentiments of confidence and trust, hymns of praise, proverbs of wisdom, readings of the moral law, interpretations of Providence, studies in the workings of destiny, rules for worship, directions for piety, prayers, prophesies, sketches of saintly character, narratives of holy lives, lessons in devoutness, humility, patience, and charity."

"There is a common impression that the Bible has created a religion for man by a positive enactment. The Bible has not made religion, but religion and righteousness have made the Bible."

"In holy books we read how God hath spoken
To holy men in many different ways;
But hath the present worked no sign nor token?
Is God quite silent in these latter days?

> "The word were but a blank, a hollow sound,
>   If He that spoke it were not speaking still;
>   If all the light and all the shade around
>   Were aught but issues of Almighty Will."

"The only safe way of meeting this danger (that threatens the Bible—the danger, on one hand, of hostility; and, on the other, of indifference), is to find, as grounds for men's continued veneration and use of the Bible, propositions which can be verified, and which are unassailable. This, then, has been our object: to find sure and safe grounds for the continued use and authority of the Bible."

LIX.—ILLUSTRATIVE SELECTIONS FROM RECENT BOOKS BEARING ON THE HIGHER CRITICISM OF THE BIBLE.*

1.—*The Infallible Book.*

In early times the use of metals was unknown, and consequently the knives which the priests of a certain religion used in connection with certain of their rites, of necessity had to be of stone. Later, when metal had come into use, we should naturally suppose the crude stone knife would give place to a better knife of metal. Not so, however! The knife originally used was of stone; nothing else therefore would ever do in any future time but a stone knife. The fact that the Book had grown to be regarded as infallible petrified the religion it taught —cut off the possibility of future progress and improvement,— made sacred every crudeness, every imperfection, every childish rite or ceremony, as well as every false doctrine which, but for the notion of a faultless Book, the people in due time would have outgrown.

Thus it is that in India a single text of the Vedas (misinterpreted, at that) resulted in the immolation of vast numbers of widows on the funeral piles of their husbands. Thus, too, it is, that we see many a religious rite practised, and many an

---

* See list of volumes chiefly selected from on opening pages—page 9.

absurd doctrine believed to-day in Christendom, which long ago would have been laid aside but for the notion of a Book whose every word must be accepted, and whose lightest injunction must be carried out to the letter, as long as time lasts. *Men can't get away from the stone knife.*"

"Another thing seems to be common with nearly all the great Sacred Books of the world, or rather with the believers in nearly all these books; and that is, that, just as soon as any one of these books comes to be set up as a Bible, it is from that time forward regarded by its adherents as the *only* Bible, and all the other Sacred Books of the world are cast out as false. In other words, the process of canonization of a book, if I may so say, or of lifting it up from a merely good book into a Bible, seems as a rule, to be a process of degradation or condemnation of all other books and religions. So the Buddhist has ever been the bitter foe of the Brahman, and the Mohammedan of the Buddhist, and the Christian of the Mohammedan. Whereas, the evident truth is, each of the world's Bibles contains a great deal that is good, with more or less that is of no value, if not positively bad. Each religion has divine elements in it, as well as elements that are very undivine, and it is a great pity that the eyes of men should be blinded to this fact. It is not only a great pity that the adherents of other Bibles and religions of the world should be blinded to this fact as regards our Christian Scriptures and religion, but it is also a pity that we should be blinded to the same fact as regards scriptures and religions which are not Christian."

"In regard to our Old Testament, as is well known, the idea of infallibility attached first to the Pentateuch, or the Five Books of Moses, or the Law, as it was called. And the infallibility of even this seems to have been something very shadowy and intangible for a long time. The part of the Old Testament called by the Jews The Prophets came next to be so regarded; while all that part then known as Hagiographa, or Chetubim, and including such books as the Psalms, and Proverbs, and Job, which are generally held to-day in higher esteem than any other of the Old Testament books, did not come to be regarded as really sacred much before the time of Christ. Indeed, at the time of Christ, all this part of the Old Testament was ranked much lower in authority, or sacredness, than the rest."

"As to the New Testament writings, the Epistles seem to have come to be regarded as authoritative, considerably earlier than the Gospels or the Acts. But for a long time—certainly for two centuries—the New Testament writings were none of them looked upon by the Christian church as equally sacred with the Old Testament. And at least three or four centuries passed away before it was decided, more than in part, which particular ones, of the large number of writings produced within a century or two after the death of Jesus, should be included in the New Testament canon."

2.—*Ideas and Forms Common to all Religions.*

"The ideas of immaculate conceptions and virgin mothers and virgin-born gods are common to many religions and Bibles besides the Jewish and Christian. The Greek god Mars was fabled to have been born by an immaculate conception of Juno. Zoroaster was supposed to have been born of an immaculate conception by a ray from the Divine Reason. Both Buddha and Krishna of India are reported to have been immaculately conceived. The Hindoo Scriptures tell us that the mother of the latter (Krishna) was overshadowed by the god Brahma. The Messianic idea, too, is one found in other Bibles besides our own. The Chinese Scriptures contain prophecies of a Chinese Messiah who was to come. The Hindoo Scriptures contain like prophecies of a Hindoo Messiah."

"In the different religions of the human race, we constantly meet the same leading features. The same religious institutions—monks, missionaries, priests, and pilgrims. The same ritual—prayers, liturgies, sacrifices. The same implements—frankincense, candles, holy water, relics, amulets, votive offerings. The same symbols—the cross, the serpent, the all-seeing eye, the halo of rays. The same prophecies and miracles—the dead restored and evil spirits cast out. The same holy days; for Easter and Christmas were kept as spring and autumn festivals, centuries before our era, by Egyptians, Persians, Saxons, Romans. The same artistic designs for the mother and child stand depicted, not only in the temples of Europe, but in those of Etruria and Arabia, Egypt and Thibet." "So also the idea of incarnation. He (the Messiah) is predicted by prophecy, hailed by sages, born of a virgin, attended by miracle, borne to heaven without tasting death, and with promise of return. Zoroaster and Confucius have no human father. Osiris is the Son of God; he is called the Revealer of Life and Light; he first teaches one chosen race; he then goes with his apostles to teach the Gentiles, conquering the world by peace; he is slain by evil powers: after death he descends into hell, then rises again, and presides at the last judgment of mankind; those who call upon his name shall be saved. Buddha is born of a virgin; his name means the Word, the Logos, but he is known more tenderly as the Saviour of Man; he embarrasses his teachers, when a child, by his understanding and answers; he is tempted in the wilderness, when older, etc."

3.—*False and Fanciful Interpretations.*

"The Brahmin, repeating Vedic hymns, sees them pervaded by a thousand meanings, which have been handed down by tradition; the one of which he is ignorant is that which *we* perceive to be the true one." "Greater violence is done by successive interpreters to sacred writings than to any other relics of ancient literature. Ideas grow and change, yet each generation tries to find its own ideas reflected in the sacred pages of their early prophets. Passages in the Veda and Zend Avesta which do not bear on religious or philosophical doctrines are generally explained simply and naturally, even by the latest of native commentators. But as soon as any word or sentence can be so turned as to support a *religious* doctrine, however modern, or a *religious* precept, however irrational, the simplest phrases are tortured and mangled till at last they are made to yield their assent to ideas the most foreign to the minds of the authors of the Veda and Zend Avesta." "This practice of interpreting into Sacred Books what later ages think ought to be in them, and out of them what later ages think ought not to be in them, is pointed out and illustrated with regard to the Chinese, Brahmanic and Buddhist Sacred Books, by Dr. Legge, Dr. Muir, Burnouf, and others."

"Illustrations of the same with regard to our own Bible are more numerous still. Indeed the whole history of Christianity is full of exhibitions of the most marvellous and unflagging ingenuity, in inventing new interpretations of Scripture, to keep pace with the growth of human thought and the progress of knowledge and science."

"Almost every scientific theory that comes into existence is found to conflict in some point or other with the theological notions which an unscientific past has handed down. But the theologians are ever on the alert ; and war to the knife is at once declared against the scientific intruder. All friends of the Bible are summoned to the holy war. The conflict rages fiercely and shows no sign of abatement *until it is seen that the scientists are getting the day ;* then, it begins to be discovered by the theologians that, after all, the new theory is harmless ! *indeed there is no discrepancy between it and Scripture !* The discrepancy that had been supposed to exist grew out of a wrong Scripture interpretation. In fact, instead of the two being in conflict, the scientific theory is really taught in the Bible."

4.—*Infallible Bibles must be Infallibly preserved.*

"Grant even that the Bible was originally infallible,—that is to say, grant that the books were written in such a marvellous way as to insure their infallible correctness at the time of their writing ; and grant that all the books which have been excluded from the canon of Old Testament and New by us Protestants, are just the ones that ought to be excluded, and that all which have been included are just the ones that ought to be included, and that all which have been lost were spurious, so that the loss does not affect at all the perfectness of the canon—grant all that ; yet even now how far have we got toward certainty that this Bible which we hold in our hand *to-day* is infallible—is infallible *as it comes to us ?* In other words, grant that the stream as it began its course away back yonder in Palestine twenty-two or twenty, or eighteen, or sixteen centuries ago, was infallible in its outset, what assurance have we that now, after wandering and winding down through the dark maze of the ages, it is *still* infallible ? For mark : after we have got the writings all infallibly written, and then after we have got them all collected together just as they should be into a canon or infallible collection, we have still got to devise a way to get them down to our time, *without error or change.*"

5.—The Translators must be Infallible.

"To-day translators are very fallible beings. Have the translators of all the ages, who have translated Hebrew into Greek and Latin, and Greek and Latin into English, and Hebrew into English, in connection with the Old and New Testament books, been miraculously preserved from making errors? If so, what mean the many thousands of errors which the great Commission of English scholars, who made for us a new English translation of the Bible, found in the common translation or version of King James?

"'The whole number of various readings of the text of the New Testament that have hitherto been noted exceeds a hundred thousand, and may perhaps amount to a hundred and fifty thousand. Some of these variations, it is true, are very slight, and in no way affect the sense. But others again are very marked, and affect the sense most materially. For example, the celebrated text (I. John v. 7, 8) of the three heavenly witnesses, which has been for a thousand years the strongest scripture bulwark of the doctrine of the Trinity, is admitted now on all hands to be an interpolation.'

"So, then, what becomes of our infallible Bible? It has melted away into thin air *if there be one single link imperfect in all the two-thousand-years-long chain of preservation and transmission of the original writings down to us.*"

6.—Miraculous Inspiration no longer Credible.

"The Bible does not claim to be infallible. While in places certain claims of superior inspiration or guidance of God are doubtless put forth, there is not even one single book of the Bible that claims to be *infallible.*"

"The doctrine of the infallibility of the Bible, in the rigid sense in which it is widely held and taught now, was unknown to the early Christian church. Indeed it did not come into existence until the sixteenth century, not having been held even by the earliest and greatest of the Reformers. The Catholic church has never adopted it."

"The doctrine of the New Testament's miraculous inspiration is no longer a doctrine that can be entertained by any person who is at the same time honest, thoughtful, and intelligent.

This is a frank expression; but I am confident it is a saying that will stand. Omit the honesty, the intelligence, or the thoughtfulness, and the saying *thus mutilated* would not hold good. Taken in its *entirety*, its force cannot be broken. Show me an intelligent man who entertains this doctrine, and the chances are ten to one that he lacks either thoughtfulness or honesty. Show me a thoughtful man who entertains it, and he must be lacking either in honesty or intelligence. Show me an honest man who entertains it, and either intelligence or thoughtfulness is a missing link in the chain of his individual completeness. For every man of honesty, intelligence, and thoughtfulness *knows* that the result of criticism is, that of the twenty-seven books of the New Testament the authorship of only four is absolutely certain. But to elevate into the position of a supernatural revelation a book the authorship of six-sevenths of which is extremely doubtful, is manifestly an unwarrantable procedure. We may be tolerably sure of the authorship of another seventh. This is the extremity of critical concession."

7.—*Higher Criticism rescues and exalts the Bible.*

"Nor could the surrender of the dogma of the infallibility of the Bible hurt the volume, as some fear, as a book of devotional and practical religion. Rather, in important respects, it would help it as such. For, as already intimated, the loss of the idea of infallibility would affect not in the least the higher and more spiritual teachings of the Bible—these portions that are 'profitable for doctrine, for reproof, for correction, for instruction in righteousness.' It would be simply the letting in of a healthy wind to blow away such chaff as has no power to feed anybody. For example, the imprecations of three or four of the Psalms; the brutal exploits of Samson; exaggerations like those that I have pointed out in connection with the number of years lived by the patriarchs, and the number of soldiers in the armies of Jeroboam and Abijah; the falsehood of Abraham when he denied that Sarah was his wife; the various contradictions between Scripture and science."

"We are driven to the alternative either of confessing that God is a superhuman tyrant, an infinite devil, or else *denying that the Bible can be infallible.* Does any one fail to see which of the two is the *religious* as well as the reasonable thing to do? Surely there is a weighty and solemn religious obligation resting on us to deny the truth of a dogma which aims so cruel a blow at the character of the Being we worship, and the validity of our moral intuitions. The highest and holiest things of religion and life are very deeply at stake. As we care for religion, therefore, we must not shrink; when we come upon representations of God in the Bible that are degrading and immoral, we *must* say, 'They are wrong; the men who wrote them had the low and imperfect ideas of their age; we, to-day, standing in the light that shines from Jesus, and from the eighteen centuries since, worship a God vastly more exalted and holy.'"

8.—*Immoral Influence of the old Ideas of the Bible, especially upon the Young.*

"Think of millions of Sunday-school children, with their young and plastic minds, being systematically taught from Sunday to Sunday, for years, such things as that it was right for Joshua to perpetrate his massacres of men, women, and babes, and for Jehu to murder all the house of Ahab, and for Hosea to break the seventh commandment, and for Moses and Aaron to lie to Pharaoh, and for the Jewish people to put witches to death and hold slaves, and the like (things, all of them, which we are told *God commanded*), and then reflect what a foundation all this lays in these millions of children, upon which to build virtuous characters and sensitive consciences, and pure and high manhood and womanhood! Can anything ever compensate for, or make good, such an utter confusion and perversion of moral ideas in the minds of the young? Can we expect anything else but that children thus instructed will have low and confused ideas of right and wrong, and blunted consciences, as well as unworthy conceptions of God, when they grow up to be men and women?

No! while we continue to hold earnestly to the Bible, we must discriminate. While we cannot appreciate too highly the rich legacy of moral and religious truth and sentiment that comes down to us in its revered pages, let us not be guilty of the fatal folly of concentrating error because it happens to be associated with truth. While we may well keep the Bible in our Sunday schools, and churches, and houses, as our great, and in a true sense, our sacred book of religion, to be studied reverently and appreciatively by ourselves and by our children, we must beware that we do not make it a curse instead of a blessing, to ourselves, and especially to them, by accepting it and teaching them to accept it as what it is *not*, viz., *an infallible book.*"

9.—*The Essential Truths of the Bible are, of themselves, Self-evident.*

"If there are errors and imperfections in the Bible—that is to say, if the Bible is not all infallible inspiration, how are we to know what parts are true and inspired, and what parts are untrue and uninspired—in other words, what parts we should keep and what parts we should cast out? This question, I know, often causes real trouble to earnest and conscientious minds, and yet it seems strange that it should; for the answer is surely very simple and plain. With reference to all scientific and historical questions, and all questions of *fact*, connected with the Bible, doubtless we are to find out what is truth and what is not truth in exactly the same way that we find out truth and falsehood anywhere else, viz.—by inquiry and investigation. By honest inquiry, and candid investigation, almost all the more important of these questons of fact can doubtless be solved. That so many remain still unsolved, is undoubtedly due in large measure to the fact that as yet so little really honest and unbiassed investigation has been made."

"And so, too, with regard to the great *spiritual* teachings of the Bible—these also all carry their credentials and authority in themselves. Such utterances as the Golden Rule, the Beatitudes, and Paul's chapter on Charity, it is impossible that men should mistake about. The whole matter reduces just to this—and nothing could be simpler—whatever in the Bible, as men read it, helps them, strengthens them, gives them nobler conceptions of God, increases their faith in humanity, widens their sympathies, purifies their desires, deepens their earnestness, brightens their hope, sends them forth with a more abiding consecration to the true, the beautiful, and the good, is certainly of God—and is to be received as such with as much assurance as if it were spoken to every one by an audible voice from the skies. Whereas, on the other hand, whatever is in the Bible, or anywhere else, that tends to degrade men's conceptions of God, or confuse moral distinctions, or lower their ideals of life or standards of duty, or dim their spiritual vision, is certainly not of God—and no ecclesiastical consecration or sanction, and no alleged attestation of miracles, or anything else, can make it their duty to do anything else than reject it."

10.—*Who are the Enemies of the Bible?*

"We are friends of the Bible. *They* are the enemies of the Bible who insist on keeping it standing upon a fictitious basis, which tends ever to melt away before free thought and candid investigation, as ice melts before fire. *They* are the enemies of the Bible who refuse to allow men to discriminate, judge, apply tests of reason and common sense—who say such utterly senseless things as that the Bible is 'either all true or all false,' and that we must 'either believe it all, from cover to cover, or else throw it all away.' If the array of facts, of so many and varied kinds, exhibited in the preceding pages, proves anything, it proves that the Bible is n't either all true or all a lie. Ten thousand things in it are true, and grandly true—but some things in it are not true. We are not necessitated, either to believe it all or else throw it all away, any more than I am necessitated to tear down a beautiful picture from my walls because there are scratches or dust specks on it, or turn my mother out of my house, because, with all her wealth of tenderness and love and goodness, there may be possible flaws or imperfections in her character, as there are flaws and imperfections in the character of us all."

11.—*How to view and use the Bible.*

"Probably there is no truer conception of the Bible than as a gold mine—a gold mine inestimably rich—yet a *mine* still. There are quartz and earth in no small measure mixed with the gold, as in all mines; but there is also gold—true gold of God, more precious than we shall ever fully find out—mixed plentifully with the quartz and the earth. Evidently, then, the part of rational men and women is, neither to resort to the folly on the one hand, of declaring that the quartz and earth are gold, nor yet the equal folly on the other hand, of throwing away all, and declaring there is no gold, because they can plainly see quartz and earth with the gold ; but the part of rational men and women surely is to delve earnestly in the mine, casting out, without hesitation, what plainly is not gold, but saving and treasuring up, with glad appreciation and thankfulness, rich stores of what clearly is gold."

12.—*How the Bible was formed.*

"The exact principles that guided the formation of a canon cannot be discovered. Definite grounds for the reception or rejection of books were not very clearly apprehended. The choice was determined by various circumstances. The development was pervaded by no critical or definite principle. No member of the synod (that might be at any time engaged in considering the subject of what books ought to be regarded as canonical) exercised his critical faculty ; a number would decide such matters summarily. Bishops proceeded in the track of tradition or authority." " Moreover, a great deal of bigotry, and partisanship, and bad blood was manifested from first to last. Bishops freely accused bishops of forgery of sacred writings and of alteration of the oldest texts, and altogether the debates and proceedings of the synods and councils that had part in settling the canon, remind one very much of some of the political conventions of our day."

" And yet, out of all this a result came, the excellence of which, on the whole, we may well be appreciative of. It is easy for the scholarship of to-day to see that the men who are responsible for our Bible being what it is now, made many and grave mistakes."

13.—*The Bible Canon always an open Question.*

" Luther was decidedly of the opinion that our present canon is imperfect. He thought that the Old Testament book of Esther did not belong in the Bible. On the other hand, in translating the Old Testament, he translated the apocryphal books of Judith, Wisdom, Tobit, Sirach, Baruch, First and Second Maccabees, and the Prayer of Manasseh. In his prefaces he gives his judgment concerning these books. With regard to First Maccabees, he thinks it almost equal to the other books of Holy Scripture, and not unworthy to be reckoned among them. Of Wisdom, he says he was long in doubt whether it should be numbered among the canonical books; and of Sirach, he says that it is a right good book, proceeding from a wise man. He had judgments equally decided regarding certain New Testament books. He thought the Epistle to the Hebrews came neither from Paul nor any of the apostles, and was not to be put on an equality with Epistles written by apostles themselves. The Apocalypse (or Revelation) he considered neither apostolic nor prophetic, and of little or no worth. He did not believe the Epistle of Jude proceeded from an apostle. James' Epistle he pronounced unapostolic, and 'an epistle of straw.'

"The great Swiss reformer, Zwingli, maintained that the Apocalypse is not properly a Biblical book. Even Calvin did not think that Paul was the author of Hebrews, or Peter of the book called II. Peter."

"As to the New Testament canon, that was never settled only in a most haphazard and utterly inadequate way. Up to the beginning of the second century, no one seemingly ever thought of such a thing as any writings ever being regarded as Sacred Scripture, except the Old Testament writings. For a long time after the gospels and various epistles came into existence, they were much less esteemed than the Old Scriptures. Indeed, up to about the middle of the second century they were not so highly esteemed as the oral traditions of the churches in which any of the apostles had preached. By the close of the second century, however, a change appears. Certain New Testament books have come into more general favor than the rest, and are beginning to be classed to a certain extent by themselves as a new collection of Sacred Scriptures. As time goes on, they grow more and more into use among the churches. Yet for centuries the various churches continued to use, side by side with the writings which make up our New Testament to-day, various books which we call spurious."

14.—*The long Period of the Bible's Growth.*

"The various histories, biographies, poems, prophecies, letters, and productions of one kind and another which make up this collection of literature called our Bible, was more than a thousand years coming into existence; some of the productions making their appearance (at least in substance, if not in their present form) in the morning of Jewish civilization, as early in the nation's history as the nation had a literature at all; while others did not come into being until the nation had passed through long and varied experiences of contact with some of the richest civilizations of the ancient world, including among others the Phœnician, the Assyrian, the Persian, the Greek, and the Roman."

"Comparing the date of the origin of our own Sacred Scriptures with the date of the origin of the other great Sacred Scriptures of the world, we see from the foregoing that no part of our Scriptures can have been written so early by probably some centuries as the earliest portions of the Vedas and Zend Avesta, which are decided by the best authorities to have been produced as far back as from 1000 to 2000 B. C. On the other hand, we see that certain portions of our Sacred Scriptures—the whole New Testament part, with possibly one or more books of the Old—were written considerably later than any of the other great Bibles except the Koran, which was not produced till the seventh century after Christ."

"The writings nearest the time of Jesus after the Epistles of Paul are the Epistle to the Hebrews (certainly not Paul's) and the book of Revelation. These were both written from 65 to 70 A.D."

"Of the existence of the Four Gospels we learn with certainty only in the fourth quarter of the second century, one hundred and fifty years after the death of Jesus. The earliest, Matthew, cannot have received its present form much before the end of the first century. The latest, John, dates from about the year 135. Possibly from a few years earlier than this, possibly from a few years later."

15.—*Date of the Birth of Jesus.*

"Popular chronology implies that Jesus was born 1896 years ago last Christmas-day. But this chronology is notoriously inaccurate so far as the year is concerned, and arbitrary as concerns the day. The Christian era, that is, the dating of events from the birth of Jesus, was an invention of the abbot Dionysius in the sixth century after Christ. Before this time events had been dated from the founding of Rome, or from the accession of this or that emperor to the throne. But the investigation of Dionysius was conducted without any critical acumen. The Gospels represent Jesus as being born before the death of Herod; but Herod died four years before the beginning of our era. Luke associates the birth of Jesus with a certain taxing of Quirinius. But this taxing was six years *after* the beginning of our era. The relations of Jesus to John the Baptist afford somewhat more satisfactory data. Reckoning from these, the average of critical opinion gravitates to a point three or four years before the beginning of our era. If Jesus was born, as Keim and others think, before the death of Herod, some three or four years earlier would be the true date, and this year of ours (1897) would properly be the year 1903, 1904, or 1905. Certainty is here impossible. It is only safe to say that Jesus was born from three to eight years before the time suggested by our popular chronology."

16.—*The Story of the Miraculous Birth.*

"The genesis of the story of the miraculous birth of Jesus is so easily accounted for without supposing any basis of reality, that one must be wilfully credulous to entertain the idea for a single moment. It is of a piece with various stories predicating the miraculous birth of famous persons, especially of famous teachers of religion. Buddha and Zoroaster share with Jesus in this doubtful honor. The fundamental Gospel tradition is wholly innocent of any such idea. So, too, are the Gospels in their present shape, beyond the legends of the infancy. Paul is equally silent where he would have been voluble enough if he had heard or given a moment's heed to such a tale. No, he is contradictory rather than silent. For when he speaks of Jesus as "born of a woman," it is only the madness of dogmatic preconception that can imagine any denial of the human father. The expression was the current phrase for human generation. But we have more emphatic contradiction close at hand in the legends of the birth and infancy. Both Matthew and Luke deduce Jesus from David *through Joseph*. What are we to infer from this remarkable phenomenon, if not that these genealogies were the invention of a time when the miraculous birth of Jesus was an unheard-of fable?

17.—*The Messianic Hope.*

"Few subjects have received more conscientious study than the Messianic hope; and now, at length, though much remains in doubt, a few clear outlines have been well made out, which we may hope will not be blurred by any future investigation. These outlines are, however, as different as possible from those of the popular Christian exposition. The gist of this exposition is that the Messianic hope originated in the time of Abraham, was cherished by Moses, attained its most complete development in the age of the prophets, from 800 to 400 B.C., and then retired into comparative obscurity for centuries, to await its consummation and fulfilment in the birth and life and death of Jesus Christ, Jesus the Christ, that is to say, the Anointed, the Messiah. Such is the popular Christian exposition, and the commentary which an intelligent and scientific criticism makes upon it is this: The Messianic hope displayed itself most characteristically and powerfully, not from 800 to 400 B.C., but from 175 B.C. to 135 A.D., and that from the birth of Jesus onward to the final extinction of the Jewish nation by the Emperor Hadrian was the period of its most remarkable growth. This criticism assures us that the Messianic element in the prophetic writings is entirely subordinate; that much that is accounted Messianic is the reflection back upon the prophets of the Messianic ideas of a later time."

"The Jewish hope of a Messiah became in the Christian the hope of Jesus' second coming 'in the clouds of heaven with great power and glory.' The forms taken upon itself through all this period by the Messianic hope were exceedingly diverse. The factor of a personal Messiah was frequently wanting altogether. But in one form or another it was omnipresent and omnipotent. From the death of Herod, 4 B.C., to the death of Bar-Cochba, 132 A.D., no less that fifty different enthusiasts set up as the Messiah, and obtained more or less following. No one of these attained to general recognition before Bar-Cochba, under whose leadership the hope was quenched in seas of blood. Some saw the Messiah even in Herod the Great! This was the lowest point reached by the Messianic ideal."

18.—*Jesus the Messiah.*

That Jesus should come at length to think of himself as the Messiah was not so strange as the simultaneous conclusion that he must be a suffering Messiah; for, the Messianic idea was so omnipresent to the Jewish mind that, for a man conscious of a great mission not to connect his mission in some way with that idea, was quite impossible. It was the grandeur of his spiritual ideal that compelled Jesus to identify his mission with the Messianic office. He remained the herald of the kingdom so long as he could consistently do so. The Messiah must be the incarnation of the highest possible ideal. To himself Jesus was this. This wonderful self-confidence on the part of Jesus did not necessitate self-righteousness, only an absolute devotion to the moral welfare of mankind,—only an absolute conviction that righteousness and love were fundamental facts in the new order. It was as representative of these that he demanded personal allegiance."

"The first thing we have to do, then, is to take the record of the facts, if we can, absolutely without the warp of any preconceived opinion, or any theological dogmatism. Looking at them so, it appears plain that what we call the Messianic consciousness of Jesus, which is so intense and even predominant towards the close of his ministry, was a comparatively late development in him. To put it in theological phrase, his generation as son of God was anterior to his appointment as Messiah of the Jews. In the language we usually apply to human experience, his vocation as a moral and spiritual teacher was recognized first ; and only as an after-result came his strong conviction that he was the chosen deliverer of his people, though by a way they could not understand or follow."

19.—*The Gospel according to the Hebrews.*

"Time was when our New Testament Matthew was thought to be a translation of the Gospel according to the Hebrews. But one of the fixed facts of modern criticism is that our Matthew is not a translation. And still its relation to the Gospel according to the Hebrews is one of the most interesting questions of New Testament criticism. The agreements of the two are many, and where they disagree the uncanonical work sometimes preserves the more reliable tradition. The Gospel of the Hebrews seems to have existed in various forms, in this respect being in no wise different perhaps from the New Testament gospels. Whether its earliest form was the germ of our own Matthew, or the two branched from a common stock, is a dilemma which impales on either horn an equal number of New Testament scholars. This much, however, is tolerably certain : that throughout the second century the Gospel according to the Hebrews enjoyed a reputation not inferior to that of our New Testament gospels. The decline of its reputation synchronized with the decay of Jewish Christianity."

"It is even possible that Matthew arrived at a written form before the destruction of Jerusalem in 70 A.D. It contains sentences that could not have originated after that event, and the crudity of the method of aggregation is evinced by the fact that these sentences are allowed to stand and bear the contradiction of events. The result at which we finally arrive, therefore, is this: *That from thirty to forty years after the death of Jesus the tradition of his life and ministry and death had shaped itself into the basis of our present Gospels of Matthew, Mark, and Luke.* The contents of this fundamental tradition (fundamental to our Gospels, but in its turn, no doubt, the result of various accretions)—the contents of this tradition are as flattering to the anti-supernaturalist as he could reasonably expect. Accounts of miracles are here, even some of the most startling; but there is not a hint of the miraculous birth of Jesus, nor of the legends of his infancy, and the tradition ends with the discovery that his tomb is empty, without a word to signalize that he was seen again by any woman or disciple. In this tradition the personality of Jesus is revealed in lines so firm and strong that the accretions of a later time add little to their force. The man behind the myth is there, no thin abstraction, but an individual with blood in his veins, and in his heart the love of human kind."

20.—*The New Testament Miracles.*

"The strangest thing of all in this connection is that the Fourth Gospel, cherishing a conception of Jesus as the pre-existent Logos, nevertheless does not avail itself of the miraculous birth, but plainly intimates that Jesus was the son of Joseph in the line of human generation."

"There is, indeed, much better evidence for the miracles recorded by St. Augustine than for any recorded in the New Testament. We come much nearer the events, and we know something of the narrators, where in the New Testament we know nothing. Never was there a place and time where and when stories of prodigy and miracle were more likely to be fashioned without any basis of reality, and to obtain credence without any evidence, than in the years immediately succeeding the lifetime of Jesus. Considering the place and time, the wonder is that the miraculous element in the New Testament is not much more obtrusive than it is, much more extravagant."

"There was no conflict here with modern science. For diseases of the imagination, to this day the most effective remedies are psychological. Much more must it have been so in the time of Jesus, when all concerned were alike under the dominion of an appalling superstition, the belief in demoniacal possession. But given a few cures of the so-called demoniacs by Jesus, also the spiritual soil and atmosphere of Palestine, and these cures would bring forth in a dozen or twenty years a crop of miracle-stories so extensive that not one quarter of its bulk could be husbanded within the limits of the New Testament. And a few cures of this sort, or temporary alleviations, are, I am persuaded, the bottom facts which underlie the entire structure of the miraculous in the New Testament, and in Christian history."

21.—*Our Synoptic Gospels.*

"Of the three Gospels that still remain to us the relative values are still in some dispute. That we are *certain* of the authorship of any one of them only a very ignorant or exceedingly dogmatic person would be likely to declare. Nor of the time when they assumed their present shapes can we be more than proximately sure. We are for the first time definitely aware of their existence as Matthew's, Mark's, and Luke's, from 170 to 180 A.D. Nor are we aware of their existence in any shape or under any name at a much earlier period. Writing in the middle of the second century, Justin Martyr quotes from certain "Memoirs of the Apostles," as he calls them, so freely that a consistent biography of Jesus might be collected from his quotations. But he never names the authors of these memoirs. His quotations from them often disagree with our Gospels, and seldom agree with them; and if our Gospels (the Synoptics) were used by him, they were used in conjunction with others which were apparently as highly, if not more highly, esteemed. If we had only external evidence to rely upon, it would be quite impossible to predicate the existence of our Synoptic Gospels earlier than the middle of the second century."

22.—*The Fourth Gospel.*

"The idea of the Logos or Word came into Jewish thought from two sides, from Persia and from Greece; from Persia by way of Babylon, from Greece by way of Alexandria. The Persian-Zoroastrian religion taught that God created all things by his *word*. The cosmology in Genesis is of Persian origin. 'God *said* let there be light, and there was light.' His word is the creative power. Before the time of Jesus this Word of God had become personified in Jewish thought, most frequently under the name of Wisdom. 'Wisdom hath been created before all things,' we read in the Book of Proverbs; 'Wisdom has been created before all things,' in Ecclesiasticus; and in the Wisdom of Solomon, 'She is a reflection of the everlasting light, the unspotted mirror of the power of God, and the image of his goodness.' The Greek influence contributed to the same tendency of thought. The later followers of Plato, the Neo-Platonists, had personified his doctrine of the divine idea or reason. They called it the first born Son of God, born before the creation of the world, itself the agent of creation. It was the image of God's perfection, the mediator between God and man. Philo Judæus, who was born about twenty years before Jesus, was possessed with these ideas and endeavored to connect them with the Old Testament teachings."

"Thus it was that the writer of the Fourth Gospel found this doctrine of the Logos; and on the other hand he found a conception of Jesus expressed in terms the most exalted, and bearing a very strong resemblance to the terms of the Logos doctrine of Philo. True, Philo had never dreamed of a human incarnation of the Logos, and Paul had never identified his exalted Christ with the Alexandrian Word. The first to do this was pretty certainly not the writer of the Fourth Gospel. It occurred to many writers at about the same time. To effect an alliance between Christianity and Alexandrian Platonism was the one passionate enthusiasm midway of the second century. Of this enthusiasm the Fourth Gospel is the grandest monument. The Fourth Gospel is not less valuable on this account. Only its value henceforth is that of a contribution to our knowledge of second-century ideas. Every true word that it contains is just as true as ever. Every beautiful thought is just as beautiful now as before."

"Of the Fourth Gospel we find no mention till the second century is drawing to its close. Of its existence we have little if any notice earlier than this. But we have ample evidence that if it was in existence midway of the second century, and back of this for five and twenty years, it was little known and less esteemed, and certainly was not regarded as the work of an Apostle. That it was meant to pass for John's there cannot be a doubt; but so was the book of Daniel meant to pass for Daniel's, who had been dead three hundred years when it was written. To seek prestige for one's own thought under the cover of some mighty name was for hundreds of years before and after the time of Jesus the commonest proceeding. It was a species of self-abnegation. The writer sacrificed his personal renown to some high cause that had enlisted his enthusiasm and demanded his service.

"'That one biography of a person is written subsequently to another is not necessarily a circumstance that is prejudicial to the later work. The latest is frequently the best. But if it is so, it must be in virtue of a closer adherence to, or a more vital appreciation of, the fundamental biographical material."

"Since the sponge dipped in vinegar moistened the dying lips of Jesus, no such service has been rendered him as that of the critics who have transferred the Fourth Gospel from the province of biography to that of theological controversy and imaginative dogma."

23.—*St. Paul's Conception of Jesus.*

"If with Ferdinand Christian Baur we accept as authentic only four of Paul's Epistles out of the fourteen ascribed to him in the New Testament, namely, Romans, the two Corinthians, and Galatians, Paul's theory of Christ's nature is quite homogeneous. If we also accept, as I am inclined to do, with the support of many able critics, First Thessalonians, Colossians, and Philippians, then we have in Paul also a development of which the starting point is found in First Thessalonians, his earliest epistle, the middle point in Romans, Galatians, and Corinthians, and the culmination in Colossians and Philippians. In Thessalonians the conception is hardly different from that of the Synoptic Gospels. In Romans, Corinthians, and Galatians it has already made a great advance. To the actual historical Jesus,

Paul was quite indifferent. He does not quote his words. He does not recount his deeds. He does not dwell on his example. His self-denial is not that of a man among men. It is the laying aside of heavenly glory, and the assumption of a human form. Paul's thought centred not in the historic Jesus but in an ideal Christ of his own conception."

"This was his first thought,—that Jesus was glorified by his death and resurrection; but this could not satisfy his speculative genius. A glory with which Christ was invested did not satisfy him. He wanted a glory for him that was essential to his personality; and so his death and resurrection became only the means of his resuming a glory which he had ages before his earthly manifestation—the glory of a heavenly, archetypal man. Henceforth to Paul the human life of Jesus was the merest episode in the career of the heavenly man, the ideal Christ of his speculative imagination; and yet lofty as was Paul's conception of the Christ, he cherished the idea that all men who would might be even such as he. Although an image of the divine glory, he was not less an image of the possible glory of the saints. It was not the character of the historical Jesus that marked Paul's limit of possible human attainment. It was the nature of the heavenly pre-existent Christ."

24.—*The Corporeal Resurrection and Ascension.*

"Article IV., of the established Church of England, reads: 'Christ did truly rise again from death, and took again his body with flesh, bones and all things appertaining to the perfection of man's nature, wherewith he ascended into heaven and there sitteth, until he return to judge all men at the last day.'"

"With his corporeal substance,—in the language of the Article, 'with his flesh and bones and all things appertaining to the perfection of man's nature'—he ascended into heaven. Assuming all this, where is the argument for our personal immortality? The resurrection of Jesus is a resurrection of the *body*; his ascension is an ascension of the *body*; his immortality is an immortality of the *body*. Now it is quite impossible for us to have any such resurrection, any such ascension, any such *corporeal* immortality. Our *bodies* moulder away. They mingle with the elements. They are taken up into vegetable and animal structures. What analogy can there be between our resurrection at some infinitely distant day and that of Jesus from twenty-four to thirty-six hours after his death? There can be no analogy whatever, and therefore there can be no argument from the one thing to the other."

"Having reviewed the testimony of the Gospels to the *corporeal* resurrection and ascension in almost every particular, what is the net result? No single account is self-consistent or agrees with any other. The different accounts are self-destructive and mutually destructive all. They agree in hardly a single particular. They differ in particulars of the first importance. Here the appearance of the risen Jesus is placed in Galilee, there, in direct contravention of his own assertions, in Jerusalem. Here his ascension is definitely placed on the first day; elsewhere, by different writers, later, but without general agreement. Here the risen Jesus is a man of flesh and blood; elsewhere a bodiless ghost; and so on through all the catalogue of difference and contradiction."

"The two from Emmaus are still talking with the eleven when Jesus stands in their midst. They are affrighted and think they see a spirit. While eating with them, he takes bread, breaks it, and gives thanks. Then they recognize Jesus and he vanishes from their sight. A body with flesh and bones capable of 'appearing' in a room whose doors are fastened, and in the same way disappearing, and vanishing like a shadow!"

"What is the amount and nature of Paul's evidence to the *corporeal* resurrection and ascension of Jesus? In First Corinthians, xv. 3, we read, 'For I delivered unto you that which I also received, that Christ died for our sins according to the Scriptures, and that he was raised again on the third day; and that he was seen by Peter, then by the twelve. After that he was seen by above five hundred brethren at once, of whom the greater part remain unto this present day, but some are fallen asleep. After that he was seen by James, then by all the apostles; and last of all he was seen by me also as by one born out of due time. . . .'

"But this concluding clause is exceedingly significant: 'and last of all he was seen of me also.' Paul makes no distinction between *his* sight of the risen Jesus and *that of the others*. That Paul had seen the risen Jesus, and that he considered *his* sight *of him* as good as any other,—so much is certain.

"'Have I not seen Jesus Christ our Master?'—This sight of Jesus must have been years after his death. That it was a sight of the *body* of Jesus which hung upon the cross there is not an intimation. . . . Whatever it was, it was something which occurred years after the death of Jesus, and it must have been something entirely different from the appearance of Jesus in the same *body* with which he died, the resurrection of which is represented with much inconsistency in the four Gospels.

"So much for the testimony of Paul.

"And now a word in regard to the ascension. Matthew does not mention it. Mark is equally silent; but in the appendix—the Spurious Verses 9-20—to this Gospel it is said that 'he was taken up into heaven, and sat on the right hand of God.' John also is silent. So, then, we have three Gospels, out of four, making no final disposition of the risen Jesus. . . . In the original tradition, there was no ascension. The resurrection and ascension were one and the same thing. This is Paul's thought as well. Though he has so much to say about the resurrection, he has not a word concerning any ascension. . . . Such is the most reasonable account that can be given of the causes that were operative in producing the New Testament tradition."

"Ascension into heaven '*with his flesh and bones*'! That men could believe this centuries ago, when the learning of the few was as superstitious as the ignorance of the many, I can easily understand. That the ignorant and superstitious of the present time, who know nothing of the laws of evidence, who have no appreciation of the inviolable sanctity of the natural order of the world, and no perception that it is men's growing faith in this which marks the hours of progress on the great dial of history,—that such can *still*, in this last quarter of the nineteenth century, believe the same is also not hard to understand. *But how any thoughfully intelligent person, in these days, can believe it passes the bounds of credibility.*"

25.—*A Parable of the Life of Jesus.*

"I have read or heard somewhere of a remarkable Indian plant or tree which grows, isolated from others, to a great height, throwing out few, if any, lateral branches, but suddenly, at the very top, bursting into a single flower of marvellous brilliancy and beauty, and with a fragrance that enchants the sense with an unspeakable delight. And then—it dies! It is a parable of the life of Jesus. Year after year it grew in silence and obscurity, sending no lateral branches, that we know of, out into the sunny Galilean air; but suddenly its top, as if drew-sprinkled with the baptism of John, as if expanded by the fierce heats of a nation's patriotic and religious zeal, burst into a flower whose beauty and whose fragrance have enriched whole centuries of time. But as we may be sure that all that patient waiting, silent growing, of the Indian tree were necessary to its one consummate flower, we may be equally sure that all the patient waiting, silent growth, of Jesus were but the needful preparation for his *brief years* of active service among men, a flower whose fragrance, even to this day, enriches every wind that blows."

LX.—MISCELLANEOUS CONFIRMATIONS—EXTRACTS FROM RECENT BOOKS.

"During the life of Buddha no record of events, no sacred code containing the sayings of the master was wanted. His presence was enough, and thoughts of the future seldom entered the minds of those who followed him. It was only after Buddha had left the world to enter into Nirvana, that his disciples attempted to recall the sayings and doings of their departed friend and master. Then everything that seemed to redound to the glory of Buddha, however extraordinary and incredible, was eagerly welcomed, while witnesses who would have ventured to criticise or reject unsupported statements, or detract in any way from the holy character of Buddha, had no chance of being listened to. And when, in spite of all this, differences of opinion arose, they were not brought to the test of a careful weighing of evidence, but the names of 'unbeliever' and 'heretic' were quickly invented in India as elsewhere, and bandied backwards and forwards between contending parties, till at last, when the doctors disagreed, the help of the secular power had to be invoked, and kings and emperors convoked councils for the suppression of schism, for the settlement of an orthodox creed, and for the completion of the Sacred Canon. We know of King Asoka, the contemporary of Seleucus, sending his royal missive to the assembled elders, and telling them what to do and what to avoid, warning them also in his own name of the apochryphal or heretical character of certain books, which, as he thinks, ought not to be admitted into the Sacred Canon.

"We here learn a lesson, which is confirmed by the study of other religions, that *canonical books*, though they furnish in most cases the most authentic information within the reach of the student of religion, *are not to be trusted implicitly ;* nay, that they must be submitted to *a more searching criticism and to more stringent tests* than any other historical books."

"In reading the above, one can hardly believe that it is not the history of the origin of our own New Testament writings and the formation of our own New Testament canon, that Prof. Müller is tracing, instead of the origin of the Buddhist Sacred Writings and the formation of the Buddhist Canon. For if we substitute ' Jesus ' in the place of ' Buddha,' the ' countries around the Mediterranean sea' in the place of ' India,' and the ' Emperor Constantine ' with one or two other Christian emperors in the place of ' King Asoka,' *we shall have an almost exact record of the origin of a large part of the literature which came into being as the result of Jesus' life and teachings*, and the manner in which a portion of this became singled out from the rest and by degrees united into essentially what is now our New Testament."

"The Jehovah of the Old Testament makes himself a local habitation, appears in the temple, walks and talks, and thinks and plans, loves and hates, gets angry, takes vengeance, and changes his mind, very much after the fashion of an Oriental despot. This is not to be wondered at ; for as water cannot rise above its source, so the human mind cannot think of God as being anything higher than its highest and best conception of what is worthy of divinity. *Humanity cannot escape itself ; and so its thought of God is always the best it is capable of thinking at the time.* As man grows and develops, so does his idea of divinity. The divine does not change ; but as you can put only twelve quarts of the Atlantic in a twelve-quart pail, so in a finite brain you can put only so much of the Infinite as the finite can contain. *As the thought of man gets larger, its contents increase.*"

"Every historic religion, that has won for itself a place in the world's history, has evolved from a core of fact, a nimbus of legendary matter which criticism cannot always separate; and which the popular faith does not seek to separate. Christianity, like every other religion, has its mythology (or legends) so intertwined with the veritable facts of its early history, so braided and welded with its first beginnings, that the myth and legend are not always distinguishable from the history. Yet the mythical (or legendary) interpretation of certain portions of the gospels has no appreciable bearing on the character of the Christ. The impartial reader of the record must see that the *evangelists did not invent the character; they did not make the Jesus of their story;* on the contrary, it was he that made them. It is a true saying that *only a Christ could invent a Christ.*"

"After all that Biblical critics and antiquarian research have gathered from the dust of antiquity in proof of the genuineness and authenticity of the books of the New Testament, credibility still labors with the fact that the age in which these books were received and put in circulation was one in which *the science of criticism as developed by the moderns—the science which scrutinizes statements, balances evidence for and against, and sifts the true from the false—did not exist;* an age when a boundless credulity disposed men to believe in wonders as readily as in ordinary events, requiring no stronger proof in the case of the former than sufficed to establish the latter, viz.:—hearsay and vulgar report; an age when literary honesty was a virtue almost unknown, and when, consequently, literary forgeries were as common as genuine productions, and transcribers of sacred books *did not scruple to alter the text in the interest of personal views and doctrinal prepossessions.*"

"And the best scholarship of the church is still unsettled about Hebrews, James, Jude, the second epistle of Peter, the second and third of John, and the Revelation.

If there be infallible books, of which to make an infallible Bible, and if these be infallibly preserved and transmitted to us, we are still undecided and in trouble, *unless we have also an infallible catalogue to tell us which they are.* If there are two or three guide-posts, and one is infallibly correct, and the others not, it matters little to us, unless some one is able to tell us which is right. And then, if *words* be so important, how comes it that the New Testament writers quote the Old loosely and incorrectly? In one place, the Septuagint is followed where its translation from the original Hebrew is blunderingly wrong, and even reverses the sense; and not only are these things so, but *there are in the Bible palpable errors and inconsistencies and contradictions that no one would think of trying to cover up, were it not for the pressing necessities of special pleading.*"

"Again, there are irreconcilable difficulties in connection with the genealogies of Jesus given by Matthew and Luke. Both these genealogies trace the ancestry of Jesus through Joseph. But having done this, both Matthew and Luke tell us that Joseph was not the father of Jesus at all. *Thus Jesus is claimed to have descended from David, because a man who is not his father descended from David.* A most extraordinary claim! Moreover, Matthew says the number of generations from Abraham to David is fourteen, and from David to the Captivity fourteen, and from the Captivity to Christ fourteen. But if we look carefully at the genealogy, as he himself gives it, the number from Abraham to David is only *thirteen*, and the number from the Captivity to Christ is only *thirteen*. Furthermore, the genealogies of Joseph, the husband of Mary (called the genealogies of *Jesus*, but not the genealogy of Jesus at all unless Joseph was Jesus' father) as given by Matthew and Luke, are radically different, agreeing in only fifteen names in the whole list, and differing in forty names. Now, when we bear in mind that these genealogies both run back in the male line, from son to father, and then grandfather, and then great-grandfather, and so on, *we see that divergence can mean nothing else but error in one or the other of the authorities, or both.* Nor may we suppose that one genealogy is that of Mary. Such a supposition rests on not a shadow of evidence, while it is positively contradicted by the language of the text."

"Neither faith, nor love, nor truth, nor disinterestedness, nor forgiveness, nor patience, nor peace, nor equality, nor education, nor missionary effort, nor prayer, nor honesty, nor the sentiment of brotherhood, nor reverence for woman, nor the spirit of humility, nor the fact of martyrdom, *nor any other good thing is monopolized by any form of faith.* All religions recognize, more or less remotely, these principles; all do something to exemplify something to dishonor them."

" He is the CHRIST. This word literally means the 'anointed,' and the idea conveyed by it is derived from the ancient ceremony of consecrating a king to his kingly office. In connection with Jesus it is clearly a figurative term, involving, however, the idea that he who bore it had been called and appointed to his office; *intimating, therefore, the existence of a higher power which had chosen him.* Hence Peter terms him 'the Christ of God'—God's Christ, that is, one anointed of God, or appointed by Him to be what he was.

" This word, we need scarcely remind the reader, is the same in meaning as the Hebrew word 'Messiah,' and the same explanation holds good of both. We learn the true value and import of the latter, when we find that it is applied, in the Old Testament, to a heathen king, *one who is made the instrument of executing a particular purpose of Jehovah.* Cyrus, the king of Persia, was the means of putting an end to the captivity of the Jews. Hence the later Isaiah says of him, 'Thus saith Jehovah to his *anointed*, to Cyrus.' Literally this might be rendered 'to his Messiah,' the same word which in Christian times is applied to Jesus under the Greek form of Christ.

" The term which was applied to Cyrus only incidentally and because of a particular purpose, *is used of Jesus as his usual and abiding designation;* and he is, therefore, Jesus the Christ, an appellation which soon passed into a personal name, and became Jesus Christ. *But this fact does not alter the relation between him and the Creator which the word denotes.* That was the same, in truth, as for the time existed between the Almighty Being and His chosen instrument the king of Persia. The one was the Anointer and the other the anointed; the one the Sender and the other the sent; the one was the Creator and the Source of power, the other the creature and the recipient of any authority or power which it pleased the Father to confer upon him."

"The term SON leads us to the same conclusion. According to our usual ideas and experience of human relationships, a *son* is, indeed, of the same nature with his father. The same or like mental and bodily powers belong to both ; and therefore it might be inferred, in the case of Jesus, that he, being said to be the Son of God, *is in all respects of the same essential nature as the Being of whom he is so often termed the Son.* And this is constantly either expressly affirmed, or tacitly assumed, by orthodox writers. But granting this, there is at least one important point in which the word necessarily implies *inferiority*, according to all ordinary ideas and the usual force of human language—except, indeed, among persons who are satisfied to set human language at defiance, and speak of ' Eternal Sonship,' and pledge their ministers at ordination to believe in it. *A son, at all events, is* younger *than his father, so that to speak of eternal sonship is something like speaking of an eternal fifty years.*"

" Of course I am aware of the cheap way of meeting these statements, which is coming to be so common, viz., sneering at them as the ' invention of infidels,' declaring that they are ' as old as Christianity,' 'and have been answered a thousand times over.' To this I only care to say—they are not the ' invention of infidels,' or of anybody else ; they are simply obstinate *facts*, that refuse to accommodate themselves to the wish of either ' infidel ' or Christian. As to their being ' as old as Christianity,' this is true ; that is to say, *careful and unprejudiced students of the Bible from the earliest ages have perceived contradictions in it*, though with the lapse of time and the advance of biblical scholarship, *the number of these contradictions discovered has constantly increased.* As to their having been ' answered a thousand times,' I have only to say, they have been *replied to* a thousand times—they have never been *answered* at all."

"So far from its being painful to give up the doctrine of Biblical Infallibility, I hesitate not to say that, just in so far as one has the spirit and love of Christ, and at the same time comprehends intelligently the points at issue, he will rejoice to be able to give it up ; and *what little comfort there may be in* thinking he has an infallible guide, he will gladly sacrifice to the larger and better results. As a matter of fact there is not the least justification for 'orthodox' writers and preachers, when they say that those who question the infallibility of the Bible are undermining the hope of man."

"Who, then, is the God of evolution? Not the mechanical contriver, or the Oriental despot of the Old Testament; not the Zoroastrian Ahura-Mazoa, ruling but half the world; not the Hindoo Brahm asleep in the heavens; not a deity dwelling in temples, and only to be sought at special altars; not the partial and implacable God of Calvin; not one sitting afar on his throne, to be reached only through mediators. The righteousness which is by evolution speaketh on this wise: Say not in thy heart, Who shall ascend into heaven to bring him down? nor, Who shall descend into the deep to bring him up? *But what saith it? God is nigh thee, even in thy mouth and in thy heart. And it says this with a reality and meaning never said before.* Or it borrows the beautiful and mystic tongue of Wordsworth, and speaks of

> 'A sense sublime
> Of something far more deeply interfused,
> Whose dwelling is the light of setting suns,
> And the round ocean, and the living air,
> And the blue sky, and in the mind of man;
> A motion and a spirit that impels
> All thinking things, all objects of all thought,
> And rolls through all things.'"

"Now, then, what can science do for religion? Science has been doing for hundreds of years one of the greatest services possible. It has been destroying the superstitions, the crudities, the falsehoods, the misconceptions of men concerning religion. For example, the doctrines of astrology, of demoniacal possession, of witchcraft, the doctrine of the material resurrection of the body, of a material hell just under the surface of the ground, and many others that were once considered central and essential parts of religion,—*these things which were only hurts and damages, barnacles on the ship that hindered its sailing,*—these things science has stripped off, and thrown away, and utterly destroyed.

"I do not wonder that men have cried out against science because it has done these things; for if once a man identifies his own thought with the very central life and thought of the universe, of course, when you touch him, he thinks the throne of God is giving way. But science has reconstructed religious thought: that is one thing that it has done for it. Another thing I have already enlarged upon. *It has heightened infinitely the objects of religion, giving us a grander God, a nobler humanity, a more magnificent universe as the theatre for human action.*"

"God has more truth than is in the Bible; and the process of the ages is but the unrolling of His divinely written scroll. What matter, then, though we do not certainly know each step we are taking? Are the children of a ship-captain less safe because they do not understand the log-book, the quadrant, the path of the vessel through the waves? *A wise head and a loving heart are in the cabin, and a strong and wakeful hand is on the wheel.* The Captain knows where He is going; and He knows His route; and the smallest, weakest, and most ignorant child shall go sailing up the harbor, and when the anchor is dropped, and the boat lowered, shall set foot on the wave-washed, sandy beach of the Everlasting Shore, just as surely and safely as the Captain Himself. Have faith, then, not in churches, nor creeds, nor councils, nor books: '*have faith in God*'; for

> 'I doubt not through the ages one increasing purpose runs.
> . . . .
> Not in vain the distance beacons. Forward, forward let us range;
> Let the great world spin forever down the ringing grooves of change.
> Through the shadow of the globe we sweep into the younger day.'

"I have a great deal of doubt of men,—their thoughts, their creeds, and their systems; but *with all my heart and soul I believe in God and the future. He has inspired and led in all the past; He inspires and leads to-day; He will inspire and lead to-morrow;* for 'He is the same yesterday, to-day, and forever.'"

PART SECOND.

PART SECOND.

"BUT I HAVE *this* AGAINST THEE, THAT THOU DIDST LEAVE THY FIRST LOVE. REMEMBER THEREFORE FROM WHENCE THOU ART FALLEN, AND REPENT, AND DO THE FIRST WORKS; OR ELSE I COME TO THEE, AND WILL MOVE THY CANDLESTICK OUT OF ITS PLACE, EXCEPT THOU REPENT."

"I KNOW THY WORKS, THAT THOU HAST A NAME THAT THOU LIVEST, AND ART DEAD. BE WATCHFUL, AND STRENGTHEN THE THINGS WHICH REMAIN, THAT ARE READY TO DIE: FOR I HAVE NOT FOUND THY WORKS PERFECT BEFORE GOD."

"AND TO THE ANGEL OF THE CHURCH IN SARDIS, WRITE:

"THESE THINGS SAITH HE THAT HATH THE SEVEN SPIRITS OF GOD, AND THE SEVEN STARS: I KNOW THY WORKS, THAT THOU HAST A NAME THAT THOU LIVEST, AND THOU ART DEAD. BE THOU WATCHFUL, AND STABLISH THE THINGS THAT REMAIN, WHICH WERE READY TO DIE: FOR I HAVE FOUND NO WORKS OF THINE FULFILLED BEFORE MY GOD. REMEMBER THEREFORE HOW THOU HAST RECEIVED AND DIDST HEAR; AND KEEP *it*, AND REPENT. IF THEREFORE THOU SHALT NOT WATCH, I WILL COME AS A THIEF, AND THOU SHALT NOT KNOW WHAT HOUR I WILL COME UPON THEE. BUT THOU HAST A FEW NAMES IN SARDIS WHICH DID NOT DEFILE THEIR GARMENTS: AND THEY SHALL WALK WITH ME IN WHITE; FOR THEY ARE WORTHY. HE THAT OVERCOMETH SHALL THUS BE ARRAYED IN WHITE GARMENTS; AND I WILL IN NO WISE BLOT HIS NAME OUT OF THE BOOK OF LIFE, AND I WILL CONFESS HIS NAME BEFORE MY FATHER, AND BEFORE HIS ANGELS. HE THAT HATH AN EAR, LET HIM HEAR WHAT THE SPIRIT SAITH TO THE CHURCHES."

"AND TO THE ANGEL OF THE CHURCH IN LAODICEA, WRITE:

"THESE THINGS SAITH THE AMEN, THE FAITHFUL AND TRUE WITNESS, THE BEGINNING OF THE CREATION OF GOD: I KNOW THY WORKS, THAT THOU ART NEITHER COLD NOR HOT: I WOULD THOU WERT COLD OR HOT. SO BECAUSE THOU ART LUKEWARM, AND NEITHER HOT NOR COLD, I WILL SPEW THEE OUT OF MY MOUTH. BECAUSE THOU SAYEST, I AM RICH, AND HAVE GOTTEN RICHES, AND HAVE NEED OF NOTHING; AND KNOWEST NOT THAT THOU ART WRETCHED, AND MISERABLE, AND POOR, AND BLIND, AND NAKED: I COUNSEL THEE TO BUY OF ME GOLD REFINED BY FIRE, THAT THOU MAYEST BECOME RICH; AND WHITE GARMENTS THAT THOU MAYEST CLOTHE THYSELF, AND *that* THE SHAME OF THY NAKEDNESS BE NOT MADE MANIFEST; AND EYESALVE TO ANOINT THINE EYES, THAT THOU MAYEST SEE. AS MANY AS I LOVE, I REPROVE AND CHASTEN: BE ZEALOUS THEREFORE, AND REPENT. BEHOLD, I STAND AT THE DOOR AND KNOCK; IF ANY MAN HEAR MY VOICE AND OPEN THE DOOR, I WILL COME IN TO HIM, AND WILL SUP WITH HIM, AND HE WITH ME. HE THAT OVERCOMETH, I WILL GIVE TO HIM TO SIT DOWN WITH ME IN MY THRONE, AS I ALSO OVERCAME, AND SAT DOWN WITH MY FATHER IN HIS THRONE. HE THAT HATH AN EAR, LET HIM HEAR WHAT THE SPIRIT SAITH TO THE CHURCHES."

LXI.—EMPIRICISM AND EVOLUTIONISM VERSUS INTUITIONALISM AND CREATIONISM.

THE various schools of Philosophy and Science—rather of scientific-Philosophy or of philosophical-Science—are now, more eagerly than ever, contending for Truth as indicated by such methods as those above named. Renascent Christianity, here, as on questions of Theology and of Ecclesiasticism in general, occupies the middle ground.

Intuition is accumulated experience : and the accumulated experience of all the past plus the experience of the present life (the present incarnation of the human individual) is what is called *empiricism*. Evolution is gradual unfolding ; and gradual unfolding is the one and only observed method of Creation. So, of the *empiricist* and of the *intuitionalist*, of the *evolutionist* and of the *creationist*, we may say: "You are both right and both wrong, the Truth lies between you." All knowledge of Truth comes, ever has and must come, to man from the gradual experience of the individual in connection with the systematized experience of the race. The Universe, in all its parts and details, is forever a gradual *unfolding and becoming* rather than suddenly created or supernaturally perfected—i. e., *mechanically* produced and controlled.

The experience of the individual hitched on to the systematized experience of Mankind, *and* individual unfoldings added to the (scientifically observed) unfoldings of the Universe, this is, seemingly, the true method of Human Knowledge and the only one that is adequate or wise.

From such interpretations of Man and the Universe many luminous and helpful teachings have come. Chief among them are the following *distinctions* which bear directly upon the general method and contents of this volume:

(*a*) Traditional or "orthodox" Christianity, from the Fourth Century downward, has been based on one or another form of what is now called *intuitionalism* in Philosophy and (mechanical or supernatural) *creationism* in Science. Its attitude has been, is, and must be face-backward. On the other hand Materialism and Agnosticism, in all their forms, have always been based on what are now called *empiricism* and *evolutionism*. Their attitude has been, is, and must be face-forward. Primitive Christianity and its present revival, which we call renascent Christianity, being essentially *eclectic*, is based on the common truths of both sides and of all sides. Hence its attitude was in the beginning, is now, and must be Janus-like—*both* backward and forward. It avoids extremes, rejects mere speculations (philosophic, scientific, and theologic alike) and combines into one ever-accreting and hence ever-living and ever-growing System, all *verifiable* facts of human experience and observation. It looks within and without, up and down, backward and forward, yes, and *all around* ("see that ye walk *circumspectly*, not as fools but as wise") and whatever it sees, and is sure it sees, that it accepts—and nothing else. It includes origins *and* results, the past *and* the future, the descent of man *and* the ascent, experience *and* intuition, evolution *and* creation, the terminus a quo *and* the terminus ad quem. The questions of traditional Christianity on the one hand and of Materialism and Agnosticism on the other are important ; but primitive Christianity revived (that is renascent Christianity) includes them all—simply because it, and it only, is *eclectic*. As to methods, the one extreme says : In order to know truth and avoid errors *pray*. The other extreme says : Prayer is superstitious and useless—*think*. Eclecticism says : Pray *and* think—the two great commandments are, first, Thou shalt think and, second, Thou shalt pray ("Watch and pray"); on these two commandments hang all the laws of safety and of salvation ; *the two must go together ;* each is a hemisphere, incomplete and worse than useless without the other. Again, one extreme teaches : Avoid the evil *in order to attain* the good. The other extreme teaches : Seek the good *in order to escape* the evil. Eclecticism says : "Abhor that which is evil *and* cleave to that which is good, . . . *prove* all things and hold fast that which is good." Error is the only evil and Truth is the only good, abhor that and love this with all thy mind as well as with all thy heart: so shalt thou walk in safety and attain to a present and perpetual experience of Eternal Life. But, *take notice;* abhorrence of Error and love of Truth is not passionate desire to get the beliefs of others overthrown and *my own* beliefs confirmed; rather is it passionate desire to get all *shams* overthrown and all *realities* confirmed—even should it involve the shattering of all *my* systems and the establishment of those I now deem heretical or false. Let *self* be forgotten, let *systems* be excluded, let nothing be hated but *shams* and nothing desired but *realities;* thus, and only thus, canst thou follow Jesus the Christ and attain the experience of his promise "Ye shall know Truth and Truth shall make you free."

(*b*) A second difference is that of *liberty* as distinguished from slavery to Law on the one hand and slavery to Logic on the other; this is *categorical* bondage and that *dogmatic*, this is called Consistency of Thought and that Conformity of Belief. Both alike are enslaving to mind and heart, and the Eclecticism of renascent Christianity breaks off the fetters and exclaims " Stand fast therefore in the liberty wherewith Christ hath made us free, and be not entangled again with the yoke of bondage."

Traditional Christianity commands all to *believe* what has always been believed—" the faith *once* delivered to the saints." Materialism and Agnosticism alike command all to *think* what the laws of thought compel—" The Categorical *imperative*." Eclecticism (which is true Christianity) rejects both the " once delivered " of Dogmatism and the " imperative " of Logic; it commands nothing, but " Be pure in heart " and " He that hath ears to hear, let him hear;" it condemns all *yokes* of Belief and *burdens* of Consistency, and commends in their place the *yoke* of Love and the *burden* of Duty—" Come unto me all that are weary (with yokes of Traditional Belief) and heavy laden (with Categorical Imperatives) and I will give you rest."

In soul-life as in body-life and mind-life fluency is essential to health and happiness. When the respiratory, circulatory or other normal motions of the body are obstructed there result distress and disease. When normal intellectual processes are interrupted there result mental distress and disease. So, and in like manner, spiritual distress and disease result from any obstruction or restraint of the normal investigations or aspirations of the soul. Fluency, in other words *freedom*, is essential to Soul-life as it is to body-life and mind-life. Hence any authority, creed, or book imposed as *infallible* and *binding* upon the Soul throttles and enslaves it—chokes its respiration, impedes its activities and ultimately produces disease and distress. No such impositions were made or permitted by Jesus the Christ, or by Apostolic Christianity:—no forced options, no compelled convictions, but (as the Book of Common Prayer well states it) "perfect freedom."

The formulated beliefs of renascent Christianity, like those of primitive Christianity, must not be strait-laced, must not divide "heresy" from "orthodoxy" by any sharp-drawn line. "There must be left over and above the proposition to be subscribed, '*ubique, semper, et ab omnibus,*' another realm into which the stifled soul may escape from pedantic scruples and indulge *its own faith at its own risks.*"

So taught the Founder of Christianity: "Why, even of yourselves judge ye not what is right? . . . Man, who made me a ruler or a divider over you? . . . Neither do I condemn thee. . . . I judge no man."

So taught also the chief Apostle: "Brethren, ye have been called unto liberty. . . . Who art thou that judgest another man's servant? To his own Master he standeth or falleth. . . . Let every man be fully persuaded in his own mind. . . . Every one of us shall give account *of himself* to God. . . . Let us not therefore judge one another any more."

(*c*) A third and final difference is the following: Materialism and Agnosticism alike are forever asking the old question of Pilate (half-doubtingly and half-sneeringly) What is Truth? and, because they ask it of *empiricism* and of *evolutionism* alone, no satisfying answer has ever yet come to them. On the other hand Traditionalism (of every sort) has forever asked the same question of *intuitionalism* and of *creationism* alone; and, as a consequence, have received nothing but the ancient half-answer (with which none but dormant minds and stagnant souls can be satisfied)—"Truth is a *deposit* long ago and *once for all* supernaturally made." Eclecticism, in the form of primitive and of renascent Christianity, asks the question of Experience *and* of Intuition, of Evolution *and* of Creation; and, from the *combined* voices, receives the reply: "Truth is God *imminent* and *incarnate* both in Nature and in Man—the eternal Logos *always* self-revealing."

New light ever makes new truth. To believe that any phase of Truth that mankind has yet observed is absolute, final, and unchangeable is "A weakness of our nature from which we should free ourselves as fast as we can. . . . I sincerely believe that this course is the only one we can follow as reflective men, . . . to be sure we must go on experiencing and thinking over our experiences, for only thus can our opinions *grow more true;* but to hold any one of them—I absolutely do not care which—as if it never could be reinterpretable or corrigible, I believe to be a tremendously mistaken attitude; and I think that the whole history of philosophy will bear me out."

These are recent words of one whom we all revere as our highest living authority in the *reverent and broad* interpretations of Philosophy and Science from the theistic standpoint—a venerable and venerated Professor in Harvard University. They only confirm what true Eclecticism has always taught, namely:—Truth, though in its *substance* unchangeable, in its *logos* or self-revealings is manifold and progressive: its *phases* are (like itself) infinite and always adapted to the expanding powers of the finite mind and the increasing immaculateness of the human heart. Therefore it must be self-evident that *New light ever makes new truth.* Also it follows; as a method, that *The desire for Truth is what brings its self-revealings.* The more eager and persistent the desire, the quicker and more fully will Truth come. Ardent desire is the soul's effective wooing of Truth; she flies to the arms of those who *ardently* desire her. As Jesus said "Be asking" (ask eagerly and persistently), "be seeking" (in the same way), "be knocking" (in the same way), and "ye shall receive, ye shall find, it shall be opened unto you." For to every one who has ever *thus* asked, sought, and knocked, Truth has responded with assuring and loving self-revelations.

LXII.—TENDENCIES TO REVERT AND TO DEGENERATE HISTORICALLY CONFIRMED.

OUT of thousands of historic confirmations of the main theory and warning of this volume, that of the reversions and degenerations of Christianity, we will here notice but one.

In 1485, the Pope who is known as Innocent VIII. issued a bull enjoining the persecution of the Waldenses, even to their extermination. He, as the mouthpiece of God, promised absolution for this life and highest seats in Paradise to whatever rogues, sensualists, or outlaws who should profess the Catholic Faith and join to exterminate the heretics. As a result, writes a Vaudois historian: "There is no town in Piedmont where some of our brethren have not been put to death. Jordan Terbano was burnt alive at Susa; Hippolite Rossiero at Turin; Michael Sonato, an octogenarian, at Sarcena; Vilermin Ambrosio hanged on the Col di Meano; Hugo Chiambs of Fenestrelli, had his entrails torn from his living body at Turin; Peter Gaymoroli of Bobbio in like manner had his entrails taken out in Lucerna, and a fierce cat thrust in their place to torture him further; Maria Romano was buried alive in Rocco Patia; Magdalena Teauno underwent the same fate at San Giovanni; Susana Michelini was bound hand and foot, and left to perish of cold and hunger on the snow at Sarcena; Bartholomeo Foche, gashed with sabres, had the wounds filled up with quicklime, and perished thus in agony at Fenilo; Daniel Michelini had his tongue torn out at Robo for having praised God; James Boridari, perished covered with sulphurous matches which had been forced into his flesh, in his nostrils, mouth, and all over the body, and then lighted. Daniel Rovelli had his mouth filled with gunpowder, which being lighted, blew his head to pieces. . . . Sarah Rostignol was split open from the legs to the bosom, and left so to perish on the road between Eyral and Lucerna; Anna Charbonnier was impaled and carried thus on a pike from San Giovanni to La Torre"—*and much more of the same sort*.

Other historians of that period record numerous similar facts such as these:—" In one year (1485) forty women were executed in Burbia as being bewitched or possessed of the Devil." " Peasants in the vicinity of Dôles were authorized, by parliamentary license, to hunt, as wild beasts, men, women, and children afflicted with the disease of Demonomania, who were called Werewolves." " In the electoral see of Trèves, within a few years, six thousand five hundred men were executed as enchanted, bewitched, and possessed of the Devil." " The ministers held it to be imperatively requisite to bring the whole power of justice against devil-worshippers; hundreds of human beings were burnt or incarcerated. The judges worked the rack actively in order to get complete confessions from the bewitched and from those who were supposed to be *sold to the Devil*." The Church itself sowed the seed and richly fertilized it through its superstitious Dogmas and fanatical Teachings: then, when the crop of *heretics* and of *fanatics* appeared it proceeded to torture them or to cut off their heads. All this at the beginning of the Sixteenth Century. And it is only a fragment of what has been done, *in the name of Christ*, by Protestants and by Patriarchists, as well as by Papists, from the Athanasian triumph at Nicæa down to this day! The latest outcroppings of the same degenerate spirit are such *et cæteras* as the Andover and Union Theological Seminary Heresy Trials; denominational exclusions of " open communionists;" sectarian excommunications of those who doubt the saving power of Atoning Blood; Papal Edicts and Pastoral Letters dictating exactly what all " true Churchmen " must hold and teach; the bitter reproaches and threatenings of "Orthodoxy" poured forth upon the devoted heads and consecrated lives of such reformers of to-day as were the late Phillips Brooks and Professor Drummond, and as are Dr. Watson, Dr. Abbott, Professor Harper, and other conservative leaders of the New Criticism—to say nothing of the unceasing condemnations and crucifixions of Unitarians and of all others who question the Supreme Deity of Jesus the Christ, on the ground that he never called himself nor in the New Testament is called by any higher name than that of Son of Man and Son of God.

> Almost every daily newspaper brings some account of Heresy-persecutions. On the date of this writing appears the following: "The Protestant Episcopal Bishop of ———, who is generally beloved for his virtues, esteemed for his talents, and admired as one who has the courage of his convictions, is accused of heresy by no less than fifty local ministers of all Evangelical Sects. Formal charges have been drawn up and signed by these ministers, and great excitement over the matter prevails in all the religious circles of the State. Denial of the Trinity, of the miraculous birth of Christ, and of bodily Resurrection are the main charges."

Degenerate Christianity has *out-paganed* Paganism in its bigotry, intolerance and persecutions for full fifteen hundred years past. Even Mohammedanism can hardly show so bitter and bloody a record. But 't is ever thus—the higher the attainment the deeper the fall, the more lofty the *genuine* Religion the more ignominious its corruption and decay.

> In an article on the late Professor Harry Drummond by "Ian Maclaren" in the May number of the *The North American Review* the following passage occurs, which is of special interest as bearing upon the recent heresy trial of its author by the synod of the English Presbyterian Church:
>
> "When one saw the unique and priceless work which he (Dr. Drummond) did, it was inexplicable that the religious world should have cast this man, of all others, out, and have lifted up its voice against him. Had religion so many men of bountiful and winning life, so many thinkers of wide range and genuine culture, so many speakers who could move young men by hundreds towards the kingdom of God that she could afford to have the heart to withdraw her confidence from Drummond? Was there ever such madness and irony before heaven as good people lifting up their testimony and writing articles against this most gracious disciple of the Master, because they did not agree with him about certain things he said or some theory he did not teach, while the world lay around them in unbelief and selfishness, and sorrow and pain? 'What can be done,' an eminent evangelist once did me the honor to ask, 'to heal the

breach between the religious world and Drummond,' and I dared to reply that in my poor judgment the first step ought to be for the religious world to repent of its sins and make amends to Drummond for its bitterness. The evangelist said it was unlikely to do any such deed, and I did not myself remember any instance of repentance on the part of the Pharisees."

A recent correspondent of "The Observer," a Presbyterian Journal of New York, has discovered the fatal defect in Professor Drummond's Theology. He attended some of his lectures and "in one of them" erroneous views were presented with reference to the Doctrine of the Atonement! The same Journal, commenting on the large number of persons recently admitted to membership in Plymouth Church, Brooklyn, exclaims: "A mere roster of converts means little unless we know what sort of converts they are!" This is the same remark long and often made " by skeptics and scoffers " with reference to the *sum-totals* of professed Christians as proffered evidences of the truth of Christianity, and in criticism of the *argument from numbers* for the superiority or spiritual worth of any particular church or sect. And it is as pertinent in the latter case as in the former. In either case and in all cases "a mere roster of converts," though it should amount to millions or hundreds of millions of names, is no certain evidence of truth or worth. *Non multa, sed multum* —not many, but much; not quantity, but quality. "And *few* there be that find it."

LXIII.—THE PRESENT DEGENERATION OF OUR CHURCHES.

At a recent Bi-Centennial Jubilee of Trinity Church in New York City a well-known Episcopal Rector was brave enough to say, as reported by the Daily Newspapers:— "The great sin of to-day is that of giving too much prominence to the rich in our Churches." "During my 15 years in New York I have seen the city's population south of Fourteenth street, increased by the addition of 100,000 souls. In the same period I have witnessed the sad spectacle of 19 churches moving farther uptown. Can any man be blind to the fact that it has been and is the policy, nolens volens, to take spacious churches away from the people who most urgently need them?" "Another thing we want *is freedom of speech* in our pulpits. We hem and haw; we wait for a cue. The times in which we live demand something more than that. Let our clergymen be *beyond the control of monetary considerations.*"

He might well have continued his criticisms, and given them especial emphasis, in application to *four main and growing evils* in all the Protestant Sects, *viz.:* Proprietorship of Pews, Rich Men's Churches and Poor Men's Churches, Fat-salaries and Starving-salaries, and Sensational-Worship instead of Gospel-Worship.

(*a*) No Church is worthy to be called Christian in which there is a square foot of space that is not open to all alike without any *stipulated* price.

(*b*) No Church is worthy to be called Christian in which the rich and the poor do not meet together with fraternal and cordial recognitions.

(*c*) No Church is worthy to be called Christian which permits what are known as its "popular" and "talented" ministers to *feast* while those who fail to attain these flattering distinctions must *fast*. As the first ministers of Christ had "all things in common," so always should there be a common fund from which all who are received as ministers of Christ should have a *community of support*, justly proportioned to their several circumstances and needs. No one should have more, and no one less, than what might fairly be called a *comfortable livelihood*. Such a method would be truly Christian and would effectually forestall that widespread bribery—in the way of luxurious salaries and large perquisites—which now ties tongues, seals lips, and elicits soft words and smooth flatteries, from what is called the Pulpit.

(*d*) And finally:—No Church is worthy to be called Christian which rejects the simplicity, fervor, plainness, and pointedness of Gospel-Worship—as pictured and patterned in the New Testament—substituting in its place the Sensational Worship of noise or of novelty, of elaborate ritual or of mere æsthetic effect. *All* of these *are* sensational; the *noise* of the Salvation Army, the *novelty* of the Pulpit-Crank, the *pageant* of the elaborate Ritual and the *studied softness and soothingness* of the Program of Service—all alike are Sensation and not Gospel. No true Christian Church ever has tolerated them or ever will; it is only degenerate Christianity that can devise or welcome them.

Whenever our Clergy will vigorously attack these "four main and growing evils in all the Protestant Sects" and continue the attack till they are somehow remedied, Christianity will *spring up anew* and begin again to be the same reforming and regenerating power in all the world that it was in the Apostolic age and in the two succeeding centuries.

To the plea for more moderate salaries and fewer perquisites for ministers of the Rich-men's Churches and more *equalized* support for all the Clergy in general, it is commonly objected that "superior talent and worth should have superior pay." To which we reply:

"*What then! Is the reward of Virtue, bread?*" Is money "the measure of the man"? In these money-grasping, every-thing-by-money-measuring days, 't is a shame that any one called a minister of Christ should be found grasping with the rest; should allow his "talent and worth" to be measured and rewarded by money, or by anything that money can procure. Magnificent church edifices, fashionable congregations, exquisite music, enriched rituals, elegant parsonages, and parson's pockets filled with gold are foreign enough from Gospel Christianity. But when they indicate " superior talent and worth" it is high time for some Clergy-rebukes and Clergy-reforms similar to those of nineteen centuries ago when money and applause, as measures of talent and worth, were rejected and trodden under foot; when one who "had his raiment of camels' hair, and a leather girdle about his loins, and his meat was locusts and wild honey," dared to say to his would-be aristocratic parishioners, "O, generation of vipers"; when one who had "not where to lay his head" said, of the magnificent temple with its magnificent ritual, crowds of formalistic worshippers, pompous priests and overflowing treasury: "Not one stone shall remain upon another that shall not be thrown down . . . hypocrites, that pray to be seen of men . . . hypocrites, that do alms that ye may have glory of men . . . hypocrites, that minister for earthly reward . . . behold, your house is left unto you desolate"; when one who had renounced the highest positions and worldly promises of his ancestral "Orthodoxy," and wrought daily at tent-making that his "own hands" might minister to his "necessities" said : "Of the Jews five times received I forty stripes save one, thrice was I beaten with rods, once was I stoned . . . to whom gave we place by subjection, no, not for an hour . . . those who *seemed to be somewhat*, whatsoever they were, it maketh no matter to me ; God accepteth *no man's person* . . . and when Peter was come to Antioch, I withstood *him* to the face, because he was to be blamed . . . and the other Jews *dissembled likewise with him* . . . but when I saw that they walked not uprightly according to the truth of the Gospel, I said *unto Peter before them all* . . . I am *crucified with Christ*, nevertheless I live; yet not I, but Christ liveth in me; and the life which I now live in the flesh I live by the faith of the Son of God, who loved me, and *gave himself* for me"; when, in short, all those ministers of the Gospel whom the world now delights to honor were, like their Divine Master, "good shepherds" who came not for salary or applause but to "lead out," to "go before," and to "lay down their lives, for the sheep."

Moreover it *is not true* that the highest "talent and worth" are found in what the world calls the "highest places"—any more in the Church than elsewhere. The discouragements, difficulties, and many-sided requirements of the obscure Mission, or of the humble Country Parish develop and (if faithfully responded to) indicate higher "talent and worth" than those required, or usually found, in the well-equipped Rich-men's Parishes where everything moves along of its own accord. Here money is superabundant for all desired externalities, hundreds of hands are ready to co-operate in all fashionable or formalistic work, the attractions of exquisite music and of luxurious surroundings avail to draw and hold the crowds, to be a member and especially a "communicant" of such a Church is both reputable and profitable; nothing then is needed or (in most cases) is even acceptable in the line of "talent and worth" on the part of the minister beyond superior attractiveness of person, manners, and voice in connection with unusual adaptations as a manager, a diplomat, and a patron of those who constitute "aristocratic" society.

In addresses delivered at the Centennial Services of a New England Parish the following significant facts, relative to one of its first and most "distinguished" pastors, were mentioned:—As a young man of twenty-six years he officiated as candidate at ——— Church. The Committee reported, "he pares an apple and lights a pipe more like a gentleman than any of the other candidates"—and so he was chosen. His subsequent popularity is suggested when we read, "The richest shippers of the city and their negro servants made up the congregations chiefly." Still more so when we learn that the Church and its pastor *remained neutral* throughout the War of the Revolution; and that their successors and descendants in the same city zealously defended Slavery and bitterly opposed the Anti-Slavery leaders. While no burning words of protest against popular wrong or in advocacy of unpopular right are quoted we find such quotations as this: "We made a fine appearance as we walked together in our gowns and cassocks." Not in Roman Catholic, Greek Catholic, and Anglican or Protestant Episcopal Churches alone are such tests of "talent and worth" found; but in all the Sects they are beginning to prevail widely.

"Verily I say unto you They have their reward"—and let them have it; only let them not have *also* the undeserved rewards of being exalted, both as those "who seem to be pillars" and as those of "superior talent and worth," above their brethren who are faithful ministers of Christ in obscure or humble stations.

As to the relative requirements of large and rich Churches on one hand and of small and poor ones on the other, the author is speaking from his own long experience as well as wide observation. Of the thirty continuous years of his ministry, the first fifteen were spent as Pastor of unusually large, intelligent, and wealthy (but, fortunately, not in any marked degree "fashionable" or "aristocratic") Parishes; the last fifteen years have been spent as Rector of small and poor Parishes. Whatever "talent and worth" he has, were both developed and demanded *less* in the first fifteen years than in the last; and, if he has any "treasure in Heaven" it has accumulated *chiefly* during this latter period, when, without any especial regard to "money or price" he has tried to be true to that sign and seal of genuine Christianity which its Founder himself authorized:—" The poor have the Gospel preached to them."

To the Clergy at large, as well as to the World at large, how deeply hidden, as yet, is the meaning of those words of Jesus, "Verily I say unto you, they have their reward"; and again (as if in explanation) "There be many that are first that shall be last and many that are last shall be first."

LXIV.—TRUE TO ONE'S OWN SELF AND WORKING IN ONE'S OWN WAY.

THE following passage is from the Table-talk of Luther:— "I am radical, plain-spoken, boisterous and disposed to be warlike. I seem born to contend against innumerable monsters and devils. It seems *my* mission to remove stumps and stones, cut away thistles and thorns, and clear the wild forests; then Master Philippus (Melanchthon) comes along, softly and gently, sowing and watering according to the gifts which God has bestowed upon *him*." So it was that each was contented to do his own work. It should ever be thus: Every man true to himself and faithfully putting to use whatever gift God has bestowed upon *him*. The radical and plain-spoken Peter must not try to copy John: if he does his Master will rebuke him and say, "What is that to thee? follow thou me." Paul must content himself with planting and leave Apollos to water. Transposing some well-known words, "You want to be like everybody else; don't do it; *one's enough*." Be yourself; and permit every other one to be himself. Do your own work; and do it in your own way—leaving results to Him who rules and overrules. Without the *radicalism* and *sharp-speech* of Peter, Paul, and Luther the *conservatism* and *soft-speech* of John, Apollos, and Melanchthon would have been as water falling upon a rock or as seed scattered upon unploughed ground.

The Peters, Pauls, and Luthers of the world—being called to agitate, protest, and reform—must always be ready to accept the martyr's obloquy and shame; but, in the midst of their essential unpopularity, they may comfort themselves by believing that "in due time," their words will be accepted and their methods approved. They who sow in tears, doubtless shall come with joy *at the harvest*, bringing their sheaves with them. *After many days*, they who cast their bread upon the waters shall find it. At any rate they *must* scatter their seed, speak their word, do their deed as Conscience bids them:

"*When Duty whispers low, 'thou must,'
The soul replies, 'I can':* "—

I can and I *will*, leaving the results to Him who rules and overrules.

"With the vision of certain duties to be done, of certain outward changes to be wrought or resisted—no matter how we *succeed* in doing them—do them we somehow must: for the leaving of them undone is perdition. No matter how we feel; if we are *only faithful*—the world will in so far be safe, and we quit of our debt toward it. Take, then, the yoke upon our shoulders; bend our neck beneath the heavy legality of its weight; regard *something else than our feelings* as our limit, our master, and our law; be willing to 'live and die in its service,'—and, at a stroke, we have passed from the subjective into the objective philosophy of things; much as when one awakens from some feverish dream, full of bad sights and noises, to find one's self bathed in the sacred coolness and quiet of the air of the night."

LXV.—A RIGHTEOUS DISREGARD OF PUBLIC OPINION.

THE terms Dissenter, Schismatic, Heterodox, Heretic, Unbeliever, Infidel, Atheist, Servant of Beelzebub, Child of the Devil are all synonymous in the popular conception and speech. In every nation, religion, and age this has been so.

It is as truly, though not as intensely, so now and here as formerly and elsewhere. The commonly accepted opinion whatever it may be, is, always and everywhere, called Orthodoxy. The true Religion, as also the true standards in Society and in State, is supposed to be whatever the masses dictate and delight in. The voice of the Populace is accepted as the voice of God. Stand with the majority, and you stand presumably on the Lord's side. Count the votes, and the overwhelming suffrage is thought to indicate the absolute and final Truth. Say what your constituents want you to say (and will pay you well to say) and you are believed to speak as "the Spirit giveth utterance." Above all things be popular; for the favor of men is considered to be the same thing as the favor of God. "Shout with the mob —if there be two, shout with the largest one":—thus you will be called a Conformist and a member of the True Church. If you do otherwise you will be a Dissenter, a Schismatic—and all the rest, as named above.

All observing travellers and all intelligent historians tell us that this is everywhere and always so—in every Nation, in every Society, in every Religion. Moreover the more barbarous the Nation, the more uncivilized the Society, the more irrational the Religion the more widely and persistently is it so. Considering this fact the true disciple of Jesus always hears a Voice saying to him, "What is that to thee? follow thou me." It is so natural to inquire, What thinks this one and that? What is the belief of the multitude? What is the opinion of the majority? The New Testament answer is: Why, even of yourselves judge ye not what is right? Enter ye in at the strait gate and narrow way though few there be that find it. Blessed are ye when men shall revile you, and persecute you, for my sake; for so persecuted they the prophets which were before you. Even if wife or husband, parents, children, kindred, friends, and all the world oppose you, still take the cross and follow me. The simple meaning of all such Bible teachings is this:—Conform if you can conform *intelligently and sincerely*, but otherwise bravely accept the Dissenter's reproach and shame.

Be " orthodox" if you can be *intelligently and sincerely*, but otherwise follow Jesus even to Gethsemane and the Cross. "*What is that to thee? follow thou me.*"

Said a popular critic to one of our greatest nineteenth-century poets, in criticism of a poem he was about to publish, " That will never do." The poet replied, " It must do; I know very well that it will be unpopular, but *it must do*." The martyr-spirited clergyman of the Church of England, whom everybody knows as author of The Eternal Hope, published and circulated that " heretical " volume, (in his own words) " perfectly well aware of the gravity of what I was doing. At last it had become my duty to express my convictions unmistakably. 'While I was musing the fire burned, and at last I spoke with my tongue.' I felt constrained to publicly repudiate doctrines which had been almost universally professed and proclaimed by Christians for fifteen hundred years. I knew that to do so was an act that would cost me dear . . . that I could not escape the most savage animadversions. The *odium theologicum* is as virulent and anti-Christian in this day as it ever was. The religious newspapers are often as unfair and remorseless as the Inquisition itself. . . . A leading clergyman of London said to me, ' You have spoken out what nearly every-one of us secretly believe '; and yet it soon began to rain denunciations. I was assailed in scores of pamphlets; annihilated in hundreds of reviews; lectured against by University professors; anathematized by Anglicans, Baptists, and Methodists. The refutations, the replies, the revilings would alone fill a small library. . . . Such is the 'eternal spirit of the populace' . . . the *anathema Maranatha* of traditional and partisan theologians."

Such is a single one out of very many recent illustrations. To proclaim and try to promulgate (or even to quietly profess) opinions that are not " orthodox " (i. e., popular) is almost as much of a reproach, requiring a martyr-spirit to endure, in the Church of to-day as in that of the so-called Dark Ages; and among Christians almost as persistently as among Moslems, Buddhists, and other Pagans. It is the same old intolerance of Orthodoxy that has prevailed through all the ages back to the Sabbath Day upon which transpired this which follows:

"And all they in the synagogue, when they heard these things, were filled with wrath; and rose up and thrust him out of the city, and led him unto the brow of the hill whereon their city was built, that they might cast him down headlong."

Let us all pray for that heroic grace of Jesus—A *righteous* disregard of popular opinion.

LXVI.—THE GOLDEN MEAN OF CONTROVERSY.

THERE is a world of wisdom in the homely words of that landlord (portrayed in one of our finest modern works of Fiction) who used to close the hot and prolonged debates of the famous literary patrons of his Inn with the exclamation, "Ye are both right and both wrong, gentlemen! the truth lies 'atween ye, the truth lies 'atween ye." It was only a plainer way of stating the old lesson of Scylla and Charybdis—*hold to the mid-stream, avoid extremes, occupy the Golden Mean.*

The author of this volume is, and long has been a believer in the Golden Mean of all *intelligently and sincerely* controverted opinions. In all intelligent and sincere controversy each side and every side presents both partial Truth and partial Error. Indeed a fraction or fragment of Truth taken for the whole Truth is Error: and the only way to overcome this kind of Error is to add fraction to fraction, fragment to fragment by the eclectic or inclusive (instead of the radical or exclusive) method.

Controversy ceases when extreme (that is exclusive) positions are abandoned. When each says to all and all say to each, "Truth is broader than any of our systems, broader than all our systems and includes them all; come and let us reason together"—then destruction ends and construction begins.

In polemic periods extremes are forced upon those who

eagerly desire to destroy some particular error: but when that error is destroyed, those who eagerly desire to construct Truth in its place abandon extremes, and select their material for construction from both sides and all sides. That is, they become *eclectics* and are no longer *partisans*. They discard self-made or party-made systems and as soon as they do this, find to their joy that "everything fits in." Truth as seen from all sides—everybody an observer, everybody a helper, everybody a "Witness for the Lord"—is what they now care for. They have ceased to defend systems and seek nothing but Truth. And Truth is infinite; co-extensive with the Infinite One, of whom it is the eternal and universal Logos, or Word, or Revelation.

This, in Religion as in every other department of human thought, is the *constructive* method. This is Eclecticism, or the Golden Mean. Such has been the method of this volume.

The author, adhering to no party or sect, has sought to draw from all parties and all sects whatever is pure, and beautiful, and good. He believes that the *common truths* of all Religions constitute True Religion; that this is what Jesus the Christ and his Apostles taught; and that this is genuine Christianity. Each party or sect observes but a single side of *infinite-sided* Truth. Assured of this no wise observer will confine himself to a party or a sect. Yesterday he stood with one group and, as a Seer, tried to *see* what they saw; to-day he stands with another; to-morrow he will stand with another; and so he will continue to do, if he be *truly* wise, "World without end. Amen." The broadest of the "Broad Churches" is the only one that he will belong to; and that must be so broad as to include in its cordial fellowship every earnest seeker and sincere lover of Truth beneath the sun. When it fails to be this, he will protest, agitate, dissent—at whatever risk of opprobrium, of poverty, or of being "cast out." He will gladly suffer the loss of all things and "count them but dung" rather than be separated from that love of God which was in Christ Jesus toward all who seek for Righteousness and Truth.

His must be the Church of the Communion Office in the Book of Common Prayer—"the blessed company of all faithful people." This is an *invisible* company; and rather than be separated in sympathy and spiritual communion from *even one* of these he will prefer to be cast out, from the *visible* Church. For he who stands with God stands never alone, but has the happy assurance that the *blessed majority* are all about him. "And Elisha prayed, and said, Lord, I pray thee, open his eyes, that he may see. And the Lord opened the eyes of the young man; and he saw: and, behold, the mountain *was* full of horses and chariots of fire round about Elisha."

Such is true Churchmanship and true Christianity.

LXVII.—FRAGMENTS.

1. *Risings and Fallings of Man.*

HUMAN History always has been and doubtless will long continue to be a succession of risings and fallings of Man, a series of "Paradise" lost and regained. In the language of Evolutionary-science—"Struggles for Existence" resulting in more or less lofty attainments, followed by Inaction and consequent decline: "Survival of the Fittest" in some ennobled characters who create and lead an epoch, then a "falling away" or reversion and degeneration of the masses. Such ever has been Human History, and such doubtless it will long continue to be; not of *necessity*, nor of the *will of God*, but simply because the inviolable law universally prevails that, *going upward requires effort and to cease from effort is to go downward*. It is difficult to rise, it is easy to fall. "In the sweat of thy brow shalt thou eat thy bread *all the days of thy life*." To cease from effort even for a day is to revert, and to revert means degeneration or going downward.

> "*This law the immortal gods to men have set
> That, none arrive at Virtue but by sweat.*"

This is recognized as a universal law, ceaseless and inviolable. Effort *propels* and inaction *repels*—alike in body, mind, and soul: the more vigorous the effort the more rapid the *ascent*, the more complete the inaction the more rapid the *descent*.

The cardinal vice, the "besetting sin" of Human Nature is Indolence: physically this is true, mentally still more true, and *spiritually truest of all*. It was this Indolence that caused the first highly evolved man and woman (whom History tells us about) to degenerate. They ceased to aspire and to struggle, then they *fell:* and a period of reversion and decay succeeded both to them and to their posterity.

This is the old story of Adam and Eve and The Fall of Man. The story began, though we have no *written* or *traditional* records of it (plenty of geological and similar records) countless ages before the evolution of "Adam and Eve"; and it has been going on, with unceasing alternations of *risings* and *fallings* ever since.

In "Adam's" rise we rose all;
In "Adam's" fall we fell all.

For countless ages to come this will be the summarized History of Mankind, as it has been for countless ages past. Such is the corporate relation (taught by Science as fully as by Scripture) of descendants to ancestors and of ancestors to descendants *forever and forever*. There are no *separate* interests, there is no such thing as *individual* salvation. The human race, (from the first Amœba-to-ape-developed man *up* to "Adam" and from "Adam" *up* to the last Kingdom-of-Heaven-established-on-Earth generation), is so bound together that—*All must rise together and together fall*. In this sense it is true that in the *first* Adam's fall "we sinned all," and in the *second* Adam's rise we all rose. *That* was "death," *this* was "resurrection from the dead." "As in Adam all died, so in Christ *are* all made alive." "I, if I be lifted up will draw all men *with me upward*." The Amœba (or whatever other lowest form of individualized life) *aspiring*, and *struggling to ascend*, starts upon the path of "Eternal Life" and carries all its progeny *upward* with it. The Ape (or whatever other higher form of evolving individual life) *contented*, and *ceasing* to struggle upward, starts backward upon the path of Reversion, of Degeneration, or of "Eternal Death" and carries all its offspring *downward* with it.

Such are the risings and fallings of Man. To be contented and to cease struggling upward is to revert, to degenerate, *to die;* to aspire and to struggle upward is to have life, and *to have it more abundantly.* This, in both an individual and a corporate sense, is a law seemingly universal, eternal and inviolable. To neglect it is to be "dead in trespasses and sins"; to conform to it is "the Resurrection of the dead, and the Life of the world to come. Amen." Moreover, to *proclaim* it, everywhere and unceasingly, is to "preach the Gospel to every creature"; to refuse to thus *proclaim* it, is to be "disobedient to the heavenly vision" and to perish with "them that perish."—"Then shall He say also unto them on the left hand, Depart from me, ye cursed, into everlasting fire, prepared for the devil and his angels; . . . Verily I say unto you, *Inasmuch as ye did it not to one of the least of these, ye did it not to me.* And these shall go away into enduring punishment."

From this point of view, common to both Scripture and Science, all the evolutionary interpretations of the Universe and all the ever-alternating facts of History are clearly explained. *An inviolable law of Aspiration and of upward Struggle; conformity to this law brings ever-unfolding life and peace, non-conformity brings the opposite.*

This explains all. All the *holy* precepts of Holy Books, all the *lofty* maxims of Sages and Saints, all the *wise* inductions and deductions of Philosophy and of Science as well as of Theology point to this one law—lead to it, and confirm it.

"Not to the *born* saint, but to the sinner *becoming* a saint the full length, and breadth, and heighth, and depth of life's meanings are revealed."

Not the absence of vice, but vice there and virtue *holding it ever by the throat*, seems the ideal human state."

The wretch languishing in the felon's cell may be drinking draughts of the wine of Truth which are untasted by the so-called favorites of fortune who, content with luxury and selfishness, have ceased to struggle for a *higher* existence—both for themselves and for that Humanity of which they are an essential part.

The ascent and the descent of man, the joys and sorrows of life, the achievements and failures of the human race, and all the processions and recessions of sentient forms of existence beneath the sun are natural consequences of conformity or of non-conformity to Nature's inviolable law—Thou shalt struggle and help others to struggle upward, *and forever upward*.

2. *Jesus the Fruitage of the Ages, and the Product of His Environments.*

THE century which opened the Christian Era was in every way remarkable. Being such it could not fail to produce remarkable men; and, among the many remarkable men, one most remarkable of all. It was the Harvest of the Ages. The great saints, sages, and prophets of Israel; philosophers, poets, and artists of Greece; law-givers, legislators, and heroes of Rome; mystics, dreamers, and "wise men" from the East (Persia, India, China) had all combined to scatter the seed which, in the first Century came to an abundant harvest. Jesus the Christ was its "first fruit," its finest product: and his Religion became its "Garner." The antecedents and environments of Jesus could not fail to produce him (in a lofty sense) any more than those of Moses, David, Isaiah, Sakya Muni, Confucius, Socrates (and hundreds more who sprang loftily forth from the teeming soil of teeming ages) could have failed to produce them.

The first Century was not only one of the Golden Eras but *the* Golden Era: the Era of Universal Empire, Peace, Culture, Refinement, Toleration, Intellectual Vigor,—*of Dogmatic Decline and Religious Resurrection, of Ecclesiastical Decay and Ethical Renewal.* Judea was the centre of it all; through it were travelling and in it were dwelling "devout men, out of every nation under heaven."

Out of this best prepared soil of Humanity and most teeming life of History, what a *miracle* it would have been had not at least one *miraculous* product issued,—one, as far superior to all others as his Era was superior (in remarkable antecedents and environments) to all the Eras which preceded and succeeded it!

Such a product was Jesus, *miraculous* and yet entirely natural; the *supreme* and yet the typical and prophetic fruitage of all the ages.

3.—*External Prosperity and Internal Decay.*

The sharp eye of him who "knew what was in men and needed not to be told" detected in individuals, and also in the institutions of Church and of State alike, the "dead men's bones" within the "garnished sepulchres"—the unreality or the "uncleanness" beneath gilded and glorious exteriors. Such *individuals*, with whom the Temple and the Synagogues were thronged, he constantly rebuked and scorned as "hypocrites"; and such *institutions*, never more glorious with external prosperities and pieties, he unceasingly predicted would be completely overthrown so that "not one stone should remain upon another."

In all religions and generations to this day the *popular* individuals and the *popular* institutions have been of the same kind; exteriors regarded, interiors unconsidered—appearances, not actualties. This is so because *popularity* (in its wide or "orthodox" sense) means the judgment of the majority; and the majorities have never yet risen to an intellectual, moral, or spiritual elevation sufficient to enable them to form anything but superficial judgments in these several departments. Taking advantage of this fact, self-seeking individuals and self-parading institutions have always flattered the majority into believing that their *vote and verdict* is the *voice of God*. Their vote has always been for externalities, their verdict for superficialities. So, pretentious Hypocrisy has flourished, and glittering Emptiness prevailed, in State and Church alike (but in Church far more than in State) to this day.

External glory may be the product of internal decay. A magnificent show of Piety may co-exist with hearts "full of all uncleanness." So that stately temples with thronged courts, gorgeous adornments, grand rituals, impressive ceremonies, and imposing formalities of Worship (even if abundant charities and humanities of the self-parading sort are added) are no certain evidences of *vital soul-life* in the Christianity of to-day more than they were in the Christianity of the fourteenth century; nor in the Christianity of the fourteenth century more than they were in *magnificently decaying* Judaism at the beginning of the Christian Era.

Thus far, in the history of every name and form of Religion, "the zenith of formalistic Piety has ever been the nadir of 'Religion Pure and Undefiled.'" If sincerity be not in the heart, intelligence in the head, and love in the life the prosperities, ceremonialisms, and splendors of Religion are "only sounding brass and tinkling cymbals." Sincerity, Intelligence, Love—these three are *co-essential;* "but the *greatest* of all is Love."

4.—*What Mankind Most Needs.*

Thus far, in the history of all Religions and Theologies, the greatest lack has been *the historic sense and the logical insight combined* by which to discriminate between fact and fiction, truth and error. Blind credulity and readiness to believe "every word that is told him" without criticism, investigation, or caution has been the fatal defect of the overwhelming majorities of mankind. "Its cardinal weakness is to let belief follow recklessly upon lively conception, especially when the conception has instinctive liking at its back. . . . What such people most need is that their beliefs should be broken up and ventilated, that the northwest wind of Science should get into them and blow their sickliness and barbarism away."

The masses of men have never read the "first and great Commandment" beyond the word *heart*—"Thou shalt love the Lord thy God with all thy heart." It is high time that

Priest-craft should not only permit but urge them to proceed to the next clause—"and mind." Simply this is what Renascent Christianity insists upon. Till the "mind" is reverenced *equally* and put to use *co-operatively* with the "heart," in the love and service both of God and of Man, it matters not how much false prophets and hireling-priests of all the degenerate Religions combined may say "Peace, Peace!"—in the name of God and for the welfare of Mankind Renascent Christianity will reply, *There shall be no Peace!*

At the date of this writing (May 12, 1897) the *New York Times* has the following significant and not at all uncommon item: "Mr. —— is one of the most worthy members of the —— Church at ——, and gives freely of his means to support it. He is a deacon, and a teacher of a Bible Class. Until a few weeks ago he was a firm supporter of the Rev. ——, the pastor of the church. Recently the Rev. —— heard that Mr. —— was inculcating the doctrine of an intermediate state, and he denounced the theory as heresy. Hot words passed between the men and the controversy has extended until it has involved the whole church. . . ."

The names given by the newspaper are here left blank. The church is located within a hundred miles of New York City and its Pastor is called a Protestant. If it were located in Central Africa or in the South Sea Islands, or if its Pastor were a Romanist or a Mohammedan; or even if such intolerant Protestants were not the rule but rather exceptions, the circumstance might pass without notice.

As it is, the least that can be said of such "Pastors" and "Protestants" is to quote the words of the Master to similar teachers and leaders of his day: "Ye have taken away the key of knowledge, ye entered not in yourselves, and them that were entering in ye hindered. . . . Blind guides, which strain at a gnat, and swallow a camel."

5.—*Faith and Works, or Answering our own Prayers.*

In a section preceding it was affirmed that Eclecticism (or Renascent Christianity) combines all that is true and good in both of the opposing Systems known as Supernaturalism and Naturalism.

The relative conceptions and methods of these three different schools of interpretation may be illustrated by the following:—A gentleman calling on friends, found a bright little girl much grieved that her brother was making a trap to catch birds. A few days later, calling again, he asked her "What about the trap?" She said, "I first went out and told the birds not to go near the trap ; but that same day one was caught. The next day I asked the Lord to keep the trap from catching them : but it caught two before noon. Then I prayed the Lord *to help me to keep the birds from getting caught*, and I went out and kicked the trap all to pieces." So the Naturalist apostrophizes Nature, and awaits results; the Supernaturalist prays to the Lord, and awaits results; the *Natural-Supernaturalist* or Eclectic prays the Lord to help, and then goes to work vigorously and *kicks the trap to pieces*. Neither Nature nor Providence ever does for man anything that he is competent to do himself, by using the faculties and powers with which he is endowed. Every man is thus endowed for the attainment of all that it is wisest for him to have in the present life ; to recognize, reverence, and use to their utmost those endowments is, *of itself*, Prayer. True Prayer asks for nothing (of a worldly or temporal nature) but that Indolence and Cowardice may be overcome, and that Industry and Courage may be aroused sufficient to do with one's might whatever one's hands find to do. To drive out Sloth and Fear and to cultivate Energy and Bravery (toward all that is true, and beautiful, and good) is to invoke both Nature and the Supernatural.

Petition for the stimulus and the will to do what one *ought and can* is the wise man's only (personal) prayer. This prayer he will pray with every effort and with every breath. In the same way for everything received or accomplished, enjoyed or secured he will devoutly give thanks.

Such are the Faith *and* Works, the Prayer *and* Thanksgiving of Eclecticism, which is *true* Christianity. "Pray without ceasing : in everything give thanks."

LXVIII.—THE SPIRIT AND NOT THE LETTER OF THE CREEDS.

IN attempting to give a modern meaning to the ancient formularies of Historical Christianity, in the preceding pages, the position was taken that, in every department of

Religious Interpretation (the same as in the Bible), it is equally and ceaselessly true that "the letter killeth, but the spirit giveth life."

The scholarly and beautifully conservative book (of one of our most Christ-like modern Divines), well known as *Orthodoxy, Its Truths and Errors*, elaborates this position in the spirit of the New Testament. We may take a fundamental illustration—that of the dogma of the "Trinity." After showing its popular errors and urging their rejection, the author says of its truth: "The Father, the Son, and the Holy Ghost are not merely different names for the same thing, but they indicate three different Revelations, three different views which God has given of His character, and which taken together constitute the total Divine Representation. . . . This Trinity of Manifestations is founded in the truth of things, and is also according to the teachings of the greatest Fathers of the Church. There is no antecedent objection to the form of the Trinity as a *threefold manifestation* of the Divine Being: and we have only to ask, Is it *true* as a matter *of fact?* Has such a threefold manifestation of God actually taken place? We reply that it is so. According to observation and experience, as well as to Scripture, we find such to be the fact. . . . According to the New Testament the Father would seem to be the source of all things: the Creator, the Fountain of being and life. The Son is spoken of as the manifestation of that Being in Jesus the Christ. The Holy Ghost is spoken of as a spiritual influence proceeding from the Father and the Son, dwelling in the hearts of believers as a source of their life—the idea of God seen in *Causation*, in *Reason*, and in *Conscience*—as making the very life of the soul itself. . . . There are these three *classified* Manifestations of God, and we know of no others. They are distinct from each other in form, but the same in essence. They are not merely three *names* for the same thing, but they are real *personal* Manifestations of God, real Subsistencies, since God is *personally* present in all of them, . . . There is, therefore, an essential truth hidden in the idea of the Trinity. While the church doctrine in every form which it has hitherto taken has failed to satisfy the human *intellect*, the Christian *heart* has clung to the *substance contained in them all*. . . . A *simple unity*, as held by the Jews and Mohammedans, and by some Christian imitators, may be a *bald unity* and an *empty unity*. This it certainly is when it shows us God withdrawn from Nature, from Christ, from the Soul; not *immanent*, but *outside* of them. This is to make Nature godless; Christ *merely* human; the Soul a machine, moved by an external impulse, not by an inward inspiration. Such is the practical view of the Trinity, *when rightly understood.*"

The substance of this citation seems to be as follows: The *letter* of the doctrine of the Trinity is that there are *three persons* in one God; its *spirit* is that there is one God in *three personal* Manifestations. Of all Unitarians and Trinitarians alike the common ground is that there is One God, and that He is a *person* in some unspeakably glorious and expanded sense of that word. This *personality* of God, being an infinite mystery, should only be affirmed and trusted in; it should not be defined except in its Manifestations. These Manifestations, as *classified*, are three—in the language of Science they are Causation, Reason, and Conscience; in the language of Theology they are Father, Son, and Holy Ghost: these Three are One, or, *One is in the Three*. Simply this is the spirit of the doctrine of the Trinity, all else belongs to the letter: and "the letter killeth, but the spirit giveth life."

LXIX.—MODERN USE OF ANCIENT IDEAS AND TERMS.

The Philosophy of which Socrates, Plato, Aristotle, and Philo were successively chief expositors (which was an Eclecticism of all widest learning and deepest thought of the entire world down to the first century), furnished Apostolic Christianity with many of its most effective ideas and terms. Among these were especially the following:

(*a*) "Logos," or Word of God: teaching (what before had been, and even now is, but very narrowly and imperfectly apprehended) the Divine *immanence* in Nature and *incarnation* in Man; or God *in* Nature and *in* Man. An *ever-present* God, not an absentee; a *speaking* God, not a silent one, who *spake* "in the beginning" and has been *speaking* ever since.

> How forcible is all this in the sense of the common German Proverb, "Speak that I may know you." No other self-revelation is so real and satisfactory as Speech. Speech is not only the vehicle of Thought but is also its incarnation. Speech is Thought embodied and "dwelling among us." Men live in their words; and if men, how much more He who is the One and the All! "The Speech (Word) was God . . . by Him were all things made. He was made flesh and dwelt among us; and we beheld His glory."

This means a God who is *here* as well as everywhere and *within* as well as without:

> "*Whose body Nature is and God the Soul.*"
> "*Shines in the stars and whispers in the breeze.*"

> "*O ye who seek to solve the knot,*
> *Ye live in God yet know Him not.*"

> "*Closer is He than breathing,*
> *And nearer than hands and feet.*"

"He is not far from every one of us; for in Him we live and move, and have our being." "In the beginning was the Divine Self-Revealer (Word), *and the Divine Self-Revealer* (Word) *was God. . . . All things were made by Him . . . In Him was life and the life was the light of Men . . . and the Divine Self Revealer* (Word) *was made flesh and dwelt among us.*" "*I and my Father are One . . . as thou Father art in me, and I in Thee, that they also may be One in us. . . . I in them, and Thou in me, that they may be made perfect in One.*"

"*In him* (Jesus the Christ) *dwelt all the fulness of the Godhead bodily. . . . Know ye not that ye* (also) *are the temples of God and that the Spirit of God dwelleth in you? . . . as God hath said, I will dwell in them and walk in them.*"

All these teachings grew out of the term Logos and the ideas unfolded from it. The term itself was in common use in all the great schools of Philosophy, especially in that of Philo. The ideas had been gradually unfolding in all the great Religions of the world, especially in the Jewish, long before the time of Socrates. The philosophers of Greece, and later of Rome, by no means *originated*, but only received and transmitted them. As Confucius said, " I only hand on," so they only *handed them on* to the Founder and Fathers of Christianity. What is true of the term Logos and its outgrowing ideas, is likewise true of what follows.

(*b*) "Threefold Revelation," or Trinity: teaching that God is *immanent* in Nature, *incarnate* in Man, and *enthroned* in Conscience. This had been taught vaguely by all the great Religions, had been made clear and emphatic by the great Philosophers, and finally became a common teaching of the Founder and Fathers of Christianity. But the term Trinity, and its dogmatic formula, Father, Son, and Holy Ghost, did not come into popular use till a later century.

(*c*) "Twice-Born" or Born Again; teaching that degree or stage of *spiritual* evolution at which a man first awakens (clearly and fully) to the threefold consciousness of God, the Soul, and Eternal Life. God-Consciousness, Soul-Consciousness, and Eternal-Life-Consciousness; these, one or all, could only be experienced by the "Twice-Born." A *spiritual* New Birth, *absolutely essential* to all true knowledge of God, of Self, or of Immortality, was a fundamental teaching of all the great Philosophers from Socrates to Philo. This teaching, too, they did not originate, but only *handed on* with new clearness and emphasis. Christianity received it as still more a fundamental teaching and as *nothing new*. Hence the surprise of Jesus when he exclaimed to Nicodemus, "Art thou a *teacher* in Israel and knowest not these things! Ye *must* be born again. Truly, truly, I say unto thee, Except a man be born again he cannot see the Kingdom of God." Apostolic Christianity made this the first and chief of all its doctrines—the New Birth, or Regeneration, or receiving the Holy Ghost, or being *made* Sons of

God, or Christ *formed within*, or the Kingdom of God *within*, or "the new man which after God is *created* in Righteousness and true Holiness," or "hath *begotten* us again unto a lively Hope," and similar terms everywhere found in the New Testament, all having a common meaning.

(*d*) "Altruism" or Self-denial and the Cross: teaching that *complete* self-consecration to God for the service of Mankind that includes every helpful, vicarious, or atoning self-renunciation,—even to renunciation of the bodily life itself. This teaching also was fundamental with all the great Philosophers (in the form of Heroism and Martyrdom) and by them was *handed on* with new emphasis to John the Baptist, Jesus the Christ, Paul and all the other Apostles and Confessors of the first centuries.

Such are illustrations of the ideas and terms which Apostolic Christianity received as a timely legacy from the great Schools of Philosophy which immediately preceded it.

LXX.—IDEAS AND TERMS FURNISHED BY EVOLUTIONARY SCIENCE TO RENASCENT CHRISTIANITY.

In like manner Evolutionary Science (which also is a similar "Eclecticism of all widest learning and deepest thought of the entire world down to the" close of the nineteenth century) has furnished Renascent Christianity with many of its most effective ideas and terms.

Among these are especially the four following:

(*a*) "Development"; teaching the humble origin and gradual evolution of every form of organic or individualized life—physical, mental, and spiritual.

(*b*) "Struggle for Existence"; teaching that nothing in the visible Universe (as thus far revealed) advances or can advance to its *ideal* unfolding and destiny except by persistent effort—physical, mental, and spiritual.

(*c*) "Reversion"; teaching that there is, in every developing form of organic or of *individualized* life, a strong and persistent tendency to *revert* (to fall back or to degenerate) to original lawless and degraded conditions—of body, or of mind, or of soul.

(*d*) "Survival of the Fittest"; teaching that only those who *struggle for existence* attain, or can attain, their "ideal unfolding and destiny"—which for Mankind, is a pure and ennobled life on Earth, issuing into *self-conscious* Life Eternal.*

Upon these ideas and terms which Evolutionary Science has received as a "timely legacy" from all the thought and research of the past (expanded, verified, and *handed on*), must the Renascent Christianity of the twentieth century chiefly depend to render itself effective and widely understood.

This volume has been written entirely in the spirit and phrase of these ideas and terms—which are now universally accepted in all departments of thought and of life (among highly civilized people) except in the religious. In the religious, too, they *must be accepted* sooner or later. To hasten their acceptance, in some even slightest measure, is the devout object and the only hoped for reward of the author of these pages.

* *By no means is meant, even in Science, much less in Religion, a merely selfish* INDIVIDUAL *struggle to exist: but a struggle of co-operation, of fellow-feeling, and of general helpfulness toward all mankind; and not only toward all mankind but also toward every sentient creature that has capacity for a higher life. A struggle to rise by helping others to rise—helping everywhere and always; this is what is meant by that Struggle for Existence which results in Survival of the Fittest, i. e., of all who are* FIT *to survive.*

The gold-paved, pearl-gated Heavens of the popular religions filled with harp-playing, self-pleasing and self-conceited "saints" are—in the words of a revered and well-known essayist—" lubberlands, pure and simple, one and all . . . tedium vitæ is the only sentiment they awaken in our breasts. To our crepuscular natures, born for the conflict, the Rembrandtesque moral chiaroscuro, the shifting struggle of the sunbeam in the gloom, such pictures of light upon light are vacuous and expressionless, and neither to be enjoyed nor understood.

"If this be the whole fruit of the victory, we say; if the generations of mankind suffered and laid down their lives; if prophets confessed and martyrs sang in the fire, and all the sacred tears were shed for no other end than that a race of creatures of such unexampled insipidity should succeed, and protract in sæcula sæculorum their contented and inoffensive (useless) lives,—why, at such a rate, better lose than win the battle; or at all events better ring down the curtain before the last act of the play, so that a business that began so importantly may be saved from so singularly flat a winding up."

What is really meant by Survival of the Fittest is, an endless continuance of aspiration and (of its essential accompaniment) effort and struggle. An effort-

less existence would be aspirationless; and an aspirationless existence would be a living death. Hence of the eternal life as of the present, and of what are called Heaven and Hell hereafter as now, every enobled soul says with Jesus, "*My Father worketh hitherto, and I work.*"—*If I am, or shall be, in Heaven, I will work so long as even a single soul remains outside. If I am, or shall be, in Hell, I will start improvements and never cease the struggle to reform both others and myself. This is Gospel as well as Law: Religion "pure and undefiled" as well as Evolutionary Science.*

In Carlylean phrase—"*Hang your sensibilities, stop your snivelling complaints and your equally snivelling raptures! Leave off your general emotional tom-foolery, and get to* WORK *like men.*"

The genuine Altruism of Science as well as of Religion, is beautifully portrayed in a poem (representing a "pure, white soul" at the gates of Heaven, refusing to enter while any are left in misery outside) of which the following are concluding stanzas:

> "' Should I be nearer Christ,' she said,
>   ' By pitying less
>   The sinful living, or woeful dead
>   In their helplessness?'
>   And the angels all were silent.
>
> "' Should I be liker Christ were I
>   To love no more
>   The loved, who in their anguish lie
>   Outside the door?'
>   And the angels all were silent.
>
> "' Did He not hang on the curséd tree,
>   And bear its shame,
>   And clasp to His heart, for love of me,
>   My guilt and blame?'
>   And the angels all were silent.
>
> "' Should I be liker, nearer him,
>   Forgetting this,
>   Singing all day with the Seraphim,
>   In selfish bliss?'
>   And the angels all were silent.
>
> " The Lord Himself stood by the gate,
>   And heard her speak
>   Those tender words compassionate,
>   Gentle and meek;
>   And the angels all were silent.

" Now, pity is the touch of God
  In human hearts ;
'T was in that way Christ ever trod
  And ne'er departs ;
And the angels all were silent.

" And He said, ' Now I will go with you,
  Dear child of love,
I am weary of all this glory, too,
  In heaven above' ;
And the angels all were silent.

" ' We will go seek and save the lost,
  If they will hear,
They who are worst but need us most,
  And all are dear ' ;
And the angels all were silent."

LXXI.—THE CHRISTIAN CHURCH AND ITS WORSHIP IN THE FIRST CENTURY.

[*From a recent issue of "Our Anglican Review," contributed by the Archdeacon of London, and Chaplain in Ordinary of Her Majesty the Queen.*]

"THE first glimpse that we get of primitive Christian worship, apart from the meeting of the Feast of Love and the Lord's Supper, is from the fourteenth chapter of the First Epistle of St. Paul to the Corinthians:

"'If, therefore, the whole church be come together into one place, and all speak with tongues, and there come in those that are unlearned or unbelievers, will they not say that ye are mad? But if all prophesy, and there come in one that believeth not, or one unlearned, he is convinced of all, he is judged of all; and thus are the secrets of his heart made manifest; and so, falling down on his face, he will worship God, and report that God is in you of a truth. How is it then, brethren? When ye come together every one of you hath a psalm, hath a doctrine, hath a tongue, hath a revelation, hath an interpretation. Let everything be done unto edifying. If any man speak in an unknown tongue, let it be by two, or at the most by three, and that by course: and let one interpret. But if there be no interpreter, let him keep silence in the church; and let him speak to himself and to God. Let the prophets speak two or three, and let the other (prophets) judge. If anything be revealed to another that sitteth by, let the first hold his peace. For ye may all prophesy one by one, that all may learn and all may be comforted. And the spirits of the prophets are subject to the prophets—for God is not the author of confusion, but of peace, as in all the churches.'

"This vivid picture, the only one of its kind, gives us a clear and instructive view of the nature and workings of church life in those early times. The first thing that strikes us is the absence of all fixed order. No hint is given of the superintendence of an individual or class of persons regulating the services in the church assemblies, even where the mention of such would most naturally be made, as in the case of the disorders spoken of in the twenty-fifth and following verses. The exercises seem to have gone on spontaneously, very much as is now the case in many social gatherings where the meeting, as the saying is, is thrown open. Individuals employed their gifts under the promptings of the Spirit, as seemed to them best, governed only by considerations of mutual regard and general utility. All enjoyed the right, yea, felt it a duty, to contribute something toward the public edification according to the ability conferred on them generally. *The idea that a special priest was necessary to mediate between the worshipping assembly and God is not for a moment entertained. Indeed, it is altogether ignored and excluded, on the supposition that all were now made priests unto God by the unction of the Spirit, and had an equal right to speak the truth that was in them, and to offer prayer.* The disorders arising from the fullest concession of this right were not regarded as an evil so great as would have risen from the repression of the Spirit that wrought in all members severally as he would. The Spirit was not to be quenched; prophesyings were not to be despised; and whatever there was of the carnal and selfish element mingling with what was spiritual and divine was to be separated and rejected by the critical faculty of the more discerning. The hearers were expected to prove all things, and hold fast that which is good. These facts should be commended to the attention of those who, in the excessive regard for having all things done decently and in order, *proceed to the extreme of repressing the spontaneous life and activity of the Church as a whole, by putting the assembly solely and entirely under the control of a special order of individuals.*"

How refreshing it is to gather an honest confession of Historic Facts, when we are constantly humiliated by such Ecclesiastical Fiction (made more offensive by the cheap and snobbish exclusiveness of those who assume to be of "The Apostolic Succession") as the following, gathered from religious publications of recent date:—" The Rev. ―― (a well-known clergyman of New York) is quoted by the *Independent* as stating that 'those who boast that they derive their office as ministers from the people should be made to know, if not to feel, that they are removed by an infinite chasm from those who derive their mysterious powers from above and are the vicegerents of heaven.' And he adds: 'Dissenting ministers should be made to feel their inferiority.'"

(*a*) *Prayer in the Church down to the Middle of the Third Century.*

In Origen's treatise "On Prayer" (De Oratione, cc. 25, 26. Opp. I., pp. 222-224) is the following:

"If we understand what prayer is, it will appear that it is never to be offered to any originated being, not to Christ himself, but only to the God and Father of all; to whom our Saviour himself prayed, and taught us to pray. For when his disciples asked him, *Teach us to pray*, he did not teach them to pray to himself, but to the Father. . . . Conformably to what he said, *Why callest thou me good? there is none good except one, God the Father*, how could he say otherwise than, 'Why dost thou pray to me? Prayer, as you learn from the Holy Scriptures, is to be offered to the Father only, to whom I myself pray.' . . . 'You have read the words which were spoken by David to the Father concerning me: *I will declare thy name to my brethren; in the midst of the assembly will I sing hymns to thee*. It is not consistent with reason for those to pray to a brother, who are esteemed worthy of one Father with him. You, with me and through me, are to address your prayers to the Father alone.' . . . Let us then, attending to what was said by Jesus, and all having the same mind, pray to God through him, without any division respecting the mode of prayer. But are we not divided, if some pray to the Father and some to the Son? Those who pray to the Son, whether they do or do not pray to the Father also, fall into a gross error, in their great simplicity, through want of judgment and examination."

In learning and talents, Origen, during his lifetime, had no rival among Christians. There was no other who possessed the same weight of character. The opinions which he expresses in the passages just quoted were, undoubtedly, the opinions of the intelligent Christians of his time.

Origen, in other passages, implies that prayer in an *inferior sense* may be addressed to the logos or Christ. In his work against Celsus, he says, for instance: " Every supplication, prayer, request, and thanksgiving is to be addressed to Him who is God over all, *through the High-Priest*, superior to all angels, the living and divine logos. But we may also supplicate the logos himself, and make requests to him, and give thanks and pray, *whenever we may be able to distinguish between prayer properly speaking and prayer in a looser sense*." What is here meant may appear from two other passages, in his work against Celsus, in which he says: " We first bring our prayers to the son of God, the first-born of the whole creation, the logos of God, and pray to him and request him, *as a High-Priest*, to offer up the prayers which reach him to the God over all, *to his God and our God*."

LXXII.—CHRISTOLOGY IN THE CHURCH DOWN TO THE CLOSE OF THE THIRD CENTURY.

PHILO, the great contemporary of Jesus, as a Jewish-Platonic philosopher in that chief city and centre of first-century learning, Alexandria, *prepared the way* for Paul, and the author of the Fourth Gospel, and the Christian Fathers, as truly as John the Baptizer and Reformer in the wilderness of Judea, *prepared the way* for the Christ and his chosen disciples. It is in the writings of Philo that we find first developed that doctrine of the Logos which is found in the Pauline Writings, characterizes the Fourth Gospel and finally is expanded into the Historic Creeds of the Church. No one then can rightly comprehend the Historic Creeds of the Church nor the Fourth Gospel without tracing them to their root-teachings as found in the elaborate philosophical writings of Philo. "According to him, considered as a *person*, the Logos is *a god*. In a passage which has been closely imitated by Origen, he says: 'Let us inquire if there are really two Gods.' He answers: 'The true God is one, but there are many who, in a less strict use of language, are called gods.' The true God, he says, is denoted by that name *with* the article; others have it *without* the article; and thus his most venerable Logos is called god without the article. 'No one,' he says, 'can comprehend the nature of God; it is well if we can comprehend his *name*, that is, the Logos, his interpreter; he may be considered, perhaps, as the god of imperfect beings, but the Most High is the God of the wise and perfect.' He represents the Logos as the instrument (ὄργανον) of God in the creation of the universe; as the image of God, by whom the universe was fashioned; as used by him, like a helm, in directing the course of all things; as he who himself sits at the helm and orders all things; and as his first-born son, his vicegerent in the government of the world. 'Those,' says Philo, 'who have true knowledge [knowledge of God] are rightly called sons of God. . . . Let him, then, who is not yet worthy to be called a son of God, strive to fashion himself to the resemblance of God's first-born Logos, *the most ancient angel, being, as it were, an archangel with many titles.'* . . . "In the beginning was the Logos, and the Logos was with GOD, and the Logos was *god*, i. e., *divine;* he became man and dwelt among us."

This conception of Philo became the common faith, and teaching (we may say of Jesus himself) certainly of all the New Testament writers and of all the Christian Fathers down to the close of the third century. It is so elaborated in the writings of Justyn Martyr and of Irenæus, but more fully and clearly by that greatest, most learned, and most saintly of the Fathers—Origen.

"Origen fully and consistently maintained the doctrine of a human soul in Jesus. Imbued with the principles of Platonism, he believed this soul, *in common with all other souls,* to have pre-existed, and in its pre-existent state to have, *through its entire purity and moral perfection, become* thoroughly filled and penetrated by the Logos, *of whom all other souls partake* in proportion to their love toward him. Thus the human soul of Jesus *became* one with the Logos, and formed the bond of union between the body of Jesus and the divinity of the Logos; in consequence of which both the soul and body of the Saviour, being wholly mixed with and united to the Logos, partook of his divinity and *were transformed into something divine.* From the illustrations which Origen uses, respecting the connection between the Logos and the human nature of Christ, it is clear that he had no conception of that form of the doctrine which prevailed after his time. 'We do not,' he says, 'suppose the visible and sensible body of Jesus to have been God, nor yet his soul, of which he declared, *My soul is sorrowful even unto death.* But as he who says, *I the Lord am the God of all flesh,* and *There was no other God before me and there shall be none after me,* is believed by the Jews to have been God *using the soul and body of the prophet as an organ;* and as, among the Gentiles, he who said,

> I know the number of the sands and the measure of the deep,
> And I understand the mute and hear him who speaks not,

is understood to be a god, addressing men *by the voice of* the Pythoness;—so we believe that the divine Logos, the son of the God of all, spoke through Jesus when he said, *I am the way and the truth and the life;* . . . *I am the living bread which has descended from heaven;* and when he uttered other similar declarations.'"

"Εἰς θεὸν μεταβεβηκέναι." . . . "Origen, here, as often elsewhere, uses θέος (god), not in our modern sense, as a *proper* name, but as a *common* name. This use of the term, which was common to him with his contemporaries, and continued to be common after his time, is illustrated by his remarks upon the passage, 'and the Logos was god' in which he contends, that the Logos was 'god' *in an inferior sense;*—not, as we should say, *God,* but a *god,* or rather, not *the* Divine Being, but *a* divine being; and in which he maintains that 'beside the True God, many beings, by participation of God *become* divine.''

Literally "*become* gods";—as said the Psalmist approvingly quoted by Jesus and applied to himself. "Jesus answered them, Is it not written in your law, I said, Ye are gods? If he called them gods, unto whom the word of God came (and the scripture cannot be broken), say ye of him, whom the Father sanctified and sent into the world, Thou blasphemest; because I said, I am *the* son of God?"

The learned Professor of Theology (Prof. Norton) from whom most of these citations are made adds, suggestively: "The full illustration of the use of the term *god* as a *common* name would, I think, throw much light upon the opinions both of the ancient Heathens and Christians."

The terms "Messiah" among the Jewish Christians, "Christ" among the Gentile Christians, and "Logos" among the Platonizing Christians (or *philosophizing* Christians) all had a common meaning; and, till the latter half of the third century, were generally received and interpreted *as above set forth.* But during the fourth century and thereafter such ecclesiastics as Athanasius, Augustine, Cyril, Leo, and their successors, *developed* this simple teaching of the Bible and of the Apostolic Church into the old Pagan Mystery of a Triad. This doctrine of a Triad is one of the oldest and most persistent *mysticisms* of the Pagan Religions. We find it broadly developed in the most ancient theology of the Bramins. Plato speculated upon it only to reject it. Philo used it as a figure of speech, or as a pictorial illustration, for the temporary help of the uneducated and unreasoning masses: he especially says—"God presents sometimes one and sometimes three images to the mental vision; *one*, when the soul, *thoroughly purified,* rises above all idea of plurality to that unmingled form of being which admits of no mixture, alone, and wholly independent; *three*, before it is initiated *in the greater mysteries*, and cannot contemplate HIM WHO IS by Himself alone, but needs the aid of something beside,"—that is, the principal "Powers of God are spoken of as *distinct persons*, only as a figurative mode of representing the operations of the Divine Being, *accommodated to the weaknesses of those who cannot comprehend Him as* HE IS."

Such were the evident conceptions of all the Christian Fathers, likewise, down to and including Origen. But Athanasius, Augustine, and their successors insisted upon retaining the ancient *mysticism* and reincorporating it—not as a "figure of speech or as a pictorial illustration" accommodated to the *spiritual and intellectual weakness of the masses*, but as a fundamental doctrine the acceptance and belief of which is, *everywhere and forever*, essential to salvation!

Did not Esaias and Jesus have in mind also this very degeneration of "Pure religion and undefiled before God and the Father" when they exclaimed—"But in vain they do worship me, teaching for doctrines the *speculations* of men!"

Originally the Hindoo Philosophers, Plato, the Jewish Cabalists, Philo, the Apostles, and the Christian Fathers all used the "Triad" as a symbol of the three *main attributes* of the One Supreme. They had no idea of them as *personalities*, except as figures of speech. As one may say "Reason governs me, Hope cheers me, and Duty directs me" without resolving himself into an *actual* "Triad" composed of three *persons;* so exactly the original and only intelligible meaning of all the Divine "Triads" was that of *attributes*. When these attributes were believed to be *actual* Persons and as such were hardened into an essential dogma, then intellectual as well as spiritual degeneration began and rapidly prevailed.

"From the shapeless, discordant, unintelligible speculations of the fourth century, the doctrine of Tri-personality of God drew its origin. These speculations it is now difficult to present under such an aspect as may enable a modern reader to apprehend their character. But the doctrine to which they gave birth still subsists, as the professed faith of the greater part of the Christian world. And when we look back through the long ages of its reign, and consider all its relations, and all its direct and indirect effects, we shall perceive that few doctrines have produced more unmixed evil. For any benefits resulting from its belief, it would be in vain to look, except benefits of that kind which the providence of God educes from the follies and errors of man."

LXXIII.—DEGENERATION IN THE CHURCH: HOW IT PROCEEDED, AND PROCEEDS.

The Council of Ephesus, A.D. 431, which *settled* the doctrine of the "Hypostatic Union," the "Motherhood of God," etc., and anathematized as a "second Judas" every one who should presume to object, was presided over by Cyril (whom the traditional Church calls St. Cyril) a "turbulent, ambitious, unprincipled man"—as were nearly all the great champions of Orthodox Dogmatism from the beginning of the fourth century downward. "Cyril prevailed in his factitious contest, through his influence with the officers of the imperial household, and the bribes which he lavished upon them; for, what was Orthodoxy was to be determined in the last resort by the Emperor Theodosius, *or rather by the women and eunuchs of his court.* 'Thanks *to the purse of St. Cyril*' says Le Clerc, 'the Romish Church which regards Councils as infallible, is not Nestorian.'" Not only the Romish Church but the traditionally Protestant as well is indebted for its "orthodoxy," in a very large degree, to the "purse of St. Cyril" and to his "turbulent, ambitious, unprincipled" leadership. The same in general is historic truth of Dioscurus who triumphed at the succeeding Council of Ephesus (fittingly called "a Council of Banditti"): of Leo who, by the Emperor's authority, prevailed at the Council of Chalcedon over the "Monophysite Heretics" in favor of the "two natures in one person"—the "road to paradise," the "bridge as sharp as a razor suspended over the Abyss,"—and of many other dogma-mongers and vote-purchasers or vote-compellers of preceding as well as of succeeding "infallible Councils" of the degenerate Church.

"The simple and sad truth is, that as soon as Christianity was generally diffused, it began to absorb corruptions from all the countries that it covered, and to reflect the complexion of all the religious and philosophic systems to which it was opposed."

"The East and West were infusing their several elements of poison into the pure cup of Gospel truth. In Asia Minor, as at Alexandria, Hellenic philosophism did not refuse to blend with Oriental theosophy: the Jewish superstitions of the Cabbala, and the wild speculations of the Persian Magi, were combined with Greek craving for an enlightened and esoteric religion. *The outward forms of superstition were ready for the vulgar multitude."*

So began the degeneration of Christianity, and so has it proceeded through all the centuries till now.

Even as late as in the fourteenth century, violent disputes arose and raged with rancorous contention over the question, whether the light which surrounded Jesus at the transfiguration was *created* or *uncreated*. Four councils of the Church were assembled and, after endless discussions, it was decided that the light was *uncreated;* and all who denied it were anathematized as " worse than all other heretics."

It is hardly two centuries since it was the common opinion, if not formal decree of the Church that the denial of witchcraft was the denial of God himself. " They that doubt of witches do not only deny them, but spirits ; and are obliquely and of consequence a sort, not of Infidels, but Atheists."

And, coming down to the nineteenth century, the " orthodox " councils, decrees, and opinions of to-day adhere to Mysticism, Speculation, and Traditional Dogma,—identifying them with Christianity and with the Christ so completely as to result in the popular verdict, that, all who do not so *identify and adhere* are heretics, infidels, and practical (if not theoretical) atheists.

What are now accepted as commonplace truths concerning the Bible were stated, with profound and incontrovertible evidences, two hundred years ago by Richard Simon, the great Oriental scholar, and restated a hundred years ago by Dr. Joseph Priestly (the distinguished leader in England and America of modern Unitarianism) in his " History of the Corruptions of Christianity." Both of these scholarly and saintly men were overwhelmed with denunciations, and their prophetic voices were silenced by the "orthodox" outcry. Now, the children of those who slew these prophets are building their monuments, and meanwhile *are themselves slaying the prophets of to-day.*

Of this, as of every past generation, it is true that lives are seen and valued only in retrospect. The "Heresy" of one generation is the "Orthodoxy" of succeeding ones. The zealous conformist or the stout faith-defender of one age is written in History as a persecuting bigot or a stoner of the prophets, while the *self-sacrificing* non-conformist or the *conscientious* "heretic" is enrolled as sage or saint. So in every period of human evolution is fulfilled the prediction of Jesus—Many that *are* first *shall be* last, and many that *are* last *shall be* first!

There is a form of degeneration, probably more widely prevailing at the present time than even in the earlier centuries (because light and knowledge, and the consequent temptations to it are largely increased),—that of more or less strictly conforming to the *ritual* or letter of Traditionalism while deliberately violating its spirit. The "orthodoxy" outgrown and inwardly rejected, but, outwardly maintained for the sake of some form of personal advantage—*peace or policy!*

As the degenerate Greeks maintained the traditional "but one meal a day" (as a Sacrament of Obligation) by feasting the whole day long; as the degenerate Jews maintained the tradition of "a Sabbath Day's Journey," by halting at the prescribed limit and *calling* it their residence, then proceeding from stage to stage at their pleasure; so the degenerate conformist for the sake of peace or of policy ever does, and now seemingly even more widely than in former times. This is the most degenerating of all forms of Hypocracy, because it is most irreverent to Conscience and disloyal to Truth. Cyril and the long line of like-spirited ecclesiastical *politicians* who preceded and succeeded him were, at least, sincere; hence "the times of that ignorance God winked at, *but now!*"—Now, recurring centuries and wide intellectual progress have brought *light* so clear and ever-increasing that the Cyrils of to-day cannot be *excused;* the ecclesiastical *politicians* of to-day must be, from selfish motives, *insincere.* All insincerity springs from selfish motives: and of all Hypocrites the insincere Religious Conformist is most noxious and least forgivable. To such it was that Jesus (quoting all the greatest prophets) said,—repeating it again and again, with prophetic *woes* added like " burning coals of fire ":

"Ye hypocrites, well did Isaiah prophesy of you, saying,
This people honoureth me with their lips ;
But their heart is far from me."

The following, as "signs of the times," may here be fittingly inserted:

"In a record of notable persons who have united with the Roman Catholic communion within the past three months, as converts from other denominations, the Paulist Fathers mention" (several names of well-known *society people* are here given) . . . "They quote Cardinal ——— as authority for the statement that there are received into the Church every year in this country 30,000 converts."—*(From a leading New York Daily Newspaper of this date, —June 7, 1897.)*

"The *Christian Advocate* says of Rev. ———, an English clergyman who has become a Romanist, that 'he is the most noted of the large number of Protestant Episcopal and Church of England clergymen who have Romanized. But there will be more to follow unless some antidote can be found to the Romanizing germs under culture in that body.'"

—And in every other traditionary "body" as well!

Inadequately verified Traditions accepted as Facts, insisted upon as History and imposed as essential Creeds—these are the "Romanizing germs under culture," the ever-growing *fungi*, the noxious *bacillariæ* of Degeneration in all Religions and in every Sect. "Romanizing" is but Protestantizing carried a step backward. Protestantizing is *Fourth-centuryizing*. *Fourth-centuryizing* is a combination of Judaizing and of Paganizing which is, again, Romanizing. So the circle is complete.—"*All are but parts of one stupendous whole*," which is Traditionalism, which is Reversion, which is Degeneration, which is *intellectual and spiritual*

Decay. The only kind of "izing" that leads forward and upward is that of simple Truth based upon such *facts* of History and of Experience as are verifiable by the processes of Reason and the methods of Science.

This is *Christianizing*—"Why even of yourselves judge ye not what is right?—Ye have made the commandment of God of none effect by your traditions." All who thus *Christianize*, though called "heretics" or "heathen," are Christians. All others travel in the *endless circle* above described.

The "tendency to revert" in Religion even more than elsewhere is always strong and persistent. It is encouraging however to note "signs of the times" in the opposite direction, such as the following, also of recent date:

> "Several progressive clergymen of nominally Orthodox Churches and of various denominations, in Boston and vicinity, have decided to demonstrate their cordial fellowship of Unitarians by an exchange of pulpits. Some even of the Episcopal clergymen also speak and act in hearty sympathy with Unitarians, as always did their great Bishop, Phillips Brooks."

> "Jew and Gentile worshipped under the same roof Sunday at the Belden Avenue Baptist Church. Rabbi ——— of the Emmanuel Jewish Church and the Rev. ———, pastor of the church in which the union service was held, preached from the same pulpit, while Christians and Jews touched elbows in the pews."

> "Rabbi ——— confirmed eleven young Jews, after which Rev. ——— and his Jewish brother each said encouraging things about each other's religion. After Rabbi ——— pronounced the benediction both congregations passed out well pleased with the novel experience."

And more encouraging still:

> "Swami Virikananda, the learned Brahmin of India, during his two year's mission in this country, has been respectfully welcomed and listened to by audiences in every large city, composed of our most refined and cultivated people."

Surely "The morning light is breaking" and the Kingdom of God is *beginning* to come!

LXXIV.—DEGENERATION OF THE APOSTOLIC MINISTRY INTO COMMERCIALISM—AS FOUND AT THE CLOSE OF THE NINETEENTH CENTURY.

" For the time will come when they *will not endure sound teaching*, but will procure for themselves *teachers after their own fancy;* because they will have itching ears; so they will turn away their ears from the truth, and turn aside to fables."

THE following extracts from a long and well-sustained letter in a recent New York Daily Newspaper will sufficiently explain the heading given to this Section:

(Additional explanations may be found in preceding Sections headed " Mercenary Conformity " and " Hireling Priests.")

" The fact is, confirmed by abundant testimony and by the reluctant admissions of men who are interested to maintain the contrary, there never was a time when a bright, clean, self-respecting, talented, and absolutely fearless young man undertook a greater personal risk in committing himself to the restless sea of ministerial supply and demand. It would require a book in place of a newspaper column to demonstrate this fact; but if ever a fact is more easily demonstrable the writer will hail it with acclamation. . . .

" The initial note in the discussion of the problem is most significant. I refer to the all-pervasive restlessness and discontent, the ill-concealed disgust with present churchly conditions, the deep underlying anxiety for prospective bread and butter, the ominous foreboding for the future which one finds reflected in the private confidences of so many ministers now holding pastorates. A prominent officer of a missionary society is reported to have said that in all his visitations among the clergy of a certain state, he had failed to discover a single incumbent who did not wish to make a change. I have in my possession a letter from a successful and honored pastor in New England, for fifteen years in one parish, but now desirous of change for weighty reasons, and who writes me: ' It makes one sick of the whole business to see the scramble for place.' Not long ago an able and useful clergyman, whose sermons are in print in a notable publication, finding it desirable to resign his pastorate, deliberately turned his attention to the study of law rather than enter upon a fierce, degrading, heart-breaking competition for another pulpit. . . . Of such testimony the writer could furnish a dismal sufficiency. . . . A certain Congregational church in Connecticut, with by no means an inviting future, received not less than 250 applications, scattered all the way from Maine to California. And such ratio is more than a thrice-told tale. . . . Indeed, *the commercial basis of modern church life is one of the most discouraging tendencies of our time.* . . . So much the worse for a system that encourages the cultivation of a spirit quite the reverse of the spirit inculcated in the Pauline maxim, that the good soldier of Christ 'must endure hardness.' Moreover, who will vouch for a state in the Union where the hue and cry after vacant pulpits is not formidably resonant? Who will name a pastorless church, East or West, that is not besieged? . . . The remorseless competition for places; the wire-pulling and pipe-laying merely to get a hearing in a vacant pulpit; the chance of being set aside in the full vigor of maturity; the alarming growth of short-term pastorates; the fact that men of decided ability sometimes wait years for employment; the reluctant conviction that influence and a 'pull' will do for a man in the ministry precisely what such factors will accomplish in politics—all these considerations are powerful makeweights in turning the attention of high-minded young men to other pursuits. Is it any wonder that out of a class of 275 at Yale—the educational stronghold of New England Congregationalism—only five study theology? . . .

(The graduating class of Harvard University for 1897 numbers 388. The Class Secretary, in response to the usual circular, has received replies as to proposed vocations from nearly 300, "not one of whom proposes Theology or the Christian Ministry.")

"The baneful conditions which underlie much of our modern church life already begin to tell as deterrent forces. . . . The writer would be grateful indeed if a more optimistic view of the ministry could be vindicated. But something more than sentiment and religious tradition will be required to dispose of the cold and repellant facts already adduced. . . . When conditions improve—if they ever do—one may return to the traditional view of the clerical profession.

The responsibility of the church for the existing condition of affairs must be reserved for another article.

"CLERGYMAN.

"New Haven, April, 13, 1897."

<small>As a specimen of what every day may be read in "religious" as well as in secular papers the following (of the date of this writing) may be given: "The Rev. —— has received a $5000 call to ——. Going to look over the field, he found a very elegant church in the most fashionable part of the city, and the congregation composed of the most fashionable portion of the population. It was all very fine and tempting . . ." *ad nauseam.* Of course "the call has been accepted," and congratulations to the "young pastor" are eagerly and widely offered. Such is the almost universal *commercialism* of the age,—in the "Church" as elsewhere. The first question is, How much salary? the second, How fine or fashionable? and the degrees of talent or of success, as well as of congratulations expected, are proportionate.</small>

The author does not recall nor, after much inquiry, has he learned of but a very few instances in which a "call" at a larger salary or wider fame has been declined, or a rich and fashionable Church voluntarily relinquished for a poor and humble one. Not only most important Missions needing highest talent as well as greatest self-sacrifice, but most important official stations also—such as that of a General Secretary, a Presiding Officer, or even a Bishop—rarely are able to secure an "acceptance" from clergymen whose salaries are larger than those proffered—unless superior honors or other *perquisites* are connected with the station. Thus is the "constraining love of Christ" held in abeyance. Thus do the *rich* have the Gospel preached to them.

"But do thou, O man of God, flee these things; and seek rather for righteousness, godliness, faith, love, patience, meekness; fight the good fight of faith, lay hold on everlasting life."

<small>In their ignorance and fear men built altars. Religion became a trade. Sacerdotalism managed and monopolized the market. The priests (and their proclaimed deities) consumed the abundant Sacrifices and dwelt in the costly temples "arrayed in purple and fine linen," while the people who brought the sacrifices and built the temples starved. *Such was the meaning of the Parable of Dives and Lazarus.*</small>

<small>"Even the great revelation of Jesus left his followers so bound by traditions that they could not escape from priestly shackles, and wove into the new faith</small>

a mass of ceremonial observances as fruitless, wearisome, and unspiritual as those of the Talmud. Not even the Pentecostal fires could transmute the baser metal into the pure gold, and it remained for the Christian religion to gradually develop a sacerdotal system more complex and tyrannical than any known to the ancient world.

"DOES NOT CARE TO SURRENDER THE LIBERTY OF SPEECH."

This, as a heading in the Daily Newspapers of this date, is so suggestive of nobility and courage—especially on the part of a clergyman—that it is deserving of permanent notice. The young, scholarly, and widely distinguished President of one of the oldest Universities of New England, who is also a Professor and a Pastor, resigns all these positions with their honors and emoluments rather than "surrender the liberty of speech" which his conservative trustees and other constituents demanded. Surely the heroic love of Truth and the spirit of self-surrender for Convictions' sake, which together constituted the crowning glory of Apostolic Christianity, are not yet entirely perished from the earth. An appropriate exhortation to many who, as yet, have not developed *the courage of their convictions* is, "Go thou and do likewise."

[*See remarks by the Bishop of New York on one of the opening pages.*]

A HOPEFUL INCIDENT.

"DECLINED THE PROFFERED DEGREE OF D.D."

"[*By telegraph to the Herald.*]

"TORONTO, Ont., *June* 30, 1897.—The Rev. ―― of this city has declined unreservedly to accept the degree of Doctor of Divinity." . . . So rare an instance of modesty deserves a permanent as well as a telegraphic record. The degree of "D.D." has come to signify nothing at all as to *essential* scholarship or worth; and yet it is amusing, as well as sad, to observe how it is sought for and paraded. They love "to be called of men *Doctor, Doctor!*"

LXXV.—SERMONS MADE TO ORDER.

(*From the Boston Evening Transcript, July* 17, 1897.)

"Seldom has there been a more glaring instance of a departure from the ethical standard of the pulpit than in a circular which comes from New York, offering to furnish clergymen with special typewritten sermons, prepared by 'a clergyman recently connected with a large church,' prices to be dependent upon the nature and extent of the work required. That the authors of the circular recognize this fact themselves is apparent in their excuse that these sermons are for ministers 'who, in the sharp competition of modern times and the multiplicity of other duties, are not able to prepare for themselves the high quality of work demanded in the pulpit.' The pitiful fact about the matter, however, is that there must be some demand for work of this sort, or there would be no one with the temerity to insult a clergyman by offering him a typewritten sermon to be passed off on his congregation as his own. Plagiarism in the pulpit is not unknown, and it may be remembered that a cultivated Englishman who visited Boston some years ago stooped to such work; but as a business, to be advertised by circular, this sermon-manufacturing is something new. The 'Outlook' has received one of these circulars, and commenting upon it at length, says:

"'We know of no way of making such a business impossible except by the cultivation of a higher ethical sentiment among clergymen themselves.' A wolf in sheep's clothing, indeed, is the man who talks to his people about honesty and sincerity and then reads to them as his own a sermon which he has never prepared."

But it is an open secret that this is widely done. The *manuscript sermon trade* is an old one in European countries and, especially in the Churches of England, is seemingly accepted as legitimate. In the American Churches, too, of the more fashionable order, one rarely can hear a sermon with any first-handed life or point in it; so that whether it is or is not original is a matter of entire indifference. *The less of it the better anyway;* and if it is smooth, and short, and melodiously delivered no questions will be asked. Even when a fashionable "orthodox" Church on the Avenue is diverted with an Easter-day *Sermonette*, made up of fragments of an eloquent sermon from a volume of "heretical" sermons, and the imposition is publicly exposed, hardly a ripple of excitement and no condemnation at all is awakened thereby! In this condition of the "ethical sentiment" it is as well to use "typewritten sermons made to order" as to use those in manuscript imported from England or those in print stolen from books.

The sermon, anyway, among *the fashionable* Protestant sects is rapidly becoming what it has long been in the Roman Catholic sect—a matter of little or of no account. "How did you like the sermon?" asked one of another as they left the church. "I do not care for sermons anyway, and as that came as near to nothing as possible I liked it well," was the reply. To fill out the program and give a breathing-spell to the singers and reciters seems growingly to be the main function of the sermon. The performance of a Ritual, or the *short and quick* discharge of a still reputable, but very distasteful, duty of "going to church" being a chief object of what is called Worship—quite naturally the increasing demand must be for *short and quick* sermons and "as near to nothing as possible." The time *has* come when "itching ears" in the Churches "no longer endure sound instruction," nor *instruction* of any sort. The "tithings of mint, anise, and cummin"—the *proprieties* of ceremonies, forms, recitings, and other *externalities*—have widely taken the place of the "weightier matters of the Law." So that it is now *old-fashioned* and extremely unpopular to "preach the Gospel to every creature." Any modern Paul who should venture to "reason of righteousness, temperance, and a judgment to come" so pointedly as to make his *aristocratic* hearers "tremble" would quickly be remanded to the madhouse (especially should he "continue his speech till midnight") with words similar to those used of both Paul and his divine Master, "he is beside himself";—or, should he *press home* his Gospel so as to make it *personal* to his whole congregation, something would certainly transpire similar to that recorded in St. Luke's Gospel, 4th chapter, 28th and 29th verses: "And all they in the synagogue, when they heard these things, were filled with wrath; and rose up and thrust him out of the city, and led him to the brow of the hill whereon their city was built; that they might cast him down headlong."

In this condition of the "ethical sentiment" it is well, *for all who are not possessed of the martyr-spirit* of *genuine* Christianity, to preach sermons that are "short and quick" and "as near to nothing as possible"—whether original, or purchased, or stolen.

What *genuine* Christianity is should be gathered from the brave, and bold, and self-forgetting voices and lives of the "noble army of martyrs" in connection with such *fundamentally essential* New Testament requirements as follows: "Ye shall indeed drink of the cup that I drink of and be baptized with the baptism that I am baptized with. . . . The servant is not above his lord, nor the disciple above his teacher; if they have called the ruler of the house Beelzebub, how much more will they so call them who are of his household. . . .

If *any man*" (and especially *any minister*) "will be my disciple let him deny himself, take his cross *every day* and follow me . . . think not that I am come to send peace on earth. I came not to send peace but a sword . . . behold I send you forth as sheep in the midst of wolves . . . if they have persecuted me they will also persecute you . . . *woe unto you when all men shall speak well of you*, for so did their fathers to the *false prophets*—blessed are ye when man shall revile you, and persecute you, and say all manner of evil against you falsely—for so persecuted they the (*true*) prophets which were before you"—all of which, *as fundamental self-surrender and self-crucifixion*, was accepted and experienced by every *true* minister of the Gospel and by every *genuine* Christian from the days of Peter and Paul to the days of Luther, Wesley, Channing, Robertson, Stanley and Phillips Brooks.

LXXVI.—TRADITIONALISM AS A MAIN CAUSE OF DEGENERATION.

IN the traditional Christian Church exactly the same thing has come to pass that existed in the Jewish Church at the beginning of the Christian era,—" making the Word of God of none effect through your *tradition*, which ye have delivered—*teaching for doctrines the commandments of men*." The degenerate Jewish Church had come to esteem traditions concerning the Law as equal to, and even above, the Law itself. The Pharisees insisted that the *written* could only be understood through the *oral;* that the Church through its Sanhedrim, and the Sanhedrim through its Succession of Priests, had received the True Faith from Moses according to which the Law must be interpreted by all. " It was the fundamental principle of the Pharisees that by the side of the written law there was an oral law (tradition) to complete and to explain the written law. It was an article of faith that in the Pentateuch there was no precept, and no regulation, ceremonial, doctrinal, or legal, of which God had not given to Moses all explanations necessary for their application, with the order to transmit by word of mouth. The classical passage on this subject is the following: 'Moses received the Traditions from Sinai, and delivered them to Joshua, and Joshua to the elders, and the elders to the priests, and the priests to the men of the Great Synagogue.' " In the end the Traditions became more sacred than the

Law, and practically superseded it. The Law was only read or heard in detached passages or "texts" just to furnish a starting point for the endless Traditions.

So now—endless Expositions, Commentaries or Sermons have taken the place of the Bible and practically superseded it. It is read or heard only as a "text," or as a *starter* for elaborate traditional interpretations. No longer is it "Hear what the Spirit saith to the Churches," but Hear what THE CHURCH says, or what POPES have commanded, or what SANHEDRIMS from the fourth century downward have decreed! The *Mishna* and the *Targums*—the Creeds and the Doctrines with their *officially authorized* elaborations are both the Law and the Gospel of "Orthodoxy" now, as they were of "Pharisaism" at the opening of the Christian Era. "Howbeit, they did not hearken, but they did after their *former manner*. So these nations feared the LORD, *and served their graven images*, both their children, and their children's children; *as did their fathers, so do they unto this day.*" (See 2 Kings, chapter 17).

A sermon just published, as preached in one of the largest and most fashionable Roman Catholic Churches of New York to "a crowded congregation, many people being turned away from the High Mass," begins as follows. "At the outset God placed at the entrance of His temple an incomprehensible mystery. Those who will enter there must accept this mystery blindly. If they will accept this mystery on the strength of His Word, then there will never be a single difficulty in their belief. . . . My lips are closed by the commands of St. Paul. I can imagine his scowling countenance if I were about to explain this mystery to you." Just so! Let your eyes be put out, your brain stupefied and your reason stultified—then there will be no further trouble; after that there will never be a single difficulty in your belief.

> "*Open your mouth and shut your eyes,
> And I'll give you something to make you wise*"—

though an old rhyme is, after all, the summarized method

of charlatanry in Religion as everywhere else. "Whether it be a proposition or a pill, *swallowing* and not questioning" is what the charlatan demands. Both the fat livelihood and the self-parading glory of the Charlatan Priest depend upon "unquestioning faith" in his fundamental proposition. That *proposition* accepted " blindly," all the rest follows—of course!

Grant the *premise* and all the conclusions *must* follow: there is no escaping them. Antichrist, in all its forms the world over, begins ever with an "incomprehensible mystery" which it forges into a fundamental or *sine qua non* dogma: this dogma once accepted becomes a *yoke*—then follow whips of Logic and goads of Consistency, *compelling* all the rest. This is the method of priestcraft in all the Religions and in all the sectarian forms of each religion. Sharp as a serpent (but *not* as "harmless as a dove") each sectarian, churchman, champion-of-the-faith, or whatever else he may be called, invariably says, as his first word: "I can do nothing with you until you accept on faith" (that is *blindly*) "my fundamental proposition." This accepted and the *yoke* of the sect, church, faith, whatever it may be, inevitably follows. Thereafter it will be "hard to kick against the pricks," —as the Voice said to Saul, who was inwardly and secretly rebelling against the whips and goads of Pharisaism, whose hard and heavy yoke of Dogmatic Consistency he had, from youth up, been compelled to bear.

Still sounds, as earnestly and as pitifully as ever, the voice of Jesus—the same that spoke to Saul on the way to Damascus—" Come unto me all ye that labour and are heavy laden, and I will give you rest. Take *my* yoke upon you, and learn of *me;* for *I am meek and lowly in heart:* and ye shall find rest unto your souls. For *my yoke is easy and my burden is light.*"

A timely illustration of the *reliableness* of Tradition is before us at this date. The "Diamond Anniversary" of Queen Victoria has called forth such endless *spurious* reports of her sayings and doings—told and retold, *printed and reprinted* as evidences of her supreme goodness, wisdom, greatness, and glory—that "she no longer attempts to refute or deny them," considering it to be a hopeless task.

"If they do these things in a green tree, what shall be done in the dry?" In these omniscient days of the Printing Press and of Argus-eyed Historic Records and Criticisms, spurious Traditions are even more widely received and believed than are verifiable Facts. What then must have been the case *increasingly* as we go backward through the centuries! What is *any* Tradition worth unless it be *historically verified* —especially any Tradition of such imaginative and credulous ages as were those which produced and "handed down" the *Mishna* and *Targums*, the *Apocryphas* and *Hagiographas*, the *infallible* creeds and *essential* doctrines of "orthodox" Christianity, Judaism, Mohammedism, Buddhism, and all the other forms of traditional religious faith. "And even now is the axe laid unto the root of the trees: every tree therefore that bringeth not forth good fruit is hewn down, and cast into the fire. . . Whose fan is in his hand, and he will thoroughly cleanse his threshing-floor; and he will gather his wheat into the garner, but the chaff he will burn up with unquenchable fire."

LXXVII.—CREDULITY AND ROME, OR FAITH AND REASON—WHICH?

For sixteen centuries the doctrine of the "Triad" in its Christianized form has been sustained, chiefly from the word Elohim in the Old Testament and from the passage known as that of The Three Witnesses in the New Testament. This last was long called, by some of its chief supporters, the "main peg upon which the doctrine hung" or the "corner-stone upon which it was built." Since the Revised Version has joined with all honest or honorable Biblical Scholarship to reject this New Testament passage as spurious, the still persistent defenders of the doctrine have fallen back upon the name Elohim—a name now clearly proved to be a *a relic of polytheism* which was permitted to survive for a time in the oldest of the Old Testament writings.

"In Amos K. Fiske's work, entitled 'The Myths of Israel,' the Elohist portion of the text of Genesis is distinguished from the Jahoist by being printed in different type, while in the Polychrome Bible the composite authorship is indicated by the four or five separate colors.

"Referring to the Elohist text, the Rev. A. H. Sayce, the greatest living authority on the Babylonian cuneiform inscriptions, in 'The Higher Criticism and the Verdict of the Monuments,' writes as follows:

"'The word Elohim takes us back again to the pre-Israelitish age of Canaan. Elohim is a plural noun, and its employment in the Old Testament as a singular has given rise to a large amount of learned discussion, and, it must also be added, of a learned want of common sense. . . . If the Hebrew word Elohim had not once signified the plural "gods," it would never have been given a plural form, and the best proof of this is the fact that in several passages of the Old Testament the word is still used in a plural sense. Indeed, there are one or two passages, as, for example, Gen. i., 26, where the word, although referring to the God of Israel, is yet employed with a plural verb, much to the bewilderment of the Jewish rabbis and the Christian commentators who followed them. It is strange how preconceived theories will cause the best scholars to close their eyes to obvious facts. . . . What can be plainer than the existence of a persistent polytheism among the bulk of the people, and the inevitable traces of this polytheism that were left upon the language and possibly the thoughts of the enlighted few?'

"The tablets of Tel el-Amarna (1887) show very clearly how it was possible that a word which formerly signified 'gods' could come to signify the one Supreme Deity."

There would now seem to be left no infallible authority for this doctrine of the "Triad in its Christianized form" other than that of infallible Councils. But infallible Councils essentially imply an infallible Church; and an infallible Church essentially implies an infallible head of the Church, which is Papacy. So that, so far as this particular doctrine is concerned, it is now and henceforth " Rome or Reason " —there is no other alternative.

Accept " Rome " and this matter, like all others pertaining to fact as well as to faith, is already closed and settled. You are forbidden to ask questions, you must not think; all that you may say is, " I believe."

" The Holy Office and Supreme Infallibility of the Vatican " has just now promulgated an Edict forbidding absolutely any further investigation of the question as to whether the " text of the three heavenly witnesses " is authentic or an interpolation. Whether it is an integral part of the original Epistle or not, taught in the Bible or not, *it is an integral part of the teachings of the Infallible Church*—and that ends the matter. For the future no Roman Catholic must call it into question, or investigate it except as an Infallible Truth. This is logical and inevitable—from the standpoint of an Infallible Church, as also from the standpoint of Infallible Councils, or of Infallible Creeds, or of Infallible Tradition or of *essential and binding* " Orthodoxy " of any sort. All these roads lead to Rome. Whoever resolutely walks in either of them should " leave all hope behind "; and the quicker *he* reaches Rome the better. Accept *any* claim of Inerrancy, whether it be creed, or book, or Pope and you are already within the territory of the Vatican. And from it there is no ultimate escape or consistent appeal except to Reason. At last the time has come, and the twentieth century will fully reveal it, when, for all *honest* people there can be but two Churches—the Church of Rome and the Church of Reason; or rather, the Church of *Credulity dictated and compelled* by Rome and the Church of *Faith directed and constrained* by Reason. Which of these will be chosen by all the *intelligently honest* is not a matter of doubt. For that intelligence *which is noble enough to be honest* will never submit to the suppression of investigations with reference to *any question beneath the sun.*

LXXVIII.—EVOLUTION OF THE TRIAD AS AN EXPLANATION OF GOD.

The conception of God as a Triad probably originated from its analogy to the human family—father, mother, and child (or children). We trace this in the most ancient Hindoo teachings, and the symbol was constantly in use by Plato, Philo, the Cabalists, and the Gnostics. The human family is *three in one*, hence the divine family or the "Godhead" must be, or probably is, *three in one*. So they reasoned, and fourth-century theologians accepted their reasoning.

Elaborating this analogy the Triad came to be the common explanation of almost everything. Among the Chaldean and all later Astrologers it explained the Universe. Sun, Earth, and Moon—Source, Product, and Reflector—were the *three in one* of the Universe. For these there were three symbols, united to form a fourth: the Circle, the Cross, the Half-circle, and these three (Sun, Earth, and Moon) as One symbolized by the "mystery-planet," Mercury, whose symbol was all three combined (half-circle / circle / cross).

Of all Astrology and of all its resulting *Occultism* " the entire symbology is built on these signs, and their arrangement conveys at once the whole of the hidden meaning. The Sun is the centre of our system; its symbol is the Circle, which is the sign of perfection. It represents spirit —the highest condition we are capable of understanding. Behind it is the Logos of our system. His Essence, pouring out life upon His children, is indicated by the dot always placed in the centre of the circle. In manifestation, energy works from the centre to the periphery. This essence is the WILL in us, or, the spirit in motion. In all Astrological calculations the Sun is the centre. It represents the I, or Individuality in humanity. The Cross represents the Earth, or matter. In form it is two straight lines athwart each other, producing four acute angles, and expressing duality as opposed to the Unity exhibited by the circle. In these two symbols, we find typified the difference between spirit and matter, in the Universe. The Half-circle represents the Moon—the collector and preserver of light. It is the great moulder of form; the illusion."

Thus was the Universe explained as a divine Triad, which the Christian theologians called the "Godhead"—using symbols peculiar to Christianity.

A still later evolution of this most ancient analogy is found in all systems of Philosophy, beginning with that of Plato.

"The symbol of the mystery-planet, Mercury, for a long time was the puzzle of Astrologers; but we now understand it as representing the perfect man. The symbol of Mercury expresses the *three in one*—body, soul, and spirit united. It finally becomes changed into the Uranian symbol of the god-like man.

"Thus the idea of God, gradually formed by man, is a reflection from his own mind. Yet, as it is an unveiling of the Divine Spirit in man, which is also the Universal Spirit, it must give a truthful, though incomplete idea of the divine nature. The doctrine of the Trinity may be true, although as formulated in creeds it gives distorted ideas of the truth. The Universal Existence may be analogous, as in the Kosmos of Plato, to the *threefold being of man*, whose physical, psychical, and rational factors are the expressions of spirit-activity in association with particular phases of matter."

"Aristotle taught that the corporeal has no dimensions outside of the three. The Pythagoreans taught that all and everything is determined through triplicity: they regarded the triad as the most perfect form in the universe; unless it were the tetrad, or four, *which is the triad more fully developed.*"

This development has at last been made in Christian Theology by the Roman Church, whose *triad* has now become a *tetrad*—Father, Son, Holy Ghost, *and* the Virgin Mary. Its ultimate Evolution is bound to be a fulfilment of the prayer of Jesus and the prophecy of Paul:

"That they *all* may be one; as Thou, Father, art in me and I in Thee, that *they also may be one in us.*"

"And when all things shall be subdued unto Him, then shall the Son also himself be subject unto Him that put all things under Him, that God may be *All in All.*"

This is simply the old teaching of the Divine Omnipresence as found everywhere in the Bible. Just now it is newly brought before us in the *fifth* of the "New Sayings of Christ" reported as recently discovered at Behnesch in Egypt—" Jesus saith . . . Wherever there is one alone there the *I Am* is with him. Raise the stone and there thou shalt find *Me;* cleave the wood and there *I Am.*" This corresponds closely with all the logia of the New Testament, which may be summed up in the simple sentence—" I and my Father are one," *as explained by the two analagous sentences above quoted.*

(*a*) DIVINE PERSONALITY.

This teaching of the Divine Omnipresence is by no means "Pantheism" in the materialistic or *non-personal* sense.

"*Whose body Nature is, but God the soul.*" The "parts" cannot be more perfect than the "stupendous whole"—nor can they be more individual or *personal.* The "ladder whose top reaches Heaven and upon which angels ascend and descend" cannot be less perfect, but infinitely more so—nor can it be less individual or *personal,* but infinitely more so than is any one of the infinite number of rounds that compose it.

Locke defines *person* as "a thinking, intelligent being." According to Dr. Paley, *personality* implies "consciousness of thought." In these higher, spiritual meanings, *divine personality is an essential characteristic* of "God the Soul"; it is *necessary* as well as reasonable to believe that the "One in us," the "All in all" is *Person* or *Personality.*

It may be reasoned out as follows:—All that in man is highest and best also *must be* in Him "Who is in man, and in Whom man is":—*the same* " highest and best," only infinitely beautified and perfected. The very "highest and best" in man is his *personality;* hence to deny or doubt the *personality* of Him "in whom we live, and move, and have our being" is an absurdity. To conceive of any of the *parts* as "higher and better" than *The All*, is nonsense intolerable. That *part* of *The All* we call "man" thinks, knows, loves, is self-conscious—that is, is a *person;* and this is his supreme glory and mark of superiority. It is then self-evident that *The All* must be a *Person* in an infinitely more glorious and complete sense—must think, and know, and love, and be self-conscious as "The All in all."

Such is the *axiom* of Divine Personality as suggested by the essential teachings of the Bible and of Apostolic Christianity.

LXXIX.—A MAIN REASON WHY SO MANY DISBELIEVE IN GOD AND IN IMMORTALITY.

That is a universal and an eternal law of Condition and of Consequence, or of Cause and of Result, which Jesus enunciated as a first utterance of his divine ministry: "Blessed are the pure in heart, for they shall see God." A law equally open to and equally inviolable by all, Jew or Gentile, Christian or Pagan, now and ever.

But, as a matter of fact, thus far in the Evolution of Humankind the immense masses of men ever have been and are very far from "pure in heart"; seemingly make no effort and do not even desire to be "pure in heart."

So, as Jesus the Christ first recognized and taught, they must, little by little, be lifted up and drawn *toward* this condition and its blessed consequence, by attractive representations of the character of God. "God is your Father, God is Love and loves you, all He does is in love for you, all that He requires or ever will require is for your good." Such was the Gospel of Jesus and of his early followers. Thus, during the first two Christian centuries half the world were *drawn* to self-surrendering, life-consecrating belief in God.

But, then and thereafter, cold, repellant Dogmatism began

to be preached, instead of the "Good News." Mercenary salvation—salvation through desire of "a hundred-fold in this life" and Heaven in the life to come, or through fear of "tribulations in this life" and Hell in the life to come, which is *Commercialism or self-interest on the part of both God and man*—began to be proclaimed instead of the Gospel of Love. As a consequence the baser motives, instead of the nobler ones, were appealed to and converts were *bought* or *compelled* into self-interested professions of Christianity, instead of being *attracted* or *drawn* by the Love of God and the Beauty of Holiness. So it was increasingly and has continued unceasingly down to the present time.

But a nobler or *less base* disposition—less open to the baser motives—now begins to prevail and, as a consequence, the proclaiming of Commercialism—which traditional Ecclesiasticism and "orthodox" Dogmatism always and everywhere proclaim—results in making unbelievers faster than in making "converts." The "accessions" to the various Churches are fewer and from the least intelligent and moral classes, while the most cultivated and virtuous classes (either quietly or with indignant protests) refuse such a mercenary religion with its mercenary God and become, many of them, agnostics if not downright unbelievers.

The blame and guilt of much if not all of this lies at the door of degenerate Christianity—rather at the door of those pseudo-custodians of Christianity who, from the fourth century downward and for sundry reasons of personal advantage, have caused it to degenerate.

That this is so and why it is so has been pointedly set forth, as follows, in a recent sermon by a well-known "heretical" clergyman of the Church of England:

"The conception of God's nature which has been laid before us for many years, has brought many men at last to turn away from it with dismay and pain. They feel that the morality of the pulpit on this matter lags behind the moral feeling of society. God has been represented, they think, and I think with them, as selfish, as seeking His own glory at the expense of His creatures' welfare, as jealous, as arbitrary, as indulging in favoritism, as condemning all for the sake of one, as insisting on forms of temporary importance and binding them forever on the conscience, *as ruining men for mistakes in doctrine, as claiming a blind submission of the conscience and the intellect,* as vindictive, as the resolute torturer of the greater part of the human race by an everlasting punishment which presupposes everlasting evil; as, in one word, anything rather than the Father revealed in Jesus the Christ. Much of this teaching remains still, though it is presented under a veil by which its coarser outlines are modified. It is accepted by many who either *do not possess a strong and individual sense of morality,* or who do not think, or *prefer not to think* on the matter, lest they should shake the fabric of their easy faith or spoil their religious sentiment. But, those who do, and whose moral feeling of right and wrong is sane and strong, turn away revolted from a God of this character, believe that to be immortally connected with Him would be degradation, even the very horror of hell.

"Not having been taught any other God, and being, to a certain degree, culpably lazy about *examining into the teaching of Christianity for themselves,* they fall back on their last resource, and disbelieve in all Religion. 'It is better to perish for ever, than to be the slave of such a ruler. We deny his existence. But, at the same time, we will be true to our sense of right and wrong; we will do what we can to help the race; we will have our immortality in the memories of the future, or in the Being of Humanity; but, as for ourselves, let us cease, for *we could not live with the Being who has been described to us.*'

"Now, I believe this to be, and no one need mistake my meaning, a *really healthy* denial of God, for it is founded on the denial of *a false God.* So far as it is founded on the assertion of *a true morality,* so far it is, though these men do not confess it as such, the assertion of *the true God.* The God who has been preached to men of late has now become an idol, that is, a conception of God lower than we ought to frame, and *a revolt against that conception is not in reality a revolt against God;* it is a protest against idolatry. I sympathize strongly, then, with that part of the infidel effort which is directed against these *immoral views* of God's character, though I am pained by the manner in which the attack is conducted—and it is my hope that the attack will lead our theologians to bring their teaching up to the level of the common moral feeling on this subject, and to reveal God as the Father of men in all the profound meaning of that term. The belief in immortality will then return, for the love of God will return to men. For it is impossible for any man to clearly see and believe in the Father as revealed in the Christ and not passionately desire to draw nearer and nearer to Him forever, and not feel that he *must live and continue to live forever*. Therefore, in order to restore to men such as I have described a belief in immortality, we must restore to them a true conception of God. This is, this ought to be, the main work of the preachers and teachers of this time. For *as long as the morality of the pulpit hangs behind the morality of religious-minded men, those religious-minded men will be infidels.*"

LXXX.—THE ECLECTICISM OF CHRISTIANITY— ILLUSTRATIONS.

In various portions of this volume, but on pages 27-34 in particular, the essential eclecticism of Christianity has been claimed and variously illustrated. In its *methods* as well as in its materials—in its *practical-workings* as well as in its theories or teachings—it is essentially eclectic; so that all of its *organic divisions*, its Denominations, Sects, or Schisms, as they are called—are Providentially overruled to the cooperative fulfilment of one great end, *viz.:* the purification and (through purification) the elevation or "Salvation" of human souls. Among other figures to illustrate this, that of a vast system of graded schools, commencing with the "Kindergarten" and extending to the University, was used. The pictorial or *object-lesson* Denominations, beginning with those which are most "ritualistic" (i. e., sensational or dramatic) take human souls in their *infantile* or least developed stages and *start* them upward. In proportion as they "*grow* in grace and in the knowledge of God" they will *graduate* from one department of organized Christianity to another, (from one Denomination to another) in each advance leaving behind the *childishness* of past developments and "reaching forward" to the *manliness* of those which are before. "When I was a child, I spoke as a child, I understood as a child, I thought as a child; but when I became a man, I put away childish things." So, from the most ritualistic (kindergarten and primary) Denominations upward, each may have its recognized function, and all co-work to one great end. Instead of sectarian rivalries and antagonisms there should be loving co-operation. Each individual should be in whatever *grade* of the Church Catholic his developments fit him for—which may always be determined by his own choice of *what interests and helps him most.* There let him remain, *helping and being helped,* till he unmistakably hears the Inner Voice saying, "Come up higher,"—graduate into a higher department of the Church Catholic. Then (in spite of what any *human* voice or *earthly* interest may say) let him change his Denomination to another better suited to his developing *manliness.* "This one thing I do, forgetting the things that are behind and *aspiring* to the things that are before, I *press forward."* So all the Denominations may have their recognized uses.

A less dignified illustration has somewhere been hinted, which the author may be pardoned for here elaborating to suit, what seems to be, the *peculiar function* of each of the best-known Denominations of Christians: "*Washed their robes and made them white*"—is one of many texts by which the figure is suggested. In any well-regulated process of "washing and making white" robes or clothes of any sort, in our day, there are several successive stages: *First,* the soaking and soaping; *second,* the boiling and scouring; *third,* the rinsing and wringing; *fourth,* the drying and starching; *fifth,* the smoothing and folding.

Using these common-place terms (as the Master did those of salt, candles, bread-making, clothes-mending, and other similar ones) it may be said (without intended offence to any) that each organized body of Christians has its own *peculiar* function in some one of the above-named processes as applied to the *sanctification* of the Church in general and of its individual members in particular.

The *first* process seems to be that *peculiar* to the more "ritualistic" bodies as the Roman, Greek, and Anglican Catholic sects; the *second*, to the more aggressive bodies as the Methodists and the Salvation Armies; the *third*, to the more puritanic bodies as the Baptists and Independents or Congregationalists; the *fourth*, to the more formalistic bodies as the Presbyterians, Broad-Church Episcopalians, and Lutherans; the *fifth*, to the more rationalistic bodies as the Unitarians, Progressive Friends, and other similar organizations of Liberal Christians.

Though a somewhat facetious illustration and commonplace indeed, yet it is suggestive and appropriate. Throughout the Bible the figure is used in such phrases as "wash me," "purge me," "cleanse me" as applied to the individual; and "without spot or wrinkle or any such thing" as applied to the Church. To fulfil any part, however primary or humble, of this Divine Process of *making clean* is no unworthy function. As to the illustration itself—"What God hath cleansed, that call not thou common."

More elegant (though less Biblical) is the illustration which, as a portrayal of the *world-wide* eclecticism of Christianity, is so forcible that it is quoted in full on succeeding pages.

[See pages 293–296.]

SOME REASONS FOR AND METHODS OF
"LITERARY CRITICISM" AS APPLIED TO THE
BIBLE AND TO CHRISTIANITY IN COMMON
WITH ALL OTHER LITERATURE AND SYSTEMS
OF RELIGION
BEING EXPLANATIONS
COMMON TO THE COMPANION VOLUMES
"ANCIENT SACRED SCRIPTURES OF
THE WORLD"
AND
" RENASCENT CHRISTIANITY."

> "Welcome each rebuff
> That turns earth's smoothness rough,
> Each sting that bids nor sit nor stand, but go!'

"For this old world of ours needs bracing up, and needs it badly. It has needed it before: granted. There were times worse than these: grant this also. But we were not living then: we are living now; and the world was never before sinning against as much light as it is now, and never before was there quite so much ingenuity displayed in calling wrong things by right names and right things by wrong names. Downright honesty of speech is a pressing need of the hour. Soft and silken phraseology is covering a multitude of sins. The men who want the earth are finding persuasive and pretty reasons for it. Mercenary considerations are in danger of becoming fundamental principles. The straight line between good and evil is getting warped; and the old questions, 'Is it right?' 'Is it wrong?' are losing their grip. We are assuming a financial attitude, instead of a moral attitude, toward things. . . It is time to change, to take on a new tone, to preach righteousness, to tell men that the supreme reason for doing right is because it is right."

> "We gain not heaven by a single bound,
> But we build the ladder by which we rise;
> And we climb to its summit round by round,
> From the lowly earth to the lofty skies."

"It is one of the noblest human instincts that we cannot feel within us the glory and power of a real conviction without earnestly striving to make that conviction pass into other minds."

"Our knowledge has run ahead of our virtue. Our scientific progress is far greater than our moral progress. The platform on which society stands is all crank-sided: the scientific side is too high for the moral and religious side. I call on you, cultivators of art and preachers of religion, that you hold up your end. I know it is by far the heavier end; but the more is the reason why you should lift heartily and with a will, and, more than all, *that you should lift all together.*"

LXXXI.—RENASCENT CHRISTIANITY AND SACRED SCRIPTURES.

(a) *Explanatory Note.*

The two volumes "Ancient Sacred Scriptures of the World" and "Renascent Christianity" are designed as companion volumes. As such the Explanations which follow are common to both.

The latter volume, which has the general title "Renascent Christianity, A Forecast of the Twentieth Century," has been especially prepared in the interest of what is now everywhere known as Higher Criticism :—most inadequate it is and utterly unworthy, but yet designed, *by its very imperfections,* to elicit and even to compel more adequate and worthy attempts. As such it would not be complete without a setting forth of some special Methods of Criticism and of Translation such as those according to which the volume "Ancient Sacred Scriptures of the World" has been prepared.

(b) *Motives.*

In spirit and in general facts, though not in personal details, the following conclusion of a notable volume may serve both as Preface and Conclusion for this and its companion volume :

"I should not speak of myself personally, were it not for the desire which every reader naturally feels to know the probable motives of one who addresses him on any important topic of practical interest. Disconnected, in a great degree, from the common pursuits of the world, and *independent of any party* or of any man's favor, there is, perhaps, scarcely an individual to whom it can be a matter of less *private* concern what opinions others may hold. No one will suppose, that, if literary fame were my object, I should have sought it by such discussions as these in which I have engaged. Even among those who have no prejudices in favor of the errors opposed, much indifference and much prejudice to the subject must be overcome, before I can expect such volumes to find any considerable number of readers. . . . I have been writing, as it were, on the tombstones of those who were most dear to me, with feelings of the character, purposes, and duties of life which my own death-bed will not strengthen. I may, then, claim at least that share of unsuspicious attention to which everyone is entitled *who cannot be supposed to have any other motive in maintaining his opinions, than a very serious, earnest, and enduring conviction of their truth and importance.*"

(c) The "retrograde movement."

Traditionalism, in its assertive and non-critical form, is just now exulting over what it calls the "scientific confirmations" of its methods in a recently published volume by a well-known author. "It may not display a scientific temper of mind, but it is a splendid tribute to Harnack's accuracy of methods, that on all sides men accept the general conclusions arrived at in his latest work *before having examined his reasoning*. Of course many of those interested have held this same conclusion *under the authority of tradition without regard for what criticism might say*, but now, *without a detailed knowledge of his argument*, they feel assured that it is the conclusion of Criticism, *simply because Harnack says so.*" Surely 't is true that a drowning man will clutch at a straw! The "straw," and the only one in the volume referred to, that can save this form of Traditionalism from going down for the "third and last time" is presented in a single sentence, by which "the colossal labor of which the book we refer to is a monument can be summed up." And what is this *summing up?* "The literature of the Christian Church, from the earliest writings of the New Testament canon to the time of Irenæus is proved by critical investigation to be 'in the main points and in most of its details, from the point of view of literary history, veracious and trustworthy.'"

In spite of the "colossal labor" and the unquestioned worth of the volume thus summed up, there is in it nothing at all but unceasing and strong confirmations of what all sifters of Tradition, verifiers of History, and "higher critics" both of the Bible and of the Church (who have called themselves Christians) from Origen, Arius, and Eusebius down to Channing, Norton, and Martineau, and from these down to all the "higher critics" of the day (who still retain the Christian name) have unanimously held and taught.—*Namely*, that "in the *main* points and in *most* of the details" the canonical Scriptures and other historically recognized "literature of the Christian Church" are "veracious and trustworthy" down "to *the time of Irenæus*."

(1) The time of Irenæus (the second century) is just the period to which unadulterated Apostolic Christianity extended, and at which strong tendencies to revert and rapid degeneration set in. Apostolic Christianity was that newborn Religion of Eclecticism presented to the world by the lips of Jesus and the pen of Paul. For a century nothing, save what those divine lips had unquestionably uttered and that truth-recording pen had unquestionably confirmed, was received or tolerated as Christianity. Then, at "the time of Irenæus," began that "falling away" and arose those "false prophets" predicted by both Jesus and Paul.

Judaism was *Platonized* into a "system" of Christian Dogmas; Christianity was *Judaized* into a "system" of Christian Ecclesiasticism and Ritual; Paganism was *Christianized* into an unverified and unverifiable "system" of Christian Traditionalism:—so began the "falling away." At the same time arose and, by the voice and vote of the semi-Heathen populace, prevailed the "false prophets"—Neo Platonizers, Neo Judaizers, Neo Paganizers too numerous to mention, down to those busy makers and stout defenders of that present Traditionalism which arrives at, and holds fast to, certain *popularized* and *profitable* conclusions "under the authority of tradition, without regard for what criticism might say:"—which Tradition it insists upon calling, and (under penalty of excommunication) requiring all others to call History! All this, and not Apostolic Christianity down to "the time of Irenæus," is what Higher Criticism objects to and rejects. It accepts, as it ever has accepted gladly—from the time of Origen, the first of the higher critics, downward—the *summing up* of Harnack's recent volume: that, the *canonical* Christian literature of the first century after the death of Jesus the Christ is "veracious and trustworthy in the *main* points and in *most* of the details." But this has no bearing—except of condemnation—upon the unverified, unverifiable, and before-that-time-unheard-of (by Jesus and the Apostles, utterly rejected) traditions which began to prevail in the Church of the third century, and have more and more widely prevailed ever since. All that Higher Criticism asks or has ever asked is that *whatever* is called History shall have *adequate* historic confirmations; and that *no one* shall henceforth be required—on penalty of either excommunication or of being branded as a heretic—to believe as History what has not been, *by commonly accepted literary methods*, historically confirmed. The "*main* points and *most* of the details" of the Bible are thus historically confirmed, and these it gladly accepts. But this does not imply the acceptance of the *whole* Bible in *all* its "points" and "details," much less the multitudinous traditions *about* the contents and meanings of the Bible which have come down to us from the third, fourth, and later centuries. Harnack's "retrograde movement" is well named if it be taken to imply, what doubtless it does imply, a going back to *original* sources and demanding that nothing shall be imposed as an *essential* Creed or as *essential* Christianity,—which is not clearly found in the canonical and *historically verified* records of the first century after the death of him, whom all the world acknowledges as The Founder of Christianity.

(d) *Special Explanations.*

"*For every word men may not chide or pleine
For in this world certain ne wight ther is
That he ne doth or sayeth sometime amis.*"

In issuing a new Edition of "Ancient Sacred Scriptures of the World" three special explanations are called for:

First,—with reference to the re-translation of some portions of the Bible, especially of some familiar phrases and words of the New Testament, which the author has made. Why not accept the received version, or at least the new revised version and leave the matter there? The author has done this invariably *except* in case of phrases and words which, as all unprejudiced critics agree, utterly misrepresent (in the accepted versions) the meanings and conceptions of the original utterances. As a matter of fact all the "orthodox" translators have read modern doctrines into certain of the original phrases; and have forced into some of the original words meanings that *were entirely foreign to them when spoken or written.* To do this is to do violence to the Historic Sense *of to-day* and to profane, as well as to pervert, History. The Bible *as History or as Literature* should be translated, in all respects, as other History or Literature is *honestly and honorably* translated. To impose one's own doctrine upon, or to read one's own meaning into, a translation or transcription of any sort is a deception or a fraud not to be for a moment tolerated by the Historic Sense *of to-day.* Everywhere else this is so (in these enlightened days) and so it must henceforth be in Biblical Criticism,—as also it must be in the Criticism of Theological and Ecclesiastical Literature in general. As an illustration:—The founders of all the great Religions of the world proclaimed themselves as Prophets of God, "one with Him" simply as His commissioned vicegerents or revealers. Their *immediate* followers so understood, received and recorded their teachings. But later generations came to believe them to be God Himself in human form and devised systems of belief and of homage accordingly. *This they had a right to do if they chose;* but to impose their belief upon, or to re-read their homage into the original records, in their translations and transmissions, *was, is, and ever must be an outrage upon History.*

Let any, even most intelligent and least prejudiced, Christian look at a picture, statue, relic, book, shrine or temple of Buddhism (or of any other Religion *except his own*) before or about which millions of devotees are prostrate, and he can easily understand how *they* read their own superstitions into their venerated object or volume. In the same way the most intelligent and least prejudiced of Buddhists (and of others) easily understand how *we*, as "orthodox" Christians, read *our* superstitions into our Bible, Traditions, and Symbols.

> "O wad some power the giftie gie us,
> To see ourselves as others see us!
> It wad frae monie a blunder free us,
> And foolish notion."

Exactly this has transpired also in all the "received" or "accepted" versions of the Bible and especially of the New Testament. From the third century down to to-day the *vox populi* of the Christian Church has proclaimed certain systems of Doctrine and of Worship as true and binding upon all. *This they (had, and) have a right to do if they choose.* But to so translate or transmit the *original records* as to do violence to their *original signification* is to profane those records, and also to commit an outrage upon History. What did that phrase mean, what did that word imply *to the speaker or the writer?*—This is the one and only question that an honest translator or transcriber will ever allow himself to ask.

(a) When the disciple said or the Apostle wrote "Rabbi" or "Adônâi" as applied to Jesus, did he *mean* "Master" or "Teacher" and *not* "God" or any word synonymous with "God"? If so, then "Master" or "Teacher" we should translate and transmit it faithfully, whether our version be "received" or not.

The persistent translation of such terms as the Hebrew Rabboni or Rabbi, and the Greek *despotēs* or *kurios* as "Lord" when applied to Jesus, while in all other cases the same terms are translated (as they uniformly mean) "Master," "Teacher," or "Sir," is a notable indication of the literary untruthfulness of Theological Dogmatism. These terms, unless immediately joined to or standing unquestionably for JEHOVAH, or ALMIGHTY ONE, or THE ETERNAL, or SUPREME GOD can never be translated "LORD" except through irreverence as well as literary untruthfulness.

It is no acceptable argument and no excuse to say that "to the Church, in a later period, was *revealed* the truth that Jesus Christ was the ALMIGHTY ONE in human form." Those who are the speakers and writers of the New Testament had no such *revelations* made to them, had no such knowledge or conception—as all intelligent critics of the Bible agree. Hence, to *make* them speak and write as if they conceived or believed *what we know they did not* is (again we say) an outrage upon History and upon Literary Criticism. The only honest or honorable way is to *begin* the use of terms, words, or phrases synonymous with the ALMIGHTY ONE as applied to Jesus the Christ *where the revelation of his Supreme Deity is alleged to have been actually made and received*,—in the writings or traditions of the second, third, or fourth century, as the case may be. But let no one, any longer, presume *to go back and force it upon the lips and pens of those to whom it was not yet " revealed"*—namely, the speakers and writers of the Bible. Against this both Historic Verity and Literary Criticism protest as falsehood and fraud.

The same may be said of all the doctrines " revealed to the Church in later periods " which have been *read into* the Bible through sectarian translations or transcriptions. Let whosoever will receive, believe, and proclaim these doctrines as " later revelations made to the Church " ; *on this ground* let him be " Churchman," " Romanist," " Orthodox," " Heterodox " or whatever he may choose. But let him not falsify the Original Records in order to establish his Church, or to maintain his Hierarchy, or to prove his Creed ! Let him not compel the speakers or writers of the Bible to testify to the verity of things which their eyes had not seen, their ears had not heard, nor their minds conceived ! To do this is to " sin against the Holy Ghost " and to " lie *both* unto men and unto God " !

The fruitful cause of all this manipulation of and doing violence to the Original Records may be traced to (what we may call) *Systemism* or, what is the same thing, Sectarianism in Religion. Some individual or individuals started with a personally pleasing or profitable proposition ; this proposition soon became a premise, the premise grew into a fundamental dogma and this became at length an Essential Doctrine or, an Infallible Creed. This proposition, premise, dogma, Doctrine or Creed once accepted all the rest inevitably followed—the School, the System, the Sect, the True Church, the Infallible Hierarchy. So have arisen the countless conflicting Religious Denominations.

Each *Systemarian* developed into a Sectarian ; and, when put on the defensive by all the others, appealed (in his straits) to the Bible and *forced from it* desired confirmation ; sometimes so translated and (in earlier periods) even interpolated it as to *make it* directly teach his fundamental proposition. As a consequence the world is full of Trinitarians, Unitarians, etc., or of Papists, Congregationalists, etc. ; and the chief aim of each one of the hundreds of Systems or of Sects is *to prove from the Bible* and thus promulgate its fundamental proposition, whatever it may be.

In Religion, the same as in everything else, what is now needed and what henceforth we must have in rapidly increasing numbers is (to use a new term) Trutharians or Truthists—LOVERS-OF-THE-TRUTH, "the whole Truth and nothing but the Truth." In Goethe's words : " I desire nothing but pure Truth and *have no system ;* so everything fits in." This is the Divine Eclecticism of Jesus the Christ and of all who, like his Apostles, "have been with and learned of him." Such *Eclectics* are the only ones *who are capable of being honest and true* as translators or as transcribers of the Original Records.

(b) When the disciples said or the Apostles wrote " Son of God " as applied to Jesus did they *mean* JEHOVAH, or ALMIGHTY ONE, or THE ETERNAL, or SUPREME GOD in human form ? Did they *mean* a " Person of the Godhead ? " Did they *mean* " Deity incarnate ? " If *not*, then let no translator or transcriber by any phrase, word, letter, or mark of punctuation even intimate that such *was the original meaning*.

And so on for various similar terms and phrases. It is not at all a question of what, *as a later revelation or unfolding*, "the Church" came to believe; but what the word or phrase *then and there* meant.

One may believe that Cæsar was Deity incarnate, or that Napoleon's or Wellington's victories were miraculous; he may formulate his belief and proclaim and enforce it as widely as possible; but he must not outrage History by translating original words into meanings foreign to them, or by transcribing original phrases into teachings never designed by those who uttered them. Once this might have been done; it has been done, unceasingly and universally, till now; *but it can be done no longer*. The Historic Sense, *newly developed and newly developing*, forbids it henceforth—with regard to the Bible as well as all other books; with regard to Church History and Religious Literature in common with all other departments of History and of Literature. With this understanding of the case a few familiar words and phrases (further explained in Preface of "Sacred Scriptures") have been translated or transcribed according to their *unquestioned original meaning* instead of the *modern dogmatic meaning* of all the "authorized" or "received" versions.

Second.—Another explanation is called for with reference to the *progress* of Higher Criticism since the main preparation of this volume was made. At its first issue, fourteen years ago, a frequent comment of its kindly disposed critics was, that it was "so far in advance of the age." Now, by the same critics, it is more likely to be pronounced "behind the age." So rapid has been the growth of *reverent* Criticism and of *rational* Religious Comprehension *combined!* And, with all the profound investigations and new light—from the time and school of Bauer down to those of Harnack—there has developed no actual refutation and no certain contradiction of a single important position taken in the published Preface and Explanations so many years ago.

Third.—An additional explanation is offered with reference to the persistent and almost universal objection of " orthodox " adherents of all Religions alike—Christians the same as Moslems, Buddhists, and the rest—to any expurgation, compilation, or change (except *traditional additions and expansions,* of which they can never have enough) of their Sacred Books. In no other department of History or of Literature in general is this objection ever made. Everywhere else expurgations, compilations, and changes *to modern word and phrase* (more expressive of original meanings) are called for. The critical study of the Bible *as literature* (the same exactly as any of the other Sacred Scriptures of the World) demands similar expurgations, compilations, and changes.

" Many persons have been taught from childhood to associate a false meaning with words and texts of the Bible. This meaning, borrowed from the schools of technical theology, is that which immediately presents itself to their minds, when those words and texts occur. They can hardly avoid considering the expositions so familiar to them, as those alone that could be obvious to an unprejudiced reader. *He who would break the associations which they have between certain words and a certain meaning, and substitute the true sense for that to which they are accustomed, appears to them to be doing violence to the language of Scripture.*

" Now these prejudices, so far as they are capable of being removed, can be removed only by establishing correct principles of interpretation, applying them to the subject in hand, and pointing out the true or the probable meaning of the more important passages that have been misunderstood."

" The literary critic—the critic of the right sort—does just this thing. He takes a book of which we wish to know, and gives us the very best it contains; he picks out its fine passages, and by so doing sets them out in a bold relief which they did not possess in the book itself; he takes the volume and sets it in its proper proportion,—gives us its historical relations, and from his store of knowledge and varied reading delivers to us a compact and vital parcel that probably carries with it far more of permanent value than we could have in any way gained ourselves from actual perusal of the book."

What Higher Criticism claims is the privilege of rendering the Bible as we do all other books, not according to *verbal meanings* (which may be numerous and conflicting as well as absurd) but according to evident or probable *original meanings*—the meanings of those who uttered the words, whether by pen or voice. This has been the principle of all intelligent translations and interpretations back to the time when Cicero elucidated it in the following words:

"What law, what decree of the Senate, what ordinance of a magistrate, what treaty or convention, or, to return to private concerns, what testament, what judicial decision, what stipulation, what form of agreement, *may not be invalidated or annulled, if we insist on bending the meaning to the words, and neglect the intent, purport, and will of the writer?* Truly, our familiar and everyday discourse would have little coherence, if we lay in wait for each other's words. There would be no domestic government, if we allowed our slaves to obey our commands *in their verbal meaning, and not in that sense in which the words are to be understood.*"

A learned professor of Theology and translator of the Bible has said: "This principle of interpretation is so constantly present to the mind of everyone, and is acted upon so unconsciously in reading all other books *but the Scriptures*, that, except in reference to them, it is scarcely necessary to announce it or advert to it."

"In many cases we at once reject the literal meaning of words, and understand them as figurative, because if we did not do this they would convey some meaning which contradicts common sense; and it would be inconsistent with our notions of the writer to suppose him to intend such a meaning. Men's minds being constituted alike, so that, when a subject is clearly understood, what appears an absurdity to one will appear an absurdity to another, we do not ascribe an absurd meaning to the language of any writer, except upon the special consideration of some well-known peculiarity of belief, or defect or cloudiness of intellect. Yet a great part of all language diverted in any way from its literal sense *will bear* an absurd meaning, that is, admit of being so interpreted as to be absurd *when the words alone are regarded.*"

"But this principle has not been regarded in the interpretation of Scripture. The believer in transubstantiation contends that we are to understand *verbally* the declaration: 'Unless you *eat the flesh* of the Son of Man, and *drink his blood*, you have not life within you.' The sect of the Antinomians would have us take to the letter the words of St. Paul, as rendered in the Common Version: 'But to him that *worketh not*, but *believeth* on him that justifieth the ungodly, his faith is counted for righteousness.' And of the believers in the doctrine of Atonement, some contend, that, when the Apostle speaks of the church as being 'purchased by the blood of Christ,' or, as they would have it read, 'by the blood of God,' we are to regard the blood of the Son as being paid, as it were, to the Father to deliver us from his wrath. All the errors connected with Christianity have appealed for support to such verbal misinterpretations of particular passages. Hence it has been said, that anything may be proved from the Scriptures. And it is true, that, if we proceed in so erroneous a method, and neglect every fact and principle which ought to be attended to in the interpretation of language, there is no meaning too false, too absurd, or too ridiculous, to be educed from the words of Scripture, or, equally, from those of any popular writing."

(*e*) The "*Received Text.*"

In all History there is not a greater fiction than is the widely prevailing belief that there is, of the Bible, and particularly of the New Testament, a "Received Text" which is reliable and final. Ascertain what the "Received Text" truly means and you have the exact and full meaning of the original speakers and writers of the Bible—is the common "orthodox" notion! To all Protestants what is commonly meant by the "Received Text" is the Greek New Testament as published at Leyden by Elcevir's Sons, in 1633, with a preface in which the publishers announced, "*Textum ergo habes nunc ab omnibus receptum.*" So said the publishers, advertising their publication as "a text now received by all"—a text *formed by an unknown editor*, in the days when what we now call Biblical Criticism was utterly unknown. This is the "Textus Receptus." It seems to have been collated from the editions of Erasmus, Robert Stephens, and Beza which were chiefly used for the King James translation into English, first published in 1611. Those editions all were, as nineteenth-century criticism has shown, crude and unreliable. Their common basis doubtless was that earliest edition of the Greek Testament printed in 1514 contained in the Complutensian Polyglot. For this "the manuscripts which were used have never been identified . . . and there has been much controversy respecting their value." We have the authority of Bishop Marsh, that the text which they have given almost invariably agrees with that of the *modern* Greek manuscripts,—such as were written in the thirteenth century or later. "There cannot be a doubt, therefore," he says, "that the Complutensian text was formed from *modern* manuscripts alone." Wetstein and other scholarly critics came to the same conclusion.

Taking this unreliable edition as their chief help, the versions of those who prepared the way for the King James translation and for the "Textus Receptus" were also unreliable.

Of the edition by Erasmus in 1516, he himself says: "*Præcipitatum fuit verius quam editum*—it was driven headlong through the press rather than edited." His publisher drove him on in order that he might issue his edition in advance of a new issue of the Complutensian Polyglot. "Only four or five manuscripts were used, all of them modern, and, with one exception, of very little value." Erasmus was a scholar worthy of the highest respect and admiration, but he edited the Greek Testament, to use the language of Griesbach, "*as he could*, from a very few manuscripts and those quite modern, with no other helps except the Latin Vulgate in an interpolated state, and the writings of a few inaccurately edited Fathers."

Stephens's edition closely follows the text as given in the Complutensian and has no original value. "The splendor of its typography, and the display of various readings, appear, however, to have given this edition a reputation to which it had no title from intrinsic merit. Its credit among Protestants was also doubtless enhanced by the fact that Stephens, who had been much harassed by the bigoted doctors of the Sorbonne, withdrew to Geneva soon after its publication, and announced himself a convert to the doctrines of the Reformation."

The only one who clearly went back of the thirteenth century Greek manuscripts was Beza. For his five editions, published in 1565-1598, he had some valuable ancient manuscripts. "But he made very little use of them. He mostly followed the text of Stephens's edition, and where he differed from it often altered it for the worse, sometimes introducing readings on mere conjecture, and frequently on very slight authority."

Such was the material out of which were developed the King James translation of the New Testament and the "Textus Receptus," both of which among Protestants have been *popularly* considered, and almost adored as infallible, for now nearly three centuries.

But during these centuries a vast amount of newly discovered critical materials have been gathered and are now available. Hundreds of manuscripts never before examined for critical purposes; vast collections of various readings made by such laborious scholars as Mill, Bengel, Wetstein, Griesbach, Matthæi, Alter, Birch, Scholz, Tischendorf, Tregelles, and many others down to Harnack; diligent, scholarly and *impartial* collations and comparisons of uncial and other ancient manuscripts, of various versions and of numerous New Testament quotations in the writings of the Christian Fathers—all this and much more has developed during the past three centuries, and chiefly during the last half of the present century. Besides this large accumulation of materials for critical purposes, the *critical faculty* and the *historic sense* —both so essential to the proper use of the materials—are the peculiar developments of the nineteenth century; indeed are just beginning to develop in their *truly non-partisan* and *absolutely unprejudiced* sense. The conclusion is that we are *just getting ready to begin* a " literary," that is an *impartially* critical and an *accurately* historic study of the Bible. Such a study is essential to its proper understanding and its highest usefulness. It is demanded by the *increasing honesty* as well as by the higher intelligence of to-day. It will constitute the most sacred task and produce the most glorious results of the twentieth century. It will end in a " Received Text " which all who intelligently accept the Christian name will gladly acknowledge; and also in " Received Translations," into all tongues, which he who runs may read.

" *And the Lord answered me and said, Write the vision, and make it plain upon tables, that he may run that readeth it.*"

[To add, even a feeble impulse, to this sacred work *just beginning* and so to contribute, even a little to its glorious outcome is the main purpose of the companion volumes— " Ancient Sacred Scriptures of the World " and " Renascent Christianity."]

(*f*) *The Polychrome Edition of the Bible.*

There is now in course of publication what is to be known as " The Polychrome Edition of the Bible." The most learned of the critical and at the same time reverent students of the Bible have found that most, if not all, of its books (both of the Old Testament and of the New) have been compiled from previously existing documents; that some of them are of composite authorship, and that many of them have been added to or changed since their first composition. To indicate these changes, additions, composite authorships and compilations the above-named Bible is now being printed, with specific colors to designate each class of departures from what were probably the original and reliable documents. The most eminent Biblical scholars of the world are engaged in the work; but only the Old Testament is, thus far, in course of preparation. We learn from a recent review that the book of Genesis is to be in eight colors, Leviticus in two,

Joshua in seven, Samuel in eight, Job in three, Chronicles in four, Ezra and Nehemiah in nine—each color indicating a distinct class of variations. Doubtless when the New Testament has been sufficiently studied, the now rapidly sharpening sense of Historic and of Literary Criticism will unravel the contents of its various books, with similar results. The prediction may be ventured that at least eight colors will be used for the book of Matthew, two for Mark, seven for Luke, eight for John, three for The Acts, four for the Pauline Epistles, and nine for the General Epistles and The Revelation. Thus, or in some other way, later if not sooner, the genuine and the important will be separated from the spurious and the unimportant in the Bible; the wheat will be garnered and the chaff burned, the trees bringing forth good fruit will stand and those that are fruitless will be cut down.

More than twenty years ago this same work of sifting and discriminating was systematically commenced and studiously continued by the author of this volume. An ardent student of the Bible from youth up, and improving every possible advantage to study it both devoutly and understandingly, he at length, as pastor of a large and critical congregation, felt the necessity of a *Compilation* of Sacred Scriptures which should (so far as possible) contain nothing but the *unquestionably genuine* and the *actually important*. No such a Compilation existed, or seemed then to be promised; so he felt constrained to undertake the task himself. Devoting the leisure (often also the midnight) hours of several successive years to the study and detail required, the volume known as "Ancient Sacred Scriptures of the World" was the result. By no means does the Compiler and Editor of that volume consider it faultless or final. It was at first, (and now again is), presented only as an humble attempt at what needed greatly to be done. Others are now beginning to do the same, and doubtless will do it in a far more scholarly and worthy manner. At the best it is designed to be only a *makeshift;* a temporary construction, anticipating and awaiting more permanent ones. As such (with many apologies for its errors and defects) it is now offered to the public in a new edition uniform with this volume—which has been prepared as its general elucidation and introduction. The Polychrome Edition of the Bible, in its completed form, cannot be issued for some time to come; and, besides being very large and expensive, can never be comprehensible or convenient for ordinary daily and devotional uses. It must be a Student's Volume, chiefly to be used for critical and literary purposes. From it *Compilations* doubtless will be made of a nature similar to that of "Ancient Sacred Scriptures of the World." When this shall have been done, so vastly superior in scholarship and in judicious selections and arrangements will they unquestionably be, that all their *forerunners* which have devoutly striven "to prepare the way" will gladly withdraw.

(*g*) *Confirming Citations from various authors.*

"No book in the world could bear such rules and modes of interpretation, as have been applied to the Bible. In all books, except scientific treatises, free use is made of metaphor and hyperbole, which are always defined and limited by what goes before and what follows, but which, taken by themselves and explained literally, would imply the most puerile and absurd notions. Now the fashion among theologians has been *to set up the seeming signification of some three or four isolated clauses in the Bible, as overweighing the clear and acknowledged tenor of the entire Scriptures*. . . . I can best illustrate the prevalent mode of Scriptural interpretation, by supposing a case. Suppose that, fifteen or twenty centuries hence, there should be remaining some two or three authentic biographies of Napoleon Bonaparte. Suppose that in these, written by admiring Frenchmen, it should be said of him: 'He was a very God among his soldiers,—adoring millions prostrated themselves before him,—he took in the nations of the earth at a glance,—his will was omnipotent.' Suppose that, though elsewhere throughout these books Napoleon was perpetually talked of as a man, and the books taken as a whole made utter nonsense upon the supposition that he was not a man, there yet should arise a set of critics who maintained that Napoleon was a divine being. . . . *These critics would aptly represent the generality of modern theologians and biblical interpreters.* . . . Lord Bacon's criticism on Aristotle applies: 'He had already decided, without having properly consulted facts as the basis of his decisions and axioms; and, having so decided, *he drags facts along as a captive, constrained to accommodate themselves to his decisions.*'"

"One curious fact shows how this doctrine is supported by the fear that, *if a single verse of the Bible is admitted to be unsound, the authority of the whole will be gone.* Scholars of all denominations admit that there are mistranslations and interpolations in our Bible which ought not to be there. Some years ago the Committee on Versions of the American Bible Society, containing *eminent scholars, all of Orthodox denominations*, prepared an amended edition of the English version. They did not make a new translation, *nor amend the errors of the old one, nor even improve the text where it is admitted to be faulty.* They only corrected some palpable misprints, and altered the headings of the chapters where these are incomplete or false, or where they are in reality comments on the Scripture. This amended version, indorsed by the secretaries, and adopted by the Board of Managers, was printed and circulated by them during seven years, *and was then suppressed.* This was done in consequence of a clamor, raised not merely by the ignorant, but in which even Reviews, Ecclesiastical Bodies, and Auxiliary Societies did not hesitate to join. I asked one of the gentlemen, who was a member of the committee, why this was done; and he said that it was owing to the fear that, *if we once begin to make corrections in the Bible, the people might lose their faith in it altogether.*"

"No one believes the 'Nautical Almanac' an *infallible* book; but it is such an authority that thousands of vessels trust themselves to its calculations, and thousands of lives and millions of property are confided to its accuracy."

"One whom I knew, one of the best of men, upright

and honorable, benevolent and kind, was called an *infidel*. When I asked him about it, he said, 'Yes, I have thought myself so, and for this reason,—when I was young, I heard a minister say, taking a Bible in his hand, Everything between these lids is the Word of God, and if you do not believe it you will be damned.' I said, 'If this is Christianity, I must be an infidel.' But now I have changed my mind. I do not think that Christianity requires me to believe everything in the Bible, and so I can gladly be a Christian.'"

(h) How the Eclectism of Christianity renders it a World-Religion.

The essential teachings of Christianity and its superiority, as an Eclectic or World-Religion, are well stated in a recent personal experience of a very learned Hindoo priest or Brahmin who, after prolonged and exhaustive studies in Comparative Religions, accepts Christianity in its rational (that is non-ritualistic and non-dogmatic) sense.

Christianity, as an intelligent, independent, unprejudiced, and unpartisan Seeker of Truth finds it is, briefly, as follows:

" I was of a religious temperament from my boyhood days. While a college student I had little time for religious study, but on entering public life I made the study of comparative religions a specialty.

" The motive back of these investigations was a consciousness of the sinful condition of man. I sought an efficient means to rid me of this consciousness and afford peace of mind. The whole thing was ethical.

" I had had opportunities to study the Bible in the mission school when I was a pupil there, but I was not as yet favorably disposed toward the Christian Religion. Consequently I began a scientific study of the Hindoo religion—that is, going back to the Sanskrit Scriptures. A deep study of these books revealed the fact that the method of salvation has not always been of one single kind. Various methods have been prescribed in various portions of the Hindoo Scriptures.

"The ritualistic form made it entirely subservient to the performance of rites and ceremonies. Personal conduct is not taken into consideration. The philosophical Hindooism has also various standpoints from which salvation is viewed. The most popular form is Yogi-ism, or contemplation.

"The next most popular is Vedantism, or pantheism. In this form of Hindooism the man feels that he is a part and parcel of the universal spirit, and that this feeling is the summum bonum of his existence, this knowledge making him divine. Such philosophical thought is no doubt interesting to a contemplative mind. But I could not regard these solutions of the problem of the future life as satisfactory and practical. I was bound to right them, for India has had men of contemplation from time immemorial, yet no progress has been made toward the improvement of mankind. So with regard to the ritualistic form of worship. Their rites and ceremonies are all symbolical. They are visionary. Observance of them makes religion appear like a pantomime. Consequently I found the system unsatisfactory.

"Next I made a study of Buddhism. The ethical element of Gautama's teaching is of a superior order. But the method of salvation is tedious and pessimistic, because man is made the saviour of himself. By a process of reincarnation, numbering probably a million births or more, he is to emancipate himself. The great defect of Buddhism is *that no prominence is given to the existence of God and the truth of His fatherhood.* No ideal of life is to be seen. The whole thing is a tiresome plodding of the way from birth to death over and over again.

"Next I was led to the study of Christianity. The first thing I was struck with was the character of Jesus. That character of his has enabled me to make a study of his religion. The secret of the power of that religion consists in the fact that it fulfils the requirements of man's weakness— *it offers God as a sympathetic father; it embraces the whole world as members of one human family, and the union amongst the members of this family is love. The religion makes pro-*

vision for the improvement of the mental and spiritual man. It offers eternal hope for his regeneration, and for enjoying the highest holy bliss in future. It teaches faith in man and God. And it proves the truth of all this by the character of Jesus.

"It is this that presented itself with the greatest force in my life and made me embrace Christianity."

(i) *A Parable of Christianity as the Religion of Eclecticism.*

[*From a Sermon by a recent Rector of St. James' Chapel, London, now a Dissenting Clergyman of England.*]

"It happened, once on a time, as men went to and fro in the world who were interested in the arts, that they discovered, at different periods, and hidden away in many countries, portions, it seemed, of exquisite statues—a foot, an arm, a torso, a broken hand. Something superb in each of these made men recognize them at once as perfect. *Each nation cherished its separate piece as an ideal of art;* each drifted into a thousand suspicions as to the author and his intention; each completed the statue from conjecture according to their own ability. At last, owing to the decay of the nations, and to the rise of one upon their ruins, all the several pieces were collected in one museum. *They were still considered as belonging to separate nations and periods of art.* Dissertations were written and lectures were delivered upon them; the ideal completions which each nation had made of its several pieces were placed beside them, and the completions studied with infinite criticism.

"One day, however, when the artist-world were collected in the museum, a man whom no one knew, entered, and slowly went from room to room examining the famous remnants one after another, but passing by the completions of each with some indifference. At last he approached the group of artists: 'Sirs,' he said, 'I have examined your famous pieces of sculpture, and their ideal restorations. The restorations are interesting as examples of art at different periods, *but worthless as a foundation for any true ideal.* But, did it never strike you that all your pieces are of the same time and by the same hand, and that you have but to *bring them together out of their several rooms and unite them?* Your ideal statue is among you, and you know it not.' When he had thus spoken, many laughed and some mocked, but a few were found to listen; the greater part, however, as the stranger grew more earnest, became indignant—for what would become of their art theories if he were right?—and drove him out of the museum with ignominy. But the few sought him out, and it is said that they entered the building by night and brought together the remnants, the stranger superintending, and found it even as he had said. They saw the statue grow, piece by piece, into unity, but at the end the head was wanting. A great cry of pity arose—'What!' they wept, 'shall we never see the ideal realized!' But the stranger, as they wept, drew from beneath his cloak the head, and crowned the statue with completeness. And as he did so, he passed away and was seen no more. But the perfect thing remained—*the pure ideal of divine art, fully realized at last*. Then those few gave up their theories, and their delight in the *separate* remnants and their restorations, and went abroad, taking with them *the perfect thing*, to preach a new kingdom of art; and when men asked them to define and theorize art, they stept aside, and unveiling the statue, said, 'Look and see; this is Art. If you can receive it, you too will become artists. This is all our definition, this is all our theory.' And some believed and others did not, but slowly the new ideal won its way, till it grew to be the rule and the model of the greater part of the artist-world.

"Of what took place at the museum when the mockers found their pieces gone—of how they fought against the possessors of the statue, and denied that it had anything to do with their lost remnants; of how they made counterfeits of these remnants, and clung to their ancient restorations as the true ideals—I need not tell; nor yet of a more pitiable thing—*of how in aftertimes the followers of the true ideal made false copies of it, modifying it, and introducing their own ideas into it, and held up these, and not the perfect statue*, for the imitation and aspiration of the world of art. Are not these things written in history? But again and again, the one effort of all true artists since has been to bring back men to the contemplation of that single figure.

"This parable illustrates Christianity. *The scattered truths of the world were truths from God.* Men wove diverse religions round the diverse truths. At last the Christ came, and *did not reject, but brought together* in himself, the previous truths—made them for the first time fit into one another, so that each took its place. . . . This is that which the Christ did for us. We have granted that many truths which he declared afresh existed before his time; but they were isolated, their mutual connection was not perceived. Hence they had no regenerative power, but little practical power. Great men worked at them, carried them out into separate philosophies, but they never got any wide popular influence, and they were finally buried under a weight of conjectures and conceits. The first enthusiasm they had created died away—nor, indeed, did they ever produce that peculiar characteristic of Christianity, *an active and unceasing propagandism.*

"But under the transforming hand of the Christ, these truths came together into a perfect whole. The truth of doing good for good's sake, became in harmony with the truth of doing good for the sake of immortal life. They had formerly clashed, and there are persons yet who think they clash. The truth that the soul is to be absorbed in God united itself with the truth of the distinct personality of the soul, and in uniting, the one lost its pantheism and the other its isolated self-dependence. The truth that men lived by faith, and the apparently opposed truth that they lived by works, found in the love which the Christ awoke to himself a point where they mingled into one. *No truth was left to sound its note alone, but all together harmonized* arose into

> That undisturbed song of pure concent
> Aye sung before the sapphire colored throne.

If this be true, it forms one of the distinctive qualities of

Christianity. No heathen philosophy had done it, no heathen religion had attempted it. In fact, they had not the materials. No Jewish Doctors had succeeded in it, though they had attempted it. One or two may have had, as had the heathen, glimpses of it—all had a vague suspicion of it; but it still remained a vision till the Christ came and supplied the magic word which gave the spiritual affinity of all truths space and power to act.

"Immediately on coming into harmony, they became inspiring principles in men and instruments powerful for practical work. They took new and vigorous developments—as, for example, the truth of immortality. The men who possessed them were conscious of power, and they labored as if they were secure of victory. *They did not mind stating apparently opposed truths;* they knew that they could give to men a higher truth, in which *the contradictories became two sides of the same truth.* And when the glorious oratorio of Christian truth was sung, with parts for every nation, and the chorus rose in which the most diverse found themselves in harmony, men said, This is unique in the world's history. Heathenism, philosophies, Oriental thought, Hebraism, Judaism, have never done work like this.

"But what was the crowning truth which completed the ideal statue?—what was the magic word which set separated truths flowing together?—what was the directing element which harmonized the varied songs of truth into a whole? It was the doctrine, or rather the fact, of the Divine Man; the truth of the Word made flesh, *the fact that God had entered into Man, had revealed the Divinity of Man, the Humanity of God. This is the central truth of the world.* This is the truth without which all other truths fall back into their isolation. This is the key to all the mysteries of life."

LXXXII.—MYSTERY OF THE DIVINE IN THE HUMAN—
OR, JESUS THE CHRIST AS " GOD MANIFEST
IN THE FLESH."

The light of day which fills any room is the Sun (shining there). But countless myriads of rooms so filled would not begin to *compass* the Sun. So (as Tertullian, the Great father of the Church, plainly taught) " God was in Jesus the Christ " (as likewise in " every man that cometh into the world "),—" filling him with all the fulness," so that he was verily " God manifest." But countless myriads of Christs so " filled with all the fulness of God " would not begin to *compass* the Deity.

Tertullian expressed the common conception of the second century with reference to the *Divine in the Human* as follows:

" When we see sunlight on the floor of a room we say it is the sun shining there ; but if we wish to distinguish between the light in the room and the far-away orb of day from which it comes, we must call the former sun*beam*, and only the latter the *sun*. Likewise we may call the spirit in the Christ divine but *must distinguish between it and the Lord of all, whence it came ;* for as no room can contain all the light of day, neither can any soul compass all the spirit of God." This is the truly Christian view,—" there was in the Christ as much of the spirit of God *as can be compassed by a living soul*, as much of the eternal *as can be contained in the temporal*, as much of the immortal *as can be joined to the mortal*, as much of the heavenly *as can be brought to our earthly abode*, as much of the Divine spirit *as can dwell within the limits of flesh and blood ;* while over and above this is the *immeasurable fulness* (of which *all souls* do or *may* partake) of ' the Most High, who inhabiteth eternity,' and who ' weaveth the ages as a garment upon a loom.' "

The much-debated doctrine of the Kenosis or *self-emptying* of Jesus the Christ is here made simple and plain. He " emptied himself " *completely* of Self (which is Selfishness) in order that he might be filled *completely* with God. So it became literally true that " in him dwelt the fulness of God (the Godhead) bodily," Or, using another figure, " The Word " (also called Light and Life), which " was God," in Jesus the Christ " became flesh." Darkness and Death (which are Selfishness and its outgrowing Sin) were *entirely* driven out: in their place came pouring in Light and Life (which " was God "), and so *entirely* filled him with the

Divine Fulness that " in him was no Darkness (or Death) at all." This Light (and Life) which was in him and *filled him with all its fulness* is that "true Light which lighteth every man that cometh into the world": *it is also " the Life" of men.*

So that the process of *becoming Christians* is also simple and plain. It is to drive out Darkness and Death (Selfishness and its outgrowing Sin) so that Light and Life (God) may become flesh and dwell *in us* " full of grace and truth."

The more complete the *self-emptying* the greater will be the fulness of God *in us*. When there is left in us " no darkness at all " (that is no Selfishness at all) then shall we be *true* Christians—filled with that same Light (and Life) which was in Jesus the Christ. " Of His fulness *have all we received*, and grace for grace."

" *Let this mind be in you, which was also in Jesus the Christ ;* who, though made in the image of God (as likewise are you and all) deemed it not a thing to be grasped at to be equal with God; but made himself of no reputation (*emptied himself*) and took upon him the station of a servant and *shared the common lot of men :* and *becoming the benefactor of man*, he humbled himself and *was obedient unto death*, even the (most shameful) death of the cross. Wherefore God also hath *highly exalted him*, and *given him* a name which is above every other name."

Again let the Apostle's words of exhortation to *us* and to *all* be repeated : " Let *this* mind (complete *self-emptying*) be in you, which was also in Jesus the Christ." So will be *experienced* the mystery of the Divine in the Human ; so shall *every man* come to be, *each in his own measure*, " God manifest in the flesh."

This simple teaching of the Divine in the Human, or of God Manifest in the Flesh, was the *fundamental teaching* of the New Testament and of the Primitive Church. It may be called the *Sum and Substance* of the Gospel—the Good-News of the Fatherhood of God and the Sonship of Man through the Indwelling Spirit. Of all the doctrines which now make up the *essential orthodoxy* of Romanism and of Protestantism this is the only one distinctly held and taught in the Church of the first three centuries. This is well shown by a scholarly Divinity School Professor of the Protestant Episcopal Church in the well-known volume " Continuity of Christian Thought " (pages 19, 20):

" None of the individual doctrines or tenets, which have so long been the objects of dislike and animadversion to the modern theological mind, formed any constituent part of the Greek theology " (or theology of the Early Christian Church). " The tenets of original sin and total depravity, as expounded by Augustine and received by the Protestant churches from the Latin Church, the guilt of infants, the absolute necessity of baptism in order to salvation, the denial of the freedom of the will, the doctrine of election, the idea of schism in the Divine nature which required a satisfaction to retributive justice before love could grant forgiveness, the atonement as a principle of equivalence by which the sufferings of Christ were weighed in a balance against the endless sufferings of the race, the notion that revelation is confined within the Book, guaranteed by the inspiration of the letter or *by a line of priestly curators in apostolic descent*, the necessity of miracles as the strongest evidences of the truth of a revealed religion, the doctrine of sacramental grace and priestly mediation, *the idea of the Church as identical with some particular form of ecclesiastical organization*,—these and other tenets which have formed the gist of modern religious controversy *find no place in the Greek theology and are irreconcilable with its spirit.*" This statement is the verdict of all the scholarship of Christendom *which is free from sectarian control.*

After the first three centuries the simple teachings of the Gospel were not so prominent as questions over which theologians disputed. " Down through the debates of Nicæa, down through the doctrinal discussions of Augustine, down through the disputes of the Middle Age, down through the time of Calvin, of the Thirty-nine Articles, and of the Westminster Assembly, and through all the endless controversies of the Christian centuries,—through all this we hear very little of the Gospel of Love, very little of the Fatherhood of God, very little of the Brotherhood of Man, very little of the Glad-Tidings of *God in man* which Jesus proclaimed to the world. All this, *the heart of the primitive Christian faith,* is subordinated *to scholastic questions,* is lost to view in the dust and noise of theologic dispute. . . ."

"The preachers of ' orthodoxy,' in upholding their position, do not go back to the fountain-head of Christianity, *but to someone or something later,*—to the Westminster Catechisms, or to the Thirty-nine Articles, or to the Augsburg Confession ; and these again go back to Calvin or some other similar authority, and he to Augustine, who in turn went to the world of sin around him, and the sin which had been in his own heart before he became a Christian ; *all going back to some man, or council, or condition of things, instead of to the Gospel of Love, the Glad-Tidings as Jesus proclaimed them.*"

To do this is to forfeit the title of being a *follower* of Jesus and the claim of being a Christian *in the New Testament and Apostolic sense.* Romanist, Protestant, Churchman, Papist ; follower of Athanasius, of Augustine, of Luther, of Calvin, or whatever else they may be ;—such as these are not *truly* Christian or *truly* followers of Jesus *the Christ.*

LXXXIII.—" THAT YE MIGHT BE FILLED WITH ALL THE FULNESS OF GOD."

(*See pages 297–301*)

One of the oldest and most common prayers of that most ancient of all sacred books, the Rig-Veda, is : " Make me to be emptied of myself and possessed of God," i. e., *filled with all the fulness of God :*—an expression, simply, of that deep-felt dependence on the Deity which leads to *complete surrender of selfishness or self.* In New Testament language, " Self-denial and the Cross," *crucifixion-of-self, self-death*—that henceforth "your life may be hid, *as was the Christ's*, in God. . . . I live, yet not I, but Christ (*incarnate*-God) liveth in me. Likewise reckon ye also yourselves to be dead indeed unto sin (self or selfishness) but alive unto God."

Traditionalism, handing down all kinds of un-Scriptural teachings from the "Fathers of the Church," has persistently neglected this, their main and plainest teaching, which was also the very heart of the Gospel, *viz.*, God *in* Man. For instance, open the "Confessions of Augustine," and on the first pages find as follows*:

<small>*Though rightly apprehending the Gospel on this point, as on many others, yet by no means is Augustine quoted as authority upon any matter *of his own dogmatic reasoning.* By his own confessions he lived a life of unbridled sensuality—from his fifteenth to his thirty-third year, depending meanwhile for pecuniary support largely upon the self-sacrificing devotions of his mother and, later, upon the patronage of those Manicheans whom finally he deserted, when he found that all the avenues to bread and fame began to open only from inside the now rich and popular Church of Rome, then, with health broken as the natural result of his prolonged immoralities, he reformed his life and entered upon his career as priest and bishop, and also as the chief expounder and defender of the Traditional Faith.

Such a career of sensuousness extending uninterruptedly over a period of nearly twenty years, could not fail to *permanently* unhinge or throw out of balance the reasoning powers, at any period of life; but inevitably and hopelessly so when begun at the tender age of fourteen years. However pious and sincere the remnant of his life, and however eloquent and true his many *expositions of the simple and self-evident* teachings of the Bible, the Sins of his Youth could not fail to result in a Harvest of rational as well as of physical decay; so that to name him as "authority" upon any matter of his *own* dogmatic reasoning—in these days of enlightenment as to *the permanent mental results of early and prolonged physical dissipations*—would be folly indeed.

"Be not deceived: God is not mocked: for whatsoever a man soweth, that shall he also reap."

Let reformed drunkards, reformed sensualists, or reformed *self-abusers* of any sort do all the good they can in the world; let them also have due encouragement and due praise. But such as these have never yet been God's "chosen vessels" for the communication of *highest* Truth or *highest* Wisdom of any sort to mankind. Only from well-tuned harps—"spirits of Just Men made perfect"—has ever yet sounded either the Music of Heaven or the Music of the Spheres. In religion, in science, in every highest department of Thought—no strained, much less broken, strings can ever produce that Harmony which alone is worthy to be called Authoritative Truth. God's recognized Prophets, in all History and Literature, have been *sound minds in sound bodies* who could</small>

" What room is there within me, whither my God can come into me? whither can God come into me, God who made heaven and earth? is there, indeed, O Lord my God, aught in me that *can contain Thee?* do then heaven and earth, which Thou hast made, and wherein Thou hast made me, *contain Thee?* or, because nothing which exists could exist without Thee, doth therefore whatever exists *contain Thee?* Since, then, I too exist, why do I seek that Thou shouldest enter into me, *who were not, wert Thou not in me?* . . . *I could not be, then, O my God, could not be at all, wert Thou not in me.* . . . Even so, Lord, even so. Whence canst Thou enter into me? for whither can I go beyond heaven and earth, that thence my God should come into me, who hath said, *I fill the heaven and the earth.* . . . But Thou who fillest all things, fillest Thou them with Thy whole self? or, since all things cannot contain Thee wholly, do they contain part of Thee? and all at once the same part? or *each its own part, the greater more, the smaller less?* And is, then, one part of Thee greater, another less? or, art Thou *wholly every where, while nothing contains Thee wholly?* . . . Oh! that Thou wouldest enter into my heart, and inebriate it, that I may forget my ills, and embrace Thee, my sole good? . . . *Narrow is the mansion of my soul; enlarge Thou it, that Thou mayest enter in.* It is ruinous; repair Thou it. It has that within which must offend Thine eyes; I confess and know it. But who shall cleanse it? *Cleanse Thou me from secret faults.*"

boldly say, " All these have I kept from my youth up."—" Which of you convicteth me of (*self-degrading*) sin?"—" I have lived in all good conscience before God until this day." Only in proportion as this could be *truthfully* said has any one, *on any loftiest subject*, been able to teach " as one having authority, and not as the scribes." And so must it continue to be—" world without end, *Amen.*"

LXXXIV.—ILLUSTRATIVE SELECTIONS FROM RECENT AUTHORS.

[*The longer selections are here used by special permission. In all the selections of this volume, to especially mark the more illustrative portions, italics have been freely used.*]

"*Our present gratitude, insures the future's good ;
And from the things we see, we trust the things to be.*

"*Others shall sing the song, others shall right the wrong ;
Finish what we begin, and all we fail of, win.*

"*What matter, we or they? Our, or some other day?
The right word shall be said, and life be sweeter made.*

"*Hail to the coming singers! Hail to the brave light-bringers!
Forward we reach, and share, all that they sing, or dare.*

"*The airs of Heaven blow o'er us, a glory shines before us,
Of what mankind shall be—pure, generous, brave, and free.*

"*Ring, bells, in unreared steeples, the joy of new-born peoples!
Sound, trumpets, far-off blown! Your triumphs are our own.*"

CHRISTIANITY IS LIKE THE SEA "INTO WHICH ALL RIVERS RUN, AND YET IT IS NOT FULL."

"*A sacred ark, which from the deeps
Garners the life for worlds to be,
And with its precious burden sweeps
Adown times dark, mysterious sea.*"

"*The seas shall waste, the skies in smoke decay,
Rocks fall to dust, and mountains melt away :
But fixed Thy word, Thy saving power remains :
Thy realm forever lasts, Thine own Messiah reigns.*"

(a) OPTIMISTIC FOREGLEAMS.

[*Prophetic Utterances of Many Brave and Hopeful Voices.*]

"I tell you it has been a pretty serious thing to try to be a minister in this past quarter of a century! With every question reopened all about us; with the very foundations of Religion threatened; with Science inviting men into its brilliant paths as the only way to any certain truth; hardly able to say a prayer without some one challenging it as an obsolete formality,—do you wonder if we have often been straggling in our choice of subjects, uncertain and defensive in our tone, and sometimes voicing more of doubt than faith? But if what I have said be true,—and it is true,—*those days are passing. The foundations have been looked to, and they remain.* Much dead wood has been cut away; but out of the storm and the testing stands out in stronger reality than ever the grand realities of Religion, with the Gospel of the Christ's Life and Word as their divinest expression, the one sure, unchanging rest for the world's weary and unstable life."

"There 's new life in the seed: sow and believe!
Clearer dew did not glisten round Adam and Eve;
Never bluer heavens nor greener sod
Since the round world rolled from the hand of God."

"So we may go forward in working for them, and spreading them, and building them up in every way we can. We may not see them perfectly—who can? We are but seekers still. *But at least we have got clear from the obscuring dogmas which have so long shut out the brightest light of God.* We look toward God, toward the Christ, and toward the solemn life to come, not setting up any small conditions of what men must believe about them, but simply sure that *there* is light, and that to the pure in heart and those who keep their faces towards it, the light shall grow more and more."

"Great truths that pitch their shining tents
Outside our wall; and, though but dimly seen

In the gray dawn, they will be manifest
When the light widens to the perfect day!"

"In this new and onward movement we shall probably pass through the same slow process of transition which has marked every moral reform that ever emancipated men from bondage and superstition. First, a period of contention and persecution; second, a period of gradual and general conversion to the new ideas; third, a period when everybody will eagerly declare, 'Why, we always thought so.' I venture to predict that *thirty years from now it will be difficult to find among intelligent Protestants any one, in any denomination, who will hold the teachings of the old theology which are to-day called in question.* What is now taught by the leaders will then be accepted by the majority. The 'heresy' of this generation will become the 'orthodoxy' of the next, and what is now called *infidelity* will become the accepted form of Christianity in the twentieth century. For all this let us give thanks. Let us devoutly praise God that it is given us to live to witness the wonderful moral transformation, the intellectual progress, and theological revolution which are now going on."

> *Gospel and Science!*
> *Hail happy age which joins these twain*
> *In bond divine,—a wondrous reign.*
> *The glorious things that are to be,*
> *Earth's waiting watchers dimly see:*
> *Pure angels sing,*
> *And heralds bring,*
> *Tidings of peace and unity.*

"The evidences of Christianity will continue to be written from different points of view, from time to time, as long as men question the historical basis of the Christian religion. Each new generation must have its new demonstration of the reality of the religion of the Christ, because with each new generation there comes an accession of knowledge, the appearance on the horizon of *new facts which compel a change of point of view.* In our own age, for instance, the scientific movement has brought about something very like a reconstruction of the view of the universe. This does not mean that all old views are given up: it means that the old truths stand in new relations to each other; that prospective and relative positions have changed. In one generation humanity on its ceaseless march sees the mountain summits in a certain order; fifty years later it has reached another point of view, and sees them in a different order. So, from time to time, *under the compulsion of new knowledge and new truths*, the old positions must be restated, and the old arguments reframed or quietly dropped out of sight while new arguments take their place."

> " Happiest they of human race
> To whom our God hath granted grace
> To read, to hear, to hope, to pray,
> To lift the latch and force the way."

"The only faith that wears well, and holds its color in all weathers, is that which is woven of conviction, and set with the sharp mordant of experience."

> " *Night's candles are burnt out, and jocund day
> Stands tiptoe on the misty mountain-tops.*"

(*b*) COURAGE AND HOPE.

"The daily life of every one of us teems with occasions which will try the temper of our courage as searchingly, though not as terribly, as battle-field or fire or wreck. For we are born into a state of war; with falsehood and disease and wrong and misery, in a thousand forms, lying all around us, and the voice within calling on us to take our stand as men in the eternal battle against these.

"And in this life-long fight, to be waged by every one of us single-handed against a host of foes, the last requisite for a good fight, the last proof and test of our courage and manfulness, must be *loyalty to truth—the most rare and difficult of all human qualities.* For such loyalty, as it grows in perfection, asks ever more and more of us, and sets before us a standard of manliness always rising higher and higher.

"'For this end was I born, and for this cause came I into the world, to bear witness to the truth.' To bear this witness against avowed and open enemies is comparatively easy. But to bear it against those we love, against those whose judgment and opinions we respect, in defence or furtherance of that which approves itself as true to our own inmost conscience, this is the last and abiding test of courage and of manliness. How natural, nay, how inevitable it is, that we should fall into the habit of appreciating and judging things mainly by the standards in common use amongst those we respect and love. But these very standards are apt to break down with us when we are brought face to face with some question which takes us ever so little out of ourselves and our usual moods. At such times we are driven to admit in our hearts that we, and those we respect and love, have been looking at and judging things, *not truthfully*, and therefore not courageously and manfully, *but conventionally*. And then comes one of the most searching of all trials of courage and manliness, when men and women are called to stand by what approves itself to their consciences as true, and to protest for it through evil report and good report, against all discouragement and opposition *from those they love or respect*. The sense of antagonism instead of rest, of distrust and alienation instead of approval and sympathy, which such times bring, is a test which tries the very heart and reins, and it is one which meets us at all ages, and in all conditions of life. Emerson's hero is the man who, 'taking both reputation and life in his hand, will with perfect urbanity dare the gibbet and the mob, by the absolute truth of his speech and rectitude of his behavior.' And, even in our peaceful and prosperous England, absolute truth of speech and rectitude of behavior will not fail to bring their fiery trials, if also in the end their exceeding great rewards."

> "*These are the living lights,*
>   *That from the Earths' green heights*
>   *Shall shine afar:*
>   *'Til all who name the name*
>   *Of freedom, to their flame*

> *Come, as the Magi came*
> *To Bethlehem's star."*

"It is in truth an ungracious and thankless office to have to tell the world what it least wishes to hear. The world lives with no end of extravagant outlay, like some luxurious lord; takes and spends so long as there is anything to spend; and, whoever ventures to reckon up the cost and call attention to the balance, is regarded as an insolent mischief-maker. . . . One must not rouse the sleeping lion, unless one is ready to fight with him for life and death."

> *"I've struggled day and night against this work.*
> *I'm worn out trying to shut up my lips.*
> *'T is useless! Speak I must: else life is death."*

"My heart was hot within me: while I was musing the fire burned; then spoke I with my tongue."

"To many it is a time of honest difficulty and trouble of spirit; they hardly know what to believe or how to guide their life; and they feel as if the foundations of faith, hope, and duty were giving way. Some say, 'Let us not ask troublesome questions, but hold fast to the faith of our fathers. Let us say our prayers and go to sleep; that will be safest.' Some strain their eyes to get a peep into the darkness; some shut their eyes for fear of seeing something, or for the sadder fear that there is nothing to be seen; some whistle to keep their courage up; some mock; and *some are calm enough to look all facts in the face, and to wait patiently for more light.*"

"There is wide dissatisfaction with the old way of putting things. In one city a prominent man said to me 'I go to the most fashionable and wealthy church. It is filled with our most influential people. We go through the motions and responses in regular order; but when we get out on the sidewalk, gentlemen say to each other, 'Do you believe that?' 'No, not a word of it; but 't is all well enough.' In another city an official member of one of the largest churches gives it as his opinion that there is not one well-informed man in the congregation who does not sometimes ask if it can be possible the minister expects the people to believe what he preaches. Intimations of this kind come from all directions. *Does it mean that religion is being outgrown? Or does it mean that what is called religion is under suspicion and challenge, because it does not deserve the name?"*

"It is not worth while to waste words on those who treat these matters with levity and scoffing; but I only report what I know, from wide intercourse, to be true of increasing numbers of thoughtful and earnest men and women. . . . These honest and intelligent objections to what is *called* religion are really *demands for a better article*—the very thing we want."

"And will you not be thankful in return, if it grows clear that the faults and deficiencies of religious people,—their errors of belief, their blundering methods, their perversities of temper, and their shocking crimes against civilization and humanity,—*are no part of true religion, but are fairly chargeable to their want of it?* Cant, rant, superstition, bigotry, obscurantism, false conservatism, hypocrisy, empty formalism, priestcraft,—what has true religion to do with these but to expel them from the heart of man, and to drive them off the face of the earth?"

"Sweep away all that is irrational in creeds or obstructive in churches; make an end of wolfish and sheepish types of piety and canting forms of philanthropy; lead mankind onward and upward into the full, clear light of reason and the large freedom of nature,—and will religion have disappeared? Only as the sun disappears when men come out of caverns and cellars, and find the mists of morning swept from the wide firmament of blue and gold."

"*We are not obliged to chose between a false religion and no religion at all;* our choice is rather between the *false* and the *true*, or between the *lower* and the *higher*,—a difference even greater than that between the candle burning at an altar and the sun shining in the high heaven. If there be indeed a Wise Spirit, working in us and presiding over the Church and the world, we shall surely outgrow much that passes for religion, and much that is now covered all over with Christian labels; but this advance will be *along the line of spiritual evolution* toward the goal at which Jesus himself points when he bids us 'be perfect, like the Father.'"

"During the time when an old form of Christian thought is slowly passing away, having exhausted all it had to give, it repeats again and again with the garrulity of old age the phrases which in its youth were the expressions of living thought and feeling. They fitted then the wants of men, and they were the means by which religious life advanced and religious truth developed. But being naturally cast into a fixed intellectual system, they remained behind the movement they began; they made men grow, but men outgrew them, *for systems become old*, but mankind is always young. It follows, then, almost of necessity, that when a certain point in this progress is reached, there will be a strong reaction against the old form of Christianity, and the reaction will contain the assertion of that which is wanting in the dying phase, and a protest against its weakness. . . . There will be many who, seeing these garments of Christianity rotting away, and hearing them declared to be Christianity itself, will believe the declaration, and attack not only the garments but the living spirit itself which is waiting to be reclothed."

"It is remarkable that the theological questions which are now most widely spoken of are no longer those which presuppose a general confession of Christianity, but other and deeper questions altogether; questions the very discussion of which shows how strongly the foundations of the religious world are moved. It is now frequently asked whether there be a God or not, whether immortality be not a mere idol of the imagination. It is plain, when society has got down to these root questions, that modern theology *in its past form* has no longer the power to do its work, otherwise these things would be axioms. It is plain that, if Christianity is to keep its ground, it must go through *a revolution*, and present itself in a *new form* to the minds of men."

"With a large majority of people, the love of approbation and the force of habit are so strong that they prefer peace to progress. They go on using customary phrases and forms, without thinking much about what their significance or influence may be; and all whose mental organization leads them to question their import, they brand as heretics."

"Thus you see that to be called a heretic is at least to be put in excellent society; indeed it is to be given a place in the great company of those noble men and women who have done the most that ever has been done, in all ages and lands, for the advancement, purification and enlightenment of Religion in the world. One need not be greatly troubled at being a heretic in such distinguished and honored company. If a short-sighted to-day stones its prophets, a wiser to-morrow comes with reverent tread to build them costly tombs."

> "Though Truth's portion be the scaffold,
> And upon the throne be Wrong,
> Yet that scaffold sways the future
> And, behind the dim unknown,
> Standeth God within the shadows
> Keeping watch above his own."

"All this shows that the main concern of us all should be, not with the question of what men will think of us, or even do unto us, but with the infinitely more important inquiry, What is true?"

"Faith gratefully and reverently acknowledges and uses the Past, but she sets her face toward the Future. . . . The outward *form* of truths held sacred by good men is destined to be remodelled by the progress of knowledge; yet in their deeper essence there is a *spirit* which will live more energetically with the development of all that is most precious and glorious in man."

"The *old in* Religion dies out,—the old error, the old dispensation, the old superstition; but not the *old Religion.*

This is for ever new and for ever fresh. For this there is no decline, no decay; because it is *the life of God in the soul.*"
. . . "It is a melancholy fact that some earnest souls, educated in other forms of faith, have been attracted by our theories only to be repelled by our practices. That pure and enlightened Hindu, Rammohun Roy, became in love with the teachings of Jesus. He went to England, expecting to find there a Christain community living together like a band of brothers. He found haughtiness in one class, servility in another; super-abounding wealth on one side, rags and starvation on the other; stately cathedrals and pompous ritual, and the worship of God made a matter of bargain and sale. And he whose sensitive, truth-seeking soul had been pained by missionaries calling him 'a heathen,' died sad and disheartened because he could not find his ideal of a Christian."

"Milan cathedral, lifting its thousand snow-white images of saints into the clear blue of heaven, is typical of that Eclectic Church of the Future which shall gather forms of holy aspirations from all ages and nations, and set them on high in their immortal beauty, with the broad sunlight of heaven to glorify them all."

"Religion is a universal instinct of the human soul; and the amount of it will never be diminished in the world. Its forms will change, but its essence never. And the changes produced by the inevitable growth of human souls will be slow and imperceptible in process, as have been the mighty changes in the physical world."

"To speak truly, there never has been in the world but one Religion; which is the aspiration of man toward the Infinite. This Religion—varied and developed in innumerable ways, and gradually attaining to an elevated point of moral purity—has often been perverted and employed in the service of the most brutal ignorance, or the most refined perverseness; but, sooner or later, it always extricates itself from what is foreign, and resumes its upward march toward the Ideal; toward Perfection."

"Let us accept different forms of Religion among men as we accept different languages, wherein there is still one human nature expressed. Every genius has most power in his own language, and every heart in its own Religion."

> "All souls that struggle and aspire,
>   ALL hearts of prayer, by Thee are lit;
> And, dim or clear, Thy tongues of fire
>   On dusky tribes and centuries sit."

"It is high time to say frankly, *The Bible is not religion; the Church is not religion; neither is any ceremony or sacrament or doctrinal belief.* Let these be valued according to their reasonable uses. Let them stand or fall on their merits, as disclosed by experience and by free and fair inquiry. About all these matters there are many open questions, and there will be honest differences. But whatever may be our conclusions or our non-conclusions of such questions, the foundations of faith and of reason need not be disturbed. *Religion is life;* and life, which is the true seat of God's kingdom, is within. O friend, it is within *you.*"

"We must cease to disparage and darken 'the light that lighteth every man.' We must appeal with more confidence to the *native instincts of the soul.* We must recognize and honor *the divine in the human.*"

"The advancing race will surely have a religion; *but it will not be built of dream-stuff;* for man will be mastered by reality. It will not be something external, something which he 'gets,' and puts on; it will be *life itself,* his own life,— the health and completeness of his being, the rational action of his faculties, and wise ordering of his conduct and relations. What more can we need? What less will meet our need? But is not this the essence and outcome of Christianity, if we go to the heart of it?"

"*We want a religion for common uses, and for home consumption.* Pure air and wholesome food will yet be sacramental; cleanliness will be baptismal; an honest day's work will be an acceptable sacrifice; our breath will be prayer, and our play will be innocent; our very flesh will be sweet, healed of the old disorders of the ages. Then churches will be as households, and households as churches; there will be seven holy days in every week. 'This is the covenant that I will make with them in those days, saith the Lord: I will put my law in their minds, and write it in their hearts; and their sins and iniquities will I remember no more.'"

"Good-by, then, to confusing and misleading echoes of the *Voice which forever speaks!* Good-by to the wornout costumes of dead generations! Good-by to tiresome routine and cumbrous ceremonial! Let us tenderly lay aside the dear old copy-books wherein we have scrawled and misspelled the holy words of faith and salvation. All honor to the monuments and mile-stones which mark the majestic march of God in history; *but our faces are to the future.* We do not desert the heavenly Leader; we move at his orders, *toward new and grander victories.* . . .

Poor, *rich* human heart! say good-by also to folly and sin; to irreverent self-will and silly conceit; to worldliness, animalism, and torpid indifference; to unbrotherly greed and ill-will; to profane uses of the day and night. Learn the truth as it is in Jesus: 'that ye put off the old man with his deeds, which are corrupt according to the deceitful lusts, and that ye put on the new man, *fashioned on the divine pattern, in righteousness and true holiness.*' Go forth to the life of *faith*, which is the life of *faithfulness!* and to *the service of man*, which is *the true service of God*. . . . O Spirit Eternal, for thy gift of life we forsake all else!"

> "*Naught shall prevail against us nor disturb
> Our cheerful faith—that all which we behold
> Is full of blessings.*"
>
> "*For the Great Shepherd reigns,
> And His unsuffering Kingdom yet will come.*"

"Christianity resembles a railway whose track is just marked out. What abysses will still require to be filled in or bridged over, what mountains to be tunnelled, how many a year will elapse, ere the train full of eager travellers, will swiftly and comfortably be borne along and onwards! Nevertheless, we can see the direction it will take: thither it shall and must go, where the flags are fluttering joyfully in the breeze. Yes, joyfully, in the purest, most exalted, spiritual delight."

"The book of Inspiration closed? Nay; it *never can be closed*, that Infinite Volume! *All flows*, said the Greek; but who shall discover the fount of *this* Sacred Nile? 'T is an eternal deep and everlasting flux, older than any outward thing."

"Christianity is an ever-flowing ever-changing, ever-fresh *revelation*—not a rigid *deposit*, or a limited, definable faith *once delivered*."

"Christianity is not a fixture but a flow: in Goethe's phrase, a *change-continuance*, a river of God: full of water; But no two persons, far less generations, bathe in or drink from the *same* stream. The column of smoke from the chimney, or vapor from the hill, or whirl of powdery snow I saw on an Alpine peak, in the Austrian Tyrol, (shifting each moment its particles while retaining its shape) is a faint type of this perpetual dissolving of texts ever interpreted and applied anew, and modified past calculation by the atmosphere of the time, which Greek Church or Romanish cannot withstand."

"But why lament the change? It is a transfiguration more glorious than amazed Peter and James and John. 'And they knew him and he vanished out of their sight.' When he retired he was revealed. His going was his *coming again* we wait for still."

"*Beneath the quietude a tempest is at work.* The time comes, when a man knows that if he is to be worth anything, he must be true, he must get rid of all conventional beliefs and understand what he means and on what he can rest. The old forms of his thought are exhausted; the old religion of his childhood has no words for him; the very enthusiasms of his youth he finds but poor images of the unreached ideals which cry aloud within him. By many impulses and events, by loves, sorrows, hates; by clashing with the world, by unexpected agonies in his own heart; by the weaving and unweaving of life—by the direct speech of God—the elements of a new being have gradually collected beneath the crust of the old. New ideas, new points of view, new perceptions of the world around, new phases of old problems, have gradually accumulated till the ancient forms are no longer able to bear the pressure. *The fulness of time has come; a revolution is necessary.* . . .

It is sore work when that day arrives, and men are often so tired then that it seems unfair that all the inner life should be again disturbed, and that, not as before on the surface, but down to and throughout the very depths of being. *But it is at the peril of our worthiness that we refuse its call, and hush its elements into a false peace; we must go through with it.*"

" ' The stone becomes a plant; the plant a beast;
    The beast a man; the man becomes a god:'
Strange words that hold the mystery of life;
    That point the path which *none may leave untrod*.

" ' From beast to man '; a long and devious path,
    Which no man living but *hath passed along;*
No stone, nor plant, nor beast, but hath to tread;
    By law which may nor work nor suffer wrong.

" ' The man becomes a god.' The lofty goal
    Is ours, but *only at a mighty price;*
No *moment's* zeal prevails, no *vague* desire,
    No deity that plays with loaded dice.

" Think ye that death hath power to change the soul?
    That yon fierce ruffian, lurking for his prey,
May throw the gates of Heaven ope for one
    Whose feet *have barely touched* the ' narrow way'?

" Through many lives we learn; for Karma rules,
    The mighty law that ever governs well.

> ' As we have sown, we reap,' *our ev'ry deed*
>   Contributes to make life a heaven or hell.
>
> " Seek not to palter with eternal right.
>   The rougher path leads quicklier to the goal.
>   The intermediate steps must needs be trod,
>   *E'en to completion*, by the struggling soul.
>
> " Life-giver to the universe and us,
>   Raise from the true sun's face its gleaming veil ;
>   While to thy sacred seat we journey, grant
>   Of duty *fully done* we may not fail."

"We have heard much, in religious teaching, of *saving souls;* but a far more important thought is, that life is the field in which souls are practically *being developed out of the germs of a soul* which every human being has at birth. Life is not altogether a summer's holiday, in which we have only to enjoy; it is also stern, hard, capricious, full of terrors and pains, baffling and disappointing us ofttimes up to our dying hour. So it must be that if the world has God in it, *the so-called hard and bad things are indispensable to making us moral and spiritual beings;* that is, it is the combating just these disagreeable things which imparts to souls some of their finest fibre and quality. . . .

Wherever we are faithfully and earnestly trying to do our best with life, keeping heart amid discouragements, looking ever for the bright sky behind the cloud,—*we are making souls fit for advancement in the Father's realm of service.* Let us be sure there will be no failure to *make a soul* when we believe that we have a soul in germ, and *do our part to unfold it* as God shows us what we ought to do."

" His teachers held that what they had to give, demanded life's devotion ; that a man should humble himself and put away all other aims and thoughts, for the sake of those dim written pages; not that the book should serve the man, who can never fitly use it unless he already stands upright, as one *who hungers and thirsts to be pure.* . . .

Whoever enters, even a little way, into that sacred land, will carry with him its glamour of golden light—a haunting presence that will outlast life itself; and will lead him back and back to the same fountains of joy until the end."

> "*Drop Thy still dews of quietness,*
>   *'Til all our strivings cease ;*
> *Take from our souls the strain and stress,*
>   *And let our ordered lives confess*
>   *The beauty of Thy peace.*"

"Then speaks the soul of the pure man, asking: 'What maiden art thou whom I have seen here as the fairest of maidens in body?'

"Then replies to him *his own law:* 'I am, thy good thoughts, words, and works: thy good law, the own law of thine own body, which would be in reference to thee like in greatness, goodness, and beauty, sweet-smelling, victorious, harmless, as thou appearest to me. Thou art like me, O well-speaking, well-thinking, well-acting man, devoted to the good law; so in greatness, goodness, and beauty do I appear to thee.'

Then the good deeds are enumerated and the soul led into Paradise."

> "*Hope not the cure of sin till Self is dead ;*
> *Forget it in love's service, and the debt*
> *Thou canst not pay the angels shall forget ;*
> *Heaven's gate is shut to him who comes alone ;*
> *Save thou a soul, and it shall save thy own !*"

So live that when thou art summoned hence this may be, from many a loving heart, thy truthful tribute :—" He has gone to Heaven! How glad the angels will be!"

"The world has grown. It is ceasing to be the battle-ground of the Creeds, which are slowly becoming *lines*, not *walls*. Ugly hatreds and prejudices still are held, but the borderland of the religions is widening day by day, as their *agreements*, not *differences*, are kept in view. . . . The tendency of all modern faiths is toward unity, simplicity, and purification; as the process continues with the widening of the suns the nations will slip off their theologies and theogonies and derive more comfort from the prophet than from the casuist,—*from the teacher than from the priest.* If, in the final outcome, all *present* forms of faith disappear and a new combination arises, the law of the Conservation of Spiritual Forces must still hold sway, and ' not one jot or tittle ' of the inspiration in the Testaments that have impelled mankind to righteousness will ever be lost. The resultant religion will not be different in spirit to the declaration of the Pentateuch, which is voiced by the Christian Gospel and finds its echo in the Bibles of many Creeds,— ' Thou shalt love the Lord thy God with all thy heart, and mind, and strength : and, Thou shalt love thy neighbor as thyself.' When the nations shall have reached these heights of Holiness and of Brotherhood the Millennium will have dawned. . . . *The end of religions will have come in the birth of Religion.*"

ILLUSTRATIVE NOTES.

I.—SUCCESS AND FAILURE.

(*See "Introductory Quotations."*)

"*He fails not who makes Truth his cause,*
Nor bends to win the world's applause;
He fails not—he who stakes his all
Upon the Right, and dares to fall."

II.—FICTION AND FACT.

(*See "Prefatory Notes."*)

"O that those who teach us Theology could have the benefit of a little legal training; enough, at least, to realize the difference between the *possible*, the *probable*, and the *proven!*—what *might* have been, what *may* have been, and what *has* been or *is!*"

III.—A MOST ANCIENT STATEMENT OF THE DOCTRINE OF THE TRINITY.

(*See pages 64 and 263.*)

One of the great Brahmin poets has handed down to us the most ancient doctrine of the Trinity, as follows:—

"*One God by Three Revealings is made known;*
Each First, each Least,—and yet the Three are One;
Swâ, Vishnu, Brahma,—these Each may be
First, Second, Third, among the Blessed Three."

IV.—IGNORANCE EVER MISCONCEIVES THE CHARACTER OF GOD. THE GROSSER THE IGNORANCE THE MORE MONSTROUS THE MISCONCEPTIONS.

(*See pages 60, 75, 113, 357.*)

The author, from childhood, has felt deep interest in and tenderness for all forms of animal life. This feeling he has ever sought to manifest to birds, fish, insects, and all varieties of animals in general, trying to win their trustfulness and gain their affec-

tionate dependence upon him as a friend. In spite of it all they
persistently misconceive his character, misjudge his motives, and
fly or scamper from his presence in terror; the more benevolent
his intentions, the greater their alarm. No doubt to their eyes
he is a monster, ever seeking to do them harm. Among them,
doubtless, tales are told and traditions are handed down (*their*
forms of doctrines and creeds) outrageously slandering his character as that of one who has doomed them all to perdition, except as they may appease his wrath or satisfy his vengeance with
untold Offerings of Agony, Sufferings, and Blood. Now and
then a few, more intelligent and widely experienced than the
rest, grow distrustful, renounce the "orthodox" Doctrines and
Creeds, and become domesticated or tamed. But their examples
are rejected, their faith condemned; and the myth-loving, tradi-
tion-keeping flocks, and shoals, and swarms, and herds croak,
and gabble, and spout, and buzz, and hiss, and bellow, and growl,
and bark, and roar at the schismatic Dissenters as "Heretics and
Infidels forever abominable and accursed." *The less the intelligence the more "orthodox" the Belief and the more unsparing the
Anathemas.* Among those higher animals called Savages, the same
suspicions and misconceptions prevail. A civilized man is a
monster and an enemy, and to become civilized is treason and
hopeless disgrace. *The more ignorant the savage, the more "orthodox" his Belief, and the more unsparing his Anathemas.* The same
conditions and consequences prevail in all the Religions of the
world—Christianity not excepted. The character of God and
the nature of His truth are grossly misconceived by ignorant
people, always and everywhere: the grosser the ignorance the
more monstrous the misconceptions. Myths and traditions are
mistaken for truths; they are woven into Doctrines and Creeds
which are pronounced orthodox and infallible,—and *Whosoever
disbelieves them shall, without doubt, perish everlastingly.* From all
this nothing can save but Enlightenment *added to* Piety. A most
essential part of every true Gospel is Intelligence, Intellectuality, or (to use the Bible word) *Wisdom.* "Let *every man* have a
reason for the Faith that is in him." Nay; it is "the first and
great Commandment"—With all thy *mind*, as well as heart, and
might, and strength shalt thou love the Lord thy God. The
"mind" has been ignored or depreciated by Priest-craft. Slave-
holders have always found it essential to Slavery to keep their

slaves in ignorance. In every Religion, as truly as in every State, this has been the case; and Christianity *monopolized by Priest-craft* has been, and is, no exception. Increased Intelligence is the only Emancipation. Non-sectarian Education on the one hand, and Non-partisan Churches on the other: these two will prove, like giant Samson's arms, the mighty powers of God for the complete overthrow of Religious Superstitions—*whose two main supports are, Priest-Craft and Ignorance.*

V.—IN EDUCATION AS IN RELIGION THE MERCENARY SPIRIT WIDELY PREVAILS.

(*See pages 112, 121, 212.*)

Sophists and Philosophers are two ever-distinct and ever-antagonistic classes in Education, as are Hireling-Priests and Prophet-Priests in Religion. Philosophers are those who love Wisdom for her own sake, and are ever ready to communicate what they know to the poorest as to the richest, to the humblest as to the highest, and without stipulation as to "money or price." Sophists are those who love Wisdom for the "**no small gain**" she will bring them, and communicate what they have learned only to *the highest bidder.* "Having food and raiment" the Philosopher is "therewith content." The Sophist can never be satisfied till he shall be "clothed in purple and fine linen, and fare sumptuously every day." The same distinctions are those of Prophet-Priests, and Hireling-Priests.

In the present age, Sophists seemingly predominate as they did in the age of Socrates: and Hireling-Priests as they did in the ages of Jeremiah and of Jesus. Almost as prevalent in our Schools, Colleges, and Universities as in our Churches, is, seemingly, the mercenary spirit—that spirit that causes money to be the measure of worth and the ruling power of life. As the Churches secure and retain pastors according to the *size of the salary,* quite certain that every minister, like other merchandise, has his price; so is it widely with our Educational Institutions. Once *the opportunity for usefulness* was the main question. Lovers of Wisdom were wont to reply with our recent Agassiz, "I have no time to make money;" or with ancient Socrates, "The fountains of Athens run with pure water, and meal is cheap in the markets, I desire nothing more:" or with a still more ancient

Refuser-of-Bribes, "If the King would give me his house full of silver and gold, I cannot go beyond the commandment of the Lord—but what the Lord saith that will I speak!" But of all Sophists, now as ever, whether they be popular Novelists, sensational Play-actors, Literary Buffoons or Mercenary Teachers, luxury-loving Professors, Hireling-Priests or whatever—the main question is, "*How much will you give me?*" And the highest price always avails to draw and to hold. A *large-salaried* Professorship or Instructorship, like a *large-salaried* Pastorship, is never vacant; even the rumor of a vacancy quickly draws an eager multitude of "candidates," while hundreds of *small-salaried* positions are forsaken or rejected: and millions of "the poor," as they have no effective "Gospel preached to them," so have no *higher advantages* of Education—if any "advantages" at all. Thus in Education as in Religion; in Schools, Colleges, and Universities as in Churches, "wheresoever the carcass (fat salary) is there the eagles be gathered together." Still there are Philosophers, as there are also Prophet-priests, in every land; hidden and absorbed in their humble stations and work, unknown to the noisy world, unheralded by popular applause, unrecompensed by pecuniary rewards—contented with Wisdom as their chief treasure and happy in doing good. "*Behold I have yet left me seven thousand in Israel, knees which have not bowed unto Baal, and mouths which have not kissed him.*"

[*See two notable and noble illustrations on page 254.*]

VI.—SENSATIONALISM IN THE CHURCHES.

(*See page 255.*)

Saturday's and Monday's newspaper in every city and larger town of the land, heralds the "musical" and other sensational attractions of the various churches which are to *draw* or have *drawn* the congregations. As a specimen, one issue of this date has several notices of "fine baritone solos," of "beautiful soprano solos," of "fine offertories," of "rich musical treats," etc., with not one word of any Gospel to be preached. No wonder that, in the same newspaper, several embezzlements, defalcations, suicides, etc., are reported as committed by "a member of the Board of Missions," by "a Church Officer," by "a Sunday-School Superintendent," etc.

"Marvellous is it in how exhausted an atmosphere the Divine Spark within will glimmer on, and even warm the darkened chambers of the human heart."

VII.—IT PAYS.

(See page 251.)

The *famous* "Evangelists" all make money. Those best *advertised* as "consecrated, self-sacrificing and successful savers-of-souls" started in poverty and ended with fine country-seats or stately city mansions—"their eyes standing out with fatness, and having all that heart can wish." The same are substantially the facts in the case with reference to the *popular and pampered* Clergy and other Officials, of every sect of Christians, from that of the Roman Catholic down. And "the people love to have it so"; being well schooled in the *wolf-in-sheep's-clothing-interpretation* of such passages as "the laborer is worthy of his hire," interpreted to mean purple and fine linen with sumptuous fare every day; and "an hundred fold in this life," interpreted to mean large salaries, costly gifts, perquisites and luxuries in general—such as were never heard of or thought of (except as warnings of the "fallings away" that were to come) in the Christian Church *till the beginning of the fourth Century:* when began that Reversion and Degeneration which is the scientific designation of what the Bible calls "backsliding," "falling away," or "Anti-Christ." There are, indeed, thousands of humble-minded, plain-living Ministers of Christ who are content to minister, as did their divine Master and his holy Apostles, for no earthly reward beyond the simple necessities of "daily bread." To preach the Gospel of Repentance and of self-consecrated Holiness "without money and without price" to the poor *even more than* to the rich —without Pew-*tax*, *pressing* Offertories, *urged* Collections, or any other form of *sine-qua-non* Exactions—is *their* chief joy. But such as these are never found "in king's houses"; are never popular or successful *in the worldly sense ;* are always "persecuted" for the Kingdom of Heaven's sake, "despised and rejected" by the lofty,—men "of sorrows and acquainted with grief," from whom the *world in general* "hides, as it were, their faces." Blessed are *these* who have "been with Jesus" and learned of him.

VIII.—COMMERCIAL BRIGANDS.

(*See pages 89-98.*)

"ROCHESTER, N. Y., Sept. 4.—At the final session of the New York Mission Society convention in the Church of Christ, in Howell Street, last evening, the Rev. ——— of St. Louis, spoke on 'Social Reform in the Church,' and created a stir by his reference to ———.

"' We have come to the day,' he said, ' when the commercial brigand stands, not on the highway, to filch the passers-by, but behind a desk, levying toll on his fellow-citizens in the form of profit. The smell of the monopolist's ill-gotten millions will not impregnate the air with one-half of the stench that do his donations to colleges and churches of the lands; for the latter are given under the mask of Religion.'"

By self-seeking Greed and its inevitable crowding-out, or treading-down, or other heartless oppression of "those who are weak" by "those who are strong"—if not by *criminal* Fraud or *illegal* Wrong—the monopolistic Schemers fill their coffers with gold. Then when Conscience pricks or Death stares them in the face, they take out a handful to build a Church, endow a College, or support a Missionary; thus they think to bribe the Supreme Judge, secure for themselves "a title clear to mansions in the skies," and at the same time build their earthly monument and win—from the fawning Clergy and other flattering Officials—glowing Eulogies of Benefactor and Saint.

To all such as these every true prophet says—with John-the-Baptist, Jesus-the-Christ, and Peter-the-Apostle boldness—

"Bring forth therefore fruits *worthy of repentance*.—Leave there thy gift before the altar, go thy way, *make restitution four-fold*, then come and offer thy gift, but *let not thy left hand know what thy right hand doeth*.—Thy gold perish with thee, *because thou hast thought to obtain the gift of God with money*. Thou has neither part nor lot in this matter: for *thy heart is not right before God*. Repent therefore of this thy wickedness, and pray the Lord, if perhaps the thought of thy heart shall be forgiven thee. For I see that thou art in the gall of bitterness and in the bond of iniquity."

Their very dogs and horses dwell in magnificence; while all about them subsist, in squalor and wretchedness, their fellow-men:—those who are "weak" in enterprise and skill, receiving no uplifting or encouraging "help" from those who are "strong." Hundreds of thousands of Pounds sterling,—millions upon millions of Dollars are spent in self-indulgence and self-parade, not only by *the royalty and the nobility*, but also by those who ape their manners and aspire to their lofty estate—aristocracy, select-circle, society-leadership, or whatever else it may be called. And whenever, out of their superabundance, they cast a gift "into the treasury" or scatter "the crumbs from their tables" to the Lazaruses at their gates, a host of obsequious clients and flatterers are ready to cry out (in substance if not in phrase) "it is the voice of a god, and not of a man."

The same condition of things as existed so long, long ago when the Psalmist wrote :

"Lo, these are the ungodly, these prosper in the world, and these have riches in possession : and I said, Then have I cleansed my heart in vain, and washed my hands in innocency.

"All the day long have I been punished : and chastened every morning.

"Then thought I to understand this : but it was too hard for me,

"Until I went into the sanctuary of God : then understood I the end of these men ;

"Namely, how thou dost set them in slippery places : and castest them down, and destroyest them.

"O how suddenly do they consume : perish, and come to a fearful end !

"Yea, even like as a dream when one awaketh : so shalt thou make their image to vanish out of the city."

Whom the New Testament Scriptures exhort and warn :

"Go to now, ye rich, *repent and reform :* for miseries are coming upon you. Your riches are corrupted, and your garments are moth-eaten. Your gold and your silver are rusted ; and their rust shall be for a testimony against you, and will eat your flesh as fire. Ye have heaped up treasures for old age. Behold, the hire of the laborers, which is of you kept back by fraud, crieth out ; and the cries of them that labored have entered into the ears of the Lord of Sabaoth. Ye have lived delicately on the earth, and taken your pleasure : ye have nourished your hearts as for a day of slaughter."

And whom the tender Jesus instructs and invites :

"Sell that thou hast, and distribute among the poor. . . . *and come, follow me.* . . . Make for yourselves purses which wax not old, a treasure in the heavens that faileth not, where no thief draweth near, neither moth destroyeth. For where your treasure is, there will your heart be also."

IX.—PUNISHMENT MEANS PURIFICATION AND REFORM, NOT RETRIBUTION OR REVENGE :—"ON EARTH AS IN HEAVEN."

(*See pages* 237, 239.)

" Do we want to know what was uppermost in the minds of those who formed the word for punishment, the Latin *poena*, or *punio*, to punish : the root ' pû ' in Sanscrit, which means to cleanse, to purify, tells us that the Latin derivative was originally formed, not to express mere torturing, but cleansing, correcting *delivering from the stain of sin.*

"In Sanscrit many a god is implored to cleanse away ('*punihi*') the sins of men, and the substantive ('*pâvana*') . . . took the signification of purification and reform. Now it is clear that the train of thoughts which leads from purification to punishment reveals a moral and religious sentiment in the conception and warning of *poena ;* and it shows us that in the very infancy of criminal justice punishment was looked upon, *not as retribution or revenge,* but as a correction and a removal of guilt. So, too, 'castigation' was originally 'chastening' (the common Bible word) ' from *Castus,* pure : ' and meaning, in like manner, a means or method of purification and reform."—(*Chips from a German Workshop, vol. ii., page 254.*)

This original meaning has been preserved and kept in force to this day by at least one isolated and simple-minded, but still admirable and happy people, as follows :

"In Iceland there are no prisons, and the inhabitants are so honest in their habits that such defences to property as locks, bolts, and bars are not required ; nor are there any police in the island. Yet its history for 1000 years records no more than two thefts. Of these two cases, one was that of a native, who was detected after stealing several sheep : but as he had done so to supply his family, who were suffering for want of food, when he had broken his arm, provisions were furnished to them and work was found for him when able to do it, and meanwhile he was placed under medical care ; but the stigma attached to his crime was considered sufficient punishment.

"The other theft was by a German, who stole seventeen sheep. But as he was in comfortable circumstances, and the robbery was malicious, the sentence passed upon him was that he should sell all his property, restore the value of what he had stolen, and then leave the country or be executed ; and he left at once.

"But though crime is rare in Iceland, and its inhabitants are distinguished for honesty, and purity of morals, there is, of course, provision for the administration of justice, which consists, first of all, in the sheriff's courts ; next, by appeals to the court of three judges at Reykjavik, the capital ; and, lastly, in all criminal and most civil cases, to the supreme court at Copenhagen, the capital of Denmark, of which kingdom the island forms a part. The island of Panaris (one of the Lipari group), is equally fortunate in having neither prisons nor lawyers, and being absolutely destitute of both paupers and criminals."

So far so good! In this one respect, at least, among this humble people, "on Earth as in Heaven," the Kingdom of God *has* come and His Will *is* done. *So may it be,* also among those people who proudly boast that they are *more highly favored and more highly civilized!*

"The abolition of prisons by the substitution of less primitive means of deterring the criminally minded from their depredations on others was advocated this week at the Social Science Conference at Saratoga. Mr. ———, corresponding secretary of the Prison Association of New York, read an able paper on the subject. He started with the proposition that *the prisons and not the crime to a great extent create the stigma of criminality.* He denied the existence of a distinct criminal class and proceeded to show how the prison population of the country, now numbering 86,000, with an enormously expensive plant, might be reduced. All minors, and in fact most offenders up to thirty years of age, were amenable to reformatory influences. The reformatory prisons of the various States, most of which accept this age limitation, *reform eighty per cent. of those treated against eighteen per cent. treated under the old system.* This would take 45,000 from the prison census. Drunkards should be removed to asylums for medical treatment, which would take 3000 more. Of the 33,000 that remain, there could be a still further reduction by the general and rigid application of *the indeterminate sentence principle and by conditional liberation in various forms.* Mr. ——— also advocated the system of domiciliary imprisonment by which, for certain misdemeanors, offenders should be *sentenced to their own homes;* and he also spoke with favor of the New Zealand system, by which law-breakers might be released on the suretyship of two responsible members of society, who should promise surveillance. *The idea of retribution or vengeance should be entirely eliminated from the penal system, and the one dominant note should be protection to society by reducing the criminal class through reformation."*

So may it be,—" on Earth as it *is* in Heaven!"

X.—GOLDEN ERAS ALL THE GREAT RELIGIONS OF THE WORLD HAVE HAD; BUT THESE WERE NO EVIDENCE OF THEIR SUPERNATURALISM NOR OF THEIR PERMANENTLY SUPERIOR WORTH.

(*See pages 6–12 and 38–48.*)

How futile the argument and how poorly informed those who argue for the essential superiority of the Christian religion over all the other Religions, from the "glorious civilization" of its golden eras—the Fourth Century and the Nineteenth! *Then* its Cult and Creed triumphed over those of surrounding "Paganism," *now* its arts and inventions outshine those of the whole Earth beside!

But every "Pagan" Religion, too, has had its golden eras in which, for many centuries, *its* Cult and Creed triumphed over those of surrounding religions, and *its* arts and inventions outshone those of the whole Earth beside. Egypt, Babylon, China, India, Greece, Rome, Arabia, even ancient Tartary, Peru, and Mexico, to a certain extent, were once, respectively, the centre of the whole world's civilization ; possessed the chief arts and inventions of our most advanced society ; built temples, elaborated rituals, extended and sustained institutions of Religion, Education, and Humanity—as magnificent, as popular, and as long-enduring (if not as widely extending) as Christianity, up to date, can boast. Were *their* religions then, each in its golden era, the only supernatural and the ultimately supreme? So every one of them, in their simplicity and ignorance, thought. So, in turn, *the popular voice and vote* of Christianity proclaims to-day. How futile the argument! How poorly informed they who thus argue? " The Kingdom of God cometh not with observation—*it is within you.*" Regenerated characters and ennobled lives ; men, women, and children "hungering and thirsting for Righteousness"; and shining with the "Beauty of Holiness"; Cults and Creeds triumphing over Superstitions and Selfishness, with arts and inventions which tend to extend Purity and establish Love in all the Earth,—these, and these only, are substantial evidences of the essential superiority of Christianity over the other religions of the World.

XI.—CHURCHES AS SPIRITUAL HOSPITALS AND MORAL REFORMATORIES.

(See pages 34 and 269.)

On the above-named pages the Church has been figured as a vast System of Graded Schools adapted, by its variety of Denominations or Sects (from the most ritualistic, sensational, or pictorial upward), to all degrees of spiritual and moral development,—beginning with the Picture-book or Object-lesson Department, and extending to that of the University or Post-University.

A more Biblical figure is that of Spiritual Hospitals and Moral Reformatories, suggested by many such passages as : " Is there no balm in Gilead ? Is there no physician ?"—" They that are whole need not a physician, but they that are sick."—" The Son of man is come to seek and save the lost."

Unceasingly and almost universally have these *primary meanings* of the Christian Church been forgotten : and that by four classes. (1) Those who are called its Ministers appeal for the most part, and some of them entirely, to those who are already of the more spiritual-minded and morally-elevated character.

(2) Those who are called Church-Members, for the most part, commend themselves as righteous or as already " saved " (as did the " Scribes and Pharisees, hypocrites "), and condemn, if they do not actually " despise " others who are not Church-Members. (3) Of those who are *outside* the churches, the more unspiritual and immoral classes, for the most part, deem themselves unworthy or unfit to become Church-Members. (4) While those who are highly moral and highly intellectual (in place of being highly spiritual), as Skeptics criticise, or as Infidels ridicule, Church-Members for their combined immoralities and stupidities.

How absurd is all this when seen in the light of the Bible's chief figure of the Church as above defined! Any one can make the application. (1) Do physicians or other officials of Hospitals and Reformatories devote themselves chiefly to those who are already convalescent in health and well-ordered in behavior? (2) Do those who are inmates of Hospitals and Reformatories go, or remain, there because they are already strong and good? (3) Do those who are sick, or criminal, remain away because they are " not worthy," or " not fit?" (3) Do those who are really strong in health and good in character criticise, much less ridicule, those whose infirmities render it essential or expedient for them to be inmates of Hospitals and Reformatories? Moreover, we may ask: (5) Do the superintendents and inmates of different Departments and Wards in these institutions *jangle and wrangle* over which is the " orthodox " Ward or Department and which the " heterodox,"—which is " high " and which " low," which is " true " and which " schismatic "?

Ask these same questions of the Ministers, the Church-Members, the Un-Churched, the Skeptics and Infidels, and of the various *jangling and wrangling* Sects (from the Romanistic *up* to the Rationalistic, or from the Rationalistic *down* to the Romanistic, as you please), and see how *utterly absurd* the widely prevailing past and present conditions of the Church have been and are among Christians, *exactly the same* as among all who are called Pagans.

With renewed emphasis let us repeat the Bible passages :
" *Is there no balm in Gilead? Is there no physician?* "
" *They that are whole need not a physician, but they that are sick.*"
" *The son of man is come to seek and save the lost.*"

To which, as rebukes of Self-Righteousness, let us add:

"*There is none righteous, no, not one.*"

"*If we say we have no sin we deceive ourselves, and the truth is not in us.*"

"*There is joy in Heaven over one sinner that repenteth, more than over ninety and nine self-righteous persons who (think that they) need no repentance.*"

And again, as rebukes of Selfishness (that Mother-Sin of all sins), let us add and heed:

"*We that are strong ought to help the weak, and not to please ourselves.*"

"*Go out into the highways and hedges and constrain them to come in.*"

"*Go ye into all the world and preach the Gospel to every creature.*"

XII.—THE ONLY UNPARDONABLE SIN IS INSINCERITY; INSINCERITY IS THE FIRST-BORN CHILD OF SELF-LOVE WEDDED TO WILLFUL (OR AVOIDABLE) IGNORANCE.

(*See pages 116 and 148.*)

However "crankish" or "heathenish," extravagant or wild, superstitious or stupid their peculiar beliefs may be, every *genuinely sincere* sect or man is (to use a figure of the Miners) "working a vein" which contains Immortal Gold. Let them work. The more *veins* discovered and developed the greater and more glorious will be the *mass* of Immortal Gold. Only insist upon it that every one shall be *genuinely sincere;* that is, shall *self-forgettingly* and *as intelligently as possible* love and seek Truth —"the whole Truth and nothing but the Truth." All such, whether called Brahmins, Buddhists, Confucians, Moslems, Romanists, Protestants, Theosophists, Spiritualists, Christian Scientists, Mind-Healers, Adventists, Latter-Day-Saints, Dunkards, Revivalists, Crusaders, Salvation Armies, Church Armies or *what not*, are common workers in the hidden and inexhaustible *veins* of God's Truth; and *let them work.* "It is the glory of God to hide a thing, and the glory of Kings to find it out." Hinder no one from finding out as much of the Hidden Truth as he can; and each in his own, *most sincere, most self-forgetting,* and *most intelligent way.*

"Forbid them not: for he that is not against us" (through the *Insincerity* of Selfishness and of willful Ignorance) "is on our side."

But, *beware* of Insincerity and of those who are insincere: *beware* of False Prophets who, for their own advantage, "speak smooth things and prophesy deceits"; *beware* of Wolves-in-sheeps-clothing (whether Pagans or Christians, Romanists or Protestants, Orthodox or Heterodox) who "care not for the sheep," but *play the shepherd* in order to plunder and destroy; *beware* of all Self-lovers who seek the "praises of men rather than of God," who "love to be called Rabbi," who "commend themselves" and all who believe as they do and "condemn others," and who (for purposes of building magnificent temples, sustaining elaborate ceremonies, and themselves living in pomp and luxury) fawn upon the rich and exact from the poor—"devouring widows' houses and, for a pretence, making elaborate devotions." In short, *beware* of Selfishness *in thine own heart and life even more than in the hearts and lives of others:* for Selfishness is the fertile spouse of Willful Ignorance whose first-born child is Insincerity; and *Insincerity is the only sin which* "*hath never forgiveness.*"

XIII.—BONDAGE TO TRADITION.

(*See pages 3, 21, 257.*)

"Sept. 5, 1897.—A letter from Bishop —— was read in all the Roman Catholic churches of the —— Diocese to-day, urging that all children be sent to the parochial schools. The Bishop quotes from a letter of the Pope to the Archbishops of Switzerland, urging that the Catholics must not have mixed schools.

"The Bishop says much can be done by encouraging parents and seconding the zeal of the pastors, which will sustain the cause of Catholic education in the midst of opposition or trial."

"The fourth Lambeth conference, which has lately ended its sessions, has tended to emphasize the fact that year by year Anglican ideas and customs are creeping into the corporate life of the Episcopal Church in America. While there is no legislative power in this conference, there is something more effective in its working, and that is, its most persuasive side-influences. All who visit the cathedrals notice the attractiveness of their ceremonies, and are naturally inclined to emulate them in this land. This has been going on for some time, together with the importation of knee-breeches and aprons for the bishops. Every Anglican feature has been so hailed with joy in certain quarters that agitation for creating the patriarchate of Canterbury ventured to make its public bow before the conference this year. The wiser heads were obliged to make known in indirect ways the inexpediency of such a movement; but whether it will appear again in another dress must be somewhat determined by the set of the tide in the American Episcopal Church."

"The granite fact of the survivals in higher religions of the imperfect conceptions of primitive cults is not to be conjured away by any devices of reasoning. Fetichistic survivals may still be detected in the stories of children and even in the forms of ecclesiastical Christianity. Dean Stanley, in his *Christian Institutions*—faithful to history—has shown how usages and superstitions have survived the lapse of centuries, some of them being beyond doubt of Pagan origin. Primitive and modern religions are one in different stages of growth. The religion of him who in the words of the dramatist might say—

> 'Indian-like,
> Religious in mine error, I adore
> The sun, that looks upon his worshipper,
> But knows of him no more'—

is not in essence different from that of him who bows in Westminster Abbey or in Notre Dame."

"When an individual soul becomes liberated from dogmatic ecclesiasticism and begins to realize that the Christ-power literally *dwells within*, then is the dawning of the new spiritual birth. Whenever a thought is born in the mind which tends to quicken one's spiritual perceptions and give new glimpses of the infinite possibilities of his own soul-forces, that moment he has entered the incipient stage of his spiritual development."

"The question that every pastor and congregation need to ask is, How can the Christian life and resources of this church be utilized for the utmost moral and spiritual impression upon this community? The Church is bound by no principles that compel it to weaken itself in doing the work of Christ. There are no orders of services or methods of work that should not be at once abandoned if others would be more effective. Traditions, associations, and customs, however venerable, must be held in rigid subordination to the work of reaching and saving men. Even the Church itself is not an end, but the means to the end of saving human souls. Those men and churches who travel most scrupulously in the old ways are often regarded by those who indulge in superficial estimates as the most loyal to the Christian idea and genius. The exact reverse is the fact. A thorough-going Christian should be always ready to leave old paths, associations, methods, and traditions the moment it can be shown that new paths and new methods are preferable, provided the innovation is not in violation of Scriptural principles. Christians should always be ready to test their observances, methods, and institutions by the New Testament."

XIV.—TRUE RELIGION IS CATHOLIC: AS SUCH IT COMBINES THE GOOD AND BEAUTIFUL OF ALL THE RELIGIONS OF MANKIND.

(*See pages 21 to 33, also 269 and 294.*)

"To which of these Religions do you belong? asked Meister. To all; for all combined constitute the true Religion."

"The true Religion of the future will be the fulfilment of all the religions of the past—the true Religion of Humanity, that which, in the struggle of history, remains as the indestructible portion of all the so-called false religions of mankind. There never was a false god, nor was there ever really a false religion, unless you call a child a false man. All religions, so far as I know them, had the same purpose; all were links in a chain which connects heaven and earth, and which is held, and always was held, by one and the same hand. All here on earth tends toward right, and truth, and perfection; nothing here on earth can ever be quite right, quite true, quite perfect, not even Christianity—or what is now called Christianity—so long as it excludes all other religions, instead of loving and embracing what is good in each. Nothing to my mind can be sadder than reading the sacred books of mankind—and yet nothing more encouraging. They are full of rubbish; but among that rubbish there are old stones which the builders of the true Temple of Humanity will not reject—must not reject, if their Temple is to hold all who worship God in spirit, in truth, and in life."

In the *Greenacre Course of Lectures* (1897):

"The Rev. Mr. ——— introduced his lecture by reading a few passages from the sacred books of the different religions, to illustrate the spirit in which he proposed to treat the subject—*the spirit of sympathy and appreciation.* After illustrating by means of a diagram the reason why none of the special religions can ever become identical with Universal Religion, the lecturer continued by drawing a series of five contrasts between Universal Religion and the world's religions; thus showing the futility of the hope expressed by devotees of each of the great religions that their own faith will eventually absorb all the rest."

In conclusion the speaker said:

"A union of conflicting systems of faith there can be none. The only possible union is one of souls not of systems; souls united on the basis of perfect liberty in perfect love for the attainment of Truth and Right. Thus will the race be lifted above all differences of caste, color, creed into one sublime universal fellowship; one in the freedom of the Truth, one in the joy of paths untrod, one in spiritual equality, in the Religion of Humanity, the Universal Religion."

"The conference at the Isles of Shoals (1897) shows more clearly than ever a disposition on the part of some prominent clergymen to unite, not only in ordinary Christian work, but in an attempt, at least, to find some common platform for union. The rank and file of the denominations have showed much more liberal tendencies than the clergy have shown.

"On the Unitarian side, there was a frank admission that the present differences were chiefly manifested in thought and speech about Jesus. With this, however, it was claimed that while the creeds differed, the sects were united by the essentials of faith, and divided by non-essentials. 'It is time,' said one of the speakers, 'to see how far we can work together on various lines of Christian work.' All this was cordially assented to on the Trinitarian side without an endeavor to state or to attenuate the admitted differences. But the friendly disposition of the Trinitarians was made more plainly apparent in a letter read from Rev. Dr. —— of New Haven, who is one of the ablest and most popular clergymen among Trinitarians in New England. He is a representative man, and has been well known as a progressive and liberal clergyman. The following quotation will show, not only his own individual views and feelings, but those also of a very large wing of the denomination. 'I sympathize with the objects of your conference, and rejoice in everything that brings our two bodies into closer relations. I feel sure that reunion will come in time. It will not come at once, but time and change of opinion on each side, with charity, will bring it about. It will not be by capitulation, nor can it be effected by management: it will come by development and because we have grown toward each other.' This coming from so distinguished a clergyman, and one who occupies one of the most important pulpits in New England, must carry with it great weight. The former polemic attitude has been exchanged for a better mutual understanding in a conciliatory spirit. The issue of this tendency, now more strongly marked than ever, is still uncertain, but is still hopeful. *Progress in the line of breaking the old blind servitude to religion, thanks to science and learning, is constant all over the world, and all attempts to stay its hand will come to naught.*"

XV.—TENDENCIES TO POMP, LUXURY, AND WEALTH AMONG THOSE WHO ARE CALLED MINISTERS OF CHRIST.

(*See pages 119 and 213.*)

"In these days of utilitarian and materialistic civilization, when everything is sacrificed to physical comforts and social ambitions, when science is prized for its industrial applications chiefly, and democratic ideas are married to the fetichism of machinery and the increasing idolatry of wealth "—it is a shame for *even one* who calls himself a Christian minister to hold his peace, much more to be himself a seeker of pomp and luxury or a grasper of gold.

An estimable and highly-educated clergyman of refined disposition and tastes, who had always refused to minister as Pastor of any pew-renting church, or to stipulate as to exact amount of salary, insisting upon receiving only free-will offerings sufficient for the modest comforts of his family, was offered a fine residence as a gift from a wealthy parishioner. He politely declined it in the following words: My divine Master had "not where to lay his head," and "the disciple should not be above his Master." With needful food and decent raiment, thus far, have I always been content; and so will I continue to the end. I prefer to say, with the Apostle, " I have coveted no man's silver or gold ": and to sing with the poet,—

> "*No foot of land do I possess,*
> *Nor cottage in this wilderness.*"

The most Christian vow that a Christian minister ever took is the vow of Poverty. Alas? that in its place the ambition for pomp, luxury, and wealth should widely prevail, and in the " Apostolic " Churches more widely than among " the Sects."

We read of a present Archbishop of the Anglo "Apostolic" Church who, in addition to private wealth, accepts a " living " of $72,000 a year, with numerous rich perquisites besides, dwells in a palace with no end to liveried servants, and fairly rivals the Pope of Rome in the state and ceremony of his official displays. Quite naturally his example is followed, so far as the " livings " will permit, by other Archbishops, and by Bishops and other Clergy of the Protestant the same as of the Roman Churches, all over the world. Of such, without undeserved rebuke, it may be said, " their eyes have they shut " to the example, and "their ears have they closed " to the voice of him who said : " It is enough that the disciple be as his Master."—" Ye shall indeed drink of the cup that I drink of, and be baptized with the baptism that I am baptized with." Of course the reply will be : All that was meant for the Apostles and Martyrs of the Early Centuries; we live in different times. How " different " let our Criminal Records and similar Statistics show ! The citation which follows is only one of a multitude of indications that the times we live in are not so " different " after all.

XVI.—THE CONDITION OF SECTARIAN MISSIONS ILLUSTRATES THAT OF SECTARIAN CHURCHES IN GENERAL AND OF THE PROPAGANDISM OF RELIGIOUS PARTISANSHIP THE WORLD OVER.

(*See every page of this volume.*)

"A writer in the *Independent* of this week—Rev. Dr. ———, a well-known Presbyterian clergyman,—claims to have discovered one of the principal causes of the financial troubles of the Missionary societies connected with the different denominations in this country. He has had for one year, in connection with the committee of one of these societies, an experience which has been one of the 'saddest and most mournful' of his whole life. The Church, he says, has lost faith in its denominational missions. The cry of debt is heard at the treasury of every one of the denominations. Thoughtful men and women in all branches of the Church have come by common enlightenment of opinion to see that the present system is not only wasteful of men and money, but is proving to be positively destructive of the higher social interests of our new communities.

"Dr. ——— proceeds to give some striking examples of the waste of money and men. He takes for illustration, the State of ———, and wishes it to be distinctly understood that this State is in no wise an exceptional one. The State missionaries—many of them are well known to the writer—are said to be laborious, faithful men, but they are victims of the system. The Methodists, Baptists, Presbyterians, Congregationalists, and Christians have each separate systems of missions. Five State missionaries are busy travelling continually over the State looking after denominational interests, doing a work which one good man with an assistant could do. They do not have separate parts of the State assigned to them, but they follow each other in the same track. Dr. ——— alludes to a little village of four hundred inhabitants with all the denominations eager to get a foothold there. The Congregational church has only fifteen members, the Methodist twelve, the Baptist twenty, the Presbyterian six, the Christian church three, and the place is probably visited by an Episcopalian and a Catholic priest for occasional services in private houses. Dr. ——— declares that this is no uncommon case. There are, actually, five or six missionaries to look after this little hamlet, and they go in Indian file, treading upon one another's heels, when one man could do the whole work; and the astounding statement is made that the salaries of these men average, with their expenses, two thousand dollars per year.

"If this statement is correct, and we see no reason to doubt it, it shows an expenditure of twelve or fifteen thousand dollars where three or four would be an ample sum. Of course each of these little churches of from six to twelve or fifteen members has a pastor, with a further waste of time and money, five or six fold above what is necessary. Again, all these churches have to be housed, when one edifice would accommodate the whole, and here is again a great waste of money. All these churches are pauperized and are supported by the charities of the churches throughout the country. Religion in this community is really a minister of disintegration. It is confidently stated that if one wishes to see and understand the condition of the West, so far as religious matters are concerned, he has but to multiply this case by thousands and tens of thousands. It would certainly be a good work for the missionary societies to thin out these churches rather than plant more.

"Some time ago, a number of promising young men from Yale Seminary were sent out to this Western field, and it was trumpeted all over the country as a most sacrificing work for the 'Yale Band.' Two of these heroic young men were sent into the destitute regions of the West and great things were expected of them. Two of them were sent to the Pacific slope. One was assigned to a feeble little church where four or five others were struggling for existence in a forlorn little town. He published a protest in some paper against his own work, and one of the officers of a missionary society stated that it cost his society thirty thousand dollars. It is reliably stated that churches are constituted in the West with two or three members; four is considered a fair number, and eight or ten are thought to furnish a very promising field.

"If these statements did not come from perfectly reliable sources, they could hardly be believed. It is no wonder that the churches, upon learning these facts, withhold their funds. *This competition among the denominations to propagate each its own theological tenets at any cost of money and time, has come to be a serious question, and it is quite time to call a halt.*"—*Boston Transcript*, Sept. 11, 1897.

XVII.—WHAT THEN IS THE REMEDY, AND WHERE?

(*See also every page of this volume.*)

The only remedy is "The Cross of Christ"—the crucifixion of that Self-Love which forever and everywhere has produced *essential* Systems, *exclusive* Schools, and *partisan* Sects; *isms, arians,* and *ists*. Self-Love is the prolific mother of the whole pestiferous brood.

Not only the numerous "orthodox" *isms, arians,* and *ists* but the "heterodox" as well—Positiv*isms*, Unitar*ians*, Free-Religion*ists*, Scient*ists*, Spiritual*ists*, Theosoph*ists*, Brahman*ists*, Buddh*ists*, and every other *ism, arian,* and *ist* to the end of the list, is in the same condemnation. Each comes with a cut and-dried "System"—an *essential* proposition or formula with its logical inferences, categorical imperatives, *sine qua non* doctrines and methods—which it thrusts into the face of the rest of the world, saying, Accept this or you are a fool, if not a heretic! Whereas they ought to say (on both sides and all sides) "Brother, Sister, this is how Truth *appears* to me; How appears it to you? This is *my* testimony for the Lord; let me now hear yours." As to *names*, none should be used but those which indicate or suggest world-wide inclusiveness and hospitality: such as Truth-lovers, Truth-seekers, Sons-and-Daughters-of-God, Followers-of-God-as-dear-Children, Workers-together-with-God,—or, better than all, and *covering them all*, the simple name *Christians*, which means nothing more and nothing less than "*Anointed* (that is, self-consecrated, and, as such, accepted or adopted) *Children of God.*" As to *methods* of Worship and Work ; all methods that are *sincere and self-forgetting or unselfish*, are equally acceptable to God and should receive equal forbearance, if not favor, from men. "One man esteemeth one day as more sacred than another, another esteemeth all alike. One eateth this, and another that. Let every man be persuaded in his own mind." That is, let there be no *essential* System, no *exclusive* Sect, based on *methods* of Worship and Work. Let all strive to be *genuinely sincere and unselfish ;* then, let them worship and work as may seem to each one most elevating and effective. "Who art thou that judgest another man's servant?" Follow the dictates of thine "own conscience" and permit thy fellowmen to do the same. All this means "The Cross of Christ"—that crucifixion of Self-love which is the only remedy for the prevalent Sectarianism of the religious world.

Where shall this "only remedy" be learned? At the feet of Jesus, beholding his example and listening to his gracious words.

"Stretching out his hands to his disciples he said : Who is my mother, and who are my sisters and brethren? *Every one that doeth the Will of my Father, who is in Heaven, the same is my mother, my sister, and my brother.*" Such was the inclusiveness of his Creed. What he meant by the "Will of my Father" he plainly states elsewhere : "*Thou shalt love the Lord thy God with all thy heart, and with all thy soul, and with all thy mind. This is the first and great commandment. And the second is like unto it : Thou shalt love thy neighbor as thyself. On these two commandments hang all the Law and the Prophets.*" And what he meant by "love the Lord" and "love thy neighbor" he beautifully and simply explains in the Beatitudes : "*Be pure in heart. Be meek. Be humble. Be merciful. Be peace-makers. Hunger and thirst for righteousness.*"

These were *his* only essential doctrines, the only requirements for *his* discipleship, the only door into *his* Church,—the only gate into *his* eternal kingdom of Heaven. Hence, every one who doeth, or seeketh to do, these plain and simple—but yet self-denying and self-crucifying—things, is a Christian (an anointed or accepted child of God) though he may be called of men by whatever rejecting and reproachful names. Not till all Churches, Missions, religious Societies of whatever sort in all the world are reorganized on this *inclusive* and *eclectic* basis of Jesus the Christ, will the Kingdom of God come and his will be done, on Earth as it is in Heaven.

The Beatitudes are the only *essential* Creed, the Two Great Commandments the only *essential* Doctrines of the Christian

Church as Jesus established it. When this is recognized *and regarded*, Systems and Sects will fall, partisanship and exclusiveness will cease, and the One Catholic Church will stretch out arms of welcome and love to all, of every nation and name, who, by the standards of The Beatitudes and The Two Great Commandments, rightly belong to " The Blessed Company of All Faithful People."

Meanwhile let those who do already recognize and regard this original and only genuine meaning of Christianity, whether few or many, refuse to take or to retain the name of any less inclusive System, School, or Sect; but (rejecting their errors and laying claim to everything good, beautiful, and true), *belong to them all*. Thus will they represent, sustain, and hasten forward True Religion—which is the Eclectic and Universal Religion of Jesus the Christ.

XVIII. SECTARIANISM AND CATHOLICITY.

(*See pages 27–32.*)

" His growing spirit found itself cramped by walls built for men of other centuries and other stature; till, at length, his secret tortures compelled him to openly renounce the Traditional Beliefs with all their worldly advantages, saying simply to his pleading friends, 'No, I cannot lie for God.' Thus did he pass fearlessly out of the Church *partial* to be a helper and a light in the Church *Universal*."

This is written of John Sterling and his experience as a clergyman of the Church of England. Equally is it the experience of every truly *Catholic* soul—from Abraham, who "went out not knowing whither he went"; and Paul, who "was not disobedient to the heavenly vision"; down to the humblest Dissenter of to-day who, "forgetting the things which are behind, and stretching forward to the things which are before, presses on toward the goal unto the prize of the high calling of God in Jesus the Christ." This " land of promise " and " heavenly vision " and " high calling of God " meant, and means, a Religion *Catholic* and Universal (in place of one *Sectarian* and Partial), as portrayed by the Revelator in the figure of the Heavenly City " having twelve gates " open, *with equal hospitality* toward the " east, and north, and south, and west," and *never to be closed*. " And the gates thereof shall in no wise be shut by day (for there shall be no night there): and they shall bring the glory and the honour of the nations into it: and there shall in no wise enter into it any that are unclean, or that make an abomination or a lie."

NOTE.

No need of *closed* gates nor of any other form of *forced* exclusion. Even now and here one could not constrain—could not, for any price, induce—those who are "unclean, or who make an abomination or a lie," to dwell in companionship with those who are " pure in heart " or who " hunger and thirst for righteousness "; 't would be a worse than Hell. How much more so when the " pure in heart " have become *holy* (perfectly pure) and the " unclean " are " unclean still."

Such is the lucid meaning of the Scriptures—" The gates thereof shall in no wise be shut "; and " there shall in no wise enter into it any that are unclean, or that make an abomination or a lie." Twelve gates *open*, with equal and unceasing invitation toward every corner of the Universe, *in no wise* and *never* to be shut: those within remain within because such is their affinity and choice: those without remain without because such is *their* affinity and choice—while, *forever and ever*, " the Spirit and the Church say, Come . . . whosoever *will*, let him take the water of life freely."

Such is the *true* Church, *Catholic* and Universal, " on Earth as it is in Heaven ": it *includes* all who are " pure in heart " or who " hunger and thirst for righteousness "; it *excludes* none but the " unrighteous " or the " unclean," —and even these are *self-excluded* by the everlasting law of Affinity and Choice.

XIX. THE INEVITABLE DECAY OF RELIGION AND ITS CONSTANT NEED OF RENASCENCE OR REFORM.

(*Chips from a German Workshop*, vol. i. *See pages 208–212.*)

" If there is one thing which the Comparative Study of Religions places in the clearest light, it is the inevitable decay to which every religion is exposed. It may seem almost like a truism, that no religion has ever continued to be what it was during the lifetime of its founder and its first apostles. Yet it is but seldom borne in mind that without *constant reformation, i. e., without a constant return to its fountain-head*, every religion, even the most perfect, nay the most perfect on account of its very perfection, more even than others, suffers from its contact with the world, as the purest air suffers from the mere fact of its being breathed.

" Whenever we can trace back a religion to its first beginnings, we find it free from many of the blemishes that offend us in its later phases. The founders of the ancient religions of the world, as far as we can judge, were minds of a high stamp, full of noble aspirations, yearning for truth, devoted to the welfare of their neighbors, examples of purity and unselfishness. What they desired to found upon earth was but seldom realized, and their sayings, if preserved in their original form, offer often a strange contrast to the practice of those who profess to be their disciples. As soon as a religion is established, and more particularly when it has become the religion of a powerful state, the foreign and worldly elements encroach more and more on the original foundation, and human interests mar the simplicity and purity of the plan which the founder had conceived in his own heart, and matured in his communings with his God. Even those who lived with the Buddha misunderstood his words. At the Great Council which had to settle the Buddhist canon, Asoka, the Indian Constantine had to remind the assembled priests that what had been said by the Buddha, that alone was well said; and that certain works ascribed to him, as, for instance, the instruction given to his son, Râhula, were apocryphal, if not heretical. With every century, Buddhism, when it was accepted by nations, differing as widely as Mongols and Hindus, when its sacred writings were translated into languages as wide apart as Sanskrit and Chinese, assumed widely different aspects, till at last the Buddhism of the Shamans in the steppes of Tartary is as different from the teaching of the original Samana, *as the Christianity of many Christians is from the teaching of the Christ.* If missionaries could show to the Brahmans, the Buddhists, the Zoroastrians, nay, even to the Mohammedans, how much their present faith differs from the faith of their founders; if they could place in their hands and read with them in a kindly spirit the original documents on which these various religions profess to be founded, *and enable them to distinguish between the doctrines of their own sacred books and the additions of later ages;* an important advantage would be gained, and the choice between the Christ and other Masters would be rendered far more easy to many a truth-seeking soul. But for that purpose *it is necessary that we, too, should see the beam in our own eyes,* and to learn to *distinguish between the Christianity of the nineteenth century and the religion of the Christ.* If we find that the Christianity of the nineteenth century does not win as many hearts in India and China as it ought, let us remember that it was the Christianity of the first century *in all its dogmatic simplicity,* but with its overpowering love of God and man, that conquered the world and superseded religions and philosophies, more difficult to conquer than the religious and philosophical systems of Hindus and Buddhists. If we can teach something to the Brahmans in reading with them their sacred hymns, they too can teach us something when reading with us the Gospel of the Christ. Never shall I forget the deep despondency of a Hindu convert, a real martyr to his faith, who had pictured to himself from the pages of the New Testament what a Christian country must be, and who when he came to Europe found everything so different from what he had imagined in his lonely meditations at Benares! *It was the Bible only that saved him from returning to his old religion, and helped him to discern beneath theological futilities, accumulated during nearly two thousand years, beneath pharisaical hypocrisy, bigotry, and want of charity, the buried, but still living seed, committed to the earth by the Christ and His Apostles.* How can a missionary in such circumstances meet the surprise and questions of his pupils, unless he may point to that seed, and tell them what Christianity *was meant to be;* unless he may show that, like all other religions, Christianity, too, has had its history; that the Christianity of the nineteenth century is not the Christianity of the Middle Ages, that the Christianity of the Middle Ages was not that of the early Councils, that the Christianity of the early Councils was not that of the Apostles, and *that what has been said by the Christ, that alone was well said.*"

XX.—THE CRITICAL FACULTY AND ITS BENEVOLENT USE.

(See Introductory Notes.)

Now and then we come across persons, particularly women known as "scrupulously orderly and neat," who seem to have *telescopic vision.* This faculty always proves very inconvenient to its possessors, and exceedingly annoying and unwelcome to those about them who are persistently in love with more or less of disorder and dirt. However, the advance from the brute and the savage depends upon the possession and use of such *telescopic vision.* The same is true of the Critical Faculty as applied alike to intellectual, moral, and religious conditions. Those who in any of these departments, but especially in the latter—possess it, and use it in the spirit of Him who "chasteneth whom He loveth and scourgeth every son whom He receiveth," must be, as such ever have been, "men of sorrows and acquainted with grief"; they must also be, as such ever have been, "despised and persecuted of men." Nevertheless upon their faithful use of this Heaven-bestowed talent depends all "preparings of the way for the Kingdom of God"—all upward advance of intellect, character, and soul.

"*He is like a refiner's fire, and like fuller's soap.*"

"*A scorner loveth not one that reproveth him.*"

"*Nevertheless, afterward it yieldeth the peaceable fruit of righteousness.*"

XXI.—MERCENARY MOTIVES.

(See pages 112, 119, 253.)

Never has any true reformer or benefactor in State or Church received, or been willing to receive, large pecuniary rewards in return for beneficent services rendered. "Our exhortation was not of deceit—nor in guile—neither at any time used we flattering words—*nor a cloak of courteousness,* as God is our witness—nor of men sought we glory—*because we would not be chargeable unto any of you*—neither did we eat any man's bread for nought, but wrought with labor and travail night and day—not because we have not power, *but to make ourselves an ensample unto you to follow.*"

For all most substantial benefits the world is least thankful and renders scantiest pay. Its luxuries, diversions, and entertainments are valued at a great price; and those who furnish them are rewarded with riches and abundant praise. But its *nourishment*—alike of body, mind, and soul—and all that stimulates and sustains its *higher life* is lightly valued : and those who proffer it have long since learned neither to expect nor desire any adequate earthly reward. The masses of mankind ever have been and still are spiritual and intellectual, as well as physical, Esaus—caring more for " a mess of pottage " than for their " birthright." Whosoever will serve them with the " pottage " is sure of wealth and honor in return. From the farmer and the mechanic up to the author and the preacher, now as hitherto, no *producers* ever grow " rich " except *producers* of superfluities and superficialities—knick-knacks, ornamentations, and gew-gaws,—novelties, novels, and nonsense : these, in all the religious and mental as well as material markets of the world, are eagerly sought for, and bring " no small gain " to whomsoever will produce and offer them. " Because wide is the gate, and broad is the way, that leadeth to destruction, and *many be they that enter in thereby*. But narrow is the gate, and straitened the way, that leadeth unto life, and few be they that find it."

XXII.—MELIORATION AND THE MELIORATORS.

(See all the pages of this volume.)

Pessimism is the belief that things are *hopelessly* bad. Optimism is the belief that things are *just about as they ought to be*. " Of the two it is hard to say which does the greater mischief. Pessimism may paralyze by leading to discouragement ; but optimism may also paralyze by inducing a supine and inert complacency. But there is a third position, which has received the rather awkward name of meliorism. The meliorist is one who tries to see things not as he wishes they were nor as he fears they may be, but *as they really are*. He considers not only the advantages of the situation, but its drawbacks, not only its dangers, but its promises : and always with a faith that *it can be improved and a determination to do his best to improve it*. He sees that it is neither as bad nor as good as it can be, but that it can be made better. The meliorist is an ameliorator.

" Unfortunately, the meliorist incurs the displeasure of both the pessimist and the optimist. The pessimist considers him an optimist for continuing to work at what seems to the pessimist a useless task. The optimist considers him a pessimist because he disturbs his complacent enjoyment by pointing out dangers and defects which the optimist would rather not see. This puts the meliorist in a very unpleasant position. On the one hand, he cannot conscientiously be silent in the face of dangers that plainly beset the cause he loves; nor, on the other hand, does he like to displease those sensitive souls who cannot bear to be told that all is not exactly as it should be. He would like as well as anybody else to be carried to the skies on flowery beds of ease; but he sees too clearly that he cannot be exempt from that law of eternal vigilance and struggle by which others fought to win the prize and sailed through bloody seas. He would like as well as anybody else to receive *that favor which men are apt to give to those who persuade them that everything is as they wish it were.*

"It is to the meliorist, and not to the contented optimist, that the world owes its progress. Amos was not a pessimist when he warned those who were at ease in Zion; nor Jeremiah, when he protested against those who healed the hurt of the daughter of his people, lightly saying, 'Peace, peace!' when there was no peace; nor Isaiah, when he rebuked the complacent and well-satisfied folk, who said to the seers, 'See not!' and to the prophets, 'Prophesy not unto us right things: speak unto us smooth things.' It was not pessimism that sent out the 'Woe unto you!' from the Master against those who had everything secure: or that made Paul, whose heart's desire was that Israel might be saved, yet warn her that her heritage was passing to the Gentile. In every such case the warning is given, not out of a lack of courage or faith, certainly not out of any fear that the right will not finally prevail, but out of grief that they to whom the talent and the opportunity had been intrusted should let them slip from their hands."

Among the recently discovered "Logia of Jesus," is the following:

"Jesus saith, I stood in the midst of the world, and in the flesh was I seen of them, and I found all men drunken, and none found I athirst among them; and *my soul grieveth over the sons of men because they are blind in their heart.*"

Such is the spirit and such, in substance, the language of every one who is a true Meliorator of Mankind.

XXIII.—SENSATIONAL WORSHIP.

(Additional to page 324.)

Similar conditions are reported to us from the Cathedrals and other churches of England during the pre-Reformation centuries:

"Chanters are found in various churches who, with inflated cheeks, imitate the noise of thunder and then murmur, whisper, allow their voices to expire, keeping their mouth open . . . now you would think you hear the neighing of horses, now the voice of a woman . . . the audience gaze, filled with wonder and admiration . . . it seems to them that they are at the play and not at church, and that they have only to look and not to pray."—*Aelred, Abbot of Rievaulx, 12th century.*

XXIV.—ANOTHER VOICE IN THE WILDERNESS.

(See all the pages of this volume.)

A well-known pastor of a well-known "Orthodox" Protestant Church in New York City bravely testified as follows, in a recent sermon:

"Preachers of the Gospel live at ease, abounding in comforts, rewarded and praised by the world. If we were otherwise the people who now honor us would not tolerate us. Canon Farrar has said that not more than four per cent. of the working classes attend church in England. A similar condition exists in this country. The great masses have been alienated from the Church, while the Church is making progress among the so-called higher classes: but that progress is gained by forsaking the teachings of him who when upon the earth gave as proof of his Messiahship the fact that the *poor had the Gospel preached to them.*

"We are winning the 'higher circles' of society *because we permit those circles to mould Christianity into their own image.* Time was when it cost something to be a Christian. It cost comfort, fortune, honor, life itself—to-day it costs nothing; it is respectable, fashionable.

"Christ says, 'whosoever does not bear the cross and come after me cannot be my disciple.' Our cross—for I take the charge to myself also—where is it? What sacrifices, what afflictions, what humiliations does our faith cause us to bear? Are we not indulging with the most worldly in that same luxury, extravagance, and worldliness that ought to give us shame?"—*The New York Times*, Sept. 20, 1897.

Verily the times seem to be here again which preceded the Renaissance in Europe, when St. Francis said to those "mutterers of prayers" who called themselves the Clergy:

"The holy martyrs died fighting for the faith of Christ. But there are in our time, preachers who by the mere telling over the deeds of martyrs, seek money and honor of men. There are also some among you who like better to preach on the virtues of the saints than to imitate their labors. . . When thou shalt have a psalter so shalt thou wish for a breviary, and when thou shalt have a breviary, thou shalt sit in a chair like a great prelate, and say to thy brother: 'Brother, fetch me my breviary!'"

Of the same pre-Renascent period, during which (as in the pre-Christian, the pre-Reformation, and the *present* pre-Renascent periods) many and magnificent churches were patronized by rich and oppressive formalists, while the masses, called the *lower classes*, were "as sheep without shepherds": when Religion, in its fashionable form, had become mere lip-service and priestly-parade: when Insincerity, Self-Seeking, and Make-Believe were the "Three in One" whom the popular clergy preached and the orthodox people worshipped—of this period (as of the similar ones mentioned) we have striking pictures also in Piers Plowman and later in the writings of Wycliffe:

"Chief guardians of the flock who busy themselves with their 'Owelles' only to pluck, not to feed, them . . . shams and insincere, 'faux semblants' . . . who traffic in holy things, absolve for money, sell heaven, deceive the simple, and appear as if they 'hadden leve to lye al here lyf after.' They laud all the saints except St. Truth. Have they ever honored her? No, never! . . . With none of the saint about them save the garb, whose example teaches the world to despise clerical dress, those who wear it, and even the religion itself that tolerates and sustains it."

Of all those who thus dared (or dare) to speak the truth, of course it was (and is) written, as of Wycliffe when his ashes were scattered to the winds: "Organum diabolicum, hostis Ecclesiæ, confusio vulgi, hæreticorum idolum, hypocritarum speculum, schismatis incentor, odii seminator, mendacii fabricator."

With such shepherds to lead the flocks no wonder, as said Dante of his times, "the sheep come home from pasture *wind-fed.*" One can well understand the sincerity of that famous English writer of the same period, who exclaimed:

"If such are the inhabitants of Paradise what have I to do there? Therein I seek not to enter. . . But into Hell would I fain go; for there fare the goodly Clerks, the goodly Knights that fall in harness, and stout men-at-arms, and all men noble—with these would I gladly go."

Though the "four per cent." as above given may not express the average of *habitual* church attendance throughout what are called Christian lands, nevertheless it is unquestionably true that the overwhelming majorities everywhere, and particularly in Protestant communities, are unreached by any form of the Gospel. They are indeed "as sheep without shepherds." Why? Among other reasons (given in various parts of this volume) the two which follow are chief. First, the Gospel itself has been *made over* to suit the sensational, or ceremonial, and the fastidious or selfish, tastes of those chief patrons of the Church who call themselves the *upper classes*. Second, of those ministers of Christ who refuse to thus *make over* the Gospel, thousands "stand idle in the market-place all the day because no man hath hired" them:—the treasuries of the Church being so scantily filled by its rich patrons, and the scant contents so largely emptied into the pockets of those who *are* willing to *make over* the Gospel for salaries, ranging from the Pope's and Cardinal's, the Archbishop's and Bishop's magnificent "livings" and the Priest's or Pastor's $20,000 *per annum* (and perquisites) downward. Suppose these thousands who "stand idle," and the thousands more from our Colleges who would gladly enter a *truly* Gospel Ministry, were assured of a *common treasury* and a reasonable *equality of support* for the entire body of accepted Ministers of Christ: with no sectarian, doctrinal or ceremonial limitations other than those of Jesus the Christ as found both in his words and in the Apostolic Church:—Suppose Primitive Christianity *thus revived!* This would be *renascent* Christianity; the world of sin and sorrow would soon again be "turned upside down," the "poor" would "have the Gospel preached unto them," and the Kingdom of God would begin again to come.

A denominational paper of this date, representing one of the largest of the Protestant Sects, has the following: "Bureaus of Clerical Supply are being called for: but let no church imagine that, through such agencies, it is going to get a first-class minister at a fourth class salary."

A fourth-class salary! "What then? Is the reward of virtue"—*Salary!* Is "the measure of the man"—*Money!* Has Christianity come to this!

In *debased* Politics, in *degenerate* Society, in *degraded* Commerce, in *demoralizing* Literature, and in *deteriorating* Art of course the mercenary spirit prevails; but every noble-souled philanthropist deeply deplores its existence even here. How much more so when that highest and holiest thing named Religion, in its highest and holiest form named Christianity is deteriorated, demoralized, degraded, degenerated, debased to such a degree as is indicated by the prevalent practice as well as by the public proclamation,—" Let no Church imagine that it is going to get a first-class Minister at a fourth-class salary."

To the present age, also, apply the words of Milton:

" Enow of such, as for their bellies' sake
Creep, and intrude, and climb into the fold!
Of other care they little reck'ning make,
Than how to scramble at the shearers' feast,
And shove away the worthy bidden guest;
Blind mouths! that scarce themselves know how to hold
A sheep-hook, or have learn'd aught else the least
That to the faithful herdsman's art belongs;
What recks it them? What need they? . . .
The hungry sheep look up, and are not fed,
But, swoln with wind, . . . "

The base Commercialism of our age stops at nothing. Nothing is too high or too holy for its irreverent trampling in the dust,—the dust of Sordid Gain. One sees, for instance, flaming advertisements of *Red Cross* Tobacco, with a figure of the blood-stained Cross as trademark; of *Trinity* Bicycles, etc. One hears of projects for still more astoundingly irreverent advertisement—too irreverent to be written here.

How shamefully in keeping with all this mercenary spirit of the age (and of the ages) is the common talk about First-Class Ministers at First-Class Salaries, Fourth-Class Ministers at Fourth-Class Salaries, Churches for the Rich and Churches for the Poor, etc.

And not only the common *talk* but the common *practice* as

well. The "tables of the money changers" hedging up the aisles of Cathedrals, and the jingling of coin, mingling with the voices of sensational choirs, indicate that the "House of Prayer" has again become "a den of thieves." Pew-*renters* and pew-*owners* frown out of their pews and away from their vicinity all whose garments are not costly and fashionable. "Pay your money and take your choice" is the rule of the Sanctuary as it is of the Theatre or the Circus. The *no pay no Gospel* system in general prevails in all the "leading" Protestant as well as Roman Catholic Churches. Should Jesus and his Apostles, or the blessed Mary and the other Marys, in their rustic or out-of-fashion garbs, approach the door of the average "Christian" Church saying, "Silver and gold have I none," they (if *incognito*) would surely be repulsed by that "respect of persons" which the Epistle of St. James so pointedly rebukes; "Stand thou there or sit here under my footstool."—Stand by the door, or sit in the meanest seat which may chance to remain vacant; or, better still, "Attend the Mission" or go to the "Missionary Service" where no offence will be given to the "Upper Classes." Such is the *policy* of the "leading" churches and the *tact* of the "prominent" Clergy. The old Gospel invitation, "without money and without price," from the fourth century downward has been increasingly ignored. The poor widow with her two mites, and Lazarus in his penury find no welcome as fellow-worshippers with Dives and the chief Pharisees of to-day, more than they found in the Temple or in the Synagogues of nineteen centuries ago. Then the Divine Man began to cry, and his loyal followers for three centuries continued the cry, "Let him that hath no money come!" But now the Gospel has become a matter of merchandise: He that *hath* money, let *him* come!—sounds from the doors and pulpits of all the "leading" Churches; while the "prominent" Clergy, as "first-class ministers on first-class salaries" bid "him that *hath no* money" *go*, with other publicans and sinners, to the Missionary Service or to the Mission!

"One place there is—beneath the Burial Sod,
   Where all mankind are equalized by death;
Another place *should be*—the Fane of God,
   Where all are equal who draw human breath."

XXIV.—" ON, HONOR, HONEST."

(*Illustrative of the above section and of pages 87-95 and 323-329.*)

These, as someone has wittily and wisely said, are the three main stages in the life of the average man,—whose "chief aim is to glorify *Self* and to enjoy *Himself* forever."

First of all, by hook or crook, *get on ;* by fair means or foul, *get on ;* without regard to the happiness or well-being of others, *get on ;* without heed to Law or Gospel, Conscience, or the Almighty Himself, *get on.*

Having succeeded in this, your money—by purchase or bribe, by benevolent gifts or pious endowments—will enable you to *get honor.* Then "join" the synagogue or the church—better still the temple or the cathedral—faithfully attend its services, generously support its officials and dignitaries ; thus—all the past being forgotten—you will get *honest.* "With all your getting" get *on, honor, honest!*

So preaches Mr. Worldly-Wiseman ; *Seek ye first all these things, and the Kingdom of Heaven (no matter about the " righteousness") will be added!* And so practice the overwhelming majorities.

"*Wide is the gate and broad the way . . . and many there be that go in thereat.*"

"*But Wisdom shows a narrow path, With here and there a traveller.*"

XXV.—GRADUAL EXTENSION OF "THE REAL PRESENCE" AS A DOCTRINE OF THE CHURCH.

(*See pages 64 to 70 and 297-303.*)

The sect of Christians known as Roman Catholics are gradually extending the doctrine of the "real presence" to include the Blessed Mary. Various reliable journals of recent date publish the following :

"Dr. ———, a German Catholic theologian, declares that we maintain the co-presence of Mary in the Eucharist. We believe that in the elements the presence of Mary is complete, that she exists there entirely, body and soul."

It is a sensuous and quite unspiritual way of stating it, and yet it is a feeble glimmering of a most glorious and fundamental truth :—the " Real Presence " not only of the Omnipresent God but also of all His "ministering angels," whom that shining Collect of the Communion Office names, " the blessed company of all faithful people."

Such limited and superstitious recognitions of this great truth are, after all, better than no recognition at all. To have one holy spot, the church or the sanctuary; to have one sacred thing, the altar or that which is upon the altar; and to have one *realized* Divine Presence *there* or in *that*, and to extend that Presence to include even one or two of the " innumerable company of angels,"—the " great cloud of witnesses with which we are compassed,"—surely this is an advance upon that *lower* than " heathen " condition which recognizes no holy spot, no sacred thing, no Divine Presence in all the Universe.

Let ever-widening Intelligence and ever-growing Spirituality take fast hold of this fundamental (but grossly misconceived and much abused) teaching of Religion " pure and undefiled," and extend it into the *everywhere and always* Real Presence of God, and of Jesus the Christ, and of the Blessed Mary, and of the " Blessed Company of All Faithful People." So shall the world gradually come to the glorious recognition of every day as a Holy Day, of every place as a Sanctuary, of every thing as an Altar, of every act as a Eucharist, of every thought as a Real Presence, and of every aspiration as a Communion of Saints.

"*And he dreamed, and behold a ladder set up on the earth, and the top of it reached to heaven: and behold the angels of God ascending and descending on it.*

"*And Jacob awaked out of his sleep, and he said, Surely the Lord is in this place; and I knew it not. And he was afraid, and said, How dreadful is this place! this is none other but the house of God, and this is the gate of heaven.*"

XXVI.—" THE TRUTH, THE WHOLE TRUTH, AND NOTHING BUT THE TRUTH."

(*Illustrative of the entire volume.*)

The common objection to all attempts to find and state " the Truth, the whole Truth, and nothing but the Truth " is : This is an *ideal*, and the masses of the people cannot comprehend *ideals*; or, this is *pure* gold, and for common use we must have *alloy*. To which we answer: Very well, *in case* we do not insist upon affirming that the low or lowered teaching is the *ideal*—the Truth "orthodox," infallible and final: and do not proceed to persecute or to oppose those who cannot be satisfied with anything less than the "whole Truth and nothing but the Truth." Very well, *in case* we honestly label our alloy as *so many carats fine* (no more, no less) and do not insist upon putting or keeping it on the market as gold *pure and unalloyed*. Jesus said openly and plainly: I speak to you in parables *because* your ears are dull, your eyes are closed and your heart is waxed gross: but to those who *are willing* to understand me I speak the highest Truths, and *whosoever* hath ears to hear, let him hear.

Paul said, with similar openness and plainness: Milk for babes, but meat for men; I feed you with milk *because* ye are and *persist in remaining* babes, though ye ought by this time (many of you) to be men, and so able to bear meat.

And the author of the Letter to the Hebrews, in other words, repeats the frequent reproof of Jesus and of Paul:

"We have many things to say, and hard to be uttered, seeing ye are dull of hearing.

"For when for the time ye ought to be teachers, ye have need that one teach you again the first principles of the oracles of God; and are become such as have need of milk, and not of strong meat.

"For every one that useth milk *is* unskilful in the word of righteousness: for he is a babe.

"But strong meat belongeth to them that are of full age, even those who by reason of use have their senses exercised to discern both good and evil."

No teacher of the Bible, or of any other form of genuine Religion, ever *lowers* his Ideal or *alloys* his Gold except as a *temporary* accommodation of it to the intellectual stupidity, or to the spiritual grossness, of those whom he seeks to teach. And, even then, he always carefully explains that he is speaking in parables or administering milk. Never does he indicate or intimate that his parables are *highest* Truth, or that his milk is meat,—that his *lowered* presentation of the Truth is the *ideal*, or that his *alloy* is the *pure* Gold.

Again and again, with his divine Master does he say, "this people's ears are dull, their eyes are heavy, their hearts are gross," and, again and again, with him does he explain, "I have many things to say unto you, but ye cannot bear them *now*."

The author of this volume will here add that, though he believes there is nothing in these pages so obscurely stated that " a wayfaring man, though a fool, *need* err therein "—yet has he not prepared it for, nor does he offer it to, the unquestioning, unaspiring masses.

Only for those who are striving to become "men" and are not contented to remain "babes,"—those who are *teachable*, that is, willing to know, anxious to know, *hungering and thirsting* to know "the whole Truth and nothing but the Truth,"—only for these has this volume been prepared ; and to these it is respectfully and humbly submitted.

"*To this end was I born, and for this cause came I into the world, that I should bear witness unto the Truth. Every one that is of the Truth heareth my voice. . . If ye continue in my word, then are ye my disciples indeed ; and ye shall know the Truth, and the Truth shall make you free.*"

XXVII.—FREE CHURCHES AND THE GOSPEL "WITHOUT PRICE."

(An Open Profession.)

By maternal ancestry the author is a "birth-right member" of the Society of (Progressive) Friends. From early teachings as well as from inheritance came a strong sense of the Anti-New Testament and hence Anti-Christian nature of a *marketable* Priesthood, called by the Society of Friends a *hireling* Ministry. Paternal influence, however, and education among the Orthodox Sects led to considerations of pecuniary advantage and a gradual suppression of the Inner Voice. "Woe is to me if I preach not the Gospel" was a conviction of even boyhood days, but mercenary motives warped it into conformity with the popular and prevailing methods. The result was an experience of nearly fifteen years as Pastor of pew-renting Churches in which the salary was *bargained for* and the Gospel preached at *marketable* prices. During all these years, however, sympathetic relations were maintained with the Society of Friends and frequent participation in their reverent and spiritual worship. But the time at length came when maturely considered convictions made it impossible, in peace or in honor, to continue a *professional* Priest or a *hireling* Minister. By no means does the author undertake to say that all *professional* Priests are mercenary. There are, as there always have been, self-sacrificing and martyr-spirited men, noble and true, among the Priesthood of every form of Religion—Brahministic, Buddhistic, Moslem, or that of other Pagan names as well as of the Jews and Christians. But they are, or have been, noble and true *in spite* of the system and not as its product. The system, ever and everywhere, is debasing in its nature and degenerating in its results. As such Jesus and his Apostles opposed it; withdrew from it; and organized a Church in which every *sanctified* member *might* be both prophet and priest, preaching and ministering for the pure love of God and man, without *bargain* as to money or price. "The Son of Man came to minister and not to be ministered unto." "I have coveted no man's silver or gold." "I seek not yours, but you."

Voluntary and "cheerful" contributions for the needful sustenance of those who devote their entire lives to the service of the Gospel is, indeed, a New Testament and Apostolic requirement. But any form of exaction or of stipulation, such as taxes or rentals of seats, admissions charged or solicited, the rich seated high and the poor seated low, or even formal collections *as a part of public Worship*—all these are utterly antagonistic to the teachings and spirit of the New Testament.

As the poor widow, commended by Jesus, quietly and gladly cast her mites into the treasury *at the entrance* of the Temple, so should every Christian—letting not the left hand know what the right is doing and permitting neither priest, nor minister, nor other official to ask How much will you give? Every man's own conscience is his own and only prompter and judge in all matters of Christian charity. And every Minister of the Gospel should uncomplainingly accept, as his means of livelihood, whatever those to whom he ministers, without bargaining or constraint, may *cheerfully and quietly* offer.

With this understanding of Christianity the author fully resolved some fifteen years ago, and as Rector has unceasingly kept the resolve, to minister to those willing to accept *free* Churches and the Gospel *without price*, as Jesus and his Apostles, according to the New Testament records, organized and ordained them. Such bodies of Christians best represent "the true Church" whether derisively called Quakers or whatever. And such is the Apostolic Ministry though it minister in a "meeting house," or (as in the early centuries) by the seaside, or on a mountain, or in an upper room, or in a private dwelling.

"Jesus saith unto her, Woman, believe me, the hour cometh, when neither in this mountain, nor in Jerusalem, shall ye worship the Father. . . The hour cometh, and now is, when the true worshippers shall worship the Father in spirit and truth: for such doth the Father seek to be his worshippers. God is a Spirit: and they that worship him must worship him in spirit and truth."

"The church in the wilderness"—"the church that is in their house"—"if the church be come together into one place"—"salute the church that is in Nympha's house"—"Paul a prisoner to the church in thy house."

"I thought it necessary therefore to entreat the brethren, that they would go before unto you, and make up beforehand your bounty that the same might be ready, as a matter of bounty, and not of our covetousness.

"But this *I* say, He that soweth sparingly shall reap also sparingly; and he that soweth with blessings shall reap also with blessings. Let each man do according as he hath purposed in his heart: not grudgingly, or of necessity: for God loveth a cheerful giver. And God is able to make all grace abound unto you; that ye, having always all sufficiency in everything, may abound unto every good work: as it is written.

"He hath scattered abroad, he hath given to the poor;

"His righteousness abideth for ever."

XXVIII.—THE "ESTABLISHED ORDER" AND THE "PROTESTANTS."

(Illustrative of Pages 257-263.)

From the Romanists down, it is practically true of all the *sects*, to-day as ever, that the "liberty" they grant to those who question their dogmas is of the same kind as that which the Puritans of Massachusetts granted to Roger Williams and the Quakers; "We grant them entire liberty to keep as far away from us as possible, and if any of them are among us to be gone as quickly as they can." The main difference is that formerly this "liberty" was backed with sword and fagot, but now with ecclesiastical stigma and social scorn.

History confirms what science proves, that in any living organism, an *established order* soon results in deterioration and decay. Whatever settles down upon a *fixed and final basis*, physically, intellectually, or spiritually, begins to die. No living thing can be to-day exactly as it was yesterday, or will be to-morrow, without stagnation—and stagnation is incipient death. Hence, whosoever with honesty, intelligence and love combined protests against the *established order* is a friend and not an enemy.

The protester has ever been the pioneer. Those whom the *established order* has ever mistaken and persecuted as dissenters and heretics have been the appointed prophets of God to lead the world not only out of Egypt, across the Red Sea, and *into* the "wilderness of Sinai," but also *through* it to the Promised Land. Unless the "trumpets of silver" be sounded and the "order of march" followed the old and oft-repeated misery will result; "Your carcasses shall fall in this wilderness, and your children shall wander in the wilderness forty years."

No soft-toned priest or smooth-tongued prophet ever availed except to bring up "an evil report of the land" and to persuade the people to remain *encamped* in the wilderness; nay, even to urge them *backward*, saying, "Let us make a captain, and let us return into Egypt." *They* are the *real* enemies,—the *real* dissenters and infidels—not the Calebs and Joshuas who disquiet the people by saying, "It is an exceedingly good land: let us go up at once and possess it, for we are well able to overcome it."

Against the soft-toned priests and smooth-tongued prophets the Divine rebukes have ever sounded forth; and whosoever faithfully reiterates these rebukes does God's service—however much he may be hated as an "agitator" and a "disturber of the public peace."

True to the Gospel as well as to the Law, to the New Testament pictures as well as to the Old—however poetically incomplete—is a poem written just one hundred years ago, from which a few lines may here be appropriately added.

"THE SMOOTH DIVINE."

(Lines by the President of Yale College, 1797.)

" Placed in some great town with lacquered shoes,
Trim wig, and trimmer gown, and glistening hose,
He bowed, talked politics, learned manners mild,
Most meekly questioned, and most smoothly smiled.

Most daintily on pampered turkeys dined,
Nor shrunk with fasting, nor with study pined.

No terrors on his gentle tongue attend,
No grating truths the nicest-ear offend.

'Twas best, he said, mankind should cease to sin:
Good fame required it; so did peace within.
Their honors, well he knew, would ne'er be driven:
But hoped they still would please to go to Heaven."

XXIX.—SCYLLA AND CHARYBDIS.

(Contributed by the author and here republished as illustrative of those extremes against which this volume is a warning. See especially pages 79-89.)

1.—*Scylla.*

"*To the Editors of the Daily Eagle:*

"'Catholicism' means toleration and inclusiveness in religion. 'A Catholic' is one who tolerates all intelligently honest religious convictions, and includes rather than excludes them. For any one of the various Christian sects to name itself 'The Catholic Church,' and to presume to address all the other sects as 'Non-Catholics' is a piece of impudence which it is high time was resented with mingled pity and scorn—pity for the ignorance and scorn for the bigotry.

"With spoken and published appeals to 'Non-Catholics' for a week or more past, a representative of the Roman Catholic sect of Christians has been telling the Protestant sects of this city about their errors as to the true Christian faith. Through long reports in one of the newspapers and shorter reports in some others, these errors have been made public, backed with illogical and Scripture-perverting statements in the form of arguments. Of course when one appeals to Cæsar, to Cæsar he should go. These appeals to the public demand public answer, unless indeed the Protestants accept them as truth and are ready to go over in a body to Romanism. Through the columns of your entirely non-sectarian paper the following corrections are offered to the same Protestant public that has been appealed to every day for more than a week past, by a visitor to our city, who is published as a chief advocate of the 'One and only true and infallible Church,' which Protestants have always held to be, simply, one of the various sects of Christians, certainly no more 'true and infallible' than are the other sects. One likes to be tolerant, and every presentation in Religion—Pagan or Christian, of the Roman sect or of any of the Protestant sects alike—should be gladly welcomed in so far as it is both intelligent and honest. But when sectarianism and priestcraft, one or both, clearly show themselves as the ruling motive—protruding like horns or ears through this seemingly innocent covering—it is time to cry out, 'Beware!'

"The sharp-eyed Taine said: 'Ninety-five out of a hundred, like sheep, blindly follow whatever leader may manage to exalt himself over them.' The sharp-phrased Milton said, and Dante long before, 'The sheep come home wind-fed and swollen.' The sharper-eyed, sharper-phrased Carlyle said: 'So many millions, mostly fools!' The fact that not more than 'five out of a hundred' have yet even begun to think for themselves in religion (or hardly in anything else requiring logical or intellectual insight) makes charlatanry easy and enables quackery, pretension, and priestcraft to widely and persistently prevail.

"In your columns for several days past you have kindly given space to long reports of the mission sermons which have been preached in one of the city churches. Everyone must thank you for this entire non-partizanship which grants an equal hearing to all religious sects alike. The practical parts of these sermons have been admirable and truly Christian. But the doctrinal parts have been entirely in defence or in advocacy of the Roman sect. These parts, too, would have been interesting and commendable had they been either logical or Scriptural. Surely there must be 'five out of a hundred' of your readers who were intelligent enough to see how utterly un-Scriptural they were, and to comprehend that their main purpose was not to make converts to the religion of the Bible, but to the Roman Catholic sect. In every sermon as reported, this main purpose protrudes; and the Scriptures are 'wrested,' and twisted, and tortured for the furthering of this main purpose. In one sermon the 'verbal infallibility' of the Bible is denied in order to enforce the necessity of an 'infallible church.' In the next, isolated texts of Scripture are torn from their contexts, and from the whole consension of Bible teachings, and forced to do service in support of some controverted dogma or ritual.

"To take an example from only one reported sermon, that of October 22d. Here the false logic as well as the false use of Scripture are easily exposed. As to the latter: The dogma of an infallible church with (or through) its infallible Pope is argued from one short text, nowhere confirmed, but everywhere contradicted, in every other portion of the Bible. The dogma of the confessional (that importation from Paganism, which is a star-chamber and a hypnotic-*séance* combined) is argued from a similar solitary text, 'if we confess our sins,' etc. This text is no more applicable to the confessional of the Romanists than to the class meeting of the Methodists, or the prayer meeting or conference meeting of any of the other Protestant sects. Indeed far less; for elsewhere it is constantly explained by such texts as 'confess before men'—'confess one to another'—'confess to God,' and nowhere is *private* confession even hinted in the whole Bible.

"What 'wayfaring man, though a fool,' may not see how false and designing is such logic as this?—'As the governor of a state must be approached for favors through his appointed agents, so men must approach to God through the confessional which Christ has established.' First, we ask, When, and how did Christ establish it? Second, If the 'governor of a state' were omnipresent, —equally and always in every house, in every heart, as is He 'who is not far from every one of us,' who is indeed, as Christ himself taught, 'within us,' the Omnipresent 'Spirit' whom all in every place alike should 'worship in spirit and in truth'—if the 'governor of a state' were such an one, what a fool as well as tyrant he would be to require or even to permit all to approach him for favors only 'through his appointed agents?' What a protest to all such teachings is the whole Bible. 'Come and let us reason together,' saith the Lord. 'The Father seeketh such to worship Him.' 'Let us come boldly to the Throne of Grace.' As one has well exclaimed, breathing out the very life of Christ and vitality of the New Testament: 'Medium or messenger betwixt I will not have, I myself am on speaking terms with God.'

"Let the ministers of the Roman Catholic sect, as of the other sects, love their cult as much as they please; let them show its reason to be, and advocate its superior worth as clearly and strongly as they can; but let them not 'wrest' either Scripture or logic in its behalf. Plainly and fairly let them say, what their chief dignitaries in the high places always do say: 'These things are so, not because they are clearly taught in the Bible or are in accord with reason, but because the infallible and only true church proclaims them so.'

"The difficulty will be to convince people who are intelligent, in these growingly intelligent ages, of the reality of this last 'because.' This accepted, all the rest will readily follow.

"A CLERGYMAN."

"October 22, '97."

ADDENDUM.

"October 23, 1897.

"On the principle that 'the partaker is as bad as the thief,' a newspaper that publishes any inadequate or misleading statement, especially on so sacred a subject as Religion, is guilty if it does not also and with equal hospitality publish any honest and intelligent correction that may be proffered. The *Eagle* is not, of course, a partizan paper, and so its columns are understood to be equally open to both sides and to all sides.

"Again in this morning's report of last evening's mission sermon appeared the same 'wresting' of texts. Let any intelligent non-sectarian take the sixth chapter of St. John's Gospel and read it through, not omitting, as the preacher has done, those marvellously explanatory verses, 60 to 64, and he can no more draw from it any dogma of 'the real flesh and blood presence,' than he could from any book in his library, or any letters from his dearest friend whose contents (the writer's or author's 'body and blood') he 'eats and drinks,' *i.e.*, eagerly consumes and feeds upon. The preacher (in the reported sermon) stops as the Jews did (whose stupid materialistic interpretation he accepts as the true one) just where the explanation of it all begins: 'It is the *spirit* that quickeneth; the flesh profiteth nothing; the *words* that I speak unto you, they are spirit and they are life.' His spiritual presence then was the promised one, and his 'words,' his teachings, or his truths were the 'meat indeed' and the 'drink indeed' (the very 'flesh and blood' of the soul), of which all must partake in order to 'have life in' them, and thus be prepared to 'live forever.' As he elsewhere says of himself, 'My meat (and my drink) is to do the will of Him that sent me,' and again, 'I have meat to eat that ye know not of.' The will of God and the truth of God he ate and drank, and his 'blessed sacrament' means that we shall do the same. How simple and plain is even this, the most mysterious teaching of the Bible, when studied with the light of reason as well as the light of grace! And how dark and dead is all when, for sectarian or selfish purposes, 'The letter which killeth' is substituted for 'the spirit which giveth life.'

"In the degenerate ages of the Classic Religions we find the superstitious and unreasoning masses under the degrading tyranny of a powerful and magnificent system of Hierophants with an 'infallible' Pontifex Maximus at their head, (whose true imitators as well as successors are the Priesthood and Pope of modern Romanism) celebrating, as their most sacred ceremony and chief sacrament of Religion, 'the real presence of the flesh and blood of Ceres and Bacchus.' Ceres, the classic name for corn, and Bacchus for wine had first become personified as beautiful figures of speech; then they grew into real personalities; then priestcraft transformed them into deities, with stories of miraculous birth, sufferings, deaths, resurrection and ascension; then came Hieromancy, ending in the 'awful mystery and saving sacrament' of eating cakes and drinking wine as 'the veritable body and blood of the Goddess Ceres and the God Bacchus.' So does History still repeat itself and the masses of mankind still yield to the tyranny of Self-exalting Powers which 'desire to have them that they sift them as wheat.'

"*Still stands Scylla, deeply planted and dangerously hidden, in the midway.*   "THE SAME CLERGYMAN."

2.—*Charybdis.*

"*To the Editor of the Daily News-Press:*

"Chancing to be at leisure last evening I was one of a large audience who listened while the great American apostle of Agnosticism told us 'What we must do to be saved.' There was a great deal of wit and eloquence in the lecture, and much timely rebuke to ministers, theologians, and churches of the traditional or non-inquiring sort. But when the lecturer opened the Bible and began to explain it, he sadly displayed both his little knowledge of that book, and his lack of spiritual comprehension. 'Shoemaker, stick to your last,' I constantly felt like calling out to him. He knows as much about the Bible and Religion in their spiritual meaning as the average clergyman does of Law Books and the interpretation of Law. To talk about them in general and to sharply rebuke bigots and hypocrites (of whom there are indeed many both in pulpits and pews) was well enough. But to expound the Bible or to explain that loftiest spiritual Truth we call Religion, alas, 'what a fall was there, my countrymen!' One could fairly hear the devils laugh and the angels weep. Mr. —— is admirable as a speaker and in his personality: a magnificent specimen of manhood, if he would only 'stick to his last.'

"His constant proposition was: 'If there be a God, man can neither help nor hinder, benefit, nor harm Him.' Evidently he has in mind the God of the child and the savage—an infinite Man, who exists entirely apart from the Universe and unaffected by anything that may happen to it. With such a God men might indeed beautify and perfect the earth or deface and defile it, might elevate and glorify human-kind or degrade and destroy, without either pleasing or displeasing, helping or hindering, benefiting or harming Him. But any reasoning about such a God is too superficial and childish to be listened to, with any patience, by those who comprehend and accept the teachings of the Bible, as of all lofty Religions, concerning God as Omnipresent; that is, imminent in all Creation. God *in* man, as *in* all living things, sorrowing in his sorrows, rejoicing in his joys, concerned with all his concerns; helped or hindered, benefited or harmed by His co-workers all. *We then as workers together with God* is a teaching the philosophy of which the lecturer seemed never to have considered.

"He told us about the God whose existence he doubted, the Christ whom he said he did not believe ever lived, the Bible, which is a hodge-podge of fiction; the Soul, which is only animated flesh and blood, and the Life Everlasting, which is only Everlasting Nothingness. 'To be saved' is to eat and drink and have a good time, and not to hinder others from doing the same, to-day, and leave to-morrow to take care of itself. 'Heaven' is to have a good digestion, with 'a penny in your pocket and a pigeon in the pot.' 'Hell' is the abode of all who are sharp-witted and wise, and 'hell-fire' is nothing but the scintillations of genius. Not that the lecturer used all these exact terms, but suggested them as the substance of all he had to say.

"His condemnation of all existing Religions and of everything that might be called Faith was wholesale and entire. His ridicule was, 'Quintessence pure sprung from the deep';—the 'deep' being the scoffings of all sharp-tongued satirists from those of most ancient times down to Rabelais and Voltaire. Satire and ridicule have their place; and when used as scourges for the back of persistent hypocrisy, or of unblushing knavery, or of unyielding superstition or stupidity, are as divine as any others of the 'angels' of God. But when used merely or chiefly to force the laugh, secure applause and fill the speaker's or writer's pocket with cash, we must think approvingly of the Bible phrases: 'The tongue is set on fire of Hell,' and 'blessed is the man that sitteth not in the seat of the scorner.' So thought the writer, as he listened to much that this chief apostle of agnosticism had to say. His sharpest stings were for 'mercenary' priests and other ministers who serve the Hierarchy or conform to Orthodoxy for praise or pay. These stings are needed and widely deserved; but 'thou that preachest a man should not steal, dost thou steal?' No hireling priest or time-serving minister could more plainly revel in the applause of his constituents. And, as for 'pay,' this chief apostle of agnosticism has derived 'no small gain' from his apostleship, plying his craft so sharply that no 'Mistakes of Moses' or 'What shall I do to be saved' can be heard except 'at theatre prices,' or read except at the most profitable rates of the pamphlet venders and of the book-markets. When 'the poor have the gospel' of agnosticism preached to them 'without price,' as they had the gospel of Jesus preached to them during the first and second centuries, then there will be a chance (but not till then) for these modern 'setters forth of strange gods' not only to escape their own sharp stings of sarcasm as to love of 'praise and pay,' but also to 'turn the world upside down,' and send forth their 'new doctrine,' everywhere 'conquering and to conquer.'

"The lecturer's favorite figure came in again near the close—the masterpiece of his rhetoric of agnosticism. Humanity in a ship whose invisible captain and invisible crew no one has ever seen, tossing on an unknown sea, no one knows whither or why!

"Then and there my soul rose to a rhythmic mood and, protestingly, said:

> This life is a voyage—not meaningless sport—
> Of which Time is the ocean, and Heaven the port;
> Our invisible Captain and invisible crew
> We confidingly trust in to pilot us through.

"So does History still repeat itself and the 'Adversary as a roaring lion walketh about seeking whom he may devour.'

"*Still stands Charybdis, deeply planted and dangerously hidden, in the midway.*

"A CLERGYMAN."

XXX.—THE RULING MOTIVE.

(Recent Illustrations.)

Two brothers equally talented, pious and devout, but one an Honor-seeker and the other a Truth-seeker, stand together at the dividing of the way. The choice of Heracles, of Moses, of Jesus, of Paul, is to be repeated. At the entrance of the *broad* way stands the invisible Tempter who whispers, "All these things will I give thee" if thou wilt choose this way. At the entrance of the *narrow* way stands invisible Truth who cries aloud, "If ye were of the world, the world would love his own—if they have persecuted me they will also persecute you—in the world ye shall have tribulation."

The brothers separate, one to find the welcomes, praises and rewards of a rich and magnificent ecclesiastical sovereignty awaiting him at every step, and to die, at last, in what the world calls the "Odor of Sanctity"; the other to meet with scorn, detraction and hatred—to experience the common lot of every hero of History and to die, at last, on the cross of popular reprobation. This one indeed drank of the cup that his Master drank of, while the other *seated himself* at the imaginary right hand of a fictitious Messianic Potentate. Of him who voluntarily became " a man of sorrows and acquainted with grief," thus choosing and persistently retaining the " narrow path," it is written :

" When the time came for him to take his degree of Master of Arts he could not conscientiously sign the Thirty-nine Articles, a step which then and long afterward was of course indispensable. It is characteristic of him that he does not seem to have hesitated about his course. He threw up his Fellowship and all his brilliant prospects rather than make any compromise with his conscience, and left Oxford forever. His brother, who by this time had been completely converted to priestly doctrines, cut him off from all private friendship and acquaintance, thereby severing him from other members of his family who were living with him. One by one all those with whom he had previously held converse turned against him and ceased to acknowledge him as a friend."

Let us leave these two brothers in the hands of that Omniscient Judge who "is a discerner of the thoughts and intent of the heart"; and who inspired His Christ to say, " Many that are first shall be last and last that shall be first—Rejoice and be exceeding glad when all men hate you and speak evil of you for great is your reward in Heaven."

Of one thing at least we may be certain : that no genuine lover of Truth, from the beginning till now, has ever failed to hear and to cheerfully accept the forewarnings of the Divine Voice, " I will show thee how great things thou must suffer for my name's sake." Such are, or become, the "Catholic Churchmen " who sing ever of their missions and their creed :

> " March on, my soul, nor like a laggard stay !
> March swiftly on ! Yet err not from the way
> Where all the nobly wise of old have trod,—
> The path of faith made by the sons of God.
>
> " Something to learn and something to forget ;
> Hold fast the good, and seek the better yet ;
> Press on, and prove the pilgrim-hope of youth,—
> That Creeds are milestones on the road to Truth."

A still more recent illustration, and on a broader or more inclusive scale, is furnished by the self-forgetting career of one who has just fallen as a martyr at his post. Representative of no Party, either in politics or in religion : tied to no System, merely because it was traditional, ancient, or popular ; a simple lover of Truth, and ever advocating it bravely without thought of consequences to himself ; throwing all that he had into the cause of righteousness, " and not deeming that enough, throwing himself " —he died on the field of battle and in the thickest of the fight, as leader of a long-struggling and much-despised minority, waging unflinching warfare against the oppressive Traditionalisms of the world as mightily entrenched in the great metropolis of America.

From his funeral orations, spoken by brave non-partisans who are possessed of his own martyr spirit, a few scattered sentences are here republished.

"He flung himself into life. He identified himself with those whose wrongs he suffered as keenly as if they had been his own. He interpreted them through his own feelings. He loved truth, but he loved it most because it served mankind. To the eradication of all wrongs by what seemed to him to be a clear and sure remedy he gave himself with a simple consecration and faith worthy of all praise, worthy of all emulation."

"Whether or not we accept his methods as the best of all methods for accomplishing this, we must honor the life that was so consecrated. Not to attend church or synagogue : not to subscribe to creeds, social or religious : not to belong to organizations, industrial or so-called Christian—not any of these things make one a follower of Christ. To give one's self to the teaching of the poor, to the uplifting of the common people, to the overthrow of every form of wrong and injustice, to establish the kingdom of righteousness and peace—and no peace without righteousness—this is to follow Christ."

"He might have had any position in political life or in journalism that he choose, if he had been willing to compromise a little with his convictions."

"He never, I believe, thought what would be the effect on himself of anything he uttered. I have stood beside him on the same platform and have heard him speak truths that were unwelcome, and which seemed to me to be needlessly unwelcome. I have read every book he has written, and have found in them unwelcome truths, uttered with no corner ground off, no sharp edges planed away. It would be difficult to find a public teacher in America who thought less of the effect upon himself and more of the effect upon others."

"He went forth to seek the Truth, and when he found her he accepted her, and told her message in language simple, plain, with the conviction of his own mind shining through it as light through a glass. He was never deterred from telling what he conceived to be true. He declared his message no matter what it struck or what was the effect. God, in His order, has established it that honesty will never fail of its reward. Time that tries all things will separate the dust from the gold. An honest utterance will fall upon thousands of minds, and awake aspirations to go and do likewise."

XXXI.—BELIEFS, THEORETICAL AND PRACTICAL.

(For the Renascent Christianity of the 20th Century.)

I.—THEORETICAL BELIEFS.

I BELIEVE in God;—"The Lord our God is one Lord, and there is none other but He; The one God and Father of all, Who is above all, and through all, and in us all."

I BELIEVE in the Holy Spirit;—"The Spirit of God that bears witness with our spirits that we are the children of God."

I BELIEVE in Jesus the Christ;—"Son of the living God; Teacher come from God, who spake not his own words, but the words which he had learned of the Father; Who was tempted in all points like as we are; Who learned obedience by the things which he suffered, and, being made perfect, became the revealer of eternal salvation unto all that follow him."

I BELIEVE in the Bible;—And that "Every Scripture inspired of God is also profitable for teaching, for reproof, for correction, and for instruction in righteousness."

I BELIEVE in the Church Catholic and Universal;—"God's Household of Faith," the accepted members of which are "All in every nation who fear God and work righteousness."

I BELIEVE in the Immortality of the soul;—"In our Father's house there are many mansions. Flesh and blood cannot inherit the kingdom of God but this mortal must put on immortality; And so shall death be swallowed up in victory."

I Believe that "The end of the commandment is, love out of a pure heart and a good conscience and a faith unfeigned"; And that "God requireth nothing of any man but to do justly, and to love mercy, and walk humbly with his God."

I Believe that "No man should judge his brother, or set at naught his brother; But every man should judge for himself what is right: And worship God according to the dictates of his own conscience."

I Believe that "God is a Spirit, and that they who worship him should worship Him in spirit and in truth."

II.—PRACTICAL BELIEFS.

I Believe that all men and *women* have equal and unalienable rights, among which are life, liberty and the pursuit of happiness.

I Believe in the Emancipation of the Poor, through the Church supplying the wants of the young, the sick and the aged who may be friendless and destitute; and through the State providing for all who are able to work, encouraging opportunities and remunerative industries.

I Believe in the introduction and impartial enforcement of a system of Graduated Taxation, with severe penalties attached against all mis-statements as to the ownership of property subject to taxation.

I Believe in the rights of Labor to adequate compensation and to protection from all oppressive monopolies of Capital in Agriculture, Manufacture and Trade.

I Believe in greater moderation in all Public Expenditures, including the reduction of all official salaries (from that of the chief magistrate down), to such a minimum as is appropriate to those alone who from purely patriotic motives accept the administration of a *democratic*—as opposed to a *monarchic* or an *aristocratic*—form of government.

I Believe in Civil Service Reform, in its three applications of (1) reducing the number of offices of all sorts to a minimum, (2) filling these by merit as determined by competitive examination, (3) making their tenure dependent upon good conduct and efficiency of service alone.

I Believe in the enactment and rigid enforcement everywhere throughout our country of severe laws and penalties for the prosecution and punishment of all kinds and degrees of *unacknowledged* adulteration of Food, Liquors, Drugs and Commodities of every sort ; including all kinds and degrees of deception in the manufacture and sale of Fabrics, Jewelry, Machineries, etc.

I BELIEVE in the limitation and stringent regulation of the traffic in alcoholic liquors, and also of what is known as the "Social Evil."

I BELIEVE in the common and equal rights of suffrage and of representation granted to all law-abiding citizens without regard to station, race, sex, or religion ; with severe penalties against all kinds of fraud, bribery, compulsion or undue influence with reference to the ballot.

I BELIEVE in restraining crime and in reforming criminals—not in *Revenge* or in *Punishment;* together with removal of the "pardoning power" from all individual magistrates, and confining it to a new trial before a lawfully constituted tribunal.

I BELIEVE in the abolition of all salaries paid by government to *distinctively religious* teachers or officials—as government chaplains, instructors in sectarian schools, etc.; in the prohibition of endowments or appropriations to sectarian Colleges, Schools, Hospitals, Homes, Reformatories, Asylums, etc.; together with prohibition of exemption from taxation of property of *any sort*, except that belonging to and exclusively controlled and used by the government for governmental, reformatory, or humane purposes.

I BELIEVE that it is the sacred duty of every religious teacher to continually hold up before the world the lofty anticipations of the New Testament, viz.: The speedy establishment of the "Kingdom of God," or the speedy bringing to pass of a "Millennium" of purity and peace upon earth ; and that in order to do this, every religious teacher should continually present, *not low, flattering or time-serving* standards of conduct, but those lofty ideals of the New Testament—"We that are strong ought to help the weak and not to please ourselves" ; "If one member suffer let all the members suffer with it" ; "*Be ye therefore perfect, even as your Father in heaven is perfect.*"

XXXII.—"REPENT YE."

(*The closing, as it was the opening, cry of this volume.*)

Something needed to be said, and the manner of saying it was forgotten in its delivery. The message, not the method, seemed the all-important thing. And for this there is highest authority. No permanently effective Truth-speaker has ever stopped to bedeck or bedizen his Truth. Two of the most potent writers of the nineteenth century—the great English apostle of Rome and the great French apostle of Reason—have said: the first—"I never have been in the practice of attempting to write well. . . . My one single desire and aim has been . . . to express clearly and exactly my meaning." And the second—"I am the least literary of writers. I would have no mention made of style. I study the thing and let the words come of themselves."

Higher authority still is that of the longest-lived, most widely and deeply effective writings of the world, those of the Bible; whose writers, all, allowed their thoughts to clothe themselves, in words however rough or in phrases however rude—to fastidious eyes or ears. "I am not eloquent," said the chief prophet of the Old Testament. "Though I be rude in speech—my speech was not with enticing words—we use great plainness of speech—great is my boldness of speech," said the chief apostle of the New Testament; concerning whom the literary critics also said, "his speech is contemptible." But the Lord had said, "Go, and I will be with thy mouth, and teach thee what thou shalt say."

"Yes, he had a meaning, a conviction, which would not let him rest until it was embodied; and literature *as a display of talent, or a thing which could be sold in the market*, he no more dreamt of dealing in than of dealing with Truth itself as a commodity or an article of commerce."

Let whoever will stop, for sake of praise or pay, to pattern their sentences after the *approved rules;*—"The ancestral abode in which you have probably passed the most delightful days of your life is in a state of inflammation!" etc. The author of this volume could only give a cry:—"Your house is on fire!"—"*Repent ye, for the Kingdom of Heaven is at hand.*"

"One who never turned his back, but marched breast forward;
Never doubted clouds would break;
Never dreamed, though right were worsted, wrong would triumph;
Held we fall to rise, are baffled to fight better,
Sleep to wake."

XXXIII.—CLOSING CONFIRMATIONS.

(Words of various authors.)

"Now I appeal to all wise men, what an excessive waste of treasure hath been within these few years in this land, not in the expedient but in the idolatrous erection of temples beautified exquisitely to outvie the papists, the costly and dear-bought scandals and snares of images, pictures, rich copes, gorgeous altar-cloths: and by the courses they took, and the opinions they held, it was not likely any stay would be, or any end of their madness, where a pious pretext is so ready at hand to cover their insatiate desires. What can we suppose this will come to? What other materials than these have built up the spiritual Babel to the height of her abominations? Believe it, Sir, right truly it may be said, that Antichrist is Mammon's son. The sour leaven of human traditions, mixed in one putrefied mass with the poisonous dregs of hypocrisy in the hearts of prelates that lie basking in the sunny warmth of wealth and promotion, is the serpent's egg that will hatch an Antichrist wheresoever, and engender the same monster as big, or little, as the lump is which breeds him. If the splendour of gold and silver begin to lord it once again in the church . . . we shall see Antichrist shortly wallow here . . . If they had one thought upon God's glory, and the advancement of Christian faith, they would be a means that with these expenses, thus profusely thrown away, . . . churches and schools might be built where they cry out for want, and more added where too few are; a moderate maintenance distributed to every painful minister, that now scarce sustains his family with bread while the prelates revel like Belshazzar with their full carouses in goblets and vessels of gold snatched from God's temple; which I hope the worthy men of our land will consider."

"To be plainer, Sir, how to solder, how to stop a leak, how to keep up the floating wreck of a decayed *Theology*, betwixt wind and water, swimming still upon her own dead lees, that now is the deep design of an *ecclesiastic*."

(The Author of "Paradise Lost.")

Everywhere but especially in Religion, and in the Christian Religion the same as in Jewish and Pagan, reversion and consequent degeneration are infallibly indicated by a tendency to *fabricate* and to both impose and accept *fabrications* for facts. " I said, in my haste, All men are *fabricators*." Entire sincerity or strict truthfulness is the noblest and rarest of human virtues, and its opposite the most debasing and universal of human depravities. Hence no words of reprobation can be too severe or too unceasing for this *germinal sin of sins;*—especially when as Superstition it contaminates, as Dogmatism corrupts, or as Priestcraft degrades such simple teachings and such a sincere and holy life as were those of Jesus the Christ.

"We turn back and think of our fathers and of the narrowness of their faith; yes, it may have been narrow, but what a hold they had upon the truth they believed, what a power it was in their daily life, *just because they had gotten that strong grip upon it, which comes, and can only come, from the exercise of the threefold intellectual power*, which God has given to every one of us.

"How many of us now, in this generation, can say that our beliefs are matters of strong conviction, that our opinions, whether in regard to letters, or art, or religion, are things which we have reached by 'thinking unto them'? *Rather, how many of us have accepted these things by tradition?* Undoubtedly, we may not disesteem traditions, but the degradation of our intellectual condition of the nineteenth century, as I regard it, is this, that the traditions on whose authority we hold things, are so often so contemptible as compared with the traditions that bound our ancestors. Though it is true that many of them were only creatures of traditions, their traditions had the dignity of antiquity, and came trailing down through the glory of past ages, ennobled as being the beliefs and opinions of men and women who had suffered and died for their faith.

"But ours—where did we get them, and how noble and how saintly, and how worthy of the position of leadership, have been the men and women in their thought and lives from whom we often derive them? Believe me, we could do no better service to our own souls than over against this one word, wholeness, to strive for *intellectual completeness*, to ask *on what grounds do I hold truth?* and to seek to discipline and call into action the power in us that thinks, and so develop a more clear understanding, whether of the truths of nature or of revelation, by the exercise of the powers God has given us, wherewith to take hold of them. . . .

"Now what is the characteristic of the age in which we live, as regards its mental attitude? It is an age of very slender and shifting beliefs, an age in which the opinions of yesterday in no individual case, as a rule, are sure to be the opinions of to-morrow. It is an age in which we are wont to find people moved out of their old moorings, and there are more people, I believe, than confess it even into the ears of their most intimate friends, who have been moved away from all possible beliefs whatever. But if this is so, I charge such a condition of things, wherever it is found, quite as largely as upon any other influence, upon the influence of what I would call *intellectual laziness*, a curse, I think of our generation, greater in proportion than in any that has preceded it, certainly for two hundred years."

(*The Bishop of New York, 1887.*)

(*The following are from various recent authors.*)

"The author who has not made warm friends and then lost them in an hour by writing things that did not agree with the preconceived idea of these friends, has either not written well or not been read. Every preacher who preaches effectively has two doors to his church—one where the people come in and another through which he preaches them out. And I do not see how any man, even though he be divine, could expect or hope to have as many as twelve disciples and hold them for three years without being doubted, denied, and betrayed. If you have thoughts, and honestly speak your mind, Golgotha for you is not far away."

Throughout the spiritual, as well as the intellectual, world of to-day "there is a deadness which can be felt, like the Egyptian darkness of old. There are some passably minor poets, some clever essayists, with *legions and legions of novelists whose friends are booming them into fame;* but creative power has ceased. There is a dull stagnation, a predominance of vulgar aims . . . which goes well with the devotion of the masses everywhere to money-making and sport—the only two forms of activity which are really carried on with zest. . . . Prediction is, perhaps, useless. 'The future is on the knees of the gods', as the old Greeks said."

"There it was—there! at Smithfield Market, a stone's throw from here, that Ridley and Latimer were burned. Over this spot the smoke of martyr fires hovered. And I pray for a time when they will hover again."

Aye, that is what this easy-going, formalistic, frivolous, money-getting, world-seeking, man-pleasing, fable-loving, fiction-reading, truth-ignoring generation needs, "the rack, the gibbet, chains, dungeons, fagots!"—or those who dare to face and defy them. When rich Pharisees adopt a standard of life that can only be maintained by devouring the weak and oppressing honest toil, "the needs of the hour will bring to the front men who will swing the pendulum to the other side. When society *plays tennis* with truths, and *pitch and toss* with all the expressions of love and friendship, certain ones will begin to confine their speech to 'yea, yea, and nay, nay.'"

When hypocrites make parade, ceremony, and pretense out of Religion and the Churches are given over to fashion and form, Divine Voices will be heard, saying, "Thou, when thou prayest, enter into thy closet and shut the door." When sharp schemers for or indolent inheritors of wealth are proclaimed saints for their noisy patronage of the Lord's treasury, the same Divine Voices will be heard, saying, "Thou, when thou doest thine alms, let not thy left hand know what thy right hand doeth." When Religion, Philanthropy, Patriotism, and all the Heavenly Graces are made matters of merchandise, or of worldly pomp and show, Voices in the wilderness, in the synagogues and temples, in the by-ways and high-ways will begin to cry out: "O generation of vipers! Ye hypocrites! Woe unto you! Woe unto you!"

"The Quaker is the best authenticated type living of the primitive Christian. That the religion of Jesus was a purely reactionary movement, suggested by the smug complacency and voluptuous condition of the times, most thinking men agree. . . . The plain garb is only a revulsion from a flutter of ribbons and a towering headgear of hues that shame the lily and rival the rainbow."

When even popes and priests, bishops and preachers, set the example of wearing "purple and fine linen, and faring sumptuously every day," such honest souls as were George Fox, William Penn, and Elizabeth Fry will be "sent from God" to rebuke and condemn by sincerity of speech and simplicity of life.

"Quakerism is a protest against an idle, vain, voluptuous, and selfish life. It is the natural recoil from insincerity, vanity, and gormandism which, growing glaringly offensive, cause certain men and women (who are scrupulously honest and genuinely true) to *come-out* and stand firm for plain living and high thinking. And were it not for this divine principle in humanity that prompts individuals to separate from the mass when sensuousness and insincerity threaten to hold supreme sway, the race would be snuffed out in hopeless night. These men who *come-out* effect their mission, not indeed by making all men 'Come-outers,' but by imperceptibly changing the complexion of the mass."

Such are "the light of the world." Such are "the salt of the earth." Such are the "leaven hidden in the meal." *Such are "Christians" who, following the Christ, are ever the Redeemers and Saviours of Mankind.*

[*The following are from the Areopagitica of John Milton—as pertinent now as then.*]

"It is no new thing never heard of before, for a parochial minister, who has his reward, and is at his Hercules pillars in a warm benefice, to be easily inclinable, if he have nothing else that may rouse up his studies, to finish his circuit in an English Concordance and a topic folio, the gatherings and savings of a sober graduateship, a Harmony and a Catena, treading the constant round of certain common doctrinal heads, attended with their uses, motives, marks, and means; out of which, as out of an alphabet or sol-fa, by forming and transforming, joining and disjoining variously, a little bookcraft, and two hours' meditation, might furnish him unspeakably to the performance of more than a weekly charge of sermoning: not to reckon up the infinite helps of interliniaries, breviaries, synopses, and other loitering gear. But as for the multitude of sermons ready printed and piled up, on every text that is not difficult, our London trading St. Thomas in his vestry, and add to boot St. Martin and St. Hugh, have not within their hallowed limits vendible ware of all sorts ready made: so that penury he need never fear of pulpit provision, having where so plenteously to refresh his magazine. But that a bold book may now and then issue forth and give the assault to some of his old collections in their trenches, it will concern him then to keep waking, to stand in watch, to set good guards and sentinels about his received opinions, to walk the round and counter-round with his fellow-inspectors, fearing lest any of his flock be seduced."

"We reckon more than five months yet to harvest; there need not be five weeks, had we but eyes to lift up the fields are white already. When there is much desire to learn, there of necessity will be much arguing, much writing, many opinions; for opinion in good men is but knowledge in the making. Under these fantastic terrors of sect and schism, we wrong the earnest and zealous thirst after knowledge and understanding which God had stirred up in this land. What some lament of, we rather should rejoice at, should rather praise this pious forwardness among men to reassume the ill-deputed care of their religion into their own hands again. A little generous prudence, a little forebearance of one another, and some grain of charity might win all these diligencies to join and unite into one general and brotherly search after truth; could we but forego this prelatical tradition of crowding free consciences and Christian liberties into canon and precepts of men."

"And though all the winds of doctrine were let loose to play upon the earth, so Truth be in the field, we do injuriously to misdoubt her strength. Let her and Falsehood grapple; who ever knew Truth put to the worse, in a free and open encounter?"

"A wealthy man addicted to his pleasure and to his profits, finds Religion to be a traffic so entangled, and of so many piddling accounts, that of all mysteries he cannot skill to keep a stock going upon that trade. What should he do! Fain he would have the name to be religious, fain he would bear up with his neighbours in that. What does he, therefore, but resolves to give over toiling, and to find himself out some factor, to whose care and credit he may commit the whole managing of his religious affairs; some divine of note and estimation that must be. To him he adheres, resigns the whole warehouse of his religion, with all the locks and keys, into his custody; and indeed makes the very person of that man his religion; esteems his associating with him a sufficient evidence and commandatory of his own piety. So that a man may say his religion is now no more within himself, but is become a dividual movable, and goes and comes near him, according as that good man frequents the house. He entertains him, gives him gifts, feasts him, lodges him ; his religion comes home at night, prays, is liberally supped, and sumptuously laid to sleep; rises, is saluted, and after the malmsey, or some well-spiced bruage, and better breakfasted than He whose morning appetite would have gladly fed on green figs between Bethany and Jerusalem, his religion walks abroad at eight, and leaves his kind entertainer in the shop trading all day without his religion.

"Another sort there be, who will straight give themselves up into your hands, make them and cut them out what religion ye please. There be delights, there be recreations and jolly pastimes, that will fetch the day about from sun to sun, and rock the tedious year as in a delightful dream. What need they torture their heads with that which others have taken so strictly and so unalterably into their own purveying ? These are the fruits which a dull ease and cessation of our knowledge will bring forth among the people. How goodly, and how to be wished were such an obedient unanimity as this ! What a fine conformity would it starch us all into ! Doubtless a staunch and solid piece of framework, as any January could freeze together."

"Methinks I see in my mind a noble and puissant nation rousing herself like a strong man after sleep, and shaking her invincible locks. Methinks I see her as an eagle mewing her mighty youth, and kindling her undazzled eyes at the full midday beam ; purging and unscaling her long-abused sight at the fountain itself of heavenly radiance ; while the whole noise of timorous and flocking birds, with those also that love the twilight, flutter about, amazed at what she means, and in their envious gabble would prognosticate a year of sects and schisms."

ADDENDA.

"Vestigia nulla retrorsum."

"Arise, O north wind, and blow, thou south, upon my garden, that the spices thereof may flow out."

"I came not to send peace, but a sword. . . . Ye shall be hated of all men for my name's sake. . . He that loseth his life for my sake shall find it."

"The kingdom of heaven suffereth violence, and the violent take it by force. . . . Thou hast hid these things from the wise and prudent, and hast revealed them unto babes."

"Negation and criticism have their value. They are symbolized, by the pioneer in the backwoods, who hews down trees, clears away stones, that he may till the soil, sow the seed, and reap the harvest. The destruction of false dogmas, and the sweeping away of superstition, are only a preparation for the birth and growth of a truer, nobler, and more inspiring faith."

"We desire to break down every intellectual and spiritual barrier, to free man's mind from all that is false, his soul from all that is superstitious; but we do not desire to leave the mind empty and the soul bereft of aspiration. We seek to clear away error that truth may live; to destroy bigotry that charity may abide; to reject all false gods and devils that the one true God may be loved and served, and the real evils of the world attacked and removed."

"For, after all, what doth it profit a man, if he has succeeded in ridding his mind of the bad geology of the book of Genesis, the mistaken astronomy of Joshua, and the imperfect physical science of Paul, unless he is led to follow truth and practise righteousness with more earnestness of purpose than he showed before—unless he is enabled to take a larger view of God's universe, and a keener delight in the unselfish service of others?"

"Truth and liberty will prevail, in spite of feverish efforts to restrain them; for the slow, toilsome, unpopular, narrow pathway, which the 'heretics' of one age tread alone, becomes in time the public highway of the world."

EXPLANATIONS.

(Explanations made to the Advance Reviewers of this volume and here made to all readers.)

1.—Why so many explanatory pages?—The critical nature of the volume and its impartial antagonism to all Sects or exclusive Systems of Religion, render expedient many explanations in order to forestall misunderstandings and to anticipate honest objections. A non-sectarian religionist, like a non-partisan patriot, must needs define himself; and, even at his best, must expect, as the Christ said to such, to "be hated of all men."

2.—Why such "antagonism to all Sects or exclusive Systems" of Religion?—As in Science, Philosophy, Society, and Politics so, and much more, in Religion the pages of History teach us that if there be anything to be hated and opposed as Satan himself it is a Sect, *that is*, an exclusive System: and, next to this, what is called Logical Consistency—that *cat-o'-nine-tails* with which partisans and bigots scourge mankind into their cliques, machines, hierarchies, and *isms*. From all "Exclusive Systems," with their "Logical Consistency," may the good Lord deliver us! Henceforth let nothing be tolerated but such Unions and Co-operations (by whatever names they may be called) as will leave every man *who is both intelligent and virtuous* free to think and to act, as well as to worship, according to the dictates of his own conscience. Such were the teachings of Jesus and the methods of his chief Apostles, St. Peter and St. Paul. Such, likewise, must be the insistent teachings and methods of that Renascent Christianity which this volume advocates.

3.—Why such a variety of Sub-topics and so many quotations?—The volume is designed to serve as a sort of Cyclopedia of much that pertains practically as well as theoretically to renascent (or revived) Christianity: such as questions of capital and labor, the rich and the poor, the lofty and the lowly, the mercenary spirit of the age, commercialism in Religion, etc.—as well as the underlying doctrines and methods.

4.—Why such incisiveness of language and even violence of criticism?—The volume is designed to be one of (at present) many Voices in the Wilderness: and, as such, needs to be "a cry," sharp and of no "uncertain sound."

5.—Why disfigure the pages with so many italicized words and unnecessary capital letters?—Emphasized utterance and pictorial effects, to the ordinary understanding, are of more account in volumes like this (rebuking popular errors and insisting upon reform) than are conventional methods as to the appearance or taste of the printed page.

6.—Why omit the author's name and (so largely) the names of those quoted from?—That the thought may not be hidden behind the thinker and that Truth may be "all in all." Balaam's ass *brayed* for the Lord as effectively as sounded the ram's horns of the priests or the two silver trumpets of Moses. It matters not about the *instrument*, the all-important question being, Is it God's Command—*Is it Truth?*

7.—Why divide up the contents into so many short chapters and sections?—The volume is not designed to be read through consecutively like a treatise, a history, or a novel: but rather, like the Bible whose simple teachings it seeks to enforce, to be read in convenient lessons, begun and ended anywhere. For this reason, too, frequent repetitions and many re-statements have been designedly made.

As for oppositions and reproaches, let us fully understand that there is no road leading upward along which one may not meet with lions that roar, and reptiles or insects that bite or sting. Let us not therefore cease to travel, much less turn backward. Rather let us learn of them who "*through faith stopped the mouths of lions,*" and of Him who said, "*I give unto you power to tread on serpents.*"

THE AUTHOR.

"The reader of this volume must prepare himself to meet with much in it, on the first reading at least, very distasteful to his own views. But he must remember that the most helpful teachers are those who make us face the facts we wish to shun, and stimulate us to the accomplishment of that to which we have not yet attained. The author's attitude is that of a reformer—a radical reformer,—and the odium he is sure to meet with is that of all those who, axe in hand, mercilessly attack men's self-blinded errors, and unsparingly lay bare their selfishness and sin."

[*Written of "Fors Clavigera," but equally applicable to every book worth the reading.*]

"To be particular, I am of that Reformed new-cast Religion, wherein I dislike nothing but the name : of the same belief our Saviour taught, the Apostles disseminated, and the Martyrs confirmed ; but by the sinister ends of Princes, the ambition and avarice of Prelates, and the fatal corruption of times, so decayed, impaired, and fallen from its native Beauty, that it requires the critical and careful hands of these times to restore it to its primitive Integrity."—*By the Author of "Religio Medici."*

"But I trust they for whom God hath reserved the honor of reforming this Church, will easily perceive their adversaries drift in thus calling for antiquity. They fear the plain field of the Scriptures. The chase is too hot : they seek the dark, the bushy, the tangled forest : they would imbosk. They feel themselves struck in the transparent streams of Gospel truth : they would plunge, and tumble, and think to lie hid in the foul weeds and muddy waters of Tradition, where no plummet can reach the bottom. But let them beat themselves like whales, and spend their oil till they be dragged ashore. Though wherefore should we give them so much line for shifts and delays ? Wherefore should we not urge only the Gospel, and hold it ever in their faces like a mirror of diamond, till it dazzle and pierce their misty eyeballs, maintaining the honor of its absolute sufficiency and supremacy inviolable ?"—*By the Author of "Paradise Lost," in his First Book of God and Man.*

"If I, indeed, upon a Sect-less Creed
Have newly strung the Jewels of Good Deed,
Let this one thing for my Atonement plead :
That Two for One I never did mis-read."
—*Persian Poet.*

TO THE TWENTIETH CENTURY.

(*An Open Appeal.*)

"What is truth?" Pilate's question had already been answered, "To this end have I been born, and to this end am I come into the world, that I should bear witness unto the truth. Every one that is of the truth heareth my voice."

The Pharisees (like the designing, self-protecting theologians of all days) were esoteric or Jesuitical—refusing to "bear witness" to any unpopular or *impolitic* truth. Nothing that would endanger *their* pay, praise, place, or personal comfort would they ever "bear witness" to. Truth was whatever was most profitable and convenient for *themselves;* all else was *private* opinion.

"In discussing the doctrine of equivocation, as to how far it is lawful on occasion, he maintained" (a Clergyman) "the Jesuitic position that the more straightforward principle is that occasionally when duties conflict, another duty may be more imperative than the duty of truthfulness. He expressed it thus: 'Make yourself clear that you are justified in deception, and then lie like a trooper.'"

As a result of this Pharisaism, Esotericism, Jesuitism (call it what you will), to-day as ever Sanhedrin*ianity*, Church*ianity*, or Sect*ianity* is the everywhere popular religion. Christ*ianity*, now as ever, is the religion of the "despised and rejected" few. Not *the Christ* (openly, sincerely, self-sacrificingly bearing witness to every feature and fraction of Truth as inwardly revealed, even though it leads to Gethsemane and the Cross), not *this* Christ of the New Testament do the popular theologians preach or the masses follow: but *my* Sanhedrin or *my* Synagogue, *my* Church or *my* Sect,—the Christ of whatever party *I* was born in or have found it convenient to adhere to.

Whatever my "theological authorities" say, is truth, vociferate the multitude—each shouting for his own party. They never stop to consider that where there are a score or a hundred, or even but two or three, parties, each contradicting all the rest, it might be wise for every man to inquire for himself and to "bear witness" accordingly. "Why even of yourselves judge ye not what is right," and "Let every man be fully persuaded in his own mind," are texts of Scripture which popular priests never preach from and their "flocks" never consider—except to confute and condemn.

"Truth is compared in Scripture to a streaming fountain : if her waters flow not in a perpetual progression, they sicken into a muddy pool of conformity and tradition. If a man believes things only because his pastor says so, or the Assembly so determines, . . . the very Creed he recites becomes his heresy. There be—who knows not that there be?—of Protestants, who live and die in as errant credulity and superstitiousness of faith as any lay papist of Loretto. . . . Protestant priest-craft also flourishes and prevails." The reason why "priest-craft" is able to flourish and prevail, among Protestants as well as among Papists, is, that wherever there are people who will not think for themselves there the gull-catchers will be gathered together. As yet it seems to be fact (as the venerable primeminister of Germany has recently said) that to the masses of mankind "truth has no value ; it is but the subjective image of their fancy or desire ; they feed on appearances ; they believe whatever they are told, or whatever may, for the moment, please or profit them most." Hence deceivers flourish and charlatanry prevails.

When Pharaoh, as also Herod and similar tyrant-kings, had become so outrageously tyrannical and cruel as to be no longer tolerable (says an Eastern writer), he ordered his chief priests to proclaim his deity and command all men to worship him. His credulous subjects at once became his obsequious slaves and adored even his most outrageous cruelties and crimes. So the priest-crafts and king-crafts of the world, in all the religions and ages, have deified Selfishness and Tyranny into an Infinite Personality who does and demands all things for " His own eternal pleasure and glory." The masses of men have been driven by threats of unspeakable tortures or coaxed by promises of personal rewards (by those who have proclaimed themselves the oracles and prime-ministers of this Infinite Tyrant) to believe or profess to believe in the reality of this demoniacal Apotheosis.

Thus, for centuries untold, Infinite Selfishness and Tyranny personified as Deity, has been supposed to be at the head of affairs in the Universe—doing and demanding all things for " His own eternal pleasure and glory." He has commanded all men to flatter and praise Him, to bow and creep into His presence, to fear and tremble before Him, to berate and defame themselves as worms and rebels fit only to be crushed or consumed, to dare approach only through His priestly messengers, to whom obsequious reverence, unquestioning obedience, and unceasing gifts of money and praise must also be rendered.

To these representations of Infinite Selfishness have been added those of Infinite Tyranny, a vengeance-taking God who has commanded all the horrible persecutions of history, instigated all the wars, and dictated all those outrageously revengeful and unspeakably inhuman penal codes which have brutalized mankind, and which prevail (in spite of all pleas for mercy and attempts at Penal Code Reforms, Prison Reforms, etc.) in the very hearts and hands of "Christians" as well as of Pagans to this day.

By such impositions and representations have prelates and priests ruled, kings reigned, oppressors and monopolists prevailed —all imitating their deified Selfishness and Tyranny by doing and demanding according to and for *their own* " pleasure and glory." So has the world been taught that Might is Right. Infinite Might is Right—*therefore must finite might be right!* If men adore that Infinite Self-seeker whom they have been taught to call God, then will they aspire to be and grow to be like Him— *to attain to might in order that they may have right.*

So, very widely and very long, the mainspring of all human ideals and actions has been Selfishness and Tyranny,—The Right of Might.

Jesus the Christ was the first great Protestant who dared to deny and defy all this Demonism of Heaven and Earth—to deny and defy even to his latest martyr-breath. There is no God but "Our Father who art in Heaven," and no divine law nor human duty other than those of Sonship and Brotherhood, said the Christ. *Right is Might* in Heaven as on Earth, and whosoever does or demands anything on any other ground than that *it is Right* (without any regard to Might) is a devil and not man— much less "Our Father who art in Heaven." All reverence and all religion, all laws of God and duties of Humankind are summed up in the Two Commandments, amplified in the Sermon on the Mount, and again condensed in the Apostolic teaching—" God is love, . . . love is of God . . . Every one that loveth is born of God. . . . Beloved, now are we the sons of God."

This was Christianity as proclaimed by the Christ and his Apostles. Is it not high time for its *renascence* or revival?

To eat, and drink, and be merry—to be "clothed in purple and fine linen and fare sumptuously"—is sad enough and bad enough as exhibitions of heartless Self-love even when only *temporal* beggars are at the door, suffering and unrelieved. But, when "clergy and laity," from prelates and millionaires downward, can feast and joke while thousands of souls are every hour going down to the unspeakable torments of countless millions who are already hopelessly groaning and wailing in Hell—alas, what monsters of Selfishness are these! Because *they* have been "saved" by the vicarious agonies of another and thereby *are sure* of Eternal Bliss for *themselves*, in cold blood—with tearless eyes and self-seeking, self-indulging daily lives—they preach sermons and recite creeds of eternal weeping and anguish for those who cannot or do not believe what they flippantly profess and proclaim! Even in this world their eyes and ears are closed to the "Agonies of the Lost"—lest their keen relish for feasts and fashion, for money-getting and money-spending, for place and power, for praise and parade, should be somewhat dulled; but in the next world, as some of them have boldly taught, a chief joy of the "saved" will be the miseries of the "damned"!

'T is time for all who are not yet lost to Pity, Reason, and Hope—from every corner of the earth—to join in one strong and long protest against these *time-and-eternity* Monsters of Selfishness who have, in every religion and in every age, trampled upon and ravaged the hearts and consciences of Mankind. 'T is time to *compel* them either to revise their creeds or else to revise their lives; to believe what is decently humane and sweetly reasonable as to the fate of their-fellow men, or else to cease the heartless pleasures and pamperings of their lives, to become *veritable* Christians—following The Man of Sorrows from his fastings in the wilderness to his agony in Gethsemane and his death-cry on the Cross. This last would be a life beautiful and humane even were there only *temporal* sorrows to relieve; but, believing in *eternal* sorrows, any other life is monstrously inhumane.

Very widely is it a self-evident fact of the Nineteenth Century that, in ecclesiasticism as in politics, in Church as in State, *partisanship* has been the chief issue, *pecuniary* or *personal* ways and means the chief object, and *sectarian* expansion or *individual* triumph the chief end. Officials with all the pay they could get, and dignitaries with all the honors, glories, titles, and degrees they could pile upon themselves, have acted as "spoilsmen" in Religion and as "bosses" in the Church.

The pure glory of God and the pure good of Humankind have been thrust behind Sect and Self. What will advance *my* party or sect? What will *my* salary be and the perquisites? What pay and praise will men give to *me* or to *mine* if I speak or act, go or come, preach or pray, preside as an officer or serve as a missionary? Such everywhere have been and are the main questions of our Ecclesiastical as well as political Nineteenth Century "spoilsmen" and "bosses."

How rarely has been, or is, heard the cry—or observed its corresponding life-devotions—Let *me* be as nobody and *my* sect or party as nothing, let *me* have " not where to lay my head " and *my* band of disciples " be scattered," leaving me to suffer and to die "alone," if thereby the pure glory of God and the pure good of Humankind shall the better be secured! By *whatever* agency or means any good shall be done or truth advanced—be it called Protestant or Roman or Greek, Jewish or Pagan, Ethical or Infidel, and be it never so unfavorable to *me* or to *mine*—" I therein do rejoice, yea and will rejoice "! Let *me* be " accursed " and let *mine* be " counted as dung " rather than that " by any means " should be hindered the pure glory of God and the pure good of Humankind!

Men and Brethren of the approaching Century, let this that has just been uttered be our united resolution, our main purpose, and our unceasing Gospel of Reform.

Let the symbol of the Twentieth Century be " The Cross of the Christ." Upon this " Cross " let *Self* and *Sect*, Personal Ambitions and Partisan Motives, be perpetually crucified. In this " Cross " let all men glory, and by it alone let every conviction, purpose, and cause seek to triumph. So shall the Lord's Prayer begin to have a speedy fulfilment—" Thy Kingdom come, Thy will be done, as in Heaven so on Earth. *Amen.*"

THE AUTHOR.

Epiphany, 1898.

TO ALL WHO SEEK THE CHRIST.

(*An Open Appeal.*)

"SIRS, WE WOULD SEE JESUS."—John xii, 21.

An immense throng of traditionalists, nineteen centuries deep, have crowded themselves in front of Jesus and hidden him from the immediate sight and presence of the world. It is high time to brush them all aside and say, with much-deserved and unyielding reprimand,—

"SIRS, WE WOULD SEE JESUS."

Self-constituted mediators, messengers and agents, professing to hold the keys from Jesus himself, lock the doors and bar the approach. It is high time to decline their patronage, deny their right and say,—

"SIRS, WE WOULD SEE JESUS."

Jesus may be seen in the Beatitudes, Summary of the Commandments, Parables and other rational teachings and gracious ministrations of the Four Gospels :—all interpolations and addenda which are contradictory to, or inconsistent with these being unsparingly and persistently rejected. Jesus may be seen in all the sweetly reasonable teachings and truly Catholic life of the Christian Church, from the Apostolic days till now. Jesus may be seen as an ever-living, ever-present spiritual personality standing and knocking at the door of every heart of man and saying, "If any man will open to me I will come in and sup with him and he with me." It is high time to reclaim the unadulterated portions of the Four Gospels, the unpolluted Catholic life of the Church, and the inalienable private rights of first-handed hospitality (which are the God-bestowed heritage of every individual), and to say, with unflinching defiance to whomsoever would hinder,—

"SIRS, WE WOULD SEE JESUS."

Simply this, no more and no less, is what is meant by the title and contents of this volume—"Renascent Christianity, A Forecast of the Twentieth Century."

THE AUTHOR.

Epiphany, 1898.

The Rapid and Baneful Growth of Tradition.

Tradition starts with a single root and grows, like a banian-tree, into a vast overarching labyrinth. Unless continuously "cut down" by "the axe" of *unsparing criticism and demands for historic verification*, its rapid self-propagation and wildly intertangled growth will so overshadow the minds of men as to shut out all light of Truth. "Ye have made the commandment of God of none effect by your Tradition."—" Now also the axe is laid at the root of the trees."

> " The tumult and the shouting dies,
>   The captains and the kings depart :
> Still stands thine ancient sacrifice,—
>   An humble and a contrite heart.
> Lord God of Hosts, be with us yet,
>   Lest we forget—lest we forget."
>
> —*The Recessional,* KIPLING.

www.ingramcontent.com/pod-product-compliance
Lightning Source LLC
Chambersburg PA
CBHW051724300426
44115CB00007B/452